Psychoanalysis AND Architecture

Editor
Jerome A. Winer, M.D.

Associate Editor
James William Anderson, Ph.D.

Guest Editor
Elizabeth A. Danze, M.Arch.

Editorial Committee
Virginia Barry, M.D.
David Dean Brockman, M.D.
Bertram J. Cohler, Ph.D.
Paula Fuqua, M.D.
Prudence Gourguechon, M.D.
Jack Graller, M.D.
Roy R. Grinker, Jr., M.D.
Meyer Gunther, M.D.
Jerome Kavka, M.D.
Christine C. Kieffer, Ph.D.
Fred Levin, M.D.
David Liberman, Ph.D.
Joanne Marengo, Ph.D.
Dennis Shelby, Ph.D.
Marian Tolpin, M.D.
Samuel Weiss, M.D.
Edward Wolpert, M.D.

Editorial Assistant
Christine Susman

VOLUME XXXIII

Edited by

Jerome A. Winer, James William Anderson, and Elizabeth A. Danze

for the Chicago Institute for Psychoanalysis

and the Chicago Psychoanalytic Society

MHR Mental Health Resources
CATSKILL, NEW YORK · 2005

The publication of this volume was supported by grants from the
Graham Foundation for Advanced Studies in the Fine Arts
and Seymour Persky.

Chapters in this volume are abstracted and indexed in
Psychoanalytic Abstracts and are included in the Psychoanalytic
Educational Publishing (PEP) archive (www.p-e-p.org).

© 2006 by the Institute for Psychoanalysis, Chicago.
All rights reserved. No part of this book may be reproduced in any form, by
photostat, microform, retrieval system, or any other means, without prior written
permission of the publisher.

Published by
Mental Health Resources
44 Bridge Street
Catskill, NY 12414

ISSN: 0092-5055

ISBN: 0-9764976-0-3 (*Annual of Psychoanalysis*, vol. 33)
ISBN: 0-9764976-1-1 (Trade edition)

Printed in the United States of America
10   9   8   7   6   5   4   3   2   1

This book is dedicated to Seymour Persky,
whose enduring interest in both
psychoanalysis and architecture
served as the stimulus
for the creation of this volume.

Contents

Contributors   xi

Introduction   1
    JEROME A. WINER, JAMES WILLAM ANDERSON,
    AND ELIZABETH A. DANZE

I
PSYCHOANALYSTS ENCOUNTER ARCHITECTURE

*Encountering Architecture: Subjective Responses
to the Basilica of the Mission Dolores*
    ROBERT F. HARRIS   9

Dreams of Architecture and the Architecture of Dreams
    EUGENE MAHON   25

*What Can Psychoanalysis Learn from an
Enhanced Awareness of Architecture and Design?*
    STEPHEN M. SONNENBERG   39

Architecture and the True Self
    F. ROBERT RODMAN   57

*Houses as Self-Portraits: Notes on Architects
Who Design Their Own Homes*
    PHIL S. LEBOVITZ   67

II
PERSPECTIVES FROM ARCHITECTURAL SCHOLARS

Building Dreams: Space, Psychoanalysis, and the City
STEVE PILE   79

FreudSpace: Architecture in Psychoanalysis
JULIET FLOWER MacCANNELL   93

An Architect's View of Introspective Space: The Analytic Vessel
ELIZABETH A. DANZE   109

Adrian Stokes: The Architecture of Phantasy and the Phantasy of Architecture
PEGGY DEAMER   125

Adrian Stokes and the "Aesthetic Position": Envelopment and Otherness
STEPHEN KITE   139

III
FRANK LLOYD WRIGHT

Frank Lloyd Wright: A Psychobiographical Exploration
JAMES WILLIAM ANDERSON   163

Frank Lloyd Wright: Power, Powerlessness, and Charisma
JEROME A. WINER   179

Raumplan: Adolf Loos, Frank Lloyd Wright, Residential Space, and Modernity
ROBERT TWOMBLY   191

IV
HISTORICAL AND CULTURAL APPROACHES

The Bauhaus *as a Creative Playspace:*
Weimar, Dessau, Berlin, 1919–1933
PETER LOEWENBERG — 209

The Designer in Architectural Practice
ROBERT GUTMAN — 227

The Myth of the Masterbuilder: A Psychoanalytic Perspective
RUXANDRA ION AND JAMES WILLIAM ANDERSON — 241

Tracking the Emotion in the Stone:
An Essay on Psychoanalysis and Architecture
PETER HOMANS AND DIANE JONTE-PACE — 261

Architecture at the Sonia Shankman Orthogenic School
of the University of Chicago
JACQUELYN SANDERS — 285

Index — 297

Contributors

James William Anderson, Ph.D. is Faculty, Institute for Psychoanalysis, Chicago, and Professor of Clinical Psychology, Northwestern University. A specialist in psychobiography, he has published essays on such figures as William and Henry James, Leo Tolstoy, Woodrow Wilson, Edith Wharton, and Sigmund Freud.

Elizabeth Danze, M. Arch. is an Assistant Professor in the School of Architecture at the University of Texas at Austin and a principal of Danze and Blood Architects in Austin, Texas. She co-edited *Architecture and Feminism*.

Peggy Deamer, Ph.D. is Assistant Dean and Associate Professor at the Yale School of Architecture and a principal in the firm Deamer + Phillips, New York.

Robert Gutman, Ph.D. is Lecturer in Architecture at Princeton University. He is the author of six books on architecture, urbanism, and related subjects.

Robert F. Harris, M.D. is a psychoanalyst in private practice in Menlo Park, California. He is a sculptor whose work has been exhibited in a number of venues in the San Francisco area, and he has long-standing interests in art and art criticism, aesthetics, and architecture.

Peter Homans, Ph.D. is Professor Emeritus of Psychology and of Religious Studies at the University of Chicago. His publications include *The Ability to Mourn: Disillusionment and the Social Origins of Psychoanalysis*.

Ruxandra Ion, M.D., **M.A.** (anthropology), **M.A.** (clinical psychology) is a doctoral student at the Illinois School of Professional Psychology. In 2004–2005 she was a Fellow at the Institute for Psychoanalysis, Chicago.

Diane Jonte-Pace, Ph.D., a specialist in the psychology of religion, is Associate Vice Provost for Faculty Development and Professor in the Department of Religious Studies at Santa Clara University, CA. Her publications include *Speaking the Unspeakable: Religion, Misogyny, and the Uncanny Mother in Freud's Cultural Texts* and *Teaching Freud*.

Stephen Kite, Ph.D. is Senior Lecturer and a member of the Centre for Tectonic Cultures at the School of Architecture Planning and Landscape, University of Newcastle upon Tyne, United Kingdom. He is co-author of the recently published book, *An Architecture of Invitation: Colin St. John Wilson*.

Phil S. Lebovitz, M.D. is Faculty and Training and Supervising Analyst, Institute for Psychoanalysis, Chicago, and Clinical Associate Professor of Psychiatry and Behavioral Science at Rosalind Franklin University of Medicine and Science/The Chicago Medical School.

Peter Loewenberg, Ph.D. is Professor of History at the University of California, Los Angeles. He is Co-Dean and Co-Chair of the Education Committee of the New Center for Psychoanalysis, Los Angeles. His publications include *Decoding the Past: The Psychohistorical Approach* and *Fantasy and Reality in History*.

Juliet Flower MacCannell, Ph.D. is Professor Emerita of English and Comparative Literature, University of California, Irvine. She is Co-Chair of the California Psychoanalytic Circle and Co-Editor of its publication, *(a): the journal of culture and the unconscious*. Her publications include *Figuring Lacan: Criticism and the Cultural Unconscious* and *The Hysteric's Guide to the Future Female Subject*.

Eugene Mahon, M.D. is Supervising and Training Analyst, Columbia Psychoanalytic Center for Training and Research, New York, and a psychoanalyst in private practice in New York.

Steve Pile, Ph.D. is Professor of Human Geography in the Faculty of Social Sciences at The Open University, Milton Keynes, United Kingdom. He has published on issues concerning place and the politics of identity, and he is the author of *Real Cities: Modernity, Space and the Phantasmagorias of City Life*.

F. Robert Rodman, M.D. (deceased) was a member of the Los Angeles Psychoanalytic Society and Institute. His books include *Keeping Hope Alive: On Becoming a Psychotherapist* and *Winnicott: Life and Work*.

Contributors

Jacquelyn Sanders, Ph.D. is Director Emerita, Sonia Shankman Orthogenic School, University of Chicago, and Faculty, Child and Adolescent Psychoanalytic Psychotherapy Program, Institute for Psychoanalysis, Chicago.

Stephen Sonnenberg, M.D. is Training and Supervising Analyst, Houston-Galveston Psychoanalytic Institute, Austin, and Clinical Professor of Psychiatry, Baylor College of Medicine, Houston. He serves on the North American Editorial Board of the *International Journal of Psychoanalysis*.

Robert Twombly, Ph.D. is Professor of Architectural History, School of Architecture and History Department, City College of New York. His publications include books on Louis Kahn, Frank Lloyd Wright, Louis Sullivan, and twentieth-century American architecture.

Jerome A. Winer, M.D. is Faculty, Training and Supervising Analyst, and past Director, Institute for Psychoanalysis, Chicago, and Professor of Psychiatry, University of Illinois at Chicago.

Psychoanalysis AND Architecture

Introduction

JEROME A. WINER
JAMES WILLIAM ANDERSON
ELIZABETH A. DANZE

A discussion between Jerome A. Winer, then Director of the Chicago Institute for Psychoanalysis, and a Board Member of the Institute, Seymour Persky, initiated the unlikely string of events that led to this volume. Persky has a great interest in architecture and the design of buildings and was willing to sponsor a conference that explored the potential connection between psychoanalysis and architecture. James William Anderson, coordinator of conferences at the Institute, became involved, and a committee to plan the conference was formed.

We recall the puzzling questions the committee faced in its initial deliberations: Is there any connection between psychoanalysis and architecture? Does psychoanalysis have anything to offer to the study of architecture? We soon realized that there is, in fact, a profound connection. Architecture refers to the built environment, the environment within which everyone lives, the residences, civic buildings, places of business, and houses of worship that people inhabit. An essential element of architecture is the experience of it. And psychoanalysis is the study of inner experience, of the interactions individuals have with the world around them, of their most intimate, emotional, and personal reception and apperception of whatever impinges on them. Architects, moreover, like all artists, design buildings on the basis of their own personal experiences, lives, preoccupations, and conflicts, and psychoanalysis offers a way of exploring the process of artistic creation.

We decided that for the sake of the conference we would limit ourselves to a single architect, and on October 4, 2003, the Institute for Psychoanalysis presented the conference: "Frank Lloyd Wright: The Architect and the Person." A much-appreciated grant from the Graham Foundation helped to support the event.

The conference, from every point of view, seemed to be a resounding success; it drew a substantial audience, and the attendees were enthusiastic in their evaluation of the presentations. When we decided to present the conference, as best we could determine, there had never before been a conference on psychoanalysis and architecture. But we later learned that two other conferences were being planned as ours was, and they also took place in 2003: one in Cary, North Carolina, on April 5–6, sponsored by the Lucy Daniels Foundation, and the other on October 24–26 at Yale University. It seemed to us that the topic of psychoanalysis and architecture, a topic that had received only sporadic attention over the years, had now become an area of considerable interest; its time had come.

We wanted to return to our original questions about psychoanalysis and architecture and provide a forum for exploring them much more broadly than we had been able to do in a one-day conference, and we decided to produce this volume. We are grateful that, once again, both Seymour Persky and the Graham Foundation generously supported our efforts. Two of us (Winer and Anderson) realized that, while we had years of involvement with psychoanalysis and with the psychoanalytic study of artistic creation, we were neophytes as far as architecture was concerned. We learned of Elizabeth A. Danze, an architect, and a scholar and teacher of architecture, who had an interest in psychoanalysis. We asked her to join us as one of the co-editors of this volume, and throughout the editorial process we have been grateful that she said "yes."

In the resulting volume, we sought for breadth in exploring psychoanalysis and architecture. Our goal is that the essays will illustrate a variety of ways in which psychoanalysis can contribute to the understanding of architecture, will offer an overview of the kind of work that has been done in this area, and will provide a springboard for further study. One of our original questions was whether there is a connection between psychoanalysis and architecture; we think that this volume shows just what that connection might be.

The first of the four sections consists of psychoanalysts encountering architecture. What might psychoanalysts, with their focus on the inner world of personal experience, say about the ways in which people take in, interact with, and react to buildings? Robert F. Harris provides the purest example of this approach. He narrates a nuanced account of his experience with a particular church, the Basilica of the Mission Dolores in San Francisco. He describes the effect the church has on him, how aspects of the design elicit his interior monologue, and how memories and feelings arise as he interacts with the architectural characteristics of the church. Eugene Mahon focuses on buildings and spaces as they are depicted in dreams. Architecture, he implies, is an essential aspect of the stuff of experience. We live in intimate relationship with the built environment, and the unconscious can use this part of experience not only to express our desires, fears, and conflicts but also to disguise and to conceal them. Stephen M. Sonnenberg's essay revolves around two encounters of a psychoanalyst with a building: Sigmund Freud's reaction to the Acropolis in Athens and Sonnenberg's own reaction to the Neue Synagoge in Berlin. He describes how the formal elements of the building, in conjunction with its historical meaning, and in interaction with an individual's personal history, promote a self-inquiry that is similar to the inquiry that takes place in clinical psychoanalysis. He also notes that some of the elements that enable a building to have a profound effect—such as its being surprising, unpredictable, and carrying the implication that change is possible—can enhance therapeutic effectiveness when embodied in the atmosphere of clinical psychoanalysis.

F. Robert Rodman, the biographer of the British psychoanalyst D. W. Winnicott, focuses on the relevance, for architecture, of Winnicott's psychological theories. He asks, and tries to answer, these questions: How does a building foster the true self and nurture the experience of being authentic and whole? How does a building enable us to "survive," to withstand fears of disintegration? How does it help resolve our conflicting needs to be alone and to be in relation with others? Phil S. Lebovitz writes about houses that architects design for themselves. He looks at four architects and inquires into their understanding of how they built the houses in which they currently live. He seeks to understand how their personal experiences, interests, needs, and characteristics led them to design buildings that were uniquely suited to themselves.

The authors in the second section are architectural scholars who each, in his or her own way, brings psychoanalysis and architecture together. As do two of the authors in the first section, Steve Pile argues for the relevance of dreams to architecture. He examines the process of dream formation and explains that a similar process is involved in the creation of space. He also notes that dreams show our underlying yearning to find a life for ourselves that is consistent with our desires, and he argues that architectural space can do much the same, it can become more fully a space for the expression of our desires. Juliet Flower MacCannell, too, puts space at the center of her essay. Scholars, she argues, often focus on Freud's use of time—for example, in his emphasis on the importance of events from early childhood—but they tend to overlook his use of space. She suggests that one might follow Freud's example when analyzing a traumatic memory; one might change the location or perspective of the person. "Spatial reorientations," she argues, "can dislodge us from the predictable traps, dead-ends, and blind corners we unconsciously cement ourselves into." Space looms large in Elizabeth A. Danze's essay, but for her it is specifically analytic space, the setting in which psychoanalysis occurs. She uses her trained eye as an architect to consider the impact the "analytic vessel," as she calls it, has on the delicate processes involved in psychoanalysis, such as introspection, therapeutic change, and the development of a new reality. The consulting room plays an intricate role in every analysis; it "speaks and participates through materials, detail, form, light, air and space."

The other two authors in this section offer perspectives on the pioneering figure in relating psychoanalysis to architecture, Adrian Stokes, an English architectural and art critic who wrote in the middle decades of the twentieth century. Stokes had an analysis with Melanie Klein, one of the most influential, if controversial, post-Freudian psychoanalysts, and he applied her theories, which emphasize the role of phantasy, to architecture. Peggy Deamer notes that Stokes, in contrast to the whole thrust of modernist architectural criticism, downplayed the importance of space and instead focused on texture and developed a theory of surface. Though critical of Stokes's approach, Deamer suggests that it leads us to see much in architecture that we might otherwise overlook. Stephen Kite argues that Stokes's major contribution was his development of the "aesthetic position," a point of view by which one synthesizes oneness and distinctness; in other words, one seeks, simultaneously, a fusion with a building and a sense of separateness.

The third section contains three essays based on presentations at the conference on Frank Lloyd Wright. James William Anderson provides an overview of Wright's life and work. His essay is in line with the traditional, psychobiographical approach that psychoanalysts have taken toward creative artists. He focuses on what he calls Wright's "two selves": one, a sense of himself as exceptional and exalted, the other, an opposing sense of himself as denigrated and a fraud. Anderson seeks to show how these two selves developed and how Wright played them out through his architectural creations. Jerome A. Winer takes a similarly psychobiographical approach but instead of looking broadly at Wright's life focuses on two key themes: 1) the particular kind of charismatic relationship Wright formed with many of the people with whom he interacted, such as co-workers and individuals who commissioned buildings from him, and 2) the psychological effect of Wright's use of space. Wright often does away with traditional compartmentalization, Winer argues, and gives users of his buildings a sense of freedom and soothing. Robert Twombly compares Wright and his contemporary, the Viennese architect, Adolf Loos. He sees their opposite reactions to modern urban life as engendering different approaches to the *Raumplan* or arrangement of interior space in houses that they designed. Loos, who reveled in city living, designed residences that made use of the opportunities provided by modern life. Wright, who saw modern life as destructive and lacking in roots, built houses that connected their residents with nature and provided an idealized space protected from urban encroachment.

The essays in the final section, while all dealing with psychoanalysis and architecture, also make use of broader historical and cultural perspectives. Peter

Loewenberg provides a historical and psychoanalytic study of the *Bauhaus*, the school of architecture and design whose first and last directors were, respectively, Walter Gropius and Mies van der Rohe. The key to the creativity of the *Bauhaus*, Loewenberg argues, is that it provided a protected space within which the masters and students could risk creative regression. Also, boundaries between individuals were dissolved so that a process of group fusion and regressive creativity became possible. Robert Gutman's essay can be viewed as an examination of how many of the same psychoanalytic principles of creativity discussed by Loewenberg can be applied to current architectural practice. He notes that often a designer comes into conflict with others in an architectural firm, such as those involved with management, yet the success of the firm depends on the smooth functioning of the designer. In his consulting practice, Gutman describes how he tries to help firms provide an environment within which the designers can undergo the fragile and precarious process that allows for creativity and originality.

Ruxandra Ion and James William Anderson examine a Romanian myth about the construction of a particular church. They argue that the myth provides an entrée into the inner experience of those who worshiped at the church. All buildings have meanings for those who use them; Ion and Anderson suggest that a psychoanalytic analysis of the myth provides an understanding of the meaning of this church for those who believed in the myth. Peter Homans and Diane Jonte-Pace call this same process, whereby a building has meaning for its users, "the emotion in the stone." They focus on two contemporary structures, the Vietnam Veterans Memorial in Washington, D.C., and the Jewish Museum in Berlin. Using psychoanalytic concepts, they examine how the buildings foster the process of mourning. They also consider how changes in the cultural approach to memory and tradition in the twentieth century provide the background for the way in which the two buildings function as memorials. In the final paper of the volume, Jacquelyn Sanders looks at the history of the design of the Sonia Shankman Orthogenic School in Chicago, a residential treatment center for children with severe emotional disturbances. Bruno Bettelheim, who began at the school in 1944, was the moving force behind the school for more than two decades. Sanders was the director from 1973 to 1993. Bettelheim and Sanders oversaw additions to the buildings and the design of the interior and at times worked with an architect, I. W. Coburn. Sanders describes the psychoanalytic principles on which they relied in seeking to provide an environment that would be optimal for the therapeutic benefit of the children who were treated there.

The essays in this volume make a case for the relevance of psychoanalytic perspectives to architecture. There are two main places of meeting. The first is in the examination of the emotional and psychological experience of interacting with architecture. From a number of different vantage points, the authors find ways of analyzing what Homans and Jonte-Pace call the "emotion in the stone," that is, how a building acts on the psyche of an individual to produce a particular result. For example, Harris, with the sensitivity of an individual who is gifted at self-analysis, provides a detailed narrative of how the features of a particular church aroused feelings and memories within him. As another example, Ion and Anderson look at a myth about the construction of a church; through their analysis of the themes of the myth, they imagine how a worshiper would respond to the church. The second area of connection between psychoanalysis and architecture is the psychological understanding of the process of creativity that the architect undergoes. For example, Winer looks at how certain themes in the life of Frank Lloyd Wright, such as his discomfort with being enclosed, led him to develop an architecture that gives a sense of freedom and transcendence. Loewenberg explains the process of creativity, as understood by psychoanalytic theorists, and argues that the success of the *Bauhaus* was ascribable to its ability to foster this process.

Yet other essays, starting with the assumption that designed space has a profound emotional impact on those who inhabit it, look at the effect of architecture on psychoanalytically oriented treatment. For example, Danze examines how the design elements of a psychoanalyst's office affect the treatment that goes on there, and, similarly, Sanders shows how the Orthogenic School was designed to optimize the treatment of the children who lived in the school.

We are surprised, as we look back, that we once were uncertain whether there was a connection between psychoanalysis and architecture, because the connection now seems to us to be fundamental. With what we have learned from this volume, we would restate the connection as follows. Psychoanalysis is the study of the inner life: of an individual's most intimate feelings, desires, assumptions, hopes, and fears. It is just this, the inner life, that motivates architecture and on which architecture acts. All architects create out of their inner lives, and their buildings play with the inner lives of everyone who sees and uses those buildings. Architecture can be defined as the external, built environment. The subject of psychoanalysis, the inner life, mediates between that environment and us.

It is our hope that this volume, by illustrating some of the ways in which psychoanalytic approaches can be used in the study of architecture and architects, will inspire others to carry on this work. Some, we hope, will pursue studies that are similar to those included here; they might explore other architects psychoanalytically and look at the "meaning in the stone" of other buildings. And others might approach the topic of psychoanalysis and architecture in ways that are yet undreamed of.

I
PSYCHOANALYSTS ENCOUNTER ARCHITECTURE

Encountering Architecture
Subjective Responses to the Basilica of the Mission Dolores

ROBERT F. HARRIS

I am driving north up Dolores Street in San Francisco, looking for the basilica of the mission that gives the street its name. Some 10 years ago I visited this church in accidental conjunction with a visit to the old mission. I vividly recall entering through a side door, from a narrow courtyard that connects the mission with the basilica, and arriving unexpectedly into a serene space. It was domed and vaulted, both spacious and embracing. The profound peace induced by the interior during that visit is the reason I've returned, to learn more about my feeling and the space that elicited it. I want to explore the building and to record my reactions as I go, to demonstrate one process of encountering architecture and becoming alive to its emotional meanings.

When I see the church emerging ahead through the palm trees, I think I must have misremembered it. The tall spires, pitched gable roof, and sharp edges don't seem to belong to the interior that I remember. I hadn't noticed the outside of the church, but over the years I've imagined it as a collection of domes and barrels, reflecting the female roundness of the inside. Actually, I've pictured Hagia Sophia in Istanbul. The exterior in front of me is male, not so much from any phallic presence in the spires as from a certain broad-shouldered aggressiveness in the square-sectioned towers from which the spires rise. The spires themselves are encrusted with lacy decorative carving, which also spills down the façade between the towers, and over the vestibule that extends toward the street. The decoration doesn't make the façade feminine, but rather seems to be a cosmetic frill, like the lace at the collar of an armored soldier in a Velazquez painting.

After parking, I walk back to the church. The neighborhood carries an air of

10   *Encountering Architecture*

FIGURE 1. View from the northeast.

FIGURE 2. The north transept and the flanking doorways.

gentrified grittiness. Freshly painted Victorians wear wrought iron grills over doors and first floor windows, the grills often reinforced with steel mesh backing. Vacant lots, protected by pushed-in chain link fences, stand next to renovated apartments or mixed use buildings with upscale shops or restaurants on the ground floor. Iron grills also wait to be pulled across the windows of fancy boutiques. Coming from the north, fresh with these impressions, I see the church from a new angle (figure 1) and in the new context of the neighborhood's contradictions. The church rises high above the surrounding buildings. The gabled façade is artificially tall, rising maybe 10 or 15 feet above the pitched roof. The high gable is vertically accented with embedded spiral columns, a long pointed window, and myriad small spires. It joins the asymmetrical towers to carry the eye up from the low mission building on the south to the climax of the soaring north spire.

It is a pleasing effect, but it's at odds with the exposed northern elevation of the building. The north flank is low-slung and plain, its lowness emphasized by the artificial height of the front. Its most prominent decorations are the double carved columns flanking each of the two doorways—the east one false—that in turn flank the north façade of the transept (figure 2). I think of the Alamo. Indeed, the building now strikes me as a Spanish fortress-church standing over the village it protects, another element in this fortified neighborhood. Looking again at the square towers and the ornate gable between, I picture two burly guards defending a wedding cake. The extended outer vestibule forms the lowest layer of the cake, but I don't feel invited to partake. The vestibule is a constriction to be passed, a low barbican that might guard the drawbridge of a medieval castle. Thinking of a castle, I now notice small false windows in the towers. These bear a resemblance to arrow slits. I can also read the side walls of the church as the curtain walls of the castle, joining the towers at the front to the north transept, which in turn guards the domed keep.

I recall again the serene and welcoming interior from my long-ago visit. Is this expressed in any way on the exterior? There is a dome at the crossing of nave and transept, but it sits like a flattened cap on a drum. Its concessions to roundness seem grudging. The façade of the transept is arched at the top, but this too is a flattened arch and in any case it is false, concealing the gable roof. Even the stained glass windows make only reluctant gestures toward roundness. Not only is roundness missing, but so is any sense of all the parts working together. There is some coherence among the elements of the front façade, where the meat-and-potatoes of the towers and the confections of the spires and façade are whipped together into powerful upward movement. But this effect is at odds with the horizontal north elevation, which itself lacks an organizing theme or focus. It's like the neglected backside of a stage set.

On this weekday afternoon, the front doors of the church are locked, and the entrance is through the old mission, as on my first visit. Nonetheless, I pause near the front doors to look at the façade. Close up, the "lace" becomes heavy arabesques and floral patterns, which soften my impression of a barbican. It's as if the castle has been remodeled into a stately official residence. It is still imposing. I pass on to the mission, through its chattering interior bustling with tourists and bright-colored statues, and cross the narrow courtyard, a dazzling patch of light and heat in the afternoon sun. The door opens into the side of the nave, just east (toward the rear of the church) of the crossing of nave and transept. The door closes behind me and I'm suddenly immersed in quiet—quiet light, quiet color, quiet sound. To my right extends the side aisle (figure 3), a series of vaulted bays set off from the nave by an arcade. The square columns are softened by rounded corners, as are the subtle capitals. The ceilings of the vaults are aquamarine. Each bay is lit by a stained glass window, colored mostly with white and pastels. The pale light washing across the aqua ceiling gives me the sensation of being at the bottom of a still, bright pool, looking up at its calm surface.

The nave is colored a soft tan, giving the space an earthy, subterranean quality. The warm and subdued light through the orange stained glass clerestory windows enhances this effect. Light from the side aisle windows pours through the arcades, not so much to illuminate the nave as to frame it. The bright light below emphasizes the twilight above and its mystery. The nave is a barrel vault, with side vaults opening off to accommodate the clerestory windows, lining up with the arches below. Decoration is minimal. Between each of the side vaults a raised rib, inlaid with a subtle arabesque, crosses the main vault of the nave. Between each rib and the pillar below is a small medallion, ringed with gold, providing a visual link between the pillars and the ribs while allowing the ribs to float lightly above. The floating ribs remind me of the human chest wall, and the rhythm of the ribs and the ins and outs of the window vaults become a kind of breathing.

The walls are traced with deep scoring between the stone blocks that comprise them. The scoring is emphasized with darker paint. All these elements enrich the space without intruding into it or unsettling the eye. I'm struck again by the feeling of being underground, in a cave of great solidity and age. I think of Ali Baba's cave, or the cellar of an ancient chateau—caves where treasure is stored. But in calling this space a cellar or mere cave, I don't do justice to its spaciousness. It is a cavern, and invites exploration.

I continue to soak in the details of the structure, and await further associations. The transept lies in front of me (figure 4). The crossing is a large dome, where the barrel of the nave opens out into a larger space. This dome is itself the base of a smaller dome above, which adds another volume of vertical space, and another invitation to allow my thinking to expand. The dark blue color of the upper dome

FIGURE 3. The side aisle ceiling with the nave beyond.

FIGURE 4. The crossing.

suggests an opening to the sky. Farther to my left is the sanctuary, a continuation of the nave that terminates in the half-dome of the apse. The walls of the apse are covered with gold leaf, setting off this space from the tan of the nave and crossing. The ceiling is strikingly decorated in a gold sunburst pattern, with a blue and gold arabesque in the space between the rays. This symbolic rendering of sun and sky carries down the actual opening to sky that is suggested in the upper dome of the crossing. The rays bring the eye down to the large crucifix which in turn points its feet toward the altar below. The ray that leads to the cross is decorated with a small polychromed relief of the Mater Dolorosa, the sorrowful mother, who looks down toward her son's sacrifice. The arch behind the crucifix is filled with a decorative screen that repeats the blue and gold arabesque from the dome above. The effect is one of unity, harmony, and convergence at the terminus of the long axis of the church, a place for my searching eye to rest. I feel the wholeness now that I missed in the façade.

I move to the back of the church, where one enters when the church is open for ceremony, and pause at the entrance to the nave (figure 5). The repeating elements—ribs, side vaults, windows, arches, columns, and pews—march down the long axis of the church and invite me deeper into the space, toward the distant altar. I move up the aisle and take a seat within the crossing, to ponder what it is that gives this space such soothing power. Part of the effect is from the in-between size of the space, neither a chapel nor a grand cathedral. There is a "rightness" about it. But right for what? It is certainly much too large for a private living space. There's nothing cozy about it. This is a public space. It could be an indoor marketplace, like the original basilicas in Rome, or one of those grand railway stations from the early twentieth century. Those are spaces for moving through, and for waiting. A church is a place for procession, and for contemplation. A church is also a theater of sorts, but the space overhead is not obliterated with balcony seats. The high vaults, and especially the dome, seem the right size to emphasize the high purpose of the ceremony—larger than any merely human drama—and to induce a contemplative stance toward it. As a contemplative space, it provides a sense of enclosure without confinement. I think again of the space as maternal, and picture a mother who stands back, attentive, yet allowing her toddler to move out and explore. The proportions of the volumes, the ratios of height to width and length, reinforce the feelings of both roominess and enclosure. Later, at home, I will check my photo of the sanctuary with a compass and find that its vault is a perfect half-circle, and that the height of the walls exactly equals the radius. This symmetry prevents the space from squeezing in, either from above or from the sides.

The serenity does not depend on the absence of angles, as I'd expected when I saw the rigid edges of the façade. I see angles aplenty at the many intersections

FIGURE 5. From the rear of the church.

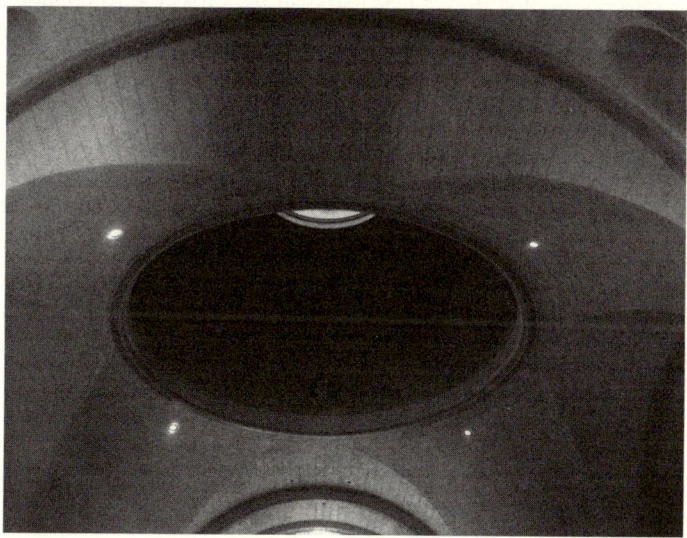

FIGURE 6. The upper dome at the crossing, with the edge of the oculus.

of vaults and domes (figures 4 and 6). These angles, though, are softened because they recede into their concavity rather than asserting themselves. There are angles also in the scored joints of the stones, and I'm surprised to realize that the scoring, unobtrusively expressing a sense of order rather than the indeterminacy of a blank surface, is an important part of what engenders my sense of peace. The staggered edges of the blocks form an interlocking pattern that conveys stability. The pattern's strong horizontal lines create a sense of solidity by accenting the curvature of the dome, with the strength such curves bring to a wall, and by showing how the weight of each course of stone rests on other solid layers.

There is also something reassuring in being reminded that this is a built space. I become aware of the degree to which my thoughts of caves have been accompanied by a sense of moving underground into dangerous places, where dark mysteries might unfold and dark rituals might be performed. I think of Christians in catacombs, and before them, pagans consulting underground oracles. I begin to realize how many sexual references are buried in the images I've had: tunnels, caves, treasure, secrets, danger—even the sense of immersion in a pool. I've not been aware of sexuality because I've been so focused on the soothing, maternal qualities of the space. It occurs to me that innocuous and uninformative words like "profound" and "vivid" that I've used earlier have referred to the quality of being stimulated, excited, as well as soothed. I form a new image of the front façade: two duennas, severe and unadorned except for their towering mantillas, closely shepherding a maiden in a lacy gown, guarding her virginity. I think too of my image of the exterior of the vestibule as a fortification. On the inside, I'd stood under the low ceiling of the narrow vestibule, and then moved out into a higher and wider space under the choir loft. From there, the nave opens suddenly and dramatically, and the sweeping expansion climaxes in the domes of the crossing. The result is indeed a consummation. I'm reminded of the gospel passage about the strait gate and narrow path that lead to paradise. Alive now to the sexual resonance, it occurs to me that marriage is one of the rituals for which this space is made, where dangerous impulses are channeled and tamed in a communal ceremony. The primitive cavern is lined with stones. Now it seems that there was more to my earlier thought of a wedding cake than I'd realized.

The image of a cavern lined with stone brings back the image of a cellar, and then of a crypt, a tomb. Certainly the slumped figure on the cross, and the altar like a sarcophagus below him, invite thoughts of death. I am touched by a sadness that is still contained in calmness. The building invites thoughts of death but also offers consolation. The parabolas formed where barrel vaults intersect with the curving dome have a soaring quality. I see a promise in this upward reach, and in the blue dome above it. I can see part of an oculus in the upper dome, with light across a

FIGURE 7. The oculus.

pale green surface (figure 6). I imagine it opens to the sky. I'm not trapped by the stone. Light from an unseen source also bathes the arcade around the altar. The base of the upper dome seems to hover over the crossing. I think of the gospel story of the Holy Spirit in the form of a dove, hovering over Jesus after his baptism, and the words, "This is my beloved son, in whom I am well pleased." The Holy Spirit is the transmitter of Hagia Sophia—Holy Wisdom; perhaps the promise of wisdom is what these upward opening spaces and hidden sources of light symbolize.

My thoughts go to the image of Mary in the sanctuary, looking down at her dying son, and "blessed is the fruit of thy womb," from the Hail Mary. I remember prayers that refer to Mary's body as the House of God. The groins of the vaults in the crossing, even more than the ribs in the nave, call to mind a ribcage. The dome above is like the inside of a breast, resting on the chest wall. In fact, it is this breast shape that the polygonal exterior dome conceals and denies. The word "groin" also reminds me of how architectural nomenclature is imbued with references to the human body. I'd earlier had, and rejected as cliché, the thought that this space is womblike. Now the word seems to capture something. There is softness in the curves of vaults and domes, like the softness and curves of a mother's body. I think of an image from Nietzsche's *The Birth of Tragedy*, of death as a return to the womb, and of the many religions that treat death as rebirth, or birth into another plane of existence. The Holy Spirit, Resurrection—these are beliefs from my Catholic boyhood that I would no longer claim. Apparently they still claim me. I register the fact that my first visit to this church was with my parents. My last two visits to a Catholic church were for their funerals. I'm moved by a sense of connection to the past: to my parents, grandparents, and long generations of spiritual seekers. The subterranean agelessness of this space stimulates this kind of experience, and its quality of unintrusive nurturance allows room for it. The nurturing space contains and tempers loss and death.

Some of this tempering is provided by the idea of the dome opening to the sky, so I move forward into the crossing to experience it. More and more of the oculus reveals itself, but for the first time since coming inside, I feel hemmed in, teased. The oculus does not open to the sky, nor does it shed light downward like a visitation of wisdom. It is barred by black metal rods in the shape of a cross, behind which is a blank surface, with only a black hole at its center (figure 7). I think of the warning sign of crossed fingers that wards off the evil eye, but now it's my expectation of release that is driven back. While the surface beyond the cross is washed with light from the sides, the effect is not of an opening out, but a closing in. Why? I chew on this and try to regain the pleasure of the space. I think of the Pantheon in Rome, where an oculus that opens to the sky requires drains below. While that would be impractical here, why not a windowed cupola over the opening, keeping out the rain but offering a glimpse of sky through its sides? Or a glass skylight?

Having been brought up short, I notice a tension in the interior that I'd not registered before, between the long horizontal axis of nave and sanctuary and the vertical axis of the stacked domes. As I stand within this spacious domed transept, the sanctuary already feels a little anticlimactic. During Mass the celebrant would stand facing the congregation, at a stone table that has been built in front of the original solid altar. The table stands in the center of the arc of the sanctuary walls, backlit from the arcade behind the altar. This sacrificial table is one focus of the liturgical drama. The communion rail sets off the sanctuary, the priestly precinct, from the body of the church where the congregation sits. The communion rail lies within the crossing. I picture the congregation moving out of their pews and filing up to the rail at communion time, and the priest coming to meet them with ciborium in hand. This meeting is the other focus of the liturgical drama, and it occurs here under the high dome. It seems fitting that the space at this point is so high, as if a blessing from above is bestowed on this coming together of priest and people, like the Holy Spirit blessing the baptism of Jesus. The sanctuary competes with this dramatic volume by its location at the terminus of the church's long axis; by its decorations (the gold leaf, the sunburst at the apex, the arabesques, the crucifix, the altar itself); and by the light that streams through the surrounding arcade. Too much visual appeal within the crossing—a glimpse of sky—would encourage us to forget the sanctuary.

I look again at the oculus, at the black cross and the blank green veil. The surface behind the cross is not flat, but is the inner curve of a still-higher dome. Looking up into this lighted, receding space, I feel again as in the side aisles, that I'm looking into a deep pool. A pool promises refreshment. Something can be imbibed from it, as from the breast. The black cross draws my thoughts back to the crucifix in the sanctuary. A grudging respect begins to grow in me for this building that rejects easy answers, but insists instead that the path to spiritual release and sustenance lies only through earthbound engagements and the suffering and losses they inevitably impose. I have a new thought about the soothing quality of the interior: in suffering, as in sexuality, we can only be soothed to the extent that we have been disturbed. This space does both. It strikes me, with a growing sense of acceptance, that the success of this interior depends upon its tensions: cave and sky, dark and light, closed and open, stimulating and soothing, mystery and revealed structure, incarnate suffering and spiritual repose.

I wonder if this realization can also resolve the tension between the interior and the exterior. What if I had entered the church through the main door, been forced to pass under those warlike towers, to press under the barbican and through its strait gate? What if I had had to survive the scrutiny of the duennas? Perhaps then the interior would have felt joined to the exterior as a destination is joined to a journey, a prize to a completed trial. In my mind I revisit the front façade. It is imposing, and the hard square towers are unscalable, raising the light spires far above reach. They do seem to repeat the message of the oculus: the only viable approach to spiritual consolation is through the narrow doors and down the long aisle to the altar and the cross. Storylines converge: the Christian story of redemption through sacrifice; the tale of the knight-errant who enters the Castle Perilous and finds the Holy Grail; the suitor who can only win his bride, and his cake, under the judging eyes of the duennas.

In these stories I find a partial resolution of the disjunction between the inside and the outside of the building, but it is incomplete. The outside does not read only as a barrier, a trial to be surmounted, but as a disguise, a concealment. I feel this especially as I think of the exterior dome and the outside of the apse. Neither the shape nor the windows of these structures reflect the interior. I think of the false door to the left of the transept, the false fronts at the ends of nave and transept, the false windows in the towers, and my early impression of a stage set. Are these elements the building's sly wink? Perhaps this exposed falseness is telling us that all is not as it appears, that we must be prepared for false leads, that the spiritual path is not transparent or obvious. God hides himself. In this building, the rewards inside are greater than what the façade promises. Still, I'm left unsatisfied. Given the incoherence of the north side, I can't be sure that there is meaning in the exposure of the false elements. I was able to reconcile my frustration with the blind oculus by integrating it into a larger message of what this building is about. The north façade resists integration, and so the disparity between the inside and the outside of the building remains largely unresolved for me.

Discussion

I've tried to demonstrate a process of engagement with architecture that begins with the registration of details of the building and its surroundings, and then follows the train of associations stirred by these elements. In using my associations to "understand" the building and its elements, as I might use them to understand a dream or my emotional responses to a patient, I've employed psychoanalytic tools and sensibilities. Thus my effort is part of a long psychoanalytic tradition of comparing a building or an artwork to a dream (Bush, 1967; Spitz, 1985; Kuspit, 1991; Adams, 1993). Others have also compared the analysis of an artwork to the analysis of countertransference (Gerhardt and Sweetnam, 2001). In this sense, it is not the building, but my experience of it, that I'm analyzing. This use of associations to internal experience as a source of information about the work is also part of an established tradition (Noy, 1968; Spitz, 1985; Rose, 1992), though I've taken my associations farther into personal and idiosyncratic directions than do other psychoanalytic commentators whom I have read (e.g., Globus and Gilbert, 1964; Wollheim, 1987). I believe that doing so sheds important light on how architecture, or indeed any art form, conveys meaning and elicits emotion. I believe, in fact, that it is the only way to illuminate how the experience of a building is cocreated between the building and a viewer, much as Ogden (2003) has described the cocreation of experience within the analytic encounter. He aptly describes how, during the analytic interaction, various experiences arise within the inner worlds of both participants in a way that precludes the attribution of exclusive authorship to either party. Others have also, in various ways, described the experience of an artwork as cocreated between the work and the viewer (Kris, 1952; Spitz, 1991; Rose, 1992; Brody, 2001).

The analyst uses his inner experiences to enhance his feeling "with" the patient, to generate previously unconsidered formulations, and to guide his attempts—through query or proffered interpretation—to elicit further material. The same processes occur in the viewer's engagement with a building, although the third element, the dialog, is modified when the encounter is with architecture or other art rather than with a person. The building will not bring forth new shapes or colors to confirm or modify the viewer's impressions. Nevertheless, the viewer's associations to his impressions do influence his further looking and can lead to confirmation. A simple example is the way that my association to a castle led me to the confirmatory observation of the narrow slit windows in the tower. More complex is my experience of the oculus, which led me to the idea that trials must be endured and surmounted before a reward could be claimed, a reading I then applied to the front façade. This led to a new and confirmatory experience of the façade, as well as to my partial integration of the inside and the outside of the building. Thus the building does supply new information when queried in a new way (cf. Kris, 1952; Spitz, 1991). I should note here that my presentation of my responses to the basilica as if they had occurred on a single visit is simply a narrative device. I actually visited several times, and in between visits I spent many hours poring over the photographs I'd taken. New images and feelings continually emerged, and new features of the building spoke to me during these repeated encounters. A number of authors have described the need for this kind of immersion in order to comprehend a work of art (Kuhns, 1983; Spitz, 1985; Wollheim, 1987; Greenberg, 1999). Lipscomb (1997) has described the need to "surrender" to the work.

One feature of the deepening relationship is that larger and larger pieces of the building become incorporated into the experience. Initially I noticed edges versus roundness, then units such as spires versus domes. From these simple structures my thoughts moved to more complex and inclusive ones: whole buildings, such as castles and tombs, and human figures, such as parents and duennas. These in turn suggested narratives, such as the Christian story, the tale of the knight-errant, and the ordeal of courtship. It's worth noting that these storylines share a similar broad structure: a desire is instigated, hardships are encountered and mastered, and a consummation is achieved. It is the nature of the desires and the trials that differs from one story to the next. While the Christian story is the one most obviously consonant with the functions of a church, the other stories provide rich undertones in the experience of this building. The process of discovering these layers of meaning in art has been described by others (Kris, 1952; Arnheim, 1977; Spitz, 1985), including the idea that fantasies are embedded within the meaning of a work (Kirshner, 2000). Brody (1953) and Sperling (1957), using data from psychoanalyses, provide further evidence that architectural features—corners in their cases—can carry unconscious meanings and fantasied elaborations.

I should emphasize that my relationship is with the building, and only in a limited and derivative way with the architect. Thus my endeavor should not be confused with psychoanalytic explorations of artists (for examples, see Spitz,

1985; Gedo, 1994). I'm describing a building that was built in 1918. While it's valid to include, for example, my associations to the surrounding neighborhood as partial determinants of my experience of the building, they tell us nothing about the architect's intentions with respect to the neighborhood of his time. Even factors more intrinsic to the building, such as its current color scheme, may or may not match the architect's specifications, and yet have a decisive impact on the viewer. While conclusions about the architect would require other sorts of data—knowledge of his other buildings, biographical information, and his cultural and stylistic traditions, to name a few—conclusions about the building and its emotional meanings require only data that the building provides. These data are supplied to a viewer, who is an individual with unique experiences and attributes. Every visitor will bring his own set of memories, desires, and expectations, and the dialog between building and viewer can be deepened by the viewer's participation in a further dialog among disparate viewers (cf. Lipscomb, 1997). Wollheim (1987) and Greenberg (1999) are among those who argue that the process of immersion in an artwork, followed by a dialog that involves pointing out to others the salient features of the experience, will weed out feelings and meanings that are consensual from those that are only idiosyncratic. With respect to what I have written here, another visitor may find something in this basilica that brings inside and outside together in an image or narrative that generates a coherent emotional response. If so, what is a flaw in the building in my reading may prove to involve a deeper integration in another reading. Of course, even these new and shared readings will be provisional and partial, subject to the experience of further viewing.

This paper and my experience of this building are already embedded in a context of dialog with other viewers of art and buildings. My visits to the church were interspersed with my review of the literature, so I no longer know which readings of others' writings preceded or followed my various readings of the building. In some instances I was undoubtedly influenced by what I had read. In other cases, I discovered in other authors ideas that felt like confirmations of my own. Arnheim (1977), for example, discusses the tension between crossing and altar. Kieckhefer (2004) has written about themes of passage—from dark to light, narrow to open, death to life—in classic churches, as well as remarking on the tension between their horizontal and vertical axes. Many have discussed the emotional equation of buildings to the human body, with both nurturing and sexual implications (Globus and Gilbert, 1964; Moses, 1968; Wollheim, 1987; Adams, 1993; Rizzuto, 2002). Others have described how buildings or other art objects elicit desires that they then fulfill or frustrate (Arnheim, 1977; Spitz, 1991; Gerhardt and Sweetnam, 2001). Kuspit (1991) has described the attunement to sexual desire in particular as one contribution that a psychoanalytic sensibility brings to the understanding of art. Varieties of tension and release (Rose, 1996) are endless, and the dialog between viewer and object and between viewer and viewer is ongoing. It is just this endless potential for deeper insight and richer emotional response that makes both architecture and psychoanalysis inexhaustible.

References

Adams, L. (1993), *Art and Psychoanalysis*. New York: IconEditions.

Arnheim, R. (1977), *The Dynamics of Architectural Form*. Berkeley: University of California Press.

Brody, M. (1953), The unconscious significance of the corner of a building. *Psychoanal. Quart.*, 22:86–87.

Brody, M. (2001), Paul Klee: Art, potential space, and the transitional process. *Psychoanal. Rev.*, 88:369–392.

Bush, M. (1967), The problem of form in the psychoanalytic theory of art. *Psychoanal. Rev.*, 54:1–35.

Gedo, M. (1994), *Looking at Art from the Inside Out: The Psychoiconographic Approach to Modern Art*. Cambridge: Cambridge University Press.

Gerhardt, J. & Sweetnam, A. (2001), The particularities of form: Reply to commentary. *Psychoanal. Dial.*, 11:107–114.

Globus, G. & Gilbert, G. (1964), A metapsychological approach to the architecture of Frank Lloyd Wright. *Psychoanal. Rev.*, 51:285–297.

Greenberg, C. (1999), *Homemade Esthetics: Observations on Art and Taste*. New York: Oxford University Press.

Kieckhefer, R. (2004), *Theology in Stone*. New York: Oxford University Press.

Kirshner, L. (2000), Panel: Art, affect, and aesthetics. *Internat. J. Psycho-Anal.*, 81:162–163.

Kris, E. (1952), *Psychoanalytic Explorations in Art*. New York: International Universities Press.

Kuhns, R. (1983), *Psychoanalytic Theory of Art: A Philosophy of Art on Developmental Principles*. New York: Columbia University Press.

Kuspit, D. (1991), Visual art and art criticism: The role of psychoanalysis. *The Annual of Psychoanalysis*, 19:1–16. Hillsdale, NJ: The Analytic Press.

Lipscomb, P. (1997), Aesthetic pleasure and the rhythms of infancy. *Psychoanal. Study Child*, 52:140–158.

Moses, R. (1968), Form and content: An ego-psychological view. *Psychoanal. Study Child*, 23:204–223.

Noy, P. (1968), A theory of art and aesthetic experience. *Psychoanal. Rev.*, 55:623–645.

Ogden, T. (2003), What's true and whose idea is it? *Internat. J. Psycho-Anal.*, 84:593–606.

Rizzuto, A. (2002), Panel: Psychoanalysis and art: A psychoanalytic view of the life and work of Cézanne. *Internat. J. Psycho-Anal.*, 83:678–681.

Rose, G. (1992), *The Power of Form: A Psychoanalytic Approach to Aesthetic Form*. Expanded edition. Madison, WI: International Universities Press.

——— (1996), *Necessary Illusion: Art as Witness*. Madison, WI: International Universities Press.

Sperling, S. (1957), The symbolic meaning of the corner. *J. Amer. Psychoanal. Assn.*, 5:250–266.

Spitz, E. (1985), *Art and Psyche: A Study in Psychoanalysis and Aesthetics*. New Haven, CT: Yale University Press.

——— (1991), *Image and Insight: Essays in Psychoanalysis and the Arts*. New York: Columbia University Press.

Wollheim, R. (1987), *Painting as an Art*. Princeton, NJ: Princeton University Press.

Dreams of Architecture and the Architecture of Dreams

EUGENE MAHON

Architecture and dreams may seem like unlikely intellectual bedfellows, except in the world of psychoanalysis where the free-associative Freudian stream of consciousness throws the most disparate elements together in the interest of unraveling the knots of neurosis and restoring psychic harmony. To a psychoanalyst, the *architecture* of dreams is a uniquely Freudian concept, since prior to Freud's extraordinary insights into the dynamic armature of dreaming, dreams were thought of as baffling, formless entities that were not considered to be serious raw material for scientific study like other identifiable phenomena in the universe. Freud changed all that by suggesting that the manifest appearance of a dream may seem nonsensical, but the latent thoughts that have been expressed through an elaborate system of disguises are anything but nonsensical and can be deciphered, if the interpreter becomes aware of the *dream-work* that has so disfigured them. If we think of the manifest appearance of dream as façade, the latent unconscious dream-work that has created this baffling façade can be thought of as the unconscious architecture that supports it—a sort of invisible blueprint that transforms urgent wishes into seemingly irrelevant disguises. A dream, in that sense, is a piece of psychological architecture, and the dream-work is an unseen architect, whose goal is to create a fancy façade that will totally disguise a trove of unconscious wishes and sneak them past the censor. An extraordinary dream-house, packed with sexual, aggressive raw material has been misrepresented as an ordinary piece of real estate with a meaningless façade; and the dreamer has been able to secure a good night's sleep, since the peculiar architecture of his dreams is really nothing for the censor to be concerned about!

If space is common to all the formal arts, painting could be conceptualized as *representing* it, sculpture as *displacing* it, and architecture as *enclosing* it

(O'Gorman, 1998). If architecture's artistic goal is to enclose space and to do so functionally and aesthetically, what space does the architecture of dreams enclose? "We are such stuff as dreams are made on" Shakespeare suggests, "and our little life is rounded with a sleep." The space of life itself is "surrounded" by the "sleep" of death, Shakespeare implies, comparing life and death and sleep and dreaming in one glorious swoop of his all-encompassing, extraordinary mind. For our purposes, I would like to suggest something far less sweepingly philosophical by arguing that the architecture of dreams encloses the vanished space of childhood by revivifying ancient longings of the infantile past in the disguised façades of dream imagery. The architecture of dreams can ingeniously augment this irony by portraying architecture itself in a dream—or at least what manifestly appears to be architecture—but may have a totally different meaning from a latent point of view. If all this sounds confusing, confusion is the dream-work's goal, after all, as unconscious intent is transformed into seemingly innocent disguise by the hidden architect behind the scenes. In other words, when architecture appears in dreams, the strangeness of its appearance is the result of the dream-work; and *disguise* is the primary intent of the unconscious, even more than the creation of a structure of any architectural solidity or integrity. Given the manifest and latent interplay the dream-work is engaged in by definition, the statement just articulated may seem redundant or tautological. But there is a further irony. If we accept the initial premise that the appearance of architecture in dreams will be (indeed must be) surreal, since dream-work is pulling the strings, can we nonetheless argue that the complex armature of dream structure itself, one that suspends a manifest façade over a latent foundation, has an integrity of its own that an architect called Freud dared to imagine a hundred years or more ago?

Freud's "dream model," if we can conceptualize it so, is such an intricate interlacing of primary processed dream thoughts and their total translation into manifest distortions of themselves that this dream model—if it could be constructed—would be as double-helical as Watson and Crick's model of DNA! (I once alarmed a colleague by suggesting that I was constructing such a model and planned to bring it to our next scientific meeting on dreams.) I believe that the aspect of psychoanalytic clinical process that deals with dreams and, day after day, connects a skein of free-associative ideas, is an actual experiential enactment of such a model, even if the "product" of such analysis does not have the concrete shape of an actual piece of architecture. If all the words and gestures and feelings of the analysis of a dream could be output by some analytic "printer," the result would be a tome of meanings, a verbal affective structure that a model builder could give shape to with nuts and bolts, or sticks and glue or whatever. If dream-work is the great unconscious architect of this complex latent and manifest structure called dream, analytic work is the great interpreter that doggedly tracks every piece of manifest façade back to the latent complexities that lie behind it. The aforementioned dream model may have no more than an academic appeal as some fanciful abstraction, but the work of analysis—the work that shows an analysand how manifest psychology is deeply intermeshed with depth psychology—is no abstraction at all, but the practical bread and butter activity of a craft called psychoanalysis.

I am implying that a piece of architecture appearing in a dream is a manifest shape crying out for the exegesis that will unite it with its latent infrastructure. Furthermore, I am suggesting that the analytic work that exposes the multifaceted connectedness between the manifest piece of architecture (house, cathedral, bridge, staircase, tower, whatever) and the free associations it arouses, will, *pari passu*, expose the hidden architecture of the formal properties of dream structure itself—expose the engine, so to speak—that drives the primary processes that produce the manifest out of the latent in the first place. Some clinical examples will make this theoretical complexity easier to grasp.

Clinical Section

An Example from Child Analysis

Miranda was four years old when her analysis began. A sensitive, intelligent child, she began to regress dramatically when her parents divorced. She became obviously sad, and refused to go to school and be with peers she had formerly loved to play with. She developed nightmares, began to lose her grip on a sense of individuation that had been flourishing, and now refused to sleep in her own bed. Gradually, analysis redressed these developmental setbacks: the analytic issues were complex, but I only want to focus on one of her dreams, which had architectural connotations.

"I was in a strange house. I was alone. I was afraid. I woke up."

Miranda loved to draw. She drew the strange house and its strange door. She commented: "A door is a tear in a house." The analyst said: "When your father left your mother and you, when he went out the door, maybe then your home felt like it had a tear in it." She was silent, and the analyst wondered if he had said the right amount or perhaps too much.

Piaget's genetic epistemology is a staggering intellectual accomplishment that has charted the development of the mind from preverbal animism to adolescent formal operations (Flavell, 1963). In a series of ingenious experiments, he demonstrated how a child develops the capacity to appreciate a sense of volume, number, space, time, and so on—that is, how the child has to wean itself from its initial, perceptually bound, magical egocentrism, a deceiving solipsism that constructs a world that is essentially distorted by its own perceptions and egocentricities. It weans itself by decentering itself from initial error, going on to eventually embrace a conceptual world of reality that is not perceptually bound and limited. For instance, the three-year-old who believes that six baseball bats must be numerically larger than six toothpicks eventually becomes the six-year-old who "knows" that six is a concept which must override the prior perceptual conviction that perceptual size must influence conceptual number. This cognitive achievement is gradually established as a child proceeds through sensorimotor intelligence to preoperational cognition, followed by operational cognition, and then, in adolescence, hypothetico-deductive or formal operational thinking. This is the barest sketch of a most elaborate thesis that shows how intelligence grows, increment by increment, as the child puts its mind to work actively on the phenomenal aliment that surrounds it.

When it comes to an appreciation of the architectural world that envelops the child so naturally (or so it seems to adult eyes that have forgotten all the developmental steps that went into the creation of the representation of reality), it is jolting and exhilarating to be reminded by Piaget that verticals and horizontals, which make up the geometric world of stable coordinates that adult perception takes for granted, are not a given—not a preformed legacy that a child inherits whole cloth—but rather a series of cognitive achievements that stumble their way toward stable verticals and horizontals before they arrive at an architecturally fixed world of consensually validated structures. It is as if a child starts out with crooked lines, shaky verticals, and wobbly horizontals before it stands on two solid feet on a stable platform of reality. If architecture reflects the human body—as Vitruvius and perhaps all architects would agree—the unstable, developmentally primitive body and mind of the child may represent the inchoate blueprint from which first spatial concepts emerge, a shaky start to what eventually may tower into a seemingly indestructible solidity.

The developmental *fluidity* Piaget has described is magically captured by Proust in a passage from *Swann's Way*, in which the dreamer tries to recover his architectural bearings as he awakens from sleep: "My body, still too heavy with sleep to move, would make an effort to construe the form which its tiredness took as an orientation of its various members, so as to induce from that where the wall lay and the furniture stood, to piece together and to give a name to the house in which it must be living. Its memory, the composite memory of its ribs, knees and shoulder blades offered it a whole series of rooms in which it had at one time or another slept; while the unseen walls kept changing, adapting themselves to the shape of each successive room that it remembered, whirling madly through the darkness" (Proust, 1970, p. 5).

These Piagetian and Proustian associative references to Miranda's dream may seem to have left the little world that she inhabits, left her very concrete worries about the stability of the home and her endangered relationship with her parents in favor of a world of abstractions; but I believe not, and that certainly is not my intention. I believe Miranda has only very recently settled into a cognitive world of stable horizontals and verticals, as well as an affective world of reliable object relations. Divorce has turned her house of stability into a house of cards, or a house in which a door has come to represent a tear, a rupture, rather than a symbol of attachment and individuation: a trusted portal of entry and exit that characterizes the stability that object constancy thrives on.

Miranda did eventually reach the psychological maturity that allowed her to appreciate a door as a useful architectural detail that makes a house easy to enter and to leave. In fact, many years later, close to termination of her analysis, when the analyst commented on the old definition of house and door, she countered somewhat haughtily, "Oh, I got over that!" Analysands "get over things," of course, by learning the workings of their own minds, the complex interrelatedness of unconscious urgencies and their more conscious expression in symptoms, character traits, normality, and pathology. In Miranda's case, she had to revisit her theory of tearing doors, and torn houses, and rescue a sound architectural view of the world from the neurotic misinformation that made the ordinary seem dangerous and extraordinary. In child analysis, this is done through play and language more than by means of the exclusively linguistic enterprise of adult analysis (though even adult analysis has its own equivalents of play and action that shadow the free-associative process, a topic which cannot be dealt with in this paper). In her play Miranda smashed, banged, and locked many playhouse doors, expressing her sadness and anger at father and mother many times. She sometimes blocked the door of the consulting room as if to insist that there could be no tear in the house of transference, if healing was to occur.

Of course, the house of transference comes with doors; and others who entered when Miranda had to leave, made it imperative for the child to reenact the old conflicts and sorrows, and to eventually master the affects and traumas in ways she couldn't initially. Her dream and her drawings depicted the sense of her plight and her mind as victims of a trauma she felt ill-equipped to deal with. Architecture was not a reflection of a stable blueprint designed by mother-architect and father-architect, in collaboration with child-architect—a blueprint that culminates in a solid structure that can weather the ups and downs of development with grace and aplomb. Architecture to Miranda was a torn blueprint that could only produce a cracked model, a crooked house. She had to learn that her own affects turned against the self were undermining the architectural security of her body-image and mind-image. The external facilitating environment and the internal psychological milieu were failing her until she could retrieve her own sense of agency and build better houses, so to speak, out of more adaptive, resourceful, non-neurotic blueprints.

Examples from Adult Analysis

The appearance of architecture in adult dreams is even more obviously conflicted, neurotic, or dynamic than the depiction of architecture in a child's dream. Two examples will illustrate this point dramatically.

Samuel was a 60-year-old lawyer whose career was flourishing, but whose emotional life had never recovered from the tragedy of his father's death when he was five years old. His father, a renowned lawyer, was suddenly felled with an acute virulent leukemia at the age of 50. Samuel felt that his father's death so overwhelmed the family that the child's needs were relatively ignored, as the grief of his mother and his older siblings upstaged his own conflicts and sorrows. Or so it seemed. In his analysis, Samuel learned how he mastered the sudden *disappearance* of his father (this was how death was experienced by the young child, as magical event rather than biological fact) by the disappearance of his own self. His superego's assaults on the indicted self were sadistic and unrelenting; self-annihilation seemed the only possible strategy. As a child, he imagined jumping from the windowsill, and eventually finding some version of revenge and masochistic love, as well as reunification with his father, in such a drastic act. Obviously, he never followed through with this fantasy, but internally it felt as if he had. Analysis over many years began to restore Samuel's confidence in a self that could feel sadness, guilt, anger, grief, joy, and conflict without turning against itself with reversals of fury. One of his dreams in mid-analysis depicts his conflicts in a striking, architectural manner, which I now want to focus on.

"I am in a two-storey house.[1] There is some terrifying sense of danger that is never clearly identified. I go to the roof. I escape down some kind of a rubber chute and land safely."

A myriad associations made it possible to see the complex latent infrastructure beneath this seemingly obvious architectural metaphor. After his father's death, the family moved to a larger house but the disappearance of the "smaller" house seemed to echo the disappearance of the beloved parent in a haunting way. The two-storey house seemed not only a condensation of these two abodes, but a punning reference to the two stories of his childhood as well. One story held a conviction that Samuel was guilty of patricide and therefore did not deserve to live, or could only live by dying and reuniting with his father in this manner. The other story held

---

[1] Throughout this paper, the British usage "storey" (for story) is maintained. Though atypical in the United States, this spelling is necessary to contrast the architectural "story" from the narrative one.

all the developmental energies of a disappointed child: the wish for a healthy father he could play with and learn from, one he could even "kill" with oedipal desires and ambitions, while being loved for such developmental "chutzpah."

The dream tried to condense these two stories with a two-storey architectural image in which infantile wish and infantile punishment plagued each other in a disguised fulfillment of contradictory wishes. "The terrifying sense of danger" that could never be clearly identified in the dream could be deconstructed in the interpretive work of analytic collaboration, as Samuel began to realize that his house need not be divided against itself forever, if he could develop the courage, through insight, not to run from himself. The escape in the dream down the rubber chute was not only a reprise of the sadomasochistic fantasy of childhood in which suicide coerces love from grief in a brutal manner, but a declaration of robust wishes for escape and safety through adaptive, aggressive action, as well. As analysis proceeded, it became very clear to Samuel that the two-storey house was no architectural reference at all, but a depiction of his need to integrate body and mind, to undo splitting tendencies, to embrace conflict as the essence of the human condition, and to leap, not to his death, based on infantile fury and grief, but into the arms of the future with birthright as his developmental mandate rather than masochism and trauma.

Marcel was a 50-year-old artist who entered analysis with a feeling that all art was vanity, and not even vanity fair, but vanity ugly, vanity foolish, and vanity useless! When the self-hatred that informed this jaundiced view of art was modified by years of hard analytic labor, Marcel's life and art began to seem less worthless, and his contempt for analysis cleared a little space for a conflicted modicum of gratitude. In this brief sketch of a portion of his analysis, I want to focus only on architectural elements in one of his dreams. A genetic preamble is essential, however, so that the context will make sense to the reader.

A pivotal early memory brings Marcel's childhood to life in a poignant, if chilling, way. At age seven, Marcel had damaged his fingers in a revolving door. His mother, who should have been taking better care of him, perceived Marcel's plight as an injury to herself, and she blamed the child for putting her through this dreadful assault on her own narcissism! Forty-three years later, every retelling of this episode made the analysand shudder, and empathy makes the analyst no passive eyewitness—or should I say ear-witness? A defensive identification with the mother's narcissism left Marcel unable to challenge her in his own developmental self-interest. His unresolved anger found its outlets in self-destructive acting out and unwitting cruelty to others, which perplexed them and indeed often puzzled Marcel himself. The psychology of all this was lost on him, until analysis laid bare the psychological depths of his seemingly thoughtless current behavior. The analysis of dreams was crucial in helping Marcel to appreciate the depths of what appeared like characterological shallowness; and as mentioned earlier, I wish to focus on only one dream which has architectural significance.

"There was a house which had no windows. Inside I see a weird fireplace with an ominous light in it, but no human warmth, no warming fire—only an eerie, uncanny light. There's a cat, that turns into a mouse, and then into a rat."

After his "usual" dismissal of the dream as insignificant, a hesitant free-associative process began to reveal to him what could not be dismissed: that if his childhood seemed like a home without any human warmth in it, given the compromised facilitating environment, the construction in a dream of a cold house with no windows in it did seem like the work of a psychological architect who was making a statement about safety, trust, self-protection, and then some! "Even the domestic animals seem to sense the ominous atmosphere" Marcel commented, as he began to ponder the meaning of the regressive metamorphosis from cat to mouse to rat. "Not a very welcoming house," he mused, "and windowless to boot. No one can see the shame of it, the pain of it, the anger of it. You can't look out. No one can look in."

If a house is an extension of the human body, a child must internalize this anatomical, architectural complexity as it differentiates its own needs from its parents' needs, its own boundaries from siblings, peers, and other objects, assisted by the facilitating environment under optimal conditions, the child remains hampered by it under suboptimal conditions. This is a complicated developmental challenge for every human being as he or she constructs and reconstructs the self out of the lost blueprints of early childhood and the subsequent infantile amnesia. Since infantile sexuality is so alarming to the child, and therefore so repressed and distorted, the daytime familiar home becomes the nighttime haunted house of the primal scene, a torn house with gashes for doors, as Miranda's imagination depicted it.

Marcel had clearly built his own fantastic dream house out of unresolved childhood conflict, and the task of analysis is to deconstruct and redress this tendency to insist on internal architecture designed by Edgar Allan Poe rather than by Frank Lloyd Wright! A schizoid, paranoid house needs to be understood in terms of the triggering emotions and defensive strategies that went into its making, before a house with a warm, inviting fireplace can be built, where a man can sit beside his purring cat in slippered, easeful domesticity. Could we perhaps argue that the use of architecture in dreams is akin to the use of playthings in childhood play—an attempt to represent the instinctual, the volatile, the emotional, in concrete terms that can then be assembled and reassembled for closer study, for safer study? We could say that *manipulation* of building blocks is a preliminary *activity* that allows the child, or dreamer in general, to portray the ungraspable volatility of emotion in a manageable fashion. That play can be disrupted, or that dream can turn nightmarish, illustrates the difficulty of playing with such psychological fire; but the ego's attempt to build a fireplace in a safe domestic setting in playroom or dream-space is one feature of the complexity of human development that can be isolated, somewhat, as we ponder the significance of architecture's appearance in dreams.

Discussion

Vitruvius's *Ten Books on Architecture* represents the philosophy of a man who, if not the founder of architecture, certainly represents a most significant early proponent. He was clearly a Renaissance man, if one can indulge such an anachronism when speaking of an artist who lived more than a thousand years before the Quattrocento. An architect, according to Vitruvius, should be well-versed in music, philosophy, mathematics, and so forth, for how could he be expected to know how to build an artifact that would reflect culture and historical context if he were only a "specialist" (Mahon, 2003, 2004)? Architecture, clearly, should reflect the cultural, artistic, and sociological *zeitgeist*. In fact, if architecture is not only an extension of the body, as McLuhan would say, but a derivative and representation of it—complete with orifices, external façade, and internal organs (rooms for sexual activity, excretory activity, oral activity, for play, for music, for reading, etc.)—a psychoanalyst can suggest that architecture in dreams is the derivative body metaphor par excellence. That is because its manifest appearance is only the façade of its meaning, of most of its secrets, latent and hidden, until analysis enters the forbidden spatial domain of its psychic depths. Did Freud have an obscure architectural metaphor in mind, perhaps, when he penned his famous citation to the manuscript of *The Interpretation of Dreams*: "*Flectere si nequeo superos, Acheronta movebo*?" ("If the upper storeys cannot be budged, I'll raise hell in the basement" is a slightly inaccurate, and more than slightly irreverent, translation.) If dreams depict the haunted house of the mind, its superior haughty façades, as well as its hellish unconscious interiors, was Freud saying, very obliquely, that such a house could only be entered through unconscious, haunted basement passageways and not by concrete, conscious steps and stairwayed entrances?

If dreams can choose any item out of the flux and flotsam of day residue to build the manifest façade that cloaks the latent dream thoughts, it should come as no surprise that architecture might be a common structure pressed into usage by the dream-work. For if architecture, as Vitruvius argued, is a representation of the body, a utilitarian derivative of the body's anatomical and physiological needs,

Leonardo da Vinci went even further. Borrowing these insights from Vitruvius, he showed how the golden section that informs the artistic measurements of all art and architecture are essentially body measurements, the human body itself being an anatomical structure that represents the "ideal" measurements to which the golden section owes its very existence in the first place. Numbers come, first and foremost, from the body. If a man had thirteen fingers rather than ten, all art and mathematics would reflect that anatomical truth, rather than the current conventional reality. Freud goes even further, perhaps, when he argues that the body's initial urgencies, represented in the mind as *instincts*, get repressed—an infantile amnesia burying the mind in the body, so to speak, as latency turns its back on the tumultuous preoedipal and oedipal dramas that characterize the first five or six years of life. If a man's life and his art takes its cues and measurements from the body, in a Freudian world, where much of the body has been buried (repressed), the measure of man is being taken by unconscious forces that make him feel like a puppet in the hands of uncanny unseen powers, rather than a free agent at all!

Proust's description of the fluid reality-testing of the awakening state of mind is very relevant in this regard: with extraordinary psychological astuteness he suggests that the "composite memory" of his "ribs, knees, and shoulder-blades" were the perceptual triggers and reminders of "a whole series of rooms" in which he had once slept! In other words, his own anatomy, and the architectural anatomy of various bedrooms, were intimately associated. Could Vitruvius, Leonardo, and Freud ask for any finer corroboration of their ideas than this uncanny confirmation of their insights coming from the psychological depths of Proust's awakening psyche?

The strange appearance of architecture in dreams, so full of manifest and latent meaning, has one additional meaning, that psychoanalysis and philosophy have never been able to conceptualize convincingly. I am referring to the concept of consciousness. Saying that the mind is a sophisticated camera, one that records the phenomenal world and stores it away in preconscious and unconscious filing cabinets, is one thing. But the mind seems to *know* that it is a sentient camera, one that not only appreciates light and processes it internally as images of an external reality, but is also conscious of the *externality* of the phenomenal world—a world that is touched by the same existential light that eventually touches the human retina, the latter being more fragile and perishable than the former. That this gives the sentient human camera a jolt of *mortality* that is painful to process has been the subject matter of art and philosophy since man came to know himself in the cave of Lascaux or perhaps even earlier. "Man is a reed that thinks" (*un roseau qui pense),* as Pascal put it. Homer compares the passing generations to leaves, and Ecclesiastes describes "all flesh as grass," but man is the only animal that records its own passing. It is this peculiar quality of the sentient camera I am focusing on; it dares to know that its mechanisms are doomed, but goes on recording anyway! How it establishes that the phenomenal world is "out there," an external reality that light falls on, before it falls internally, an infinitesimal moment later, defines a relativity that puzzled Einstein, and is a puzzle that psychology has addressed, but has never "solved," in my opinion.

I believe architecture in dreams addresses this phenomenon, as well as all the rest of the conceivable latent and manifest meanings the free-associative process tries to make sense of. One awakens from a dream in which architecture has been treated like plasticine that the human mind can bend to its purposes any way the dream-work chooses. Awakened, the dreamer steps out of bed into the world of horizontals and verticals he has learned to take for granted since he was a child. But is he not jolted by the realization that once there was a world of unstable coordinates that his developing mind, in collaboration with the facilitating environment, had to "create"—not out of solipsism alone, but out of tradition, inherited *anlage* as well as out of unique experience? The "out-thereness" of the world has always had to be "internalized" by the sentient camera and then externalized again in what we have come to call reality testing, without always realizing how complex the commerce is between internal and external, as consciousness and unconsciousness take the measure of the world.

This capacity of the human mind to not only "take in" the light into its retina and record it, but to be able to know the location of the stimulus and perceive its "out-thereness" as well, even as it internalizes it, is an ego function, or an amalgam of ego functions, that must form the complexity of what has been conceptualized as *reality testing*. I am bringing attention to it without being able to clarify it further. I believe habituation allows us to ignore the wonder of it, the mystery of it, just as the child, who once lived in an uncertain architectural world where the horizontals and verticals were far from being established with the precision Piaget has documented for the older child, forgets all about the crooked coordinates that spawned him, once his feet and eyes get used to a more stable terra firma. But dreams do not let go of these regressive memories. In dreams our certainties are challenged. We are reminded again of the uncertainties that are the cornerstones of our convictions, and the resultant humility is surely a good and sobering thing.

By highlighting architecture in dreams, I am trying to bring attention not only to the content of dreams, but to their form as well, and how an understanding of one facilitates our understanding of the other. If the initial ego is a body ego, as Freud maintained, and much of the body is "buried" and its desires repressed, the strangeness of architecture in dreams reflects not only the strange dynamics of human conflict, but the mental engine that produces those conflicts as well.

Samuel's two-storey/two-story house dream reflects his divided self and his lifelong struggle to not only keep it divided but to integrate the two divided parts as well. But it reveals more than his dynamics and conflicts. It shows how the mind of the child is preserved in the mind of the adult, how the child's primitive psychology is still in the driver's seat, even as the mature mind tries to assert its developing autonomies. If the task of the Piagetian mind is to wean itself from primitive, perceptually bound intelligence and replace it with more sophisticated *conceptual* reality, to de-center itself from initial ego-centric error or distortion, the task of the Freudian mind is even more arduous. If the child initially lives in an animistic world of architecture in which horizontals and verticals are not clearly established, the immature child can emerge from this strange, crooked world only once his preoperational intelligence is superseded by the more cognitively advanced operational achievements. The Freudian mind cannot de-center from its neurotic ego-centricities, or all neurosis would be swept aside by advancing cognition and reality testing and there would be no need for psychoanalysis. The Freudian body is well hidden, in other words: its desires are deeply repressed by the power of infantile amnesia. It can only be reclaimed by development and experience and, when they fail, only by psychoanalysis.

Architecture in dreams is intriguing for these reasons, since it reminds us of the strange, wobbly world of unstable coordinates we all emerged from. By embracing the weird regressive implications of it, by walking on its shaky platforms, so to speak, by entering its windowless buildings, by addressing the ambiguities of its two-storeyed structures, by becoming startled by doors that tear open, not only the very fabric of a house, but our own definitions of hearth and home, we ironically become more solid in our appreciation of what we build in dreams and what we build when awake. We come to appreciate what in *Beowulf* is called "the bone-house of flesh," and that what it builds is as fragile as the bones and flesh that build it (Mahon, 2002). We come to appreciate that the limitations of our mortal bodies can still build buildings that outlast us, and be a generous legacy to future generations. Architecture in dreams, by challenging the very foundations we stand on or dwell in, forces us to revisit our concepts of solidity and stability, and how we define our most emotional convictions and certainties, or lack of them. Dream architecture asks us to consider the architecture of the mind itself, and by doing so, helps us to analyze the structure of our philosophy of life and death, the foundation of our sublimations and adaptations, the blueprint of all our aspirations, and the very cornerstone of human discourse and dialogue, which is, of course, the compromise desire must forge with reality, if any building of permanent psychosocial, rather than narcissistic or provincial character, is ever to be constructed.

References

Flavell, J. H. (1963), *The Developmental Psychology of Jean Piaget*. New York: Van Nostrand Reinhold.

Freud, S. (1900), The interpretation of dreams. *Standard Edition*, 3 & 4. London: Hogarth Press, 1953.

Heaney, S. (2000), *Beowulf: A New Verse Translation*. New York: Farrar, Strauss, and Giroux.

Mahon, E. (2002), Beowulf's barrow: An essay in honor of Lester Schwartz. *J. Clin. Psychoanal.*, 2:321–333.

——— (2003), The Freud–Vitruvius dialogues. Presented at Lucy Daniels Foundation, Raleigh, North Carolina, April, 2003.

——— (2004), Freud–Vitruvius dialogue. *Art Criticism*, 19(1):75–92.

O'Gorman, J. F. (1998), *ABC of Architecture*. Philadelphia: University of Pennsylvania Press.

Pascal, B. (1932), *Pascal's Pensées*, trans. W. Trotter. London: J. M. Dent.

Proust, M. (1970), *Swann's Way*, trans C. K. Scott Moncrieff. New York: Vintage Books.

Vitruvius, M. (1999), *On Architecture*. Loeb Classical Library. Cambridge, MA: Harvard University Press.

What Can Psychoanalysis Learn from an Enhanced Awareness of Architecture and Design?

STEPHEN M. SONNENBERG

Psychoanalysis is undergoing a paradigm shift (Kuhn, 1962). The hegemony of ego psychology and its postulates, including Freud's second theory of anxiety, drives, defenses, unconscious fantasy, and conflict and compromise formation is giving way to new models of mind (Wallerstein, 2002). The belief that therapeutic action results from making the unconscious conscious, reconstructing early experience, and resolving conflict is being replaced with perspectives which focus on the nature of the experience of both analysand and analyst of their analytic relationship (Blum, 2003a, b; Fonagy, 2003; Hoffman, 1994). Detailed discussions about how to conduct an analysis once stressed Freud's technique papers; today, such inquiries focus on the two-person analytic situation, and include ideas about the self, object relations, attachment, intersubjectivity, interpersonal experience, and the dialectical nature of social constructions. In this state of flux, where there has been such a dramatic shift in what is considered useful information for analysts reconsidering a theory of mind and a theory of therapeutic action, applied analysts no longer simply attempt to impart analytic wisdom to scholarly pursuits in other fields. Rather, applied analytic investigators now look to the scholarship of other fields for insights which will illuminate the psychoanalytic enterprise. Examples

---

The author wishes to thank Dr. Chana C. Schuetz, the Curator of the Neue Synagoge and the Deputy Director of the Stiftung Neue Synagoge Berlin–Centrum Judaicum, for her assistance during the preparation of this essay. The photographs of the Neue Synagoge which appear in this essay were taken by the author, and are published with the permission of the Stiftung Neue Synagoge Berlin–Centrum Judaicum.

include the integration of mathematical models into theories of mind (Galatzer-Levy, 1995, 2004), and the use of the experience of working as an applied analyst in the realm of political science to enhance one's clinical work (Sonnenberg, 1993a). Adherents of the typical structure of the analytic situation, who stressed anonymity, abstinence, neutrality, frequency of sessions, free association, and the use of the couch have been replaced by more flexible investigators who ask, "What makes for an analytic environment which promotes effective self-inquiry?" In that regard a focus on the environment, on architecture and design, on form, on space and structure, might offer useful insights into how analysis works, and how it might work better. If that is so, what better place to start than with the naturalistic experiment that Sigmund Freud conducted when, as a man of 46 years, he visited the Acropolis?

Freud at the Acropolis

Freud wrote of this visit in a letter to Romain Rolland, in 1936, in honor of Rolland's seventieth birthday (Freud, 1936). He wrote at the age of 80, focusing on his disturbance of memory at the Acropolis. This is an outstanding example of his self-analysis, in which he demonstrates the ongoing challenge of exploring his oedipal conflicts. He also illustrates in this letter the interplay of past (memories from his childhood and of his experience at the Acropolis 34 years earlier), present (his personal admiration for Rolland and the event of Rolland's seventieth birthday), and transference (he notes that Rolland and his brother, Alexander, who was with him at the Acropolis, are both ten years his junior) when exploring an event from the psychoanalytic perspective. Today, this concurrence of focal points is still often used as a guideline in assessing what constitutes an excellent interpretation or a good analytic hour.

Freud's letter has been the subject of scholarly scrutiny, most often focusing on its text, and additionally on what is known about his transference relationship and correspondence with Rolland (Blum, 1995; Bouchard, 1995; Guillaumin, 1995). In these investigations, oedipal and preoedipal themes in Freud's self-analysis have been examined, as well as his views on mysticism (Guillaumin, 1995; Masson and Masson, 1978), the concept of the oceanic feeling (Masson and Masson, 1978), war and aggression (Werman, 1977), narcissism and homosexuality (Guillaumin, 1995), disavowal (Guillaumin, 1995), splitting (Guillaumin, 1995), and religion (Halpern, 1999). Also, the role in Freud's development of childhood loss (Bouchard, 1995), infantile seduction (Masson and Masson, 1978) and sexuality (Slochower, 1970, 1971), and ambivalence about his Jewishness (Gedo, 1992; Halpern, 1999) have been considered. This scrutiny constitutes a very wide-ranging exploration, illustrating how varied are the possible interpretations of what went on in Freud's mind as he first experienced the Acropolis and then re-experienced it self-analytically, probably many times, leading up to his 1936 letter.

Yet in all this scholarly inquiry there are only occasional references to what Freud specifically encountered on the Acropolis, and hypotheses as to how that may have motivated or stimulated his self-analysis. Flannery (1980) writes that Freud could well have experienced the frieze carvings on the Parthenon, including the carvings removed and in the British Museum, in an oedipal framework, relating these to what at that time he was exploring within himself. Flannery hypothesizes that Freud unconsciously identified with the carved figures as he visualized what was there and imagined what wasn't, with the help of a guidebook. Another writer, Harrison (1966), emphasizes that monuments and memorials, whether natural or man-made, elicit powerful reactions from inspired observers, stimulating a response that organizes these observers into a cohesive group. This leaves open the possibility that Freud was so moved.

The Lens of Self-Analysis at the Neue Synagoge

Today the majority of analysts stand on the shoulders of Freud in their practice of self-analysis; and when reading Freud's letter to Rolland, there is an opportunity to explore how that process might have been facilitated by the place on which Freud stood when he experienced his disturbance. In this essay I, a clinical analyst, will examine Freud's self-analytic experience on the Acropolis through the lens provided by another naturalistic experiment, my experience at the Neue Synagoge in Berlin, Germany. I shall focus on the physical characteristics of each place, aspects of which were originally planned by architects, artists, and designers, and aspects of which were created by other forces, including the erosion of structure over time, the effect of the removal of parts of structure by people taking antiquities for display elsewhere, and restoration efforts after the devastation of the Holocaust and World War II. In the end, I shall try to use an architectural and design perspective to understand how my psychological experience and Freud's were facilitated by the environments that motivated each of us to engage in self-inquiry. Finally, I shall try to answer a question: What does an architectural perspective suggest to us about what in the analytic environment promotes effective inquiry, be it in self-analysis or clinical analysis? I believe this will provide fresh insight into how we might do our clinical work more effectively.

Earlier, in a series of articles, I described my practice of self-analysis, and the range of applications of my self-analysis, including clinical work (Sonnenberg, 1991, 1995), teaching (Sonnenberg, 1990), writing (Sonnenberg, 1993b), and

FIGURE 1. The Rear Wall, Neue Synagoge, with reinforcing glass structure.

performing applied analytic research (Sonnenberg, 1993a). At that time, between ten and 15 years ago, I emphasized the usefulness of disciplined self-exploration, and offered examples of how I actually processed my own associations when I systematically self-analyzed. However, I also noted in something of an aside, that my self-analysis often took place more spontaneously, in a less formal way, while listening to patients, sitting at my desk, lying in bed at night, or taking a walk (Sonnenberg, 1991). More recently, I have noted that such less formal self-analysis was more important as a source of self-understanding than I had previously appreciated (Sonnenberg and Myerson, 2004).

Recently, while in Berlin, I visited the Neue Synagoge. Construction of the Synagoge began in 1859, and prior to the Holocaust it was the home to a very large,

FIGURE 2. The Rear Window, Neue Synagoge.

successful, and culturally assimilated Jewish congregation (known in Germany as a community). The building was desecrated by the Nazis, and suffered a great deal of war-related damage from aerial bombardment. After the war, the damaged sanctuary, which had seated more than 1,500 congregants, was not rebuilt, reflecting the fact that the once robust Jewish community was now very small. That small community gave permission for the demolition of the sanctuary, with the stipulation that the front part of the structure remain standing, as a memorial to the Holocaust and the historical importance of the Jewish community of Germany. The demolition took place in 1958. Then, in 1988, one year before the fall of the Berlin Wall, efforts at restoration of the Synagoge began with a grant from the East German government. The start of the restoration was timed to commemorate the fiftieth anniversary of Kristallnacht.

Today the Synagoge is a memorial, and houses a museum, a center for the study of Judaism in Germany before the Holocaust, and an archive of those once thriving Jewish communities. As can be seen in figure 1, by using very large panes of glass an outside wall was constructed out of what had once been the entrance to the sanctuary and the supports of two tiered balconies at the rear of the sanctuary. This wall was reinforced by a large structure, also made mostly of glass, which defines an outdoor space where the indoor sanctuary stood. On one of those lower windows (see figure 2) a photo has been placed, so that the viewer standing within the outdoor space, semi-enclosed by glass, can look into the building and both view and imagine an indoor space, a sanctuary, where he is actually standing while outside. In a subtle way, my experience as the outdoor viewer involved a loss of spatial and temporal orientation, as I found myself both inside and outside, experiencing today and yesterday, in a way which is unusually fluid. In more familiar psychoanalytic language, standing outside looking into the structure of the Neue Synagoge, through a photo which depicts an indoor sanctuary which no longer exists, I experienced a blending of intrapsychic space, inner space in the form of fantasy, and outer space, in the form of my perception of a photograph, and of the space now outside where once the sanctuary stood. It was there that I had a spontaneous self-analytic experience.

As I became aware that my experience involved loss of the customary boundaries of inner and outer, concrete and imaginary space, and as past and present space converged within my mind, my emotions were intense. For while standing there I began to imagine what it might have been like for me to be a congregant of the Neue Synagoge during the rise of the Nazis, when so much of what I experienced created in me emotional turmoil, profound confusion, disbelief, and disorientation. I thought of how I might have worshipped there, and how I would have experienced a sense of community with others who a few years before had held positions of great and unchallenged importance in the cultural, economic, and academic life of Berlin and Germany. I realized that for all of us becoming societal outcasts, non-Germans, or even worse, non-humans, was unthinkable, unimaginable. From there I began to associate to my psychoanalytic work on war, which in the past focused on the Holocaust (Sonnenberg, 1974), the Vietnam War (Sonnenberg, Blank, and Talbott, 1985), and the United States–Soviet Union nuclear relationship (Sonnenberg, 1993a). I thought about the experience of Holocaust survivors I had treated, recalling that an important source of trauma in many who were lucky enough to escape internment and the loss of immediate family members was the experience of being designated an outcast, a person rejected by his own country and culture. I was struck at how, standing alone in that place, I felt a more powerful identification with those former patients, a more complete sense of unity and empathy with them than ever before. Despite years studying the Holocaust and working with survivors, my sense of their experience as their societies crumbled and their identities fragmented became far more vivid.

From there I thought about the trauma of war, and I focused on what are to me two familiar themes: The dehumanization of everyone connected with warfare, including non-combatants, and the ubiquity of what I see as an effort in

FIGURE 3. The Acropolis, showing ruins. Photograph courtesy of the School of Architecture's Visual Resources Collection, the University of Texas at Austin.

the survivor to reestablish one's humanness in the face of survivor guilt. Then I associated to a focal point in my ongoing self-analysis, my experience of oedipal conflict during World War II, when, as a small child, I was confronted with the frightening possibility of an oedipal triumph should my father be called away for military service (Sonnenberg, 1991). I reflected on how that experience had shaped my studies of war and the experience of the survivor, and how issues of survivor guilt and competitive advantage were ubiquitous subjects in my clinically related self-analysis. Some specific clinical situations came to mind, and I pondered them, though I will not elaborate on them here. I realized, too, that my thoughts about my childhood experience during World War II were intensified just then, because my father's ancestors had lived in Germany before migrating to the United States. I knew that my awareness at that moment of the role of survivor guilt in my life was directly catalyzed by my being in that indoor–outdoor space at the Neue Synagoge.

I left the Synagoge and reflected on what I had just experienced, and soon realized that it was similar to what analysands experience when they share with me the intense intimacy of our analytic relationships. Like the Neue Synagoge, the analytic environment invites the analysand to abandon usual orientations in place and time, and move more fluidly among memories and imaginings about the past, present perceptual experiences, and transferences.

This brings me back to Freud at the Acropolis. As I noted earlier, little is made in the literature of the physical characteristics of where Freud stood, over what he walked, and what he saw. Using the lens of my experience at the Neue Synagoge, I now hypothesize that the openness of the Acropolis, its beautiful structures and the irregularities of its deteriorated state, and the distant vision of the tourist of an ever-shifting sea, all affected Freud as he tread cautiously over broken pieces of stone, and used his guidebook and his mind's eye to visualize frieze carvings now in a distant museum, and buildings once in pristine condition (see figure 3). Freud might have experienced a sense of the fluid interplay of inner psychological space and outer perceptual space, then a loss of temporal and spatial orientation, followed finally by the use of his imagination as he constructed a picture of what the Acropolis was once like. In that frame of mind, I suggest, we can understand how Freud, given the psychodynamics of his relationship with his father and, more broadly, his psychodynamically complex mind, was vulnerable to the disturbance of memory he described, which he was able to recognize as a false recollection of doubting the existence of the Acropolis while a child in school. Given that this was a disturbing and puzzling experience we can also intuitively understand why it became an organizer for an ongoing and intense experience of oedipally focused self-analysis. Finally, we can also hypothesize how that experience could serve an important adaptive function as Freud wished to pay tribute to Romain Rolland, a man toward whom he experienced both present admiration and a powerful transference, one manifestly involving his ten-year-younger brother, Alexander, but probably a transference infused with oedipal concerns, as suggested by the body of formulations concerning the reasons for Freud's Acropolis experience, and his motivations for writing about it to Rolland.

The Perspective of the "*Informal*": Chaos and Complexity

Now we can articulate a question which has important implications for our understanding of the process of clinical analysis, per se, and self-analysis, which is an important goal, and hopefully a part, of every clinical analysis: From the perspective of architecture and design, can we more precisely conceptualize what it is about the Neue Synagoge and the Acropolis that stimulated Freud's and my own self-analytic efforts, and what, if anything, these environments have in common? The answer to this question, in my view, underlies the answer to the question proposed earlier as the central goal of this paper. That question, again, is, "What does an architectural perspective suggest to us about what in the analytic environment promotes effective inquiry?"

For help with these questions I shall turn to an examination of the thinking of Cecil Balmond, an engineer who has worked with leading architects in designing and constructing several important contemporary building projects. Balmond is described as a consulting engineer who is interested in the nature of form and its relationship with science, art, music, numbers and mathematics (Balmond with Smith, 2002, p. 394). Writing about Balmond's conceptualization of his work, the architectural historian and critic Charles Jencks notes that he believes that phase change takes place ubiquitously in nature, and that new patterns of organization emerge spontaneously. The result of this orientation, Jencks adds, is that Balmond's work is both biomorphic and free-form: "On every design on which he has collaborated he has pushed the structure in different ways, or allowed new assumptions to interact, so that surprising patterns emerge . . . Aesthetic and intellectual appreciation demands a minimum provocation, something that spurs us to see and think anew" (Jencks, 2002, pp. 5–8).

Balmond, reflecting on his own history as an engineer and designer working with architects, notes that he experiences buildings as more than simple spaces, but rather as opportunities to be in the world creatively, unshackled from old, routine, and rigidified emotional, cognitive, and perceptual aspects of human existence. The building is to him a vehicle opening up his mind to new, expansive ways of being, thinking, feeling, and designing. In explaining his approach to his work (Balmond with Smith, 2002), which he has named the "*informal*," he writes:

> At first I assumed a certain subservience in engineering, as an enabling science to the act of putting up buildings . . . Then I began to question what these regular framings of closed squares and rectangles were; were they containers of an empty inanimate space? I looked again. I did not believe in this restriction . . . [I came upon] the contemporary idea of complexity as an unfolding, simultaneous and self-similar pattern . . . Chaos theory produced impossibly beautiful structure . . . surprising and ambiguous answers arise . . . As long as our brain kept to tramlines of reasoning the [old] model persisted. Now that the world is being accepted as not simple, the complex and oblique and the intertwining of logic strands gain favour. Reason itself is finally being understood as nascent structure, non-linear and dependent on feedback procedures. Beauty may lie in the actual processes of engagement and be more abstract than the aesthetic of objecthood. Ultimately it may really be a constructive process [pp. 13–15].

Balmond offers us specific reactions while collaborating with architects on design and construction projects. For example, "As one journeys through the building, structure reveals itself not as mute skeleton but as a series of provocations; sometimes explicit, at other times ambiguous. Structure emerges with different styles, in some locations graceful and flying, elsewhere awkward and stolid and rooted to the spot . . . in short chunky columns stuck to the roof and floor. The varying rhythms and ad-hoc strategies yield a hybridization that wraps around the visitor" (Balmond with Smith, 2002, p. 105). "The consequence," he adds, "is an architecture full of surprise. Now you can see it, now you don't. *Informal* is that chameleon, a change-artist . . . [this building is] a crucible of such elusive bad behavior" (Balmond with Smith, 2002, p. 107).

Balmond writes that "the *informal* steps in easily, a sudden twist or turn, a branching, and the unexpected happens—the edge of chance shows its face . . . Delight, surprise, ambiguity are typical responses; ideas clash in the *informal* and strange juxtapositions take place. Overlaps occur. Instead of regular, formally controlled measures, there are varying rhythms and wayward impulses . . . Uniformity is broken and balance is interrupted. The demand for Order! In the regimental sense is ignored: the big picture is something else" (Balmond with Smith, 2002, p. 111).

He then goes on to emphasize:

In the *informal* there are no distinct rules, no fixed patterns, to be copied blindly. If there is a rhythm it is in the hidden connections that are inferred and implied, and not necessarily made obvious. Order, in a hierarchical and fixed sense, is taken as furthest removed from the natural state of things. . . . Quite the opposite is the Formal, rigid, hierarchical. Its chief characteristic is analysis which needs reference, as the past comes with close grid of argument . . . it is a reductionist process . . . [Yet] The creative impulse jumping out of nowhere is scary . . . In the face of such turbulence, order is endorsed as the safe fortress. But it misses the point: that the nature of reality is chance and that "order" may only be a small, local, steady state of a much larger random [pp. 114–115].

Then, writing about the use of the spiral in a specific project, he notes that "A cherished symmetry and insistence of right-angled forms rejected, and the old paradigm of fixed centre left behind, the . . . Spiral vaults into new space. *Inside is outside* [italics added]. Floors are denied columns, and walls offer no vertical short cuts for gravity. Structure and architecture become one immediacy" (Balmond with Smith, 2002, p. 191). Significantly, he closes his comments on that project noting that "Perhaps intuition has an internal mapping of its own, of non-linear algorithms. Testing this further is a task of the *informal*" (Balmond with Smith, 2002, p. 215).

Finally, he writes:

> The *informal* is opportunistic, an approach to design that seizes a local moment and makes something of it. Ignoring preconception of formal layering and repetitive rhythm, the *informal* keeps one guessing. Ideas are not based on principles of rigid hierarchy but on an intense exploration of the immediate . . . It . . . [is] a methodology of evolving starting points that, by emergence, creates its own series of orders . . . The more subtle approach is to seek the notion that chaos is a mix of several states of order. What is an improvisation is in fact a kernel of stability, which in turn sets sequences that reach equilibrium. Several equilibriums coexist. Simultaneity matters; not hierarchy . . . The *informal* gives rise to ambiguity. This means interpretation and experiment as a natural course of events [Balmond with Smith, 2002, pp. 220–227].

I believe that Balmond is telling us that the *informal* environment promotes surprise and the potential for psychological state change in both the creator of a structure and a space, such as an architect or a design engineer, and the user of such a structure and space, such as the visitor to a museum or memorial, or the resident of, or worker in, a building. That is possible, Balmond suggests, because that environment is itself characterized by surprise and psychological and physical state change.

In my view, my description of what has been done to preserve the Neue Synagoge and memorialize those who once occupied it and their culture and community, and my experience of it, is consistent with Balmond's description of the *informal*. Balmond's emphasis on the surprising, unconventional pattern which promotes freedom of thinking, perception, and experiencing, with resulting psychological state change, is based on contemporary mathematical ideas about chaos and complex systems, and his notions of what becomes possible for a person within such an *informal* environment or structure certainly fits with my experience at the Neue Synagoge. Therefore, I think we now have a perspective, in the language of contemporary architecture and design, on what characterizes a physical environment which promotes freedom of thought, a capacity to experience surprise, and to perceive and experience oneself suddenly outside the box.

I believe the Acropolis, existing as it does with partially intact and partially crumbling structures, structures with parts removed and transported elsewhere, with ever-changing patterns of water in the distance, has evolved into an environment which is unpredictable, unconventional, and surprising, an environment which the visitor experiences in a way similar to the visitor's experience at the rear, mostly glass wall of the Neue Synagoge. I believe, then, that the Acropolis is now an *informal* environment, and that it was that quality which propelled Freud to begin a self-reflective process which lasted for decades: The Acropolis was a place which stimulated Freud to experience a psychological state change, in the form of a disturbance of memory. I believe, too, that we have identified what the Neue Synagoge and the Acropolis share as environments which encourage self-analysis.

Discussion: A Psychoanalytic Restatement of the *Informal*

Galatzer-Levy (1995, 2004) has applied the mathematical concepts of nonlinear equations, chaos theory, and the theory of complex systems to the study of clinical psychoanalysis. He has explained that these concepts do not mean that what happens in the psychological world is simply not linear, nor is it chaotic in the intuitive sense. Rather, because of the complexity of human development and human existence, rigid and unimaginative formulations of normality do not help the clinician to understand the patient, nor the patient to understand himself: A more effective orientation holds that different people develop in different ways, and different end points can constitute the normal. He goes on to note that traditional psychoanalytic perspectives teach clinicians that development not only proceeds in predictable, small increments, with predictable outcomes, but that significant psychological and behavioral shifts do not take place at what would appear to be dramatic rates of change. This, he asserts, is simply incorrect, and he adds that surprising, abrupt psychological state changes occur in the course of normal development. Galatzer-Levy thus offers a message of great significance, which dovetails with much of my long experience as a teacher and consultant: Psychoanalytic shibboleths have created a clinical technique that emphasizes a kind of orderly and programmed inquiry, orchestrated by an orderly, programmed and only seemingly non-intrusive analyst, working in a very stereotypical way, in a very stereotypical environment. In effect, the agenda is set by an analyst who comes to the clinical enterprise with a preformed view of what will transpire, slowly, over time, and even with a preformed view of clinical outcome. That view then shapes the experience of both members of the dyad.

This oversimplified summary, and my own reaction to it, do not do complete justice to the elegance of Galatzer-Levy's ideas, but they do make the point I wish to emphasize here. Using the perspectives of Balmond and Galatzer-Levy, I believe that my powerful experience of empathy and identification with a group of victims of the Holocaust at the Neue Synagoge was possible because I was placed in an environment in which I was encouraged to step emotionally out of a place fixed by the conventional boundaries of a room or a building, a rectangle or a sphere, an enclosure or a courtyard or a park, into a world where inside and outside, past and present, and imaginings and perceptions were permitted to mingle within me in a spontaneous, vivid way. I was encouraged to experience disorder and disorientation, even confusion, as I tried, for a split second, to figure out where I was as I looked through a window and a photograph, seeing myself inside and being outside, seeing myself in the year 1935, being in the year 2003. This was an experience of dramatic psychological state change, made possible by an *informal* environment. Further, that experience led me to reflect on it over time, and drew me back to it repeatedly. Long before this *Annual* called for papers on architecture and psychoanalysis, I found myself engaged in a self-inquiring experience, a self-analytic exploration of what had happened to me and why it had happened. I can assure the reader that this essay would have been written if the *Annual of Psychoanalysis* had never undertaken publication of this volume.

My hypothesis, already stated, is that the Acropolis, with its irregularities, its orderliness and its disorder, its missing frieze carvings and its remaining ones, and its view of a changing sea, promotes the same sort of experience in one who visits there. That visitor must negotiate a complex terrain with his or her eyes, legs, and mind. And at that point, if one is preoccupied with an aspect of one's own antique past, then those preoccupations may dominate that person's psyche. The Acropolis certainly does not promote in the visitor the kind of relatively predictable aesthetic response he or she would have within, or standing before, a pristine structure, or in a hall filled with polished frieze carvings at the British Museum. It evokes in the viewer an experience of the *informal*.

A Clinical Example and an Appeal for Analytic Listening with Shared Perplexity

I now want to conclude this essay by returning to what lessons might be learned from this investigation of Freud's experience on the Acropolis, my experience at the Neue Synagoge, Galatzer-Levy's ideas about psychoanalysis, and Balmond's ideas about design. The goal, of course, is to develop a deeper appreciation of what promotes both effective self-analysis and clinical analysis. I should add explicitly that, in my view, effective introspection and creative inquiry about oneself has much in common, whether it takes place with the help of a second person or is conducted alone. For that reason, I believe lessons from self-analysis shed light on how to conduct clinical analysis, and that the reverse is true, as well. Obviously, that belief constitutes a basic assumption of this essay.

This paper suggests that much is lost when the analyst works with the belief that he or she is possessed of certain knowledge about what is possible in human development, or in the effort to heal a patient: When that analyst cannot take seriously an analysand's assertion that he or she has experienced a sudden and helpful change in psychological state, especially when the analysand says that this has taken place as a result of analysis, the disbelieving analyst deprives both members of the dyad from embracing, understanding, and making further use of something beneficial. While we know that our theoretical biases inevitably influence what we hear and how we hear it, it seems to me that the analyst needs to try to approach each analysand in each analytic hour with a willingness to consider that he or she, and the analysand, will learn something new and surprising. That process requires a willingness to believe that new perspectives can emerge, and emerge rapidly, no matter what seems to have been happening in the clinical situation. Recall, for example, that at the Neue Synagoge I had a new appreciation of something I had studied for decades. It also requires that the concept of the continuity of mental functioning be modified to accept the idea that at times the nature of that continuity will be obscure or even impossible to discern, and even, in the way we usually think about continuity, not there at all. It means, and this is especially important, that the analyst should be prepared to share his or her surprise with the analysand. It requires the analyst to respond to disorientation openly and without hesitation, in effect to create an interaction in which both members of the analytic dyad share in the experience of confusion and perplexity. This, in effect, is the clinical equivalent of the *informal* environment that has been created by the combination of chance and careful design at the rear wall of the Neue Synagoge, and on the Acropolis.

I want to make clear that I am not proposing that the analyst abandon the interpersonal restraint reflected in the technical concepts of anonymity, neutrality, and abstinence, and the ways the physical environment of the consulting room incorporates those concepts. Yet I am proposing that those traditional guidelines be employed in a way that allows for the analytic environment to be more compatible with the goals of the *informal*: surprise, shared perplexity, and wonder at what sudden psychological development and change is possible. I am proposing that all of this should be encouraged by the analytic environment. Let me illustrate with a clinical example.

Many years ago I analyzed a very inhibited woman, who had grown up in a home where both parents were very rejecting of her and where both told her over and over again that she was basically incapable of successful interpersonal relationships. She had come to me after her husband had shocked her by filing for divorce after decades of marriage, and she felt desperately alone and hopeless. The subsequent analysis lasted for over ten years, and for the most part was conducted, in a formal sense, in a very traditional way: We used the couch, she was seen four times each week, and I never lost sight of the usefulness of appropriate abstinence, neutrality, and anonymity. Much of the analysis focused on how lost this woman felt in the social world, how shy she felt, and how unknowing she was of how to enjoy others and how to determine whether they enjoyed her.

Something had happened very early in our relationship which troubled my patient for several years, and resulted in her feeling very inhibited and disconnected from me in the analysis. Indeed, for long periods of time she was barely able to speak, after lying on the couch. It had seemed to her that initially I was warm and friendly, and she very specifically reminded me that I had smiled at her a lot very early in the consultation, but not at the end of it. For several years I simply had no understanding of what she was talking about, was frankly skeptical that it had happened that way, and came close to insisting that all she was talking about was the difference between her experience of sitting in a chair and facing me during the consultation, and lying on the couch when the analysis formally began. But, in the face of this stereotypical analytic assumption and response, this shy, often silent, and always inhibited woman insisted that I was missing the boat.

From the start, this woman knew something about my family. The person who had referred her to me was an academic colleague, but not a psychoanalyst, and he felt that because of the configuration of my family I could understand this woman, and told her so. This was why she knew quite a bit about my daughter, and that at least in terms of academic achievement she and my daughter had a great deal in common. From time to time she would associate to my daughter, but I never connected these thoughts and feelings with her difficulties speaking on the couch.

Several years after this analysis began, my daughter's photograph appeared in a newspaper, accompanying the announcement of her forthcoming marriage. My patient saw this, and congratulated me. When she did this, I had a sudden insight. As I was picturing the photograph in my mind's eye, I realized that my patient and my daughter resembled each other in two ways: They were both high academic achievers, and they looked alike. And suddenly, I realized that because of her appearance, when I had first laid eyes on this patient, I had related to her, unconsciously, as if she were my daughter. Simply because of her facial features I had felt an immediate and very strong paternal concern for her. She was right, I realized: I had smiled very warmly at her over and over again when I first met her, with the warm smile of a father trying to soothe a troubled daughter. She was correct, too, that by the end of the consultation I had stopped smiling in that way, for without my being conscious of any of this, as the consultation process progressed and she settled down, I felt less of that fatherly need to soothe her. I decided to tell all this to my patient, and I did, and she suddenly felt relieved. She felt that her experience in the analysis was now understood by us both. And then things began to change very rapidly, as the analysis took off and my patient was able to associate freely, analyze effectively, and begin a process that resulted in a greatly enhanced capacity to relate intimately to me and to others.

I believe this vignette illustrates how for several years after my analysand and I began a formal analysis our efforts to establish intimacy and an atmosphere of analytic inquiry had been stymied, because of my inability to consider that I had induced a surprising, sudden state change in my potential analysand, during the consultation. It also illustrates how, once I was able to experience a sudden and surprising awareness of my effect on my patient, and convey this to her, she was immediately able to undergo a major, responsive change.

This example suggests that an effective, *informal* clinical environment promotes an effective analysis, and that this is made possible by the analyst's mindset. It illustrates vividly that when the analyst is able to create an environment characterized by an openness to surprise and state change, especially his or her own surprise and state change, surprise and state change becomes much more likely for the analysand.

I will end with a specific suggestion about analytic technique. In recent years we have added ways of analytic listening to Freud's suggestion that evenly hovering attention is the order of the day. Today we listen, as well, with evenly hovering role responsiveness, a willingness to accept the patient's projective identifications, a desire to understand the patient's point of view, and an awareness of the importance of close process monitoring. We should add to those modes of experiencing the patient the need to listen in shared perplexity and curiosity as we hear about new and surprising ideas, and sudden changes in psychological state. In this way psychoanalysis can become, in and of itself, a different kind of developmental experience, which will make possible surprising and sudden growth in the analysand.

But there remains one more point to be made. As a clinician, I have attempted to use environmental experience and a perspective incorporating the disciplines of architecture and design to examine and enhance my understanding of interaction within the analytic dyad, and of psychoanalytic technique. I have also noted above that, as regards the physical environment in which psychoanalysis is conducted, I do not advocate radical change. However, I do have many questions about what in that physical environment might optimize the experience of both analysand and analyst. Answering those questions is beyond the scope of this paper, because it is beyond my expertise. Perhaps some of the contributions of architects and designers in this volume will offer insight into that area of inquiry.

References

Balmond, C. with Smith, J. (2002), *informal*. Munich: Prestel Verlag.

Blum, H. P. (1995), Freud correspondence. *J. Amer. Psychoanal. Assn.,* 43:869–873.

——— (2003a), Repression, transference, and reconstruction. *Internat. J. Psycho-Anal.,* 84:497–503.

——— (2003b), Response to Peter Fonagy. *Internat. J. Psycho-Anal.,* 84:509–513.

Bouchard, F. (1995), Sigmund Freud and Romain Rolland: Correspondence 1923–1936. *J. Amer. Psychoanal. Assn.,* 43:883–887.

Flannery, J. G. (1980), Freud's Acropolis revisited. *Internat. Rev. Psycho-Anal.,* 7:347–352.

Fonagy, P. (2003), Rejoinder to Harold Blum. *Internat. J. Psycho-Anal.,* 84:503–509.

Freud, S. (1936), A disturbance of memory on the Acropolis. *Standard Edition,* 22:237–248. London: Hogarth Press, 1971.

Galatzer-Levy, R. M. (1995), Psychoanalysis and dynamical systems theory: Prediction and self similarity. *J. Amer. Psychoanal. Assn.,* 43:1085–1113.

——— (2004), Chaotic possibilities: Toward a new model of development. *Internat. J. Psycho-Anal.,* 85:419–441.

Gedo, J. E. (1992), Art alone endures. *J. Amer. Psychoanal. Assn.,* 40:501–516.

Guillaumin, J. (1995), Sigmund Freud et Romain Rolland, correspondance 1923–1936. *Internat. J. Psycho-Anal.,* 76:1056–1060.

Halpern, J. R. (1999), Freud's intrapsychic use of the Jewish culture and religion. *J. Amer. Psychoanal. Assn.,* 47:1191–1212.

Harrison, I. B. (1966), A reconsideration of Freud's "A disturbance of memory on the Acropolis" in relation to identity disturbance. *J. Amer. Psychoanal. Assn.,* 14:518–527.

Hoffman, I. Z. (1994), Dialectical thinking and therapeutic action in the psychoanalytic process. *Psychoanal. Quart.,* 63:187–218.

Jencks, C. (2002), Preface: Changing architecture. In: C. Balmond with J. Smith, *informal*. Munich: Prestel Verlag, pp. 5–8.

Kuhn, T. S. (1962), *The Structure of Scientific Revolutions*. Chicago: University of Chicago Press.

Masson, J. M. & Masson, T. C. (1978), Buried memories on the Acropolis: Freud's response to mysticism and anti-Semitism. *Internat. J. Psycho-Anal.,* 59:199–208.

Slochower, H. (1970), Freud's déjà vu on the Acropolis—A symbolic relic of "mater nuda." *Psychoanal. Quart.,* 39:90–102.

——— (1971), Freud's Gradiva: Mater nuda rediviva—A wish-fulfillment of the "memory" on the Acropolis. *Psychoanal. Quart.,* 40:646–662.

Sonnenberg, S. M., (1974), Children of survivors. *J. Amer. Psychoanal. Assn.,* 22:200–204.

——— (1990), Introducing psychiatric residents to psychoanalysis: A visiting analyst's perspective. *J. Amer. Psychoanal. Assn.,* 38:451–469.

——— (1991), The analyst's self-analysis and its impact on clinical work: A comment on the sources and importance of personal insights. *J. Amer. Psychoanal. Assn.*, 39:687–704.

——— (1993a), Self-analysis, applied analysis, and analytic fieldwork: A discussion of methodology in psychoanalytic interdisciplinary research. *Psychoanal. Study of Society*, 18:443–463.

——— (1993b), To write or not to write. A note on self-analysis and the resistance to self-analysis. In: *Self-Analysis, Critical Inquiries, Personal Visions*, ed. J. W. Barron. Hillsdale, NJ: The Analytic Press, 1993, pp. 241–259.

——— (1995), Analytic listening and the analyst's self-analysis. *Internat. J. Psycho-Anal.*, 76:335–342.

Sonnenberg, S. M., Blank, A. S. & Talbott, J. A., eds. (1985), *The Trauma of War: Stress and Recovery in Viet Nam Veterans*. Washington, DC: American Psychiatric Press.

Sonnenberg, S. M. & Myerson, W. A. (2004), The educational boundary: Recognition, management, and why it can be managed. Paper presented at the 43rd Congress of the International Psychoanalytical Association, New Orleans, Louisiana.

Wallerstein, R. S. (2002), The growth and transformation of American Ego Psychology. *J. Amer. Psychoanal. Assn.*, 50:135–169.

Werman, D. S. (1977), Sigmund Freud and Romain Rolland. *Internat. Rev. Psycho-Anal.*, 4:225–242.

Architecture and the True Self

F. ROBERT RODMAN

Fostering the True Self

One lovely day in 1994, my wife and children and I had lunch at a café near one of the chateaux in the Loire region of France. The café was adjacent to an expanse of lawn with scattered trees. The usual gravel base lay beneath the outdoor tables that were shaded by umbrellas. For reasons I do not completely understand, I like the gravel in such settings; it brings me a kind of peace. It may be in part because the gravel absorbs surrounding sounds.

It was a sunny day, and I felt good. I drew the scene. In a state of relaxation usually associated with travel, I often sketch. The result, though amateur, is valuable to me as a memento of an event; it provides something personal. In sketching one has to take one's time, make observations, choose what seems to matter, make the marks on the page, and perhaps use a few dots of color from a watercolor box.

In such a circumstance, I feel free to express my true self. The main point I want to make in this essay is that certain architectural situations foster such expressions and are valued for that. What I have described is not a building; it is a space. But I suppose I could have found an example in the form of a building. What comes to mind are the book alcoves in a library where, as an undergraduate, I reviewed the semester's reading in preparation for final exams. It was a quiet location; the sound-deadening effect of the books may be analogous to the sound-deadening

---

F. Robert Rodman presented the original version of this paper on April 6, 2003, in Raleigh, North Carolina, at a conference on "Architecture and the Self: Explorations of Inner and Outer Space," sponsored by the Lucy Daniels Foundation. Before his death in 2004, he submitted the paper for this volume. James William Anderson edited the paper for publication, with the permission of his widow.

effect of the gravel in France. I could concentrate. I could be even-tempered. My state of mind could be sustained over many hours. For a break I could just walk out into the surrounding areas and, in those days, have a cigarette. That whole place has stood the test of time in my mind, a place where I could unfold, where my true self could emerge.

No doubt the true self is related to ideas of being real or authentic that have a long history in Western thinking. I am using the concept of the *true self* as developed by Donald W. Winnicott (1960a), an English psychoanalyst (also see Rodman, 2003). For Winnicott healthy development featured conditions that facilitated the development and expression of the true self, as opposed to the false self that, he believed, came about in response to demands made by the environment. It was not that a person could consist only of a true self. It was always necessary and inevitable that some degree of the false self would develop, because people follow social rules. One tends to accept that the question, "How are you?" is actually only a way of saying "hello," not an actual question that would have metaphysical import. When you answer "fine," you are summarizing and are undoubtedly concealing all that cannot be subsumed under the word "fine."

Why did I feel so good in France that day, and what circumstances, specifically, what architectural circumstances, can facilitate such good feeling? Might one apply a criterion to built structures: Do they facilitate the expression of the true self or do they not? There is an obvious difficulty in answering this question: buildings are so variegated, so complicated, so shaped by purpose, the demands of clients, the skills and artistic vision of the architect, the period of history in which they are constructed, and I suppose the kind of weather in the location of the relevant structure.

And how would one measure a building's power to nurture the true self? In a way the difficulty of assessing such a factor is analogous to the difficulty psychoanalysts have in deciding which of their theories is most correct. There is a consensus that develops over the years, but that consensus does not constitute proof in the way that a scientific experiment might. The number of variables is too great to be tested in a controlled way.

The difficulties involved, however, do not provide a reason to cease trying to capture the human essentials of architecture. So I offer the idea that one criterion of the value of an architectural creation is the extent to which the structure fosters the expression of the true self. It is undoubtedly true as well that the uses of a building will vary over time and therefore entirely novel conceptualizations will become necessary to address this topic. During that 1994 trip we also went to the Chartres cathedral, a monument I had studied in college and in Henry Adams's book. I was unprepared for the darkness within. There were few people present. We wandered around. I recognized the Rose Window and others. As I think of the cathedral, it occurs to me that the hundreds of years of artistic and skilled labor that went into its construction, aimed to the greater glory of God, points to a different attitude toward the self than we have today.

At times in the past, a person was seen as a sinful being who was expected to struggle to oppose the straightforward expression of one's own wishes. Wishes were all too often evil. What sort of an architecture might grow up in such times? A narrow one, I would imagine: one in which the dominant value is in the direction of human discipline and restraint as opposed to expansive freedom. I think of Salem at the time of the witch trials, on the one hand, and of buildings in modern Rio de Janeiro, on the other. But still it does not seem that buildings that appear oriented to the fostering of the expression of the true self are the likeliest to lead to such an outcome either. For certain kinds of buildings that show a traditional plainness, certain arrangements of buildings that adhere to a quasi-religious probity may provide the background for the emergence of what is unique to individuals in that environment. I am thinking of Oxford and Cambridge and of some of the eastern university campuses in the United States.

It strikes me now that it is impossible to consider a building's capacity to nurture the true self without considering the interaction between the buildings and the people who use it. I once heard that an Englishman wrote an article entitled, "There Is No Such Thing as a Building," by which he was referring to the inescapable fact that buildings and people go together. The title was a play on Winnicott's comment, "There is no such thing as an infant" (Winnicott, 1960b, p. 39). Winnicott was making the point that a baby is unthinkable—and literally cannot exist—separate from the relationship with the mother or other caretakers.

Two Patients

In further pursuing my topic of the meaning that architecture has for people, I would like to consider some material involving architecture that emerged in the psychotherapies of two patients.

In the early 1980s, a 30-year-old man who is married, the father of three children, dreams of a storefront with rooms within. He would like to have the storefront. He pictures living there alone. He imagines beautiful fabrics, painted wood. This could be an apartment building, he thinks. But there is a problem. He would be visible through the front window. How could one get light to come in through the window without being seen? There is lots of natural light in the other rooms. The second floor has a skylight, but someone else occupies it. He keeps thinking that somehow he will be given the second floor, but he is not. (It is probably relevant that my office is on the second floor of a building. He thinks of me as being in possession of the very thing he himself seeks.)

He has a conflict between being seen and admired and being shamed. He tells me he realized that when, in the dream, he was considering the idea of living alone, he knew he would miss his family. He knows he has a conflict between privacy, an ideal he has described to me many times, and the life he lives with his family.

If we pursue any strand of this dream sufficiently far, we will enter deeply into this man's dynamics. These strands reveal a conflict between being seen and being hidden. How can he receive the light without being seen? How can he express himself without running the risk of being seen? He is a man with extraordinary imaginative capacities who has successfully turned them into novels and stories that have been widely admired. But he never stops suffering over the possibility that, in expressing himself, he has run the risk of appearing to be a fool.

The dream is an architectural fantasy that embodies his conflicts. One might think that if this man were to ask someone to design a house for him, he would request having lots of light but with no chance of his being seen. In that context, his sense of safety would help him to write. Being seen would then be satisfied by the publication of his work.

Another patient, born and raised in a Middle Eastern culture, is preoccupied with the question of whether to build a new house for a family. For a long time he has been considering getting married. In a recent discussion, what emerged was the idea that the father is represented by the hard shell of the protective house, while the softer and more vulnerable interior is the mother. This is his concept of how a marriage may be represented by a house, an enclosure for a family that combines the attributes of the married couple. He is also concerned with maintaining the possibility of being alone at times, though married. It is difficult for him to imagine himself actually married—in more than the technical sense—and yet still able to be himself. When he sees a design that tells him that there would be places he could go if he wanted to be alone, he is reassured. A gym would be one such place. The sense of impending architectural change is closely related to his state of mind in our work. The resolution of his problems can be embodied in a bricks-and-mortar representation. This man requires an architectural assurance that his true self will be able to survive both marriage, as he understands it, and the reconstruction of a dwelling which represents that marriage. It is not uncommon for men to fear marriage. Many men may be concerned with the survival of their true selves within the context of marriage.

These two cases illustrate the conflict between being alone and being in a state of relatedness. This is to me a fundamental opposition in human life, not always raised to the level of conflict as seen in these men, but part of the ongoing background in people as they try to live lives that feel both free and real. In psychoanalysis there is a school of thought that says that from the very start of life we are related to others; we have what are called object relationships. This puts the aspect of relatedness first and foremost and generates an approach to problems in which early relationships are the raw material of conflict—and also, therefore, the raw material of possible resolution. Adherents to classical psychoanalysis, as developed by Sigmund Freud, do not agree that object relations are there from the beginning. They think that there is an early time in which babies cannot discern mothers as objects and that young children have to develop sufficiently to reach that point. To me this understanding of early development implies aloneness at the beginning. Being well mothered will provide relief from this aloneness, but the source of the relief will not be discernible until some months have passed.

In the 1960s, Winnicott (1963) emphasized the permanent "incommunicado" nature of the true self. This seemed to represent a shift in his thinking. Prior to this time he had written on what he called the spontaneous gesture as the expression in action of the true self. He was referring above all to the baby's gesture to the mother, but also, by implication, to later human gestures that came from deep within, gestures aimed at those whom one loves, the gestures of artists, and others. Now, beside the communicative aspect of the true self, he concluded that there is another part that intends to be hidden, or, better, could not express itself even if it wanted to. It is permanently "incommunicado." This was a turn that underscored the original duality in human life that exists between the communicating self that wishes for relatedness (and in fact cannot survive without it) and the more withdrawn aspect of the self, the part that is inaccessible and remains so. Winnicott, regarded as one of the founders of the so-called object-relations school of psychoanalysis, never embraced the notion of object relations from day one. In this area, he was rooted in Freudian thought. This may seem to be a minor distinction, but, in fact, the ripple effect of such viewpoints is widespread and deep.

One may then wonder about architectural design in terms of a true self that wishes both relatedness and privacy. This is not to say that a design that embodies these two elements will cure someone's conflict. But when an architect has perceived the needs of the client and imagined into being a finished building in which both major trends may be satisfied, the client may well have a sense of comfort. I imagine that both togetherness and separateness are basic principles of design; I am attempting to provide for this concept a slant that emanates from the world of psychoanalysis.

The patient who dreamt about the storefront used to feel that he was avoiding taking up space in his home. This was a state of mind, a fantasy of his. He noted in himself a definite predilection to avoid free movement at home. Clearly, he had an ongoing preoccupation with not existing in the way most of us take for granted. That his wife stored items of significance to him in the basement of their home—that is, did not display them the way she did other items that had more to do with herself—fit right in with his renunciation of his home as a place in which he dwelt. He was denying that he was living his life. For him, being totally absorbed inside his imagination was the only possible life. Relationships could not be acknowledged; they were somehow invalid. He was exercising a kind of omnipotence over his life as a whole, as if it were up to him whether to grant the status of living to aspects of his life. Most of this was entirely undetectable to others. He was, outwardly, an affable and accessible person, and his books themselves could be described in the same terms. One reviewer wrote that the reader "was immersed in the fictive world that was visible from the first word of the first chapter."

Against this background it is possible to see how the dream of the storefront could appeal to him, the only drawback having to do with the two-way nature of windows. Light in, but visibility too. How could he live and not be seen to be living in the world at the same time?

I doubt that architects encounter such a set of conflicts and struggles out in the open when they consult their clients in the design of a house. Perhaps they deal with this by offering designs that elicit reactions, and alter the design in accordance with approval and disapproval. But underneath this empirical method—which is undoubtedly better than spending a number of hours collecting unconscious fantasies from the client—there are these other lurking conflicts. I can conceive of a case study, for example, in which the design and construction of a dwelling is accompanied by psychoanalytic work with the clients. Some insight would probably emerge. But, of course, time is short for that sort of thing and in the end it is not necessary, even if it were interesting.

Survivability and the Built Environment

Many people would agree that the built environment, by its very survivability, provides a reliable setting for the disorderly inner lives that we all lead. The built environment is distinguished by its structural presence, its quality of survivability. The monumentality of certain structures, such as the pyramids, cathedrals, and the remains of Greek temples, gives us a sense of abiding value. We cherish such buildings partly because they have *survived*; they speak of relative permanence in the flux of time. This much seems obvious. As human beings, made of flesh and blood, subject to the vagaries of the body and ultimately unable to escape from death itself, we value that which can be relied upon to continue, that which can protect us by its intrinsic strength. We value people above all, but we also value what is built, particularly the place in which we live. What I want to say here is that the ongoing non-destruction of the built environment reassures us. Again, this seems obvious. Within each of us is a flux of thought and emotion that, on the surface, follows no particular order. Also, relationships between and among people are disorderly. This condition lurks behind the fiction that each of us is a unitary construction capable of volition and fully responsible for our actions. This fiction is required because responsibility is a *sine qua non* for any sort of social arrangement. But this does not change the underlying reality.

I would go from here to consider the ubiquity of destructive urges among humankind. It has been theorized that in strong human relationships there is always an urge to destroy the other and that the fact that the other person continues to be there, visible and functional, accords him or her special status, the capacity to be of use. It is not a simple idea, that we are all the time destroying a person, or more than that perhaps, that we are not passive recipients of sensory impressions of what is external to us, but that we are active both in our perceptions and in wishing to destroy what is out there. Certainly such urges are not, as a rule, readily available to consciousness. Such an idea would not seem applicable to the world at large; there is so much in any individual's world that cannot be subjected to a destructive intent. But it seems possible to me that we are aware that anyone or anything, human or nonhuman, can be the recipient of an urge to destroy; consequently, we can have a sense of presence and importance for anything that survives. But this is counterintuitive. One would imagine that what is most valuable would evoke a preservative urge first and foremost.

In working with a sculptor, I have found the idea useful that when we are confronted with something beautiful, some of the intensity of positive response comes from the recognition that the object has survived and that it exists, when it could easily have been destroyed, at some point along its pathway of having come into being. The sense of astonishment upon seeing a great painting, or any other masterpiece that can be named, derives, I am contending, not only from its intrinsic properties, but from the fact that it has survived. From this I would extrapolate further similar principles as they might apply to the built world. We cherish buildings in part because of their survival, not simply as an aspect of their going on being over time, but because of their survival of fantasized destruction. This survival adds to the reassuring nature of the built world that surrounds our disorderly lives.

I suppose that everything in a theory like this depends upon the question of whether ongoing unconscious destructiveness is a fact of human life or not. How can it be proven or disproved? And you may ask why it makes any sense at all, to which I would respond with reference to our original condition in the womb as omnipotent sovereigns. The urge to destroy comes, according to one psychoanalytic view, from recognition of the fact that what is out there in the world is beyond one's sovereign control. That is the principle. Gradually, what is out there, beyond control, and therefore subject to an urge to destroy, comes into one's purview, through predictability at least. There is a sort of sovereignty that goes with knowing where things are, what they look like, and how they are likely to behave. This probably applies as much to people as to things. So the *persistence* of aspects of the external world comforts us by addressing the enduring infantile attitude of one wanting to be in charge.

Having lived in the same house for 32 years, I have to ask myself whether I have just provided a rationalization for the way I happen to be, that I do value continuity and persistence, which might not be an attitude shared by everyone. The overall consideration, though, has to do with finding a circumstance in which one's true self may express itself and thrive.

The built environment provides the illusion of order in which the work of creating order out of disorder is relieved, thereby making energy available for the expression of the true self and providing a temporary victory over the internal disorder. This is all related to destructive urges.

Here I am juxtaposing the internal disorder of the mind with the abidingness and structural integrity of the built environment in which we largely dwell. There is a considerable expenditure of energy in finding order in the disorderly world of the interior life as well as in the world of relationships. Winnicott thought that the effort to discern the borderline that separates two people required an energy output that was no longer required where such borderlines need not be kept in mind. He was speaking of the transitional world in which mother and baby first were blurred together and, later on, the cultural world described in "The Location of Cultural Experience" (Winnicott, 1967). One of the benefits of hearing music or looking at art is in the mixing up of what is being perceived and what is within the perceiver. This is a world free of a need to make distinctions and is therefore replenishing. To attain and reattain order takes effort, sometimes noticeable, sometimes not detected, but always there.

I probably do not need to provide evidence for the disorderliness of the inner life, and perhaps the stabilizing effect of architectural locations is self-evident. This stabilizing effect, in addition to contrasting with the disorderly inner life, also acts as a bulwark against the destructive urges that are part of the unconscious of everyone. To some extent, those urges will have been structuralized in the putting-together of the dwelling or other building, deflected, for example, from the breaking down of a piece of wood into the nailing together of such pieces in a larger-scale wall that will survive and provide shelter. Margaret Little (1981), an

English psychoanalyst, emphasized the idea that there could be no construction without destruction.

Integration Versus Disintegration

Donald Kuspit (2001) has recently reviewed the development of modern art in a book, *Psycho-Strategies of the Avant Garde*. In his study of the work of Manet and Seurat, he discusses the disintegration of painting in the form of patches and dots, a disintegration that echoes the experience of people in the modern era who are juxtaposed but destroyed as entities by the confusing crowds in urban existence. He quotes Theodor Adorno who uses the word "shudder" for the first intimation of relatedness within that context. Shudder indicates an overcoming of disintegration, the entry-point of that human element of relatedness that brings the pieces together. One of my patients, the sculptor, speaks of a "shiver" when the stone seems right, that is, when the parts seem to form a totality. These are the physical manifestations of the intuition of relatedness, in contrast to the condition in which parts are juxtaposed. The subject here is integration versus disintegration, the death that is intrinsic to disintegration versus the life that goes with relatedness. Poets who speak of the hair raised on the neck and the chill down the spine as a criterion of poetry worthy of the name are in the same territory. The body is speaking, and we tend to trust the body more than the split-off intellect, no matter how learned and brilliant one is.

The activity of the viewer who unifies the work of art through active engagement in perception must be factored into the equation. The painting in modern times is a vehicle by which the subjectivity of the artist is engaged by the subjectivity of the viewer.

For those who can no longer be calmed by traditional beliefs, by abiding myths that encompass the meaning of the life cycle, there is an angst that is preoccupied with the questions of Gauguin's triptych: Where have we come from? Where are we? Where are we going? The bewilderment of modern man would perhaps call for an architecture that provides a shelter for the mind and not only the body. In what would such a shelter consist? I feel at the moment that I have overstepped my limitations in speaking of this subject as if I knew the answer. I can only extrapolate from the experiences of my own life and those of people I knew in depth, including patients. The balance between the need for solitude and the need for relatedness seems most fundamental, and here I am speaking of dwellings.

Frank Gehry's comment that his billowing metallic buildings remind people of breasts, coming as it does from one who is acquainted with psychoanalysis, leads to the notion of a protective mother as an appealing model. This would be an extreme manifestation of the needs of modern man for comfort. The external nature of buildings tend toward the notion of the masculine, the protective shell within which the emotions may be manifested, while Gehry's capacity to introduce curvature to the extent he has prompts us to conceptualize in another way. His work may be thought of as feminist architecture.

Can we ask whether it is true that the disintegrating people of our time, mindful of the forces of destruction pressing in upon them during the twentieth century and now in its bloody aftermath, turn now to motherly tropes for comfort?

References

Kuspit, D. (2001), *Psycho-Strategies of the Avant Garde*. Cambridge: Cambridge University Press.

Little, M. I. (1981), *Transference Neurosis and Transference Psychosis*. New York: Aronson.

Rodman, F. R. (2003), *Winnicott: Life and Work*. Cambridge, MA: Perseus.

Winnicott, D. W. (1960a), Ego distortion in terms of true and false self. In: D. W. Winnicott, *The Maturational Processes and the Facilitating Environment*. New York: International Universities Press, 1965, pp. 140–152.

────── (1960b), The theory of the parent–infant relationship. In: D. W. Winnicott, *The Maturational Processes and the Facilitating Environment*. New York: International Universities Press, 1965, pp. 37–55.

────── (1963), Communicating and not communicating leading to a discovery of certain opposites. In: D. W. Winnicott, *The Maturational Processes and the Facilitating Environment*. New York: International Universities Press, 1965, pp. 179–192.

────── (1967), The location of cultural experience. In: D. W. Winnicott, *Playing and Reality*. New York: Penguin, 1980, pp. 112–121.

Houses as Self-Portraits
Notes on Architects
Who Design Their Own Houses

PHIL S. LEBOVITZ

The psychoanalytic approach to art is based on the premise that artists express themselves through their creations. The artistic product reflects and works with the artist's concerns, needs, preoccupations, conflicts, and preferences. It flows from that which is inner and fundamental to the creator.

While this approach can be extended to architecture, one limiting factor is that architects usually work closely with their clients; in designing buildings they have to conform to many requirements. But when architects design their own homes, they need pay little attention to external personal preferences. These architects are largely free to design houses that are in accord with their personal wishes. To an extent, these houses can reflect who the architects are and how the architects see themselves. An architect's self-designed home is analogous to a painter's self-portrait. Psychoanalytic scholars (e.g., Meissner, 1993; Bock, 1998) have argued that self-portraits are the purest expression of a painter's inner self. This paper is an initial attempt to consider whether the same might be true for architects' homes. I interviewed four architects in the Atlanta area who had designed their own houses, and explored with them the meaning of their homes and how the designs arose from their life histories and their personal concerns and preferences. While making no claim that I will show definitively how these houses connect with the architects' inner psychological world, I hope that this essay will provide some suggestions of the ways an architect's self-designed home expresses abiding themes and concerns in the architect's life and personality.

Jerome Cooper

In contrast to the other three architects whom I interviewed, Jerome Cooper embarked on his house design early in his career.

He and his wife were about to have a third child and wanted to have appropriate space for their family. A central feature of the house he designed was a recessed living room with a semicircular sunken couch in front of a fireplace. In order to sit on the couch, one has to step down into the space. The space creates an enveloping coziness in which the family can congregate intimately and can feel insulated from the world around them (see figure 1). Cooper's roots are in an extended family, and he places a premium on maintaining connections and on obtaining strength and protection from his familial ties. He sought to achieve a sense of safety and shelter with his design and sees the sunken living room as playing a central role in accomplishing that purpose.

Cooper sought to integrate nature in such a way that the house would feel in harmony with is surroundings. His use of space, choice of materials, and the interrelating of the house with its setting were all ingredients in his trying to achieve this goal. He characterizes his home as "my cabin in the woods." He kept almost all of the trees on the site, except for those that interfered with the footprint of the house, and designed a house that gives the impression of being within a small forest. He also placed a priority on using natural materials, wood and stone in particular, in order to reinforce a sense of synthesis with the surrounding forest-like, hilly terrain. The house is intended to be a refuge, a sanctuary, a place in which one may screen out the world and commune with nature. "Being in touch with the land is a peace-giving quality," Cooper commented. A space of major importance to Cooper is the high vaulted living area with a clerestory that prompts one to look up from the hearth to the sky.

In talking about how he became an architect, Cooper recalled the influence of his tenth-grade teacher, Eva Dodson. After asking him to stay after school one day, she said to him, "Do you like washing cars? Because if you don't get to work, that's what you will end up doing. And if you want to attend Georgia Tech, get on with your studies." Cooper responded by applying himself academically and went on to study architecture at Georgia Tech. The home seems to me to have the tranquility and calmness characteristic of maternal figures such as this teacher and other influential women in Cooper's life.

Cooper privileges the child's perspective in his home design. The windows in the house extend all the way to the floor because traditional windows have their sill above the child's eye level; in this house the children can look out, and down, from the safety of their shelter to see their father driving into the driveway.

FIGURE 1. Cooper residence.

Cooper also created a workspace that sustains the dual themes of sanctuary and of integration with nature. The studio has a large amount of window space and reaches out into the trees; being there feels something like being in a tree house. For Cooper the studio is also reminiscent of the attic of the house in which he grew up. He spent many hours in that attic building model planes; his work as an architect, he noted, is a transformation of his immersion in this activity during his childhood.

Mack Scogin

Several years ago the remnants of a major hurricane uprooted a tree that crashed into Mack Scogin's home. He set out to design a new house that would replace the damaged structure. Scogin noted that an architect's house designed for himself "is the most self-revealing expression of self." Designing one's own home, he added, is a selfish endeavor because the project is not done for anyone else, such as a client who has commissioned the building. Scogin characterized a house as "a live-in sculpture."

Scogin developed an appreciation for aesthetics through his father's work, constructing items for an interior decorator at a department store in Atlanta. His father made many items to decorate their house as well. Scogin notes that he derived from his father a sense of pride in workmanship and recalled the influence of watching his father work skillfully in his workshop in the evening. While an undergraduate at Georgia Tech, he became interested in a career in architecture. He recalls being enthralled by the discovery that others could appreciate what one's imagination produced.

In his work, Scogin's emphasis is on natural light. He devises ways that light can stream in without one having to sacrifice privacy. Light is a restorative element for Scogin, and he sees it as providing comfort.

Scogin works closely with his wife, Merrill Elam, who is also his partner in their firm. In answer to my question about mentors, he spoke about his wife as his mentor and as "the most fascinating person I've ever met."

He and his wife travel extensively for their projects. Scogin, in designing their house, wanted to create a place to which they could return for calmness and rejuvenation after spending several days sleeping in hotels. He made extensive use of glass so that the house emits a glow at night like a beacon.

The glow is also a function of a unique and deeply personal design feature incorporated into the house. He constructed a lap pool on the upper level of the house; the pool runs alongside the master bedroom and alongside the front of the house in a way that conceals it from any passersby (see figure 2). The pool creates an ever-changing kaleidoscope of colors that is simultaneously stimulating and restful and that, he notes, evokes the calming, comforting nature of a child's nightlight. For Scogin's wife, the water is an overt childhood referent because of memories she retains about growing up on a lake.

Scogin's youthful delight in seeing his father construct interior decorations pervades his enthusiastic description of his work now. Nowhere is this more vivid than when he talks about his experience of waking each morning, opening his eyes, and having the sensation of looking through concrete. He described how he created this effect. He designed frameless windows set perpendicular to each other. There is a concrete wall extension of one of the windows with a tree behind the concrete wall. The experience is of seeing the actual tree, but in reality one sees it only as a reflection. He speaks of this as a "magical moment" that gives him the feeling, as he put it humorously, that "I can do anything. I'm atomic man."

Stanley Daniels

Stanley Daniels emphasized a point that each of the four architects independently noted: designing one's own house is an unending process; it is never fully completed. This perspective is consonant with the psychoanalytic view that personality evolves continuously and is modified by encounters with significant emotional experiences, including psychoanalytic treatment.

FIGURE 2. Scogin residence.

Daniels readily affirmed that his home reflected his personality. "My house is orderly," he noted, "and people do describe me as that: obsessional, careful about details." In concert with Scogin, who characterized an architect who creates his or her own house as courageous for attempting such a public self-expression, Daniels called it a daunting process because "you risk the judgment of your colleagues about the very personal statement which you have made with your house."

Daniels's identity as an architect represented for him an evolutionary process rather than a process of discovery. He recalled as a small child liking to build with Lincoln Logs and Erector Sets. Two events are vivid in his memory. When about nine or ten years old, he spent his summer vacation living with his favorite aunt, his mother's next older sister. Her husband had died recently, and she made significant changes in her house that summer. She contracted with a custom furniture maker to build cabinets for her. It was a new venture for him, and she was his first significant customer for this work. Daniels recalls his fascination upon seeing the components of the cabinetry and watching the project come together. About a year later his parents purchased a new house and employed an interior designer and a contractor; Daniels found himself interested and thinking about designing the building of houses, including all of the details.

Daniels notes that his decision to become an architect occurred when he took

FIGURE 3. Daniels residence.

mechanical drawing in high school and the teacher began to show him floor plans. A particularly vivid influence on Daniels's passion for architecture was his best friend's father. Daniels was so enthralled with this man's devotion to being an amateur artist that his friend was occasionally annoyed with Daniels for spending more time watching his father paint than playing with him.

Daniels's house has a meticulous quality to it. As I drove up to it, I was struck by its pristine contemporary design with large windows and carefully groomed landscaping; the line of the house created an impression of precision. The inside sustains that perspective. In addition, the arrangement of space creates a sense of expansiveness and allows light to pour into the area in a way that highlights the orderliness of the lines of the design. Daniels highlighted the asymmetrical quality of the design, though he emphasized that spatial relations in the house were formal and are in tune with that dimension of his personality. "I'm a formal person, not laid back," he said. Most of his work has regularity to it in the way spaces flow and create a spatial sense, he added (see figure 3).

Daniels emphasized that his house has features similar to those he and his partners seek in their public work: a spatial feeling, a progression of spaces, and an interrelationship among spaces. For his house he and his wife reflected on how they were going to live in the space, and how they would use the space. They both desired a light, bright house with a lot of glass. He does not try to blend his structures with nature. He sees his house as the natural environment, while its openness provides a crisp contrast to its surroundings.

"The creative process is unexplainable," he commented, "because you just try out ideas until you say, 'that's it.'"

FIGURE 4. Ventulett residence.

Thomas Ventulett

Thomas Ventulett embodies the interrelatedness of the plastic arts. Since he was a child, Ventulett liked to draw and paint. "I painted everything I could, even my first car; I painted the engine white." Ventulett has a tendency toward dramatic expressiveness in his public work and in his house. "I'm reserved as a person, but I let loose energies in my work that I don't express in my personality. I do things in my house so that people will be aware of where they are. An example is the precariousness of a perch [in my house], and I use no rails on my stairs there." In one of his public buildings he used a glass rail on the stairs so that people would experience the entire space. In the CNN Center in Atlanta, he designed the longest freestanding escalator.

A consistent and pervasive theme that thrills him is the creation of dramatic spaces. He feels that walking into space touches the human spirit (figure 4). "People," he says, "remember the spaces, not the building." Designing one's own home, he observed, is something that "permits you to be more artistic, more expressive, and [brings you] closer to [creating] a sculpture."

He was unambiguous in his recognition that the work of architects reflects their personalities. Designing one's own house, he noted, involves having "a strong ego in a positive sense." The other three architects I interviewed expressed the same idea with different phrasing. From a psychoanalytic perspective, the presence of a substantial amount of healthy narcissism is often beneficial. Daniels said his house is not primarily a monument, though "you hope it will have that effect."

"[My] house embodies my excitement in architecture," Ventulett noted. He emphasized the use of wood and stone to bring nature into the house. The drama in his design appears in the way the house sits on the site, dramatically cantilevered over a pond. Ventulett's home is situated in a woodsy, hilly area. He placed the house on an east–west axis with the rear facing south. Cooper and Scogin also spoke of how their homes were integrated with nature. Ventulett's idea was for "the light, angles, and reflection of the sun in the angles of the windows [to work] so that . . . you see the sun rise and the sun set, [making] it a place to be home, [a place you] want to return to, come to, [a place that gives a] restful, enfolding feeling."

In the morning he awakens to a large window through which he sees his favorite pine tree. As he eats his morning cereal, he looks out at the pond. Both he and his wife delight in a feeling of living in the treetops. During winter, the branches of the trees sparkle when there is ice on them and the sunlight reflects off the pond and up to the ceiling. Extensive use of floor-to-ceiling windows, particularly along the southern exposure, is in tune with his interest in sunlight. In a home office/studio that is also part of the east-west axis and southern exposure, he created a dramatic effect. He designed the angles of the windows to meet in a way that produces an illusion that the sun is visible as though there is no distinction between sunrise and sunset. He focuses on incorporating nature "for its elemental impact of security, solidity, and familiarity."

Ventulett's career was shaped by a few particularly influential figures. An uncle recognized his fascination with drawing and said he would pay for Ventulett's education if he went to Georgia Tech and became an architect. He had received Ds and Fs in high school until he took a drawing course, in which he earned an A. He cited that as a turning point because he learned how to study after that. His uncle's work ethic was an invaluable gift from a mentor. He remembers it poignantly because his uncle died at the age of 49 while Ventulett was in graduate school. He completed an architecture fellowship under Louis Kahn, whom he also views as a mentor.

His enthusiasm for drawing is largely associated with an aunt, his mother's sister. He remembers her as "an incredible painter." One painting of hers remains vivid in his memory; he can recall each of its details though he has not seen it in years because it was stolen.

Concluding Thoughts

For all four of the architects, an essential theme was whether, or how, to incorporate nature into their homes; for three of the four the aim was to incorporate nature in order to provide a sense of comfort, familiarity, restfulness, and refuge. Inferences about "Mother Nature" and the maternal nurturing inherent in the term suggest that their relationships with their mothers and other maternal figures may have nurtured their architectural creativity. Each architect focused on a different element of nature in the effort to achieve the sense of refuge. Cooper did so through the extensive use of stone and wood, a sunken family area in front of the stone fireplace, and many windows that extended from floor to ceiling. Scogin emphasized the flow of light into the house, creating a prism of light at night that emanated from the built-in lap pool, and the presence of water in the pool alongside the master bedroom. Ventulett integrated sunlight extensively with its warming familiarity and an open expanse of glass that also revealed the starry night sky.

The essential role of mentoring influences warrants attention as well. Each of the architects easily recalls having at least one, and often several, major influences. Most of their memories about mentors focus on processes that involve developing identities and solidifying self images: Cooper's tenth-grade teacher; Ventulett's uncle and aunt; Daniels's friend's father; and, for all, their teachers of architecture.

This essay is meant to be a first step in viewing the houses that architects have designed themselves as being like self-portraits in that they reflect so much of the architects' personalities and inner worlds. I am aware that it would take a far more extensive examination of an architect's life and experiences to provide a comprehensive portrait of the connection between an architect and his or her work. But, it seems to me, the results of this preliminary exploration are suggestive. With all four of them, even with relatively brief interviews, it is unarguable that there were significant connections between their houses and their personal experiences. All of them spoke about early experiences that played into their approach as architects. All of them could describe connections between their creations and their personalities. All of them recognized the special and personal nature of their homes.

References

Bock, C. C. (1998), Henri Matisse's self-portraits: Presentation and representation. In: *Psychoanalytic Perspectives on Art*, vol. 3, ed. M. Gedo. Hinsdale, NJ: The Analytic Press, pp. 239–265.

Meissner, W. W. (1993), Vincent: The self portraits. *Psychoanal. Quart.*, 62:74–105.

II
PERSPECTIVES FROM ARCHITECTURAL SCHOLARS

Building Dreams
Space, Psychoanalysis, and the City

STEVE PILE

> The reform of consciousness consists *entirely* in making the world aware of its own consciousness, in arousing it from its dream of itself, in *explaining* its own actions to it.
> —Karl Marx, 1843, p. 209

Some time back I attempted to make some preliminary links between psychoanalysis and Henri Lefebvre's study of the production of space (Pile, 1996; see also Lefebvre, 1974). At the time, putting psychoanalysis and space together seemed like a strange thing to do. The analysis of the psyche, on the one hand, seemed to have little to do with space, on the other, because space was commonly thought of as being only the abstract, external, asocial, cold stage upon which human dramas played out. However, other understandings of space, as suggested by people such as Lefebvre (and many others), are not based on the assumption that space is abstract, ahistorical, invariable, immortal. Instead, space is seen as something that is socially produced. In this understanding, it is not hard to imagine that the psyche might also produce space: be it city space or architectural space. More than this, space—including city space and architectural space—might even act back on the psyche, in a dynamic interaction, with each (overtly and covertly) modifying the other. The possibility of a dynamic interrelationship between space and the psyche, though, begs questions—questions, naturally, with many possible avenues of approach and argument. In this paper, I will use dreams as a way of simultaneously evoking something social, something psychic, and something spatial. I would like to argue, as strongly as possible, that dreams provide us with a model for understanding the place of the psychological in the production of space, regardless of whether that is city space, architectural space, or personal space.

This paper is broken down into two parts. Initially, I will outline Freud's account of dream-work, which illuminates just how thoughts and emotions are shifted along chains of association in various, intricate, ways. Indeed, thoughts and emotions are constantly arriving and leaving, constantly being worked and reworked. Much the same can be said of the time and space of the dream. Such an interpretation might help us interpret the meaning and significance of architectural and city space. To think through this argument, I look at Walter Benjamin's analysis of Berlin, which at key moments depends on a sense of the city's dreaminess. Of course, Freud's understanding of dreams informed Benjamin. However, a Freudian rereading of Benjamin's work provides a greater sense of the importance of the dreaminess of the built environment, partly through an enhanced appreciation of the dynamism and intermeshing of social and personal worlds. Significantly, and as both Freud and Benjamin would wish, using dreams as a breaching point between the personal and the social opens up possibilities for building different dreams (see figure 1; also, for a related argument, see Pile, 1998).

First, let us look at how dreams are built.

Dream Works

Though basic tenets of Freud's dream analysis are now well-known (see Flanders, 1993 and Marcus, 1999), it is nonetheless helpful to spell out key aspects (as I see it) of his account of dream formation. Freud's basic insight was that dreams were meaningful. He forcefully argued throughout *The Interpretation of Dreams* (1900) that it was not possible simply to decode dreams as if symbols always and inevitably referred to one thing—such that, for example, dreaming of being in rough seas means insecurity, or that vivid colors represent a turning point in one's life. Instead, Freud argued that tracking back to the underlying content of the dream would require following the devious and intricate operations that the psyche had performed in order to construct the dream. It is the sheer deviousness and intricacy of dreams that is interesting, because it suggests a world of meaning and significance that is not simply fixed or manipulable. There is an ever-present openness, flexibility, and creativity in dream worlds: dream worlds, I suggest, both sleeping and waking.

Freud argues that dreams do not arrive in the mind fully formed. Dreams have to be made. A constellation of dream thoughts provide the material from which the dream will emerge. These thoughts are described by Freud as being the latent content of the dream. Latent content is immanent within the dream, but there is no straightforward access to these thoughts because they contain material—and form into a wish—that cannot be directly expressed, because it is too troubling.

FIGURE 1. Mural in Sydney, Australia.

Therefore, latent material—from which the dream is made—has to be *translated* into the manifest content of the dream. This translation is necessarily devious and intricate. Freud identifies four basic forms of work that go into dream formation; the most important are condensation and displacement, these being aided and abetted by issues around representability and secondary revision. From my perspective, condensation and displacement are *spatial* operations, about convergence and divergence on/from specific elements in the dream. Secondary revision becomes important in thinking about space because it writes a narrative through the dream and gives it a façade. As it is for dreams, I argue, so it is for the production of city and architectural space.

Let us use one of Freud's dreams as an example. I have chosen "A Pleasant Dream" in part because it is implicitly set in the city (in analysis, revealed as Vienna) and partly because Freud discusses both condensation and displacement in terms of it. The patient's dream (Freud, 1900) goes like this:

> *He is travelling in a large party to X Street, where a modest hostelry is located* (which is not the case). *A play is being performed in its rooms; one moment he is a spectator, the next an actor. Finally someone says they will have to change their clothes and return to town. Some of the party are directed to rooms on the ground*

floor, others to those on the first floor. Then a quarrel ensues. The ones up above are annoyed that those down below are not yet ready, so that they cannot come down. His brother is up above, he himself is down below, and he is annoyed at his brother that he is being hurried so. (This part is unclear.) *In any case, it was already decided and disposed on their arrival who should be up above and who should be down below. Then he is walking by himself up the rise made by X Street towards the town, and his steps are so heavy, so laborious, that he cannot stir from the spot. An elderly gentleman joins him and rails against the King of Italy. Then at the end of the rise he walks with much greater ease* [p. 217].

As ever, Freud's analysis of the dream is over seven times longer than the dream itself. For Freud, this greater quantity of thoughts in the analysis compared to the dream is significant. He argued that analysis showed the sheer mass of dream-thoughts available to the mind in the process of dream-formation. These thoughts, however, need to find their way into the dream: there are various paths to take. Freud argues that one dream element can represent many different dream-thoughts. Certain dream-elements are admitted to the dream because they are points of *convergence* or contact for many trains of thought (Freud, 1900, p. 216, pp. 223–224). The work that goes into making these points of intersection into dream-elements is described as *condensation*. Significantly, this means that dream-elements are overdetermined: "the elements formed into the dream are drawn from the entire mass of dream-thoughts, and in its relation to the dream-thoughts each one of the elements seems to be determined many times over" (Freud, 1900, p. 217).

For example, one element in the above dream is about difficulty in walking. This element refers simultaneously to difficulty in breathing once experienced by the patient, due to the inhibition of movement in response to an anxiety, and to a cautionary poem by Alphonse Daudet. This is one element, determined three-times over, or one element with three trains of thought running out from it. By following the chains of association, it is possible the track the trains of thought further and further. Daudet's poem, indeed, allows Freud's patient to make links to a love-affair with an actress, who lives on X Street. In this way, Freud can show that dream-thoughts can be represented more than once and that trains of thought can intersect and interact with one another. In analysis, certain elements can set in train further chains of association. The hostelry reminds the patient not only of where he met his lover, but also of a conversation with a cabby at the time. In this conversation, a further link is drawn between the hostel not being a proper hotel and to vermin, with vermin being a particular phobia of the patient's. From there, the patient remembers another poem and a further train of thought is opened up. This one leads to an association between the actress and his wet nurse. And so on.

Thus, "it is not only that the elements of the dream are determined *many times over*, but also that the individual dream-thoughts are represented in the dream by several elements. The path of associations leads from one element of the dream to several dream-thoughts; and from one dream-thought to several elements" (Freud, 1900, p. 216).

Condensation works to admit dream-thoughts to the dream—and to avoid censorship of the dream-thoughts—by using other thoughts: through association, collaterals, combination, composition, substitution, surrogation, congruence, proximity, "just like" logical relations, and reversal into opposites. *Displacement* is allied to this work and uses its operations. Its role, however, is to ensure that the dream is *"centered differently"* from the mass of dream-thoughts (Freud, 1900, p. 232). This is to suggest that there is a transvaluation in the psychic value and intensity of the dream, so that the wish, or affect of the wish, that lies behind the dream is placed somewhere away from the center of the dream itself. This transvaluation involves placing the latent psychic intensity of a thought at a remove. This is often achieved by using situations that are reminiscent of the affect of the dream, but that do not lead back to the affect of the dream-thoughts. This effectively disguises the motivating wish of the dream, yet allows the dreamer to feel that the wish has nonetheless been fulfilled.

In many ways, displacement works by *divergence*, either by off-centering the dream from the affect (the affect stays in its proper place) or by off-centering the affect from the dream (the dream's affect moves) (see Freud, 1900, pp. 298–299). Most commonly, displacement uses "reversal into opposites" to shift one value or affect away from another, but it can also work through using parallels (where one affect is just like another), subsumption (of one intensity into another), and diminution (making the affect lesser in intensity than warranted). In "A Pleasant Dream," Freud argues that displacement ensures that the center of the dream-thoughts, which circulate around anxieties about sex with women of a lower class, is replaced by a series of simultaneously social and spatial psychodramas in which people are placed above or below one another. Now it is possible to see that the spatial relations persist (though they are commonly reversed), while the sex, desire, and anxiety have become both remote and suppressed. Even so, it is through the *realness* of the dream-affect that the dream itself lays "claim to be accepted as one of the really deep and formative experiences of our soul" (Freud, 1900, p. 299).

Issues around *representation* again revolve around the necessity of evading the censorship of the wish contained in the dream (Freud, 1900, p. 259). The dream, therefore, is formed out of struggling factions in the psyche, some attempting to gain representation, with others blocking the way. Intense feelings are at play, so dream-work also acts to suppress affect and alter the tonality of the dream. Dreams, then, are related to inhibitions (Freud, 1900, pp. 305–306; see also Freud, 1926) as well as the remembrance of anxieties and desires in past experiences, especially childhood (Freud, 1900, pp. 311–317; see also Freud, 1917 and 1919).

The fourth and final aspect of dream-work that Freud identifies is called *secondary revision*. Freud notices that "not everything contained in the dream comes from the dream-thoughts, but rather that a function of the psyche indistinguishable from our waking thoughts can make some contribution to the dream-content" (Freud, 1900, p. 319).

A critical agency within the psyche can be brought to bear on the dream. The dream is given a working-over to make it intelligible, both while dreaming and also after waking. Secondary revision fills in the gaps in the dream structure making it more coherent and less absurd. An intelligible pattern is woven out of the dream elements by adding further elements. Freud suggests that a façade is built onto the structure of the dream, but only where there is material available that fits the forming dream. Conceptually, secondary revision blurs the distinction between the mental processes of the sleeping and waking mind: indeed, they can sometimes be indistinguishable.

Finally—for understanding how dream-work is implicated in the work that goes into the production of city space and architectural space—how elements are located in dreams is also of significance. This is to say that the spatial settings that constitute the dream are worth pursuing. The dream is formed out of locations, journeys, and localities (see also Freud, 1900, pp. 246–247). Its elements can be *composites* (the formation of new unities), made up, through condensation, of different trains of thought that converge at certain points (Freud, 1900, pp. 244–247). In general, Freud prefers to see locations and localities as if they were people or sometimes moments in time. The significance of locations, then, is that they refer to many things (see "hostelry" above). That is, spatial relations are also used in dream-formation: for example, up and down can be used to indicate hierarchies of various kinds. In this case, the dream places the brother above the dreamer, a reversal of their "waking" positions. Similarly, movements can be associated one with another; thus climbing staircases can be used in dream-formation to refer to sexual intercourse. Directions, such as going up or down, and placing things side by side, can be used to imply connections or relations between things. I have far from exhausted the possibilities here. What is important is that *spatial relations* are not somehow outside of the dream, but *part of their very construction*.

Freud's discussion of dream-work suggests that different aspects of the psyche are brought to bear on dream formation at different points, significantly, both while asleep and awake. Indeed, Freud blurs any hard and fast distinction between the mental processes governing sleep and wakefulness. This idea has implications for how we think about the creation and experience of city and architectural spaces. Thus, it is possible to argue that the space-work that goes into making city and architectural spaces is *never* free of the kinds of psychological work that goes into making dreams. So, I believe that the idea of dream-work is important because it enables us to see *not only* the ways one might track fantasies through the objects of city life, and also following the placements of affect in space, *but also* the ways that city, architectural, and personal space is worked over many times by familiar stories—creating a coherence and intelligibility that might tell us more about the unconscious thinking of city life. I would like to show what is at stake by examining the way in which Walter Benjamin uses dream analysis to uncover the structure of the dreams and nightmares at the heart of modernity and city life.

Psychoanalyzing the Asphalt: Walter Benjamin and the Dream City

For Freud, secondary revision is akin to daydreaming; put another way, secondary revision blurs the distinction between the sleeping dream and the waking dream, each casting shadows into each other's worlds. In some ways, Walter Benjamin was working in the shadowy zone between sleeping and waking, a daydream of city life. For Benjamin, this was no romantic or empirical nicety, for dreams were at the very heart of his revolutionary theory (see Pile, 2000). Here, however, I am as interested in how dreams might allow access to *other* (perhaps suppressed) meanings contained within cities: meanings soldered to the other side of its façades. Of course, Benjamin was paying attention to these dreams because he thought that they might be used to liberate their meanings, and put revolution in their service. In Freudian terms, then, Benjamin was siding with the unconscious against censorship and suppression. Let us look at one piece of Benjamin's writing to see how this played out.

In "A Berlin Chronicle" (1932), Benjamin begins to reconstruct Berlin through a series of reminiscences, about places, about people, about the times and spaces of Berlin. Instead of reconstructing a "true" account either of the city or of Benjamin's autobiography, the chronicle weaves in and out of the places of memory (see Gilloch, 1996; also Pile, 2002; on the place of memory, see Nora, 1989). The result is a labyrinthine piece that journeys in time and space, through a simultaneously psychological, physical, and urban imagination. And, I would argue, the dreamlike quality of Benjamin's writing is no accident: he is trying to evoke this quality of modern city life.

To begin with, Benjamin starts his tales of Berlin by inviting the reader to meet characters from the past who have held meaning for him. Indeed, he envisages a map of Berlin in which significant relationships are traced out. Moreover, Benjamin also outlines a method of mapping the city, by walking the streets and by losing one's self in the city *as if* losing one's self in a forest (Benjamin, 1932, p. 298). Giving yourself up to the city is not simply about immersion in the city, it is also about being able to pay attention to the fragments of city life, including not just buildings but also architectural features such as staircases, walls, and windows. This technique finds its fullest exposition in Benjamin's *One-Way Street* (1925–1926). Fragments of modernity are picked up and turned around to reveal new aspects of objects, whether it be stamps or railway stations, fortune-telling machines or shopping arcades. From each object, Benjamin traces out an association, a thought image. Thus, the fragments of the modern city are tracked to other thoughts, other situations. In this, Benjamin is seeking to uncover the desire or wish that went into constituting the object—a wish, or desire, which Benjamin sees as both forgotten and as revolutionary.

Benjamin wishes to put modernity in touch with its lost thoughts. Clear links can be traced to Freud's dream analysis. Boldly stated, fragments of the city are *just like* fragments of a dream. To be clear, Benjamin is not asking the world to wake up from its dream of itself, but instead to get in touch with the wishes that the dream contains (much as Marx suggested in the opening quote of this essay). This is a reading of Freudian dream analysis that sees the truth of the dream as being woven into the making of the dream: truth is not found on waking from the dream to reality, but on seeing the reality in the dream. For Benjamin, the city becomes a dreamlike site of memories and wishes. Indeed, he wished to be able to evoke the quality of those memories and desires, though they normally remain as tantalizing as a "half-forgotten dream" (1932, p. 316). In his Berlin chronicle, Benjamin's intention is to put himself back in touch with these memories and desires, not to wake up to the reality of the modern city (as if this were possible).

That Benjamin took dreams to be a real part of life is evidenced in his recounting of dreams as part of his exploration of the city. One memory is associated with a particular house, 10 or 12 Blumeshof (he cannot recall exactly). Many happy hours of his childhood were spent in this house. He was allowed to listen to the piano and read books. Also, at this place, Benjamin (1932) says,

> I am met on its threshold by a nightmare. My waking existence has preserved no image of the staircase. But in my memory it remains today the scene of a haunting dream that I once had in just those happy days. In this dream the stairway seemed under the power of a ghost that awaited me as I mounted, though without barring my way, making its presence felt when I had only a few more stairs to climb. On these last stairs it held me spell bound [p. 329].

From this recollection, Benjamin goes on to describe the spatial layout of the rooms in the house. He remembers his grandmother, and how he had to cross a large room to reach her. The memories seem disconnected: ghosts, grandmothers, staircases, rooms, going up, going across—except when put side by side, that is. The house is a place of memories, of ghosts, of the past. (I doubt it is a coincidence that Freud also dreamt of ghosts who blocked his path: see his "non vixit" dream.) Further, the house is represented as dreamlike. It is not just that architectural features figure prominently in the dream, or that these are available for interpretation (walking up stairs sometimes being associated with sex; see above), but that architectural spaces in waking life become the material of dreaming— both while sleeping and waking. Thus, Benjamin is using the bifocal insight that significant memories persist in dreams and that significant dream elements persist on waking. The psychodramas of the dream and of 10 or 12 Blumeshof, we can see, are intimately related: indeed, inseparably so.

For Benjamin, something vital always takes place between the psyche, the city and its architectural features. Thus, at one point, Benjamin (1932) remembers:

> It was on this very afternoon that my biographical relationships to people, my friendships and comradeships, my passions and love affairs, were revealed to me in their most vivid and hidden intertwinings. I tell myself it had to be Paris, where the walls and quays, the places to pause, the collections and the rubbish, the railings and the squares, the arcades and the kiosks, teach a language so insular that our relations to people attain, in the solitude encompassing us in our immersion in that world of things, the depths of a sleep in which the dream image waits to show the people their true faces [p. 318].

On this afternoon, it occurs to Benjamin that Paris held a sway over the imagination and, despite the harshness and indifference of encounters and interactions within cities, love and passion endure and are indemnified in memory (p. 318). Each fragment of Paris like a dream-thought, available for being built into a dream—a dream called Paris, but made up of a mass of thoughts. Much the same can be said of Berlin. Yet, for Benjamin, dreams allow for other insights, too. They can also reveal surprising aspects of city and architectural spaces. For example, Benjamin (1927–1940) recalls this dream:

> The dread of doors that won't close is something everyone knows from dreams. Stated more precisely, there are doors that appear closed without being so. It was with heightened senses that I learned of this phenomenon in a dream in which, while I was in the company of a friend, a ghost appeared to me in the window of the

ground floor of a house to our right. And as we walked on, the ghost accompanied us from inside all the houses. It passed through all the walls and always remained at the same height with us. I saw this, though I was blind. The path we travel through the arcades is fundamentally just such a ghost walk, on which doors give way and walls yield [p. 409].

The dream ghost's movement through the city and its architectural spaces (doors, walls, shopping arcades) reveals something of how people "sleepwalk" through their lives—and something of how spaces are produced so that they offer as little "resistance" as possible, lest people wake from their sleepwalking. From the dream, Benjamin learns about the production of the arcades as a particular kind of space, haunted by people who are free to move as if there were no doors and no walls. The ghost allows Benjamin to see the free-floating, uninhibited, phantasmatic movement of people through modern city spaces. At this point, we might begin to think about how contemporary shopping malls create a similarly deterritorialized space, permitting easy movement—only once you're inside, that is. The arcade, in this light, creates an interior space that is also an exterior space, much like a dream.

In some ways, the production of city, architectural, personal space draws the veil of sleep over life, yet the dream images patiently wait to reveal people to themselves. In other ways, the city acts as a mass of thoughts (and by this I mean much more than simply what goes on in people's heads). Not only are thoughts embodied in objects—such as people, kiosks, rubbish, and so on—each object triggers further reflections. More than this, the city is constituted through affect: passions, love, comradeship, indifference, harshness, and melancholy, to name but a few. Benjamin's mapping of the city proceeds in dreamlike fashion, from particular moments or elements of the city, building a labyrinthine picture of the thoughts that underlie city life. In this way, the city becomes a dream: an imagined space, a map of moods and affect, an intertwining world in which there is no clear boundary between the internal and external world. The world of dreams traffics the personal and the social, freighting feelings and memories across a never clear, but never simply open, border.

Before I conclude this paper, I would like to make one more observation. Neither Benjamin nor Freud believed that this traffic in memories and affect was either simply free or simply released into the world. In fact, a whole range of agencies line up to do exactly the opposite: to suppress affect, to censor thoughts. Various agencies within the mind, whether waking or asleep, are constantly shifting thoughts around, struggling to find means of expression, forming alliances and compromising over what eventually comes to mind. From this perspective, the latent is never in a separate world, cut off from manifest ideas and actions. Instead, the latent and manifest are opposing aspects of a relation across a supposedly clear-cut boundary—between waking life and dream states. City and architectural spaces, following this logic, are produced in analogous ways to dream spaces: they would be—as in a dream—conflictual, mutable, transformative, devious, disguised, suppressed, and full of compromises. It is this imaginative *work* (condensation, displacement, nonrepresentability, and secondary revision) that the spaces of dreams and dreamlike spaces share. Space, instead of being uniform and infinite, is worked over, constantly. In this sense, city and architectural spaces are always available for being reworked, reimagined, differently felt, and differently centered. Now, it is possible to draw some conclusions about the relationship between dreamwork and (what we might call) space-work.

Building Dreams and Space-Work

Dreams are not merely the personal product of an individual's mind, personal though dreams are. Nor do dreams stay only in the head, neatly cauterized from the external world. From this perspective, dreams might even provide a model for the operation of the mind in both sleeping and waking states. (Is this so fanciful? Do we leave our dreaming brains behind us when we wake?) It is for this reason that some psychoanalysts have argued that subject formation and object relations are formed through processes of dream work (see, for example, Bollas, 1992). And I have sought to extend this argument to understanding the *work* that goes into making city and architectural space. For me, the production of dream, city, and architectural spaces are constituted by the psychic, social, and spatial relations that traverse and circulate within them. This is to argue that the interior dreaming, psychic world and the exterior city, architectural world do not exist independently of the relationships between them, which is *not* to say that one is the mirror of the other. Consequently, I have suggested that city and architectural spaces have to be understood as *never* less than fantastic or phantasmagorical, as Walter Benjamin might have it.

At this point, the politics of dreams becomes significant. Of course, political rhetoric has often made use of the word, dreams, as a counter-image to the world as it is (as we saw in figure 1): sometimes to suggest a better future ("I have a dream"); sometimes to convey a sense that reality itself is a delusion ("We need to wake up" or "The alarm bell is ringing"). Indeed, dreams themselves have been seen as a liberation from reality (as Freud noted). In fact, the rhetoric of dreams often draws attention to the injustices and inequalities of the world: not simply because of the political rhetoric bound up in utopian dreamings, but because of the censorship and repression that ensures dream-thoughts cannot find free and easy expression in the dream. Both Freud and Benjamin nonetheless saw in dreams the possibility that something vital could be liberated that would allow such injustices and inequalities to be both expressed and addressed. This possibility remained, like a half-forgotten dream, tantalizingly out of reach. It still does. However, it is possible that by tracking dreams across interior and exterior worlds, we might better map the things they have to teach us. But I would suggest that the significance of dreams is neither to occupy them nor to wake up from them. If dreams are a royal road, then this is a two-way street, and what we might have to learn is to see the dreams in our realities and the realities of our dreams. Moreover, in this undertaking, a blend of spatial analysis and psychoanalysis should be invaluable.

If there is a political injunction (as Benjamin would wish), then it will be more important to understand what it is that the dream is saying, than trying to wake up from it or relegate its significance to insignificance. Dreams may, indeed, be an archaic cry for justice: a struggle to represent the unrepresentable; to declare an affect that cannot be expressed; to deal with a world that constantly off-centers desires by forever wrapping them in less meaningful experiences. Fortunately, we might also take the lesson that city and architectural spaces are dreamlike as a source of hope. From this perspective, they already express the inexpressible; they gather together unlike elements and work them into a plausible, intelligible pattern, despite its obvious absurdity and incoherence. If city and architectural spaces offer hope, then it is that they can become more dreamlike, more imagined, more open to compromises and alliances, more connected to the yearnings that motivate them. As dreams rely on a mass of thoughts, so do cities and buildings. Indeed, they are spaces full of building materials—a mass of thoughts through which dreams might yet be made concrete.

References

Benjamin, W. (1925–1926), One-way street. In: W. Benjamin, *One Way Street and Other Writings*. London: Verso, 1979, pp. 45–104.

——— (1927–1940), *The Arcades Project*. Cambridge, MA: Harvard University Press, 1999.

——— (1932), A Berlin chronicle. In: W. Benjamin, *One Way Street and Other Writings*. London: Verso, 1979, pp. 293–346.

Bollas, C. (1992), *Being a Character: Psychoanalysis and Self Experience*. London: Routledge.

Flanders, S., ed. (1993), *The Dream Discourse Today*. London: Routledge.

Freud, S. (1900), *The Interpretation of Dreams*. Oxford: Oxford University Press, 1999.

——— (1917), Mourning and melancholia. In: *On Metapsychology: The Theory of Psychoanalysis* (Penguin Freud Library, vol. 11). Harmondsworth: Penguin, 1984, pp. 251–268.

——— (1919), The 'uncanny.' In: *Art and Literature: Jensen's 'Gradiva,' Leonardo Da Vinci, and Other Works* (Penguin Freud Library, vol. 14). Harmondsworth: Penguin, 1985, pp. 339–376.

——— (1926), Inhibitions, symptoms, and anxiety. In: *On Psychopathology: Inhibitions, Symptoms, and Anxiety, and Other Works* (Penguin Freud Library, vol. 10). Harmondsworth: Penguin, 1979, pp. 237–333.

Gilloch, G. (1996), *Myth and Metropolis: Walter Benjamin and the City*. Cambridge: Polity Press.

Lefebvre, H. (1974), *The Production of Space*. Oxford: Blackwell, 1991.

Marcus, L, ed. (1999), *Sigmund Freud's* The Interpretation of Dreams: *New Interdisciplinary Essays*. Manchester: Manchester University Press.

Marx, K. (1843), Letters from the Franco-German yearbooks. In: K. Marx, *Early Writings*. Harmondsworth: Penguin, 1975, pp. 199–209.

Nora, P. (1989), Between memory and history: les lieux de mémoire. *Representations*, 26:7–25.

Pile, S. (1996), *The Body and the City: Psychoanalysis, Space, and Subjectivity*. London: Routledge.

——— (1998), Freud, dreams, and imaginative geographies. In: *Freud 2000*, ed. A. Elliot. Cambridge: Polity Press, pp. 204–234.

——— (2000), Sleepwalking in the modern city: Walter Benjamin, Sigmund Freud, and the world of dreams. In: *Blackwell Companion to Urban Studies*, eds. S. Watson & G. Bridge. Oxford: Blackwell, pp. 75–86.

——— (2002), Memory and the city. In: *Temporalities, Autobiography, and Everyday Life*, eds. J. Campbell & J. Harbord. Manchester: Manchester University Press, pp. 111–127.

FreudSpace
Architecture in Psychoanalysis

JULIET FLOWER MacCANNELL

> I believe that the task of inventing better futures may stagger the imagination and paralyze hope, but we cannot relinquish this holy call.
> —Emilio Ambasz, architect

Although Freud thought structurally (early on he employed the word "architecture" to designate the peculiar organization of hysteria; Freud, 1897), his theories never inspired the experimentation in spatial thinkers that they did in narrative and visual artists—among whom filmmakers perhaps hold pride of place. (Lacan is the more usual link with film, but other studies have also emphasized Freud. See MacCannell, 2000.)

True, Freud rarely neglected to mark the site-specificity of the key mental events that set off his speculations—events befalling him or his patients, or even whole civilizations: the Acropolis, Vienna, Thebes, Egypt, Sinai. Yet space hardly seems as crucial to his theory as the newly effracted dimensions Freud discovered in time. Thus we recall his awakening to long-repressed memories when he finds himself on the Acropolis, and not the architectural wonders surrounding him in that spot (Freud, 1936). We focus more on the phobias induced in "Little Hans" by the horses in the streets of Vienna than on the streets themselves, or on the splendors of the Schoenbrunn Palace (although, it too, plays its part in Hans's mental disturbance; Freud, 1909). And we think more about the unconscious desires of the son and his oedipal guilt (or his perverse enjoyment) than about the particular spatial arrangements of his mother's bedroom, although Freud sometimes offers such details (Freud, 1909).

If Freud uncovered the melodramatic return of a repressed ancient Thebes,

Egypt, or Sinai in today's mental and cultural acts, we nonetheless regard his use of these sites more as historical turning points in subjective life than as particularized locations, specific built environments, or divine and natural landscapes. As for the way Rome figures in Freud, it is not its monumental architecture that counts, only the way it symbolized his father's lack of place in civic life (whence his own fearful fascination with the Eternal City). True, Freud did employ the excavation of Rome as a forceful analogy for Proustian "time lost" and repressed memories; for him, the archaeology of the Forum's layer upon layer of buried histories chronicled the past of vanquished peoples and indexed the time of unremembered events. Yet even here Freud used the way the earth conceals three-dimensional objects to illustrate how psychical time superimposes one memory over another, without hinting at the reverse.

What seemingly matters most in Freud's style of psychoanalysis, then, are those temporal, historical events whose connections to the present are hidden, lost, and dropped out of the sequential narrative of life, but which have never actually been severed from it. Analysis attempts to recuperate these by means of an unrelentingly retrospective process: by pinpointing the moment of the trauma and by elaborating protocols of timing for the pacing and rhythm of the analyst's interventions to reach it. That is, psychoanalytic procedures are devised in order to arrive at a singular, primal event, the moment when the original object of satisfaction was lost: an object whose loss is subsequently masked (and yet indirectly indicated) in myriad everyday disguises in the ordinary, familiar objects that are its substitutes, appearing as our wishes, daydreams, hallucinations, or delusions. A moment, then, is dropped from the history of the subject, but nonetheless impacts the whole ensuing chronicle of its mental life.

In contrast to Freud's uncompromising pursuit of and systematic investigation into the obscure operations of unconscious mental time, we find (at first blush) no parallel effort with respect to space. Nor do the manifestations of the unconscious in three-dimensional reality command a great deal of Freud's attention. Freud, that is, does relatively little probing of spatial thinkers beyond, say, the sculptures of Michelangelo and the peculiar landscapes of Leonardo, although he obviously made some fuss over the spaces in which he himself worked at 19 Berggasse. Still, to mention Freud and space in the same breath brings mainly to mind his various two-dimensional sketches, his schemas of the topological systems, or his cartoonish graphics delineating the logically separated yet oddly continuous-contiguous mental spaces of id, ego, and superego—slashed through smartly by a gap called "repression." Freud's miniaturized pictures of mental structure even manage to reduce the collective mentality of entire social groups to diagrammatic flatness, as when he illustrates the process whereby a leader becomes a focal object that replaces his followers' individual ego ideals (Freud, 1922, p. 116).

Freudian flatness, Lacan would eventually remind us, relates primarily to his enduring attention to the ego and its imaginary structuring—an ego that ceaselessly draws a controlled circle around itself while warding off the alternately graceful or awkward pirouettes of instinctual vicissitudes. Even Freud's descriptions of the arcs and oblique circuits of drive are more like pencil drawings of serpentine lines than like constructs with mass, and more like verbal tropings (the twisting and turning aside from normal linguistic meaning and usage) than like three-dimensional architectural objects.

In Freud, that is, space seems to play analytical second fiddle to the temporality of psychical events. And so it seems, where the architectural object is concerned, it was up to Jacques Lacan and those he influenced to fill in the void of Freudian spatial inspiration. Lacan paid elaborate attention to Moebius strips, Klein bottles, knots, mathematical topology (1973), Baroque architecture and *trompe d'oeil* (1986), "Little Hans's" maternal bedroom (1994), and anamorphosis (1973). Lacan's seminar of 1964 (1973) developed the concept of the *démontage* ("dismantling": sometimes translated as "deconstruction") of the drives, which in turn "influenced" Jacques Derrida. Derrida is considered the French thinker who has most affected recent architectural practice, mainly through his critique of Heidegger's "enframing" using Kant's *parergon*; his work directly informs Peter Eisenman's deconstructive architecture (see Ledofsky, 2004, pp. 42–45). A long detour is required, then, to mark out Freud's architectural fortunes.

More pointedly, it seems clear that our traditional sense of space has not been much budged by Freud—or certainly not as much as our conventional understanding of time, which at length has yielded to Freud's complex rhythms of temporal contradictions and reversibilities. And yet, a case might be (and certainly remains to be) made that Freud's own sense of space was equally revolutionary, and that we may have simply failed to acknowledge, much less appreciate, his radicality in its regard (see MacCannell, 2003a).

Let us for a moment reconsider the *space* we encounter at the end of an analysis. Here we will have reached the very first time that space was framed for the psyche. Poised on the threshold of an aperture, we look back through it to the beginning of the patient's subjective time, looking toward the empty place of the missing object of satisfaction—an object whose loss will have motivated the entire psychical history of that subject.

Even the most successful analysis, however, never "finally" arrives at this lost object. If it is true that the primal scene of the object's dramatic cleavage from us is never actually accessible directly, this is due less to its loss in the "mists of time" than to the special mental *space* its loss has shaped: a space fashioned around and formed by a fantasy unconsciously constructed to obscure the object's loss. Unconscious fantasy *locates* the object of satisfaction as somehow still in the picture—still there, or rather, *not yet* lost. This fantasy models or determines all of the subject's subsequent desires in a very particular way. It frames all "real" objects by mobilizing them to fill in for the missing object: they will promise, yet can never deliver, its form of satisfaction. Unconscious fantasy thus makes the reality experienced through its frame appear isomorphic or symmetrical with one's *desire*. It governs how the subject historically (or autobiographically) apprehends and systematically distorts reality.

Unconscious fantasy achieves distorted expression in visual and spatial forms. Fascist spectacles, for example, are notoriously centered and symmetrical, intended to be seen only head-on. This makes the viewing subject feel he is at the center of things; in reality, of course, the whole design dwarfs and belittles him. It offers him the glory of reveling in "total" fulfillment, but its psychical appeal requires a subject who feels utterly devoid of power and satisfaction: the fantasy supplies their lack. An American architectural example, not directly connected with fascism, is Philip Johnson's AT&T Building in New York. Johnson's rather traditional skyscraper ends in a roofline designed to honor (by imitation) the top of a Queen Anne style dresser or highboy. The architect is establishing that there is no distinction between domestic and public, social space; the ease of the architectural simile provides the viewer a familiar, comforting place in public, civic space: he is there as though in his own living room; no anonymous citizen, but the king of his home. (The AT&T building was not loved, however; efforts to reinforce the subject's sense of its "true" place in the fantasy often fall flat when they are too obvious or direct.)

Across the opening delineated by the fantasy frame, in fact, there is drawn something that absolutely divides the subject from its own lost object—at the same time as it is also the screen on which the subject projects its unconscious amendment of reality. Slavoj Žižek (1997) vividly paints fantasy's frame:

> Fantasy is the very screen that separates desire from drive: it tells the story which allows the subject to (mis)perceive the void around which drive circulates as the primordial loss constitutive of desire. In other words, fantasy provides a *rationale* for the inherent deadlock of desire; it constructs the scene in which the *jouissance* we are deprived of is concentrated in the Other who stole it from us [pp. 33–34].

(*Jouissance* is the French word for enjoyment, bliss, orgasm, and a number of other nuances. Lacan uses it to mean the satisfaction of a drive, not an instinct. The word is now commonly used in English in its French form. See MacCannell, 2003b.)

The task of analysis would then seem to be to grasp the unconscious fantasy mechanism at work behind the screen that curtains off the *jouissance* that lies just behind, or just on the other side, of the gap or aperture that fantasy screens. Focused on this singular moment, analysis becomes largely a procedure for revealing the secrets of the patient's vanished time, and the discordant, warring temporalities that disturb and destroy his or her mental balance.

Yet if we begin to attend to space as well as time, we realize that once an analysis has reached this point, Freud actually makes a new departure, and does something that no temporal approach anticipates. He does not attempt to gain access to the lost moment, nor does he try to pierce the veil of fantasy that conceals it. Not directly. Instead he presents a fundamental alternative to the patient's time and history, an alternative devoid of temporal character. To divine what is hiding in the unconscious, Freud sets up what he calls a "construction" (Freud, 1937 and 1918).

Freud was certainly the first to bring out starkly the two-step, interrupted time of trauma and the unseen manner in which the past continuously places a warp into conscious memory and present perception. But he is rarely acknowledged for being equally innovative in inventing the *construction* as a *spatial* metaphor for its treatment: a singular construction, in which moment and place, time and space, are not easily separable. In perhaps the most notable example, Freud's patient, the "Wolfman," has a dream in the course of his analysis that is so vividly visual he is able to draw Freud its picture. The Wolfman describes the dream this way: a window sash is suddenly thrown open to reveal a tree outside in which several white wolves with upright tails sit staring at him.

After searching together through the patient's childhood fairy tale books for a historical or biographical source of this precise image, Freud decides to take a different tack. Rather than trying to cross the barrier the patient has raised in front of his trauma, Freud now rearranges the setting that appears in the Wolfman's screen-dream. The theory is that the Wolfman's fantasy is erected on the very site of the original trauma; a site Freud calls the "primal scene." This scene is not the object of a perception or the subject of historical verification, for it is neither real nor unreal, neither an actual event nor a fantasied one. Freud reaches it only indirectly. He will not break through the fantasy screen, but he will subject its dreamscape to a remarkable series of *spatial reversals* that will mark out the presence of the trauma it conceals.

Freud first rotates the dreamer's position inside the dream: now the window that flies open is not something looked *at* but something looked *through*: the aperture becomes the infant's own eyelids, startled suddenly apart. The infant, who is now the one who sees (and not the one stared at by the set of pale wolves), finds its visual object transformed into the darkly hirsute figure of his own lupine father, as he mounts the child's mother the same way that a furry, four-legged animal sexually enters his female (Freud uses the Latin phrase for "from behind": *a tergo*). The scene's *trauma* is constituted by the alternate appearance and disappearance of his father's penis; an alternation that makes this into the scene, then, of the Wolfman's encounter with castration (Freud, 1918; 1955, p. 45).

Freud has thus redesigned the setting of his patient's traumatic scene by carefully but dramatically shifting the spatial coordinates of the subject embedded in the fantasy scene that had masked or screened it off. Once Freud turns his patient's dream space around, he *rearticulates* the Wolfman to his fantasy constructs in an entirely new way, so that the truth of the castration anxiety hidden in them can now be "seen."

Lacan (1973) eventually offered Freud's radical reversals of space a proper name: *anamorphosis*. But from the very start, Freud already granted due weight to the spatial element in mentation: his story of the origin of the infant's mental life begins with its turn away from the source. In *The Project for a Scientific Psychology* (1897–1903, p. 283), Freud theorizes that normal mentation quite simply arises from the anamorphic spatial turn, when the baby turns aside from its frontal view of the breast—the fount of satisfaction—so it now sees the breast only in profile. This evokes the formation of a mental image of the now-absent breast: one that still satisfies, but only *imaginarily*.

Freud's therapeutic move with the Wolfman is the same move as the baby's in reverse: by reorienting his patient's mental space completely crosswise to the space of the fantasy that harbors and preserves the trauma, Freud turns his patient's glance aside, which then permits him to (re)construct the Wolfman's primal scene, where he finds the stillness at the center of the Wolfman's whirling drive energy—the whole history of the patient's recurrent failures in life and love, and his compulsion to replicate again and again the lost causes of his peculiar sexuality. (The Wolfman, for example, falls in love with any woman he happens to see from behind in a kneeling position, fixating sexually her posterior.) Freud builds an alternative construction of the primal scene in order to supplant the Wolfman's already-in-place fantasy edifice, and to redirect his patient's drive energy down different paths.

At a certain moment, that is, the analyst–patient couple had reached the point where *time* was at a stop, the time of the patient's history and of the progression of the analysis. This sticking point is a dead, unmoving instant, which has nonetheless been the power source of all the psychical energy transporting the patient through time and motivating the shape of his psychical "reality."

At this point of stubbornness, the adamancy and immovability of his traumatic, buried memory resists any and all change that might be wrought by time and experience.

And as Freud found, this point remains to be grasped less as a *moment in time* than as a *point in space*. For there, in the middle of the coursing stream of subjective time stands something petrified, stony, unbudging—something with dimensionality, with *weight*, yet empty and insubstantial. An opaque, traumatic spot, a *thing* of obdurate resistance to time, change, and reality. The very thing, indeed, that amplifies the natural nervous energy gushing past it, by converting it into something far more powerful than the stream of experience generated by itself: a psychical turbine, so to speak, in the middle of the river of time that constitutes the subject's history, a history that has flowed from this spot at the same rate as his conscious memory has fled from it. (Lacan makes this analogy: "a hydroelectric plant set midstream in a great river, the Rhine, for example" ["*une usine hydraulique électrique qui est en plein milieu du courant d'un grand fleuve, le Rhin par exemple*"]; by cumulating and augmenting natural forces [energy] it contributes to the constructed, fantasmatic character of *Wirklichkeit* [reality]. Lacan 1994, pp. 32–33).

Once Freud makes his "construction," time loses its simple orientation. The past tense becomes indivisible from an *other* past that is inexplicably and unbearably still *present* in it. Freud calls this uncanny point of time-space "drive"—death drive— and Lacan calls it *pulsion* ("impulsion": Lacan distinguished drive from natural instinct, and translated Freud's *Trieb* into this quasi-mechanical equivalent). Death drive is the transubstantiation of time into space: into a compulsive circling that has all the trappings of a temporal movement, but which is actually stuck, cycling around a traumatic point of fixed, almost mineral immobility. With drive, time is trumped by space, and Kant's antinomian mental coordinates are discovered as coeval and co-equal.

Truth and Consequences

Once the threshold of fantasy has been crossed figuratively by analysis, where do we go? Two clear directions have appeared since Freud, the one speculative and temporal and the other plastic and three-dimensional. The philosophical, speculative option takes a good hard look at fantasy and suggests that the subject should realistically resign himself to the fact that if the fantasy frame is deconstructed, the death-drive that motivated its construction will appear in all its stark horror. The philosophical option accepts a "dead end" to analysis, just as it accepts the same of time and history. The other, "architectural" option adopts a somewhat sunnier view of human possibilities and sheds a different light on what Freud's spatial method might bring.

The consequences to disattending the spatial dimension of Freud's analysis are grave. Slavoj Žižek, who calls himself a "philosopher of psychoanalytic ontology" (1997), faces squarely the fact that the screen and frame of fantasy are never finally or fully breached. Analysis, he points out, ends with a "traversal of the fantasy" that "suspend[s] the fantasmic frame of unwritten rules that tell us how to choose freely" (p. 29). But this does not mean breaking "through the screen" (p. 30) or liberating ourselves from the restrictive viewpoint of fantasy. Žižek instead emphasizes, using the late Lacan, that at the end of analysis, the subject at last apprehends that death drive alone lies beyond the screen of projected desires: "Once we move beyond desire—that is to say, beyond the fantasy which sustains desire—we enter the strange domain of *drive*: the domain of the closed circular palpitation which finds satisfaction in endlessly repeating the same failed gesture" (p. 30).

According to Žižek's interpretation, a successful analysis destroys all the illusions fashioned to dissimulate the finite character of death drive, which Žižek calls "a radical closure" (p. 31)—or nothing other than the "end" of time.

Žižek argues vigorously that what one usually thinks of as the aim of analysis (as "opening" the subject to his or her possibilities), is simply a way to "maintain [a] false opening (the idea that the excluded choice might have happened)" (p. 33). Any analysis that supported this vain hope is destined for disappointment. Instead, Žižek affirms the end of analysis to be an impasse where the drive that endlessly cycles around an impossibly lost object is finally and fully realized.

Moreover, Žižek counsels acceptance of this "unbearable closure of being" (p. 30); thus, he asks: "What if 'traversing the fantasy' involves the acceptance of a radical ontological closure? The unbearable aspect of the 'eternal return of the same'—the Nietzschean name for the crucial dimension of *drive*—is the radical *closure* this notion implies: to endorse and fully assume the 'eternal return of the same'" (p. 31).

Such acceptance, Žižek goes on to say, actually yields another sort of enjoyment, one more profound than its original model: a joy-in-death-drive, if you will. Like all revolutionary fervors, it comes from *renouncing* any hope and all faith in the false promises of "opening." He writes that in "the 'eternal return of the same' . . . we renounce every opening, every belief in messianic Otherness" (p. 31); moreover, "in 'traversing the fantasy,' we find *jouissance* in the vicious cycle of circulating around the void of the (missing) object, renouncing the myth that *jouissance* has to be amassed somewhere else" (pp. 33–34).

Satisfaction is (philosophically at least) rediscovered at—and *as*—the *last moment*.

But Žižek's hyperbolic conclusions are clouded somewhat by his deeper neglect of space. Just as his mesmerizing analyses of cultural objects spiral round and round their several possible interpretations (following an essentially Hegelian time, with its own end to history), his "psychoanalytic ontology" presents itself in *The Plague of Fantasies* as one-sidedly *temporal*. For Žižek, the opposite of time is not space, but *eternity*; and like Hegel's, this is an essentially religious viewpoint. Žižek "endorses and fully assumes" an "end-time" that realizes itself as a perpetual whirl emptying into a void.

Žižek (1997, p. 31) assumes that "the point is . . . to oppose the radical closure of the 'eternal' drive to the opening involved in the finitude/temporality of the desiring subject." But what, after all, is Žižek's "unbearable closure of being" when looked at spatially? Surely it is no more, nor less, than that final empty space, the one awaiting us all at the end of our time: the grave. When we are face to face with time's deadest point, psychoanalytic ontology, even at its most radical, must stop; logically so, for it is organized by what *is*.

Žižek's antisentimental view of the analytic experience, while plainly consonant with Freud's demystifying spirit, is nonetheless more than just quizzically awry with respect to Freud's analytic aims. If the orientation of psychoanalysis is primarily retrospective, then Žižek would be correct that its final goal has to be to reach the zero point of time where drive energizes the fantasy that masks it, and where *eternity* offers the only alternative perspective on that time.

But, to turn the tables a bit, let me ask whether the spatial reorientation of the fundamental fantasy Freud effected in the Wolfman does not offer an entirely different resolution to the traversal of fantasy from the resignation Žižek envisages (and recommends)? Aren't there other possible lines of flight from this stillest of all points? After all, Freud took full responsibility for shifting the Wolfman off his position in the fantasy scene. Everything had been nicely arranged in his fantasy so as to screen off knowledge of the primal scene of his trauma. With the anamorphotic shift in subjective perspective that Freud insists on for the Wolfman's dream, a wholly different prospect materializes for his patient and provides them both with a crucial perspective on the Wolfman's truth.

Once it is space, not time, that is psychoanalytically reversed, the architectural option for traversing the fantasy emerges. A "radical" architecture, set toward new departures (not ending up back at the uterine enclosure), can also move us around inside our fantasy spaces: a radical architecture that turns its subject *sideways*, making him look in the unexpected direction—back through the fantasy frame that obscures his past and present realities. The stake of spatial psychoanalysis and radical architecture alike would be to re-start subjective time by treating it with space, providing a *spatial* prospect for a mental gaze blinded by the fantasy of what "is" to the critical importance of what "is not."

Architecture in Psychoanalysis II: Critical Space

Let me begin where Freud so often did, with everyday reality (the one I am saying is shaped by unconscious fantasy). Everyone knows from the daily papers what intense emotional reactions innovative architecture stirs up whenever it appears to establish some new or aberrant kind of object: an object that departs in an elemental way from the ordinary "objects of desire" that constitute our world, by substituting for and screening off the lethal satisfaction of our final objective, death drive.

When it comes to the passions this type of created object brings out, psychoanalytic insight is rare. This is understandably so, since psychoanalysis has tended to give priority to time over space, which it often sees largely as the surrogate or stand-in for the lost object. For example, a psychoanalyst friend once remarked: "Don't you think architects love their mothers too much?" The remark indicated to me that he regarded the task of analysis as chiefly a matter of reversing time, with space as little more than the representative of the time outside of human time. He also obviously took it for granted that architected space was a container or enclosure; that architectural space symbolized either a return to the womb or foreshadowed the tomb. (In a recent paper for Yale University 2003, I question this fundamental assumption.)

Something more fundamental is nonetheless at stake in the question of space in and for psychoanalysis. To repeat my original question: why do so few objects (apart from legendarily scandalous art objects) raise as much emotional commotion as architectural ones? And why do those who react so viscerally to architecture do so in such highly affective and extremely personal ways? It is as if innovative architecture disturbed some deep layer of existence that puts the fundamental structure of the world (or our fantasy place in it) in danger—or at least in doubt.

Consider a whole host of unique architectural projects proposed in the last few years for San Francisco: Rem Koolhaas's new Prada store, wrapped in a stainless steel exterior pierced at regular intervals by uniform holes, was immediately hated and labeled a big "cheese grater"; the new, copper-clad de Young Museum in Golden Gate Park by Herzog and de Meuron features a tower people instantly found reminiscent of a prison. Visceral, emotional reactions to architecture are often characterized by a tendency to link the new architectural object to some familiar, everyday object (for example, a cheese grater) that, in its gigantic appearance as a major edifice, are then deemed ridiculously "out of place." Yet in contrast, objections to "developments" that blanket hundreds or thousands of acres with uniform, unimaginative houses are generally voiced affect-neutrally, and couched impersonally: expressing, for example, fear of potentially negative environmental consequences, not how uneasy they might make us feel. One objects to them, as it were, for the sake of "nature," and not because these built environments might well produce negative mental effects. This is because uniform and completely predictable buildings, installed in conventional, gridded spaces, model a ready-made psychical reality into whose fantasy picture we have already fitted ourselves in a conventional location, our "proper place."

What, then, would a Freudian *revolution* in space look like architecturally—or to put it another way, what kind of architecture could invert the reactions noted above? As I researched this paper, I found that it probably would not look like "postmodern" architecture. Postmodern architecture deploys the same neo-Hegelian temporality as Žižek's, which invokes the "end of history"; similarly, postmodernism promotes the infinite "recycling" of established forms. While the postmodern avoids the trap of neoclassicism by deploying discordant techniques to collage forms from long-ago historical styles and disparate cultures, its aim is still the same as the one outlined by Žižek: to collapse or telescope time into a greater "all-time" that, in fusing with the end of time, becomes an imitation of eternity and a *jouissance* of an "eternal return of the same."

There are nonetheless architectural indicators of other possibilities. It would seems obvious to begin with Frank Gehry, the architect who so clearly challenged the customary way we "see" ourselves in space. His Bilbao Guggenheim breaks away from the conventional framing of space that supports our fantasies of the familiar. But there is more to be learned from another contemporary architect, Emilio Ambasz. At least that was my first, and now lasting, impression of his work.

To look at Ambasz's work is to wonder, "What if, instead of trying to go through the rabbit hole or the fantasy frame to the horror behind it—the missing object; the whirling void of death drive; or the end of time—we refused to question the frame and simply turned aside and looked through the frame anamorphically?" What would happen, that is, if we looked upon the kind of life that might materialize before our now repositioned gaze. Wouldn't it mean that the endpoint of fantasy's frame could no longer be considered only as the bottomless pit of unreal foundations, but a revolutionary vantage point on ourselves, and our future selves?

Emilio Ambasz: The Architectural Object versus the Lost Object

Emilio Ambasz has described his architecture as the "pursuit of alternative futures" (Sorkin, 2004, p. 108). Ambasz's creations are often portrayed as having a distinctly uncontemporary, almost atemporal feel; some even argue they purvey the sense of the mythic time before time, while others honestly describe their reactions as the opposite: that Ambasz seems to be looking towards an enigmatic future in which our entire relation to time, space, and nature will be fully disclosed.

Neither orientation—past or future—is quite adequate to his opus. His enigmatic architecture, at the very least, reverses the retrospective temporal orientation, and thereby the directives, usually ascribed to psychoanalysis—and that psychoanalysis usually ascribes to architecture. Still, what Ambasz really engages is not entirely obvious. His best interpreters agree that time seems somehow implicated in his architecture, but also that it is secondary to, or even dependent on, his innovations with space. Lauren Ledofsky, for example, describes Ambasz as "bring[ing] forth the earth" when he half-buries more or less "canonical" buildings (such as a Mediterranean villa), and thus enables what Ledofsky calls the "emergence of the earth over and against architecture" (Ledofsky, 2004, p. 44). Indeed, the motto of Ambasz's architectural enterprise is "Green over Gray," or, in other words, landscape over architecture (Ambasz, 2004).

In Ambasz's world, the habitants of the earth appear to be comparatively few and they seem not to have marked (or ruined) nature in any highly visible or indelible way. Yet they are not dwarfed by the "nature" they dwell in, either. Ambasz's works are unmistakably human-oriented creations that—although indeed often half-buried, with unclear exits and entrances and with no obvious ways of escape or lines of flight from them—are nonetheless often islands of a peace and a harmony that simply do not appear in a vertical, temporal perspective (eternal time) in which man is under earth and both are under God. It is not the unruffled calm of a perfect consonance with nature that Ambasz's buildings exhibit.

For his buildings, while pictured as balanced in and not merely on the earth, are nonetheless suffused with a striking potential energy that could break in any of several ways, some terrifying, some radiant. In fact, the seemingly obvious idea of green-over-gray does not really describe how Ambasz's architecture actually relates to the earth. In one project, for example, he attempted to build a lake in a park that tilted at a 45-degree angle. His fellow architects are often quickest to comprehend that Ambasz's earth is perhaps as far from "natural" as possible. As Ettore Sottsass remarks, "Ambasz's earth is not at all the picturesque botanical compendium of the pastoral" (cited in Ledofsky, 2004, p. 42), while Robert Wines terms Ambasz's a "Daliesque Landscape" (Wines, 2004, p. 89).

Some writers suspect Ambasz of an undue "maternal attachment" because he sets his architectural objects into their landscapes in such a way that they cannot really be detached from them: they could not be constructed just anywhere. But this view ignores that he subjects his buildings' landscapes to the same powerful stresses, the same distinctive viewpoints, that he brings to bear on his constructions—and this

FIGURE 1. Casa de Retiro Espiritual, Emilio Ambasz, Córdoba.

aspect of his architecture runs completely counter to the belief that Ambasz exalts ground over construct.

Indeed, Ambasz's architectural objects are neither laid in the earth—that is, fully swallowed by the grave—nor do they completely ignore this possible "end" to their history the way a housing development does. But it is also the case that Ambasz's architecture is simply not looking toward time past as it cycles into a future that will merely repeat it, at a higher or lower level. He is instead moving space off of the opposing yet fused temporal axes we try to reduce it to—vertical, synchronic, eternal time; flowing diachronic time—that hold it within a familiar, fantasy framing.

In Casa de Retiro Espiritual (figure 1), this marvel of a house, Ambasz disorients space in an especially anamorphic way: as if a wall that should surround was swiveled aside, and the stairs that should lead to an interior look at first as if they go nowhere, and then seem to lead the visitor out before they lead him in. The result: the house makes a departure, disclosing a direction for time and experience that only a twist in space can really convey. Instead of unearthing the natural past or the archaic legacy of buried horrors, Ambasz's architectural objects materialize a space that confounds our fantasies of nature and history and produces something else—which is, for Lacan, *the* elementary form of desire: "*le désir d'autre chose*" (the desire for something else) (Lacan, 1994, p. 303).

Of his own work, Ambasz writes that "sometimes I fancy myself to be the last man of the present culture, building a house for the first man of a culture that has not yet arrived" (in Sorkin, 2004, p. 86).

In this paper I have argued that space for Freud was as crucial a factor as time in the work of analysis, and that contemporary practitioners might be advised to reconsider its potential importance in treatment. If a fundamental fantasy shapes the patient's subjective life, and operates specifically by blocking access to his or her initial trauma, the effort to break its frame—to reach the time before the original traumatic moment—are not necessarily the only, or even the most effective, approach. By its very nature, fantasy bars the way to the time before its construction; and though a philosopher of will like Žižek might believe we can force a face-to-face confrontation with our subjective origin (and end) by traversing the fantasy, the result is ambiguous at best: we meet the death drive in ourselves, and this becomes its own form of satisfaction.

A rather different path is available to the analyst, with a different possible outcome. That is to take the fantasy for what it is, a *spatial* conceit. The analyst's task would be to discover where the subject has positioned himself and secreted his lost satisfactions in this unconscious fantasy picture; and then to reorient the subject's spatial position inside the fantasy. Apocalyptic breakthroughs to original time are rendered unnecessary, because the positional shift opens its own vista on what the subject has hidden away in the fantasy: a sense of its overwhelmingly defining loss (e.g., the Wolfman's fear of castration). It can do this, moreover, without forcing the ultimate destination—subjective destitution before death drive—that postmodern psychoanalytic ontology stipulates.

Architecture, wherever its spatial reorientations can dislodge us from the predictable traps, dead-ends, and blind corners we unconsciously cement ourselves into, can offer this same opening. At its most imaginative, that is, architecture may serve as one of the finer metaphors for the significance of Freud's achievement in making a space where we can see our "world"—and ourselves in it—*otherwise*.

Good art can make the same subjective difference good analysis makes: artists, Freud said, are out ahead of analysts, who only follow their path. In this essay, I hope to have made this case also for radical architecture, which can begin to take its place as a powerful guide to a new, spatially oriented form of psychoanalytic treatment. Great architecture—anonymous, quotidian, or produced by a singular brilliance—can even perhaps now be defined as something that creates a "new" *scene* for human dreaming, by performing its own virtual/virtuoso analysis of where culture is "stuck" and where we are "stuck" in it (or with it) by virtue of our unconscious fantasies. Any transformative, revolutionary effect that architecture may realize will parallel—and will not simply imitate—Freud's crucial method: identifying the conservative unconscious indirectly expressed in conventional fantasies, and articulating how we are caught up in and by it.

References

Ambasz, E. (2004), Emilio Ambasz, Inc., website: http://www.emilioambaszandassociates.com.

Freud, S. (1887–1902), The project for a scientific psychology. *Standard Edition*, 1:295–399. London: Hogarth Press, 1950.

——— (1897), The architecture of hysteria, in: Draft L; letter to Fliess. *Standard Edition*, 1:248–250. London: Hogarth Press, 1966.

——— (1909), Analysis of a phobia in a five-year-old boy ["Little Hans"]. *Standard Edition*, 10:3–152. London: Hogarth Press, 1974.

——— (1918), From the history of an infantile neurosis ["The Wolfman"]. *Standard Edition*, 17:7–122. London: Hogarth Press, 1955.

——— (1921), Group psychology and the analysis of the ego. *Standard Edition*, 18:67–144. London: Hogarth Press, 1955.

——— (1922), Group psychology and the analysis of the ego. *Standard Edition*, 18:69–143. London: Hogarth Press, 1955.

——— (1936), A disturbance of memory on the Acropolis. *Standard Edition*, 22:239–248. London: Hogarth Press, 1960.

——— (1937), Constructions in analysis. *Standard Edition,* 23:255–270. London: Hogarth Press, 1964.

Lacan, J. (1973), *Le Séminaire IX: Les Quatres Concepts Fondamentaux de Psychanalyse.* Paris: Les Éditions du Seuil.

——— (1986), *Le Séminaire VII: L'Éthique de la Psychanalyse.* Paris: Les Éditions du Seuil.

——— (1994), *Le Séminaire IV: La Relation d'Objet.* Paris: Les Éditions du Seuil.

Ledofsky, L. (2004), Peripheral vision. In: Sorkin (2004), pp. 40–63.

MacCannell, J. F. (2000), *The Hysteric's Guide to the Future Female Subject.* Minneapolis: University of Minnesota Press.

——— (2003a), Breaking out. Presented at Yale University School of Architecture, October, New Haven, Connecticut.

——— (2003b), Jouissance. In: *Glossalalia: An Alphabet of Critical Keywords*, ed. J. Wolfreys. Edinburgh: Edinburgh University Press, pp. 157–166.

Sorkin, M., ed. (2004), *Analyzing Ambasz.* New York: Monacelli Press.

Wines, R., (2004), Emilio Ambasz: Soft and hard, in Sorkin (2004), pp. 86–108.

Žižek, S. (1997), *The Plague of Fantasies.* London: Verso Books.

An Architect's View of Introspective Space
The Analytic Vessel

ELIZABETH A. DANZE

The room is his space, not mine. It has his things in it and I look at it almost every day. After a while they start to become mine, too, but not in the same way they are his. I don't know their history and I don't know his, but I start to overlay mine onto them. The primitive, handmade sculptures connect me to him, to those who made them, to other places around the world, outside and beyond myself, while I look deeply inside. They are his things, but they belong to all of us; our pasts, our present, and the future somehow are coalesced in this room. If the natural light is diffused, the room has a dreamy quality. If it is bright, I'm less in touch with my feelings and more aware of what I'm thinking. The shadows cast by the blinds are beautiful. The stillness of the room is interrupted by this reminder of our ancient attachment to the universal and fundamental qualities of the earth and our humanness in it. It is a simple reminder, too, of the passing of time. The blanket on the couch is soft, but durable, and has an open weave; obviously hand woven, it is reassuring. It was designed to protect the couch, but because I touch it, I am holding the hand of the weaver. The window lets me escape when I am resistant to the work. The visual relief quells anxiety borne of the intimacy and closeness of the analyst. The room is reassuring and consistent when I need it to be and it is an open box of treasures stimulating memories and feelings.

—Anonymous analysand

If we believe the essence and objective of psychoanalytic work is personal transformation, then the exchange, and over time the relationship, between analyst and analysand is the milieu by which this transformation takes place. This personal exchange is psychologically charged, as is the *site* of the exchange. Two unique individuals meet in a specific location, the analytic setting. This special room becomes the explicit and specific territory of this uniquely formed relationship. There is no other architectural space that has precisely the same programmatic demands as this one. All five senses are engaged in this intimate and sublime relationship and place.

By interrogating the physical and spatial qualities of the analytic room from one point of view—in this case, that of a designer and architect—ideal architectural and spatial circumstances for the work of a specific psychoanalysis might be made more evident. The couch, itself a powerful physical object in the room, has been accepted and established as an indisputable part of psychoanalytic treatment to the point of being taken for granted (Moraitis, 1995, p. 275). Why then should we not speculate about the optimal physical and architectural characteristics of the entire setting for analysis?

The analyst's office can be intimidating for some because it is spatially perceived by the patient as the analyst's territory. It is the setting in which the patient reveals and exposes the full range of human emotion, inner thought, vulnerabilities, and circumstances. Like the creation of an analysis that seeks to transform the patient, the actual, physical creation of a space and building involves enormous powers of transformation. The creative act of making *architecture* is, out of necessity, violent. The earth is ripped and rended. The ground and vegetation are often uprooted and displaced. The analytic room and the working construction site each confront and hold a multitude of powerful natural forces. The construction site is a literal scene of the transformative power of creativity; the new architecture changes the existing place and sometimes the very essence of the previous site forever. Like a construction site, the analytic setting is vibrantly active, messy, and thrillingly alive with some degree of simultaneous predictability and *un*predictability. This change may be slight or radical, but any provocation of change will—whether in the internal or external world, the construction site, or the analytic room—be met with some degree and measure of resistance. In the case of analysis, the room may appear as a physical counterpart to the inevitable appearance of emotional resistance and transference. The analytic space is then both a natural witness and powerful participant in the psychoanalytic relationship.

Several specific conditions occur in the design of the analytic space. These may seem mundane, yet are charged with architectural meaning and consequence for analysis: the couch or chair; the relative positions of the analysand to the analyst; and the design of the room itself specifically with regard to objects, windows, views, natural light, and the sequence of entering, including the specific transition across thresholds from one space to another.

FIGURE 1. Sigmund Freud's study, Freud Museum.

The Couch and the Space between Analyst and Analysand

The conventional physical position of the analyst and the analysand is for the analysand to be lying on one's back on the couch and for the analyst to be seated behind, out of view. There are many valid reasons for the patient not to face the analyst directly during the work of analysis. In regard to this Sigmund Freud (1913) writes that

> it is the remnant of the hypnotic method out of which psycho-analysis was evolved. But it deserves to be maintained for many reasons. The first is a personal motive, but one which others may share with me. I cannot put up with being stared at by other people for eight hours a day (or more). Since, while I am listening to the patient, I, too, give myself over to the current of my unconscious thoughts, I do not wish my expressions of face to give the patient material for interpretation or

to influence him in what he tells me. The patient usually regards being made to adopt this position as a hardship and rebels against it, especially if the instinct for looking (scopophilia) plays an important part in his neurosis. I insist on this procedure, however, for its purpose and result are to prevent the transference from mingling with the patient's associations imperceptibly, to isolate the transference and to allow it to come forward in due course sharply defined as a resistance [pp. 133–134].

From an architectural point of view there exists perhaps another reason, a *spatial* one, why this direct looking between persons may not be the most beneficial configuration for analytic work. When two people sit face-to-face in contact and conversation, they create a focused, defined, condensed space between them. This space is intimate yet limited; but when the analysand is looking up, out, or over, and looking not at any particular focal point, there is made to exist a spatial openness, an implied spatial potential for infinity. This applies to and is true for the analyst as well. Space, and hence *relational opportunity*, is expanded, enhanced, limitless, and open-ended. The relationship is not bound by the physical space between them. Each is a free-floating object, surrounded by a bubble of space, gazing independently. The two exist in the room together yet are able to roam imaginatively and psychically, freely apart. The *edges* of the room then contain the analysand and analyst together and independently simultaneously (see figure 1).

Traditionally the analyst usually sits above and behind the analysand, looking *down* on the patient, situated to observe facial expressions. Disregarding all other factors, the relative position of the parties in the room establishes a particular kind of spatial hierarchy. We might say the analyst is privileged from a very specific position of *prospect*, much like a surveyor, a voyeur, or a judge. Assessing, looking, and judging, without being seen in return by the analysand, is a particularly powerful spatial position to hold. From the point of view of the patient being watched, it can be a particularly alarming and disconcerting spatial alignment. This spatial configuration is blatantly nonsymmetrical and reinforces a nonsymmetrical relationship. The belief that the analyst and analysand are learning together, that theirs is a shared experience with transference and countertransference, is potentially compromised by this physically dynamic condition. A spatial equivalency does not exist in the relationship of the analyst's chair to the couch, and the effect is felt both consciously and unconsciously. Once hierarchical arrangements have been introduced, they tend to be self-perpetuating. There are many ways of interpreting this physical relationship. It is reminiscent of a chef leaning over the stove, creating or "fixing" something, or of the carpenter leaning over the carpenter's worktable, "repairing" a broken object. The image of "working on" or fixing what is broken by an ever-present, omnipotent figure is particularly powerful and formidable. The space, then, between the analyst and analysand, regardless of fantastic imagery, is much like the space between perception and reality. The analyst provokes dreaming and ultimately the reorganization between perception and reality and does so from this very specific spatial location.

The Couch

It is in the beginning of an analysis, while the analysand is sitting, that rules of engagement are laid out and agreements are established. Once the analysand is invited to lie on the couch, in the reclining position, disorientation, reconfiguration and instability all naturally and fundamentally ensue. The shift from being grounded, upright, mobile and physically in control, from being in command of one's physical location, to being passive, at rest, in the posture of the observer, an observer of one's self, is one of the most subtle and powerful physical adjustments that initiates transformation. Whether adjacent to or touching a wall, or floating, surrounded by space, the couch induces in the analysand a state of suspension. "As soon as we become motionless, we are elsewhere; we are dreaming in a world that is immense. Indeed, immensity is the movement of motionless man. It is one of the characteristics of quiet daydreaming" (Bachelard, 1964, p. 184).

Significantly, the word *attitude* is defined both as a feeling or emotion toward a fact or state as well as the arrangement of a body or thing in space. This double meaning applies to the analysand and the couch. The physical shift in *attitude* (position) initiates and encourages awareness and change in attitude (feeling and emotion). In this new position on the couch, the analysand hovers in space and place, transferring and alleviating a sense of gravity and of the "weight of the world." The experience of hovering and suspension is profound and this new position and point of view transforms the space of the room from a passive container to a full participant in the work.

The Active Room

The room itself has the power to initiate and sustain a shift in the analysand. By examining some of the room's special spatial and sensual qualities—characteristics of proximity, separation, materials, sound, and light—we see how the room actively participates (Frank and Lepori, 2000, p. 57). The room is envelope and backdrop for what goes on in it, a sensitive vessel that holds all actions and movements, containing and holding the patient. The room is a constant, much like the shared relationship between analyst and analysand; the stability of the room then holds the stability of the relationship.

The architectural space and its essential character of *muteness* is an essential backdrop offering literal resistance and a familiarity. Yet the room is not neutral; rather, it is a biased container invested with personal interpretation.

Donald W. Winnicott (1975) describes the setting of Freud's work:

> This work was done in a room, not a passage, a room that was quiet and not liable to sudden and unpredictable sounds, yet not dead quiet and not free from ordinary house noises. This room would be lit properly, but not by a light staring in the face, and not by a variable light. The room would certainly not be dark and it would be comfortably warm. The patient would be lying on a couch, that is to say comfortable, if able to be comfortable, and probably a rug and some water would be available [p. 285].

The description suggests certain qualities of the setting, specifically that the analysis should occur in a *room*, a space with a sense of *place* and stability rather than transience. Also, the statement "not free from ordinary house sounds" suggests a familiar setting, certainly not one that is sterile or institutional:

> The intimacy of the room becomes our intimacy. And correlatively, intimate space has become so quiet, so simple, that all the quietude of the room is localized and centralized in it. The room is very deeply our room, it is in us. We no longer *see* it. It no longer *limits* us, because we are in the very ultimate depths of its repose, in the repose that it has conferred upon us. And all our former rooms come and fit into this one [Bachelard, 1964, p. 226].

The size of the room, the position of the furniture in the room and the space between objects in the room, establishes the sense of intimacy, familiarity, and safety. Every room has spatial hierarchies, reinforced by the width and height of ceilings, doors and windows—all elements which define the structural or architectural envelope. Partitions, furniture, and objects establish secondary sets of horizontal and vertical relationships with the two bodies measuring and defining the scale: "Understanding architectural scale implies the unconscious measuring of an object or a building with one's body, and projecting one's bodily scheme on the space in question. We feel pleasure and protection when the body discovers its resonance in space" (Pallasmaa, 1994, p. 36).

The room should be safe and neutral, a chamber that encourages safe separation from the analysand's existing world and the outside. The room is, after all, the center of the world, managing separateness between analyst and analysand the way that an architectural loggia creates a space of simultaneity—of exposure and refuge, inner and outer sanctums, mediating the physical and the psychic.

The Window and Natural Light

The defined and bounded space of the room makes clear the dialectics of inside and outside. The window lets in the outside space of the *immeasurable* while reinforcing the intimacy of the inside. The intimate space of the room becomes familiar and known while the space outside, especially the space through the window of the long view, to the horizon, is undetermined. Lying on the couch and being *aware* of the window in the room is a tangible reminder of the analysand's unique position, that of looking both inwardly and outwardly. The window mediates the interior and the exterior, as does the analyst with the patient.

The wide, external view, if too expansive or too wide, may risk losing the sense of the room as a safe nest. A window that is too large may also be visually distracting. At the same time the presence of a crack, an opening, or evidence of the outside world where distance is brought near and the near is extended, may be reassuring. Seeing the horizon or a distant view tangibly introduces the feeling of infinity while the closeness of the interior reminds us of the finite and tangible. Every polarity, after all, requires the other for fulfillment. The window and the view out is the fulfillment of the close, inward-looking view. To be positioned in a place of prospect highlights the closeness of the analyst—literally looking out, but from a position of safety and refuge:

> Our gaze strokes distant contours and edges, and the unconscious tactile sensation determine the agreeableness or unpleasantness of the experience. The distant and the near are experienced with the same level of intensity. The eye is the sense of separation and distance, whereas touch is the sensation of nearness, intimacy and affection. During overpowering emotional states we tend to close off the distancing sense of vision; we close our eyes when caressing our loved ones. Deep shadows and darkness are essential, because they dim the sharpness of vision and invite unconscious peripheral vision and tactile fantasy. *Homogeneous light paralyzes the imagination in the same way that homogenization eliminates the experience of place*" [Pallasmaa, 1994, p. 34].

Natural light is desirable in most habitable spaces, but it may be particularly poignant in the analytic setting (figure 2). The quantity of light is not as important

FIGURE 2. Change of light on wall over the course of an analytic session.

as the *quality*. Variations of light, from the brightest light to the deepest shadows, bring out shape, texture, and stimulate our senses (Rasmussen, 1962, p. 189). The temporal quality of natural light is by its very nature transformative. The room, through the quality and changeability of light over the course of an hour, a day, and a year, bears the recognition of time. Watching a shadow cast and formed is a particularly potent marker of time and a reminder of constant, slow-moving change: "The perceptual spirit and metaphysical strength of architecture are driven by the quality of light and shadow shaped by solids and voids, by opacities, transparencies, and translucencies. Natural light with its ethereal variety of change, fundamentally orchestrates the intensities of architecture and cities. What the eyes see and the senses feel in questions of architecture are formed according to conditions of light and shadow" (Holl, 1994, p. 63).

Returning to the same room repeatedly and over time has a particular and special effect—it takes on a special familiarity, an ownership, and a special connectedness for both analyst and analysand. "For not only do we come back to it, but we dream of coming back to it, the way a bird comes back to its nest or a lamb to the fold. This sign of return marks an infinite number of daydreams, for the reason that human returning takes place in the great rhythm of human life, a rhythm that reaches back across the years and, through the dream, combats all absence" (Bachelard, 1964, p. 99).

And yet the room does not divulge all that it contains. There exists a secret, hidden component to the room, an inner tension, not overtly expressed, but present and perhaps intuitively understood—the inner forces of weight, gravity, bearing, and holding that reside and are resolved within the walls of the room. We know it is there, we feel it, but we do not visually see it. This balance of what is revealed and understood and what remains hidden is embedded in the psychoanalytic setting.

Acoustic Intimacy

The room functions primarily as a safe haven for the analysand. There are advantages to the acoustic quality of the room being primarily mute or a least safe from sudden noises. "Differently shaped rooms and different materials reverberate differently" (Rasmussen, 1962, p. 224) and the sound is hard or soft, reflected or absorbed, in response to them. The room activates daydreaming while protecting and sheltering the daydreamer, and a simple, quiet room provokes the primitiveness of refuge. By experiencing the primitiveness of refuge we "return to the field of primitive images that had perhaps been centers of fixation for recollections left in our memories" (Bachelard, 1964, p. 30). As Pallasmaa (1994) notes,

> the most essential auditory experience created by architecture is tranquility. Architecture presents the drama of construction silenced into matter and space; architecture is the art of petrified silence. After the clutter of building has ceased and the shouting of workers has died away, the building becomes a museum of waiting, patient silence. . . . An architectural experience silences all external noise; it focuses attention on one's very existence. Architecture, as all art, makes us aware of our fundamental solitude. At the same time, architecture detaches us from the present and allows us to experience the slow, firm flow of time and tradition [p. 31].

Adjacent sounds, far or near, pose questions of proximity, safety, and threat. The sounds of the surrounding street, voices in the office or room next door, the waiting room—all stimulate the imagination:

One who has half-risen to the sound of a distant train at night and, through his sleep, experienced the space of the city with its countless inhabitants scattered around its structures, knows the power of sound to the imagination; the nocturnal whistle of a train makes one conscious of the entire sleeping city. Anyone who has become entranced by the sound of water-drops in the darkness of a ruin can attest to the extraordinary capacity of the ear to carve a volume into the void of darkness. The space traced by the ear becomes a cavity sculpted in the interior of the mind. Sound measures space and makes its scale comprehensible. We stroke the edges of space with our ears [Pallasmaa, 1994, p. 30].

Territory and Objects in the Room

Most analysts also use the analysis room as a personal office; as a result, the consulting room is usually populated and decorated with furniture, personal objects, belonging to the analyst. Personal items that establish the office as the *territory* of the analyst—especially diplomas, which might be seen as trophies—may increase an initial sense of intimidation and intrusion on the part of the analysand. At the same time, the objects, items, and art present in the room might provide opportunities for association.

In the process of analysis, the analysand's memories, feelings, and thoughts are laid out similarly to the analyst's objects in the room: to be mentally rotated in space, scrutinized, and reconstructed. Associations and identification with the analyst are made through the objects positioned in the room. These items are not neutral, but rather hold and present opportunities. Freud populated his own study with specific objects. As Gamwell (Gamwell and Wells, 1989) notes,

> Freud's selection and placement of his antiques also pointed to their role as audience. Almost every object Freud acquired is a figure whose gaze creates a conscious presence and his collection was predominantly sculpture, which by its nature has a more physical presence than painting [p. 27].

Objects of art, as well as ambiguous props are invitations to dream and imagine. The objects are representations of imagination: first the imagination of the maker, and then the imagination of us, the viewers. These representations or objects become conveyors of imagination and expression for both. For the analysands, there is the purity that these objects hold, having no previously known specific and no personal story attached; they are ripe for symbolic interpretation. The objects and pictures are blurred of their original meaning. They hold great potential for provocation, but at the same time might be seen as emptied and mute—a void waiting to be filled:

> When we look at objects or buildings which seem to be at peace within themselves, our perception becomes calm and dulled. The objects we perceive have no message for us, they are simply there. Our perceptive faculties grow quiet, unprejudiced

and unacquisitive. They reach beyond signs and symbols, they are open, empty. It is as if we could see something on which we cannot focus our consciousness. Here, in this perceptual vacuum, a memory may surface, a memory, which seems to issue from the depths of time. Now, our observation of the object embraces a presentiment of the world in all its wholeness, because there is nothing that cannot be understood. There is power in the ordinary things of everyday life, Edward Hopper's paintings seem to say. We only have to look at them long enough to see it [Zumthor, 1998, p. 17].

Photographs or paintings in the room depict flat, two-dimensional or elevational imagery, or three-dimensional perspectival images. Three-dimensional images in any medium suggest depth or movement in space; these perspectives open up space, allowing the patient to transpose through visual and imaginary connection. Two-dimensional imagery suggests surfaces, patterns, and colors with their attending perceptual and associative powers.

Art is especially potent, as the hand that crafted it is present; the artist comes into the room with the analyst and analysand. The primitiveness of the object stirs earthy, tactile feelings, reminding us of something familiar—of *sensing* the past, the previous, the old, and perhaps the universal. The machine-made, the technologically refined, suggests a distancing from the hand and the body for some. What touches the body, the fabric of the couch, the pillow, blanket—is it soft or rough, was it constructed by hand? By machine? Is it perceived as durable or fragile? What does it tell us about the person who chose them, the personal qualities of the analyst? As Holl (1994) writes,

> The haptic realm of architecture is defined by the sense of touch. When the materiality of the details forming an architectural space become evident, the haptic realm is opened up. Sensory experience is intensified; psychological dimensions are engaged. Today the industrial and commercial forces at work on the "products" for architecture tend toward the synthetic; wooden casement windows are delivered with weatherproof plastic vinyl coverings, metals are "anodized" or coated with a synthetic outer finish, tiles are glazed with colored synthetic coatings, stone is simulated as wood grain. The sense of touch is dulled or cancelled with these commercial industrial methods, as is the texture and essence of material and detail displaced. The total perception of architectural spaces depends as much on the material and detail of the haptic realm as the taste of a meal depends on the flavors of authentic ingredients. As one can imagine being condemned to eating only artificially flavored foods—so in architecture the specter of artificially constituted surroundings imposes itself [p. 91].

We can say the creative effort between patient and analyst is like that of other creative collaborations. Architect Peter Zumthor (1999), when referring to his work in conjunction with his clients, says "I try to enhance what seems to be valuable, to correct what is disturbing, and to create anew what we feel is missing" (p. 24). This might be an aspiration for architects, psychoanalysts, or other creators. While the psychoanalytic process is a continual act of creating and re-creating, the room is the container, the locale, and the three-dimensional, physical canvases onto which and into which the work unfolds. Like a canvas, the room establishes the context and limits of words—like paint is contained within the bounds of the edges of the frame. Zumthor (1999) again writes that

> a good building must be capable of absorbing the traces of human life and thus taking on a specific richness. Naturally in this context I think of the patina of age on materials, of innumerable small scratches on surfaces, of varnish that has grown dull and brittle and of edges polished by use. But when I close my eyes and try to forget both these physical traces and my own first associations, what remains is a different impression, a deeper feeling—a consciousness of time passing and an awareness of the human lives that have been acted out in these places and rooms and charged with a special aura. At these moments, architecture's aesthetic and practical values, stylistic and historical significance are of secondary importance. What matters now is only a feeling of deep melancholy. Architecture is exposed to life. If its body is sensitive enough, it can assume a quality that bears witness to the reality of past life [p. 24].

The smallest of details—whether it is a part *of* the architecture, of the room, or a piece of an object or work of art *in* the room—can be a gate opening to the entire world. The smallest of observations, magnified, is like a fresh examination, enabling one to see what was not seen before.

Spatial Sequence and Transition, Thresholds and Boundaries

It is not possible to speak of the room proper without considering the space adjacent to it, outside of it, and, particularly, preceding it. The sequence of arrival contains multiple thresholds, subtle and powerful elements in establishing territory and the dialectic between inside and out (Malner and Vodvarka, 2004, pp. 231–230). The building lobby, foyer, stairs, elevator, antechamber, and waiting room are examples of sequential spaces traversed prior to "arriving." As one enters the building's precinct and proceeds towards the analytic room, layers of space are penetrated slowly, at a walking pace, preparing *for* the inner sanctum, while insulating the analysand and the analyst *from* the outside world. Only when our physical position has changed can we look back, and forward, with a literally new perspective. Movement is required for *re*location, and this relocation stimulates internal shift and movement.

One of the most poetic and beautifully designed thresholds for arrival is the entry sequence from the park into the Kimbell Art Museum in Fort Worth, Texas, designed by Louis Kahn. The changing spatial, visual, and sensual experience is at once dynamic and subtle. Crossing the expansive, public, manicured lawn, punctuated by large oak trees—and approaching the linear, water fountain calibrated to flow at a speed to produce a particular sound quality and decibel level—replaces and exchanges the noise of the surrounding city in anticipation of the quiet of the museum to come. Through a U-shaped courtyard one passes under a grove, a low canopy of miniature yaupon holly trees. Here the scale is compressed significantly, yet not unpleasantly. You are made aware of the crunching sound of your feet as you proceed now more slowly on crushed granite, with your gaze directed downward. The grove prepares one by mitigating the intimate scale of the museum with the scale of the park and its connection to the larger, outside world. Walking a few steps up onto the platform at the museum's entrance, you are covered and exposed simultaneously. As the door is pushed open, your body weight meets the weight of the door. The sequence of spatial and tactile experiences prepares the visitor for a closer, more inwardly oriented experience of viewing and engaging the art inside—in contrast to the urban world situated outside the museum's transcribed boundaries.

Kahn carefully scripted the spatial and sensual qualities of the sequence of entering the museum; he understood the connection between architectural configuration, sequence, and time and the corresponding psychological impact. It is the *way* the building prepares the museumgoer that is so assuring. Repeated trips to the museum, at different times of the year and of the day, reveal the changing seasons, weather, clouds, and sun, etc. Thus, this readying to enter is always the same, yet delicately different. The building responds to its time and place yet it gently beckons. As Pallasmaa (1994) writes,

> There is an inherent suggestion of action in images in architecture, the moment of active encounter or a promise of uses and purpose. A bodily reaction is an inseparable aspect of the experience of architecture as a consequence of this implied action. A real architectural experience is not simply a series of retinal images; a building is encountered—it is approached, confronted, encountered, related to one's body, moved about, utilized as a condition for other things, etc.
>
> A building is not an end to itself; it frames, articulates, restructures, gives

significance, relates, separates and unites, facilitates and prohibits. Consequently, elements of an architectural experience seem to have a verb form rather than being nouns. Authentic architectural experiences consist then of approaching, or confronting a building rather than a façade; of the act of entering and not simply the frame of the door, of looking in or out a window, rather than the window itself. The authenticity of the architectural experience is grounded in the tectonic language of building and the comprehensibility of the act of construction to the senses. We behold, we touch, listen, and measure the world with our entire bodily existence and the experiential world is organized and articulated around the center of the body. Our domicile is the refuge of our body, memory and identity. *We are in constant dialogue and interaction with the environment, to the degree that it is impossible to detach the image of Self from its spatial and situational existence. "I am the space, where I am," as the poet Noel Arnaud established* [p. 35].

The building allows the participant to engage the most fundamental of human experiences—the physical, sensual world—and to see and know ourselves in relation to it. Similarly, entering and exiting are part of the analytic experience. Whether deliberate or not, readying occurs when shifting from the external to internal world and back again.

Boundaries are made physical in space but they are done so in many different ways. Some are literally visible, some are invisible, and some are implied. There is often much spatial ambiguity when identifying boundaries; they might be as simple as a ray of light, a scent, specific spatial form, a material change, a piece of furniture, or the distance between furniture—like the distance of a chair or a couch to a wall. Boundaries are often only implied, but nonetheless fiercely felt, both physically and emotionally.

The role of architectural connective space is to join inside and outside, to mediate oneness and separateness, and to fuse polar nodes. A threshold, then, is that moment or space of crossing. This crossing from outside to inside is usually a compilation of many moments moving from one realm to another. When entering the analytic space, many longer or deeper thresholds have been crossed, some subtle, some overt. After making these transitions, the analysand is greeted by the analyst and then followed into the consulting room. The entire sequence—starting at the outside door, entering alone or with others, waiting for the therapist and entering his or her office—is one continuous movement, one fluid experience with accentuated sensual events along the way. The different sensations within any spatial sequence evoke a variety of associations, each corresponding to recognition of previous similar experiences.

Upon arrival, the office itself becomes a vital transitional space, in-between inside and out, old and new, the previous and the soon-to-be. Experiencing the office as a destination of spatial ambiguity or spatial certainty, for the patient, is a formidable opportunity. The same is true for the traversal of space—walking past and through the room to get to the analyst's chair and couch. The significance of the *shared* space—even if only occupied as two bodies moving through, following, or crossing one another—leaves a spontaneous *trace*; the shared space has been provisionally demarcated. The real and imagined boundaries of the room remind us—and demonstrate in space—of both the real and imagined boundaries of the relationship. Noting the physical boundaries as part of the verbal exchange is an opportunity to examine the intimate personal boundaries of the work.

The quality of the unique relationship between the analyst, the analysand, and the space where the analysis occurs is shaped not only by the cognitive context but also by the immediate and pervasive physical context. The analytic room should have the capacity to evoke different kinds of associations and be able to accommodate richly variegated desires of the occupants. The effect of the architecture on the analytic relationship, and hence the analysis, in direct and indirect awareness, is profound:

> All experience implies the acts of recollecting, remembering and comparing. An embodied memory has an essential role as the basis of remembering a space or a place. Our home or domicile is integrated with our self-identity; they become part of our own body and being. In memorable experiences of architecture, space, matter and time fuse into one single dimension, into the basic substance of being, that penetrates the consciousness. We identify ourselves with this space, this place, this moment and these dimensions, as they become ingredients of our very existence [Pallasmaa, 1994, p. 37].

The process of architectural design requires a synthesis of inward drives and outward pressures, one that is like the struggle to resolve the power of creation and the power of resistance. This architectural process is similar to the synthesis that takes place between analysand and analyst. In the design of a building, and in the creation of an analysis, a larger reality that cannot be grasped prior to its arrival is present; this new reality—for analyst, analysand, or architect—is itself a creative act. Places, with all of their sensuousness, are obviously recalled within the context of memory and imagination; place of some kind is always involved in memory, as a backdrop or context, having a more active or passive role. The analytic room is the immediate place of action. It is a silent backdrop, sometimes mute, sometimes assertive, but always present. The room speaks and participates through materials, detail, form, light, air, space, and through silence. The room, regardless of its specific spatial configuration and detail through its architecture or objects, whether more symbolically mute or active, wants to possess an atmosphere where the sense of time can shift, and memory with it. What is real and what is symbolic are always intertwined and the "real" of the room is bound to find its way in the symbolic through memory and asssociation. In the end, the analytic space is both witness *to*—and powerful participant *in*—the psychoanalytic relationship.

References

Bachelard, G. (1964), *The Poetics of Space*. Boston: Beacon Press.

Frank, Karen A. & Lepori, R. Bianca (2000), *Architecture Inside Out*. London: Wiley-Academy.

Freud, S. (1913), On beginning the treatment. *Standard Edition*, 12:121–144. London: Hogarth Press, 1958.

Gamwell, L. & Wells, R. (1989), *Sigmund Freud and Art: His Personal Collection of Antiquities*. Binghamton: State University of New York / London: Freud Museum.

Holl, S. (1994), Questions of perception—Phenomenology of architecture. In: S. Holl, J. Pallasmaa & A. Perez-Gomez, *Questions of Perception, Phenomenology of Architecture*. Tokyo: A+U Publishing, pp. 39–120.

Malner, J. & Vodvarke, F. (2004), *Sensory Design*. Minneapolis: University of Minnesota Press.

Moraitis, G. (1995), The couch as a protective shield for the analyst. *Psychoanalytic Inquiry*, 15:275–279.

Pallasmaa, J. (1994), An architecture of the seven senses. In: S. Holl, J. Pallasmaa & A. Perez-Gomez, *Questions of Perception, Phenomenology of Architecture*. Tokyo: A+U Publishing, pp. 27–38.

Rasmussen, S. (1962), *Experiencing Architecture*. Cambridge, MA: MIT Press.

Tanizaki, J. (1977), *In Praise of Shadows*. New Haven, CT: Leete's Island Books.

Winnicott, D. (1975), *Through Paediatrics to Psycho-Analysis*. New York: Basic Books.

Zumthor, Peter (1999) *Thinking Architecture*. Basel: Birkhauser.

Adrian Stokes
The Architecture of Phantasy and the Phantasy of Architecture

PEGGY DEAMER

It is characteristic of Quattro Cento buildings to afford a heightened awareness of approximations and of distinctness, and therefore of contrasts in which an approximatory element lingers to stimulate the unifying power of fantasy. The reflections in the mirror do not only contrast with the face of the stone in terms of their mobility and light and shade. I would say that they belong to the architectural impression since they evince further the already existing parable of the stone. Such strong art collects surrounding phenomena within its own terms: the visual dogma becomes entirely satisfying. When objects of the senses compel in the percipient the profoundest emotions of the contemplative state, the soul is at peace. We then have the sense that what we are looking at has rolled up the long succession of the mind in spatial, instantaneous form: and that the relationship between the objects seen, exemplify a perfect harmony of inner and outer things.
—Adrian Stokes, 1945b, p. 111

Stokes, Klein, and Freud

Adrian Stokes was an English art and architecture critic, 1902 to 1972, whose most popular works, *The Quattro Cento* (1932), *Stones of Rimini* (1934), and *Colour and Form* (1937), were written between 1930 and 1937. During this exact time, he was in analysis with Melanie Klein, although the writings of this period do not make distinct reference to her or to Stokes's analysis with her. After World War II, with books such as *Inside Out* (1947), *Smooth and Rough* (1951), and *The Invitation in*

Art (1965), his writings become more overtly psychoanalytical and less accessible to the lay public and his fellow critics.

It is perhaps important to qualify the description of Stokes as a "critic." He was not writing criticism in the sense of examining and commenting upon contemporary works of art. Rather, he was interested in a more general, ahistorical, moral/didactic/reparative view of the aesthetic object, much in the tradition of John Ruskin. Where Ruskin's moralism regarding the work of art and architecture came from religion, Stokes's came from psychoanalysis. But both looked to a building's form and material to tell a story of its makers' ethico-psychic position as well as the potential lessons to be learned by the viewer/inhabitant.

For those investigating the relationship between architecture and psychoanalysis, Stokes is interesting not just as a "translator" of Kleinian principles in architectural terms, but the manner in which he mines her concepts of phantasy and symbolization to establish a framework to evaluate, indeed proselytize, the virtues of architectural form. This endeavor is singular for architecture, a discipline that has never—beyond generic, vernacular discussions of shelter, hearth, attics, and "home"—had psychoanalysis investigate issues of design and authorial intent (of architecture, that is, and not just building). It is relatively singular in psychoanalysis as well, since, for the most part, psychoanalysis's aesthetic engagement has always stayed on the level of content—such as Hamlet's true mental state; Michelangelo's psychic motives; an odalisque's angst—but not on form. Precisely because architecture is largely a nonrepresentational art, it has repelled a sustained engagement with psychoanalysis.

This is not to say that the writings of Stokes offer comprehensive or correct programs for formal architectural analysis. Rather, they provide evidence of someone who is struggling with and working out his own neuroses on the written page as much as pursuing an objective, stable psychoanalytic analysis of architecture; he exposes his own weird misreading of Klein (and perhaps hers of Freud) as he struggles to establish why architecture matters so much to his own sanity. Nevertheless, the manner in which he enacts his Kleinian "translation" both expands a theory of phantasy and produces a highly evocative form of architectural analysis.

Melanie Klein's work can be described as a reworking of Freud's three phases of the id, replacing this paradigm with her structure of two positions, the paranoid-schizoid and the depressive. In the first, the child cannot take in whole objects extended in time and space but only the part objects of immediate sensory experience. These objects are either satisfying (as in the good breast that provides the milk) or frustrating (as in the bad breast that is denied). This position is characterized by the ego splitting into its good and bad parts or by confusion with the object in projective identification. The second position assumes a child who can recognize whole objects, especially the mother, as complete and enduring, as possessor of both the good and the bad breast. This is depressing to the child not only because it learns about the nonpurity of what it considered to be "good," but because it apprehends its own destructive desires in attacking the mother or the breast. This is the onslaught of guilt, but also of a healthy, realistic approach to the exterior world, in which the ego is integrated and exposed to the conflict of the contradictory impulses.

Klein also suggests that the superego is in evidence much earlier than Freud had assumed. She said that while children can't relate to whole objects like the father or the mother before the phallic stage and the Oedipus complex, they could nevertheless relate to "part objects"—in particular the mother's breast—well before this. Klein came to believe that it isn't merely the internalized father figure that peoples the inner life of the superego, but an entire world of part objects, both paternal and maternal—breasts, nipples, tongues, penises, and such. (Indeed, the displacement of the father figure as the central, internalized figure of the superego as well as replacement of the phallus as the dominant object of envy or feared lack, made her a figure of feminist appreciation.)

These part objects are powerful, threatening internal figures. Both they and the mechanisms of defense required to control them are violent. For Freud the main mechanism of defense is repression, but for Klein, drawing on Abraham and Ferenczi, there are four principal mechanisms of defense. The first two are projection and introjection, both of which have their origin in the pure pleasure principle. The ego wants to introject into itself everything that is good and project everything that is bad. (Projection, wherein the ego disowns its own impulses and attributes them to the exterior world, is characteristic of paranoia; introjection is based on the earliest oral impulse to eat the object.) The third mechanism is identification, which in one direction takes the object as its model, defending itself against the object's loss, and in the other direction takes the subject as model, resulting in narcissism. The fourth is the splitting of the ego, which involves the bifurcation of the ego into the normal part, which attends to reality, and the other libidinal part that detaches itself from reality and plays its phantasy out. Splitting is associated with fetishism.

Phantasy is the principal means by which these mechanisms of defense (and the drives that require them) operate; it represents the sexual instincts in terms of the appropriate object (the biting mouth, the warm breast, etc.). Symbolism is the principal means by which these phantasies attach themselves to reality, the everyday objects of the world that surround us. Phantasy was a peripheral concept in Freud's cosmology but underlay many of his assumptions regarding the ego's ability to synthesize the pleasure principle and the reality principle. He writes, "With the introduction of the reality principle one species of thought-activity was split-off; it was kept free from reality-testing and remained subordinated to the pleasure principle alone. This activity is phantasying" (Freud, 1911, p. 220). He continues, "It will rightly be objected that an organization which was a slave to the pleasure principle and neglected the reality of the external world could not maintain itself alive for the shortest time, so that it could not have come into existence at all. The employment of a fiction like this, however, is justified when one considers that the infant . . . does almost realize a psychical system of this kind" (p. 220). In Freud's view, instinct can only be perceived by its mental representation, and unconscious phantasy is this mental expression. Freud's position vis-à-vis introjection, in which he describes how the ego absorbs into itself sources of pleasure—"I should like to take this into myself and keep that out" (Freud, 1925, p. 237)—is, the Kleinians believed, a description of unconscious phantasy. It explains the link between the id impulse and the ego mechanism.

For Klein, phantasy-forming as a function of the ego assumes a greater role than it did for Freud. Phantasy is not an escape from reality, but, rather, the particular way that the child "sees" and interprets reality and copes with being in the world. Introjection and projection become the principal way that she describes the child's "object relations," at first introjecting all that it loves and preserves and projecting out all that it loathes, but later also introjecting things that it fears (to contain them) and projecting part-objects that it loves (to protect them from its own destructive forces). Klein describes, thereby, a whole inner world of part-objects that take up position in the child's psyche and are taken to be, and are seen to match up with, the outer world. It is an inner world that is robust, active, changeable, aggressive, and deeply spatial in structure.

Klein's ego epistemology is not only dense, it is highly visual; image and the pictorial presentation of phantasy are foregrounded as the child's means of thinking. In this, she follows a certain lead of Freud's. Despite accusations that he was "anti-visual,"[1] he indicates, in *The Interpretation of Dreams* (as well as in his reconstruction of the first wish of the child as a mental image) that thinking is done in images. Freud (1900), regarding even secondary process thinking, said that "thought is after all nothing but the substitute for a hallucinatory wish" (p. 237). Likewise, he pointed out that the ego was the perceptual organ in both the

---

[1] I am indebted to Nancy Olson for elaborating on the debate about Freud's sensitivity to visual imagery in a paper, "Pictures Into Words: Visual Models and Data in Psychoanalysis," given at the "Architecture and Psychoanalysis" symposium at Yale School of Architecture in October 2003.

direction of the inner world and the outer world. But Klein goes farther than Freud. In analyzing how the ego functions perceptually to direct the figures populating the id/superego inner world and their application onto and absorption of the external world, Klein, unlike Freud, depicts an ego that is almost entirely described by its image management. Her conceptual shift from Freud's "stages" of development to her "positions" is significant not only because it is a spatial as opposed to a temporal paradigm, but because it assumes a place taken up vis-à-vis the world, or, I might say, its visual unfolding. She also goes farther in depicting a particularly rich visual content. The floating, swarming bodily-parts that are the objects of the child's lust are thick, aggressive, swarming, and assertive. Vision in this case is the opposite of transparent; it is bulky and layered. Moreover, because the child has no real sense of itself as an integrated ego, the vagaries of these phantasies don't just project from the child, they *are* the child. Thus, both what the child perceives of the outer world and experiences of itself in the inner world are fully fleshed, in/on the layer of sight.

Stokes and Psycho-Aesthetics

The appeal of Klein's topology for someone like Stokes—interested in space, image, and architecture—is obvious. But he, in turn, enacted a further distortion on Kleinian/Freudian theory, taking it and its reference to childhood defense mechanisms into a more general, hermeneutic realm. Stokes, first of all, was as interested in the outside world available for phantasy consumption as much as in the inner world that demanded substitution. He also had a psychic history of trying to get out of himself (fear of his own homosexuality) and seeing himself mirrored/objectified in and on the external world. He describes his personal awakening when he arrived in Italy for the fist time through the Mont Cenis tunnel and saw the world for the first time clearly, as distinctly itself and other than him, and thereby the proper manifold for self-discovery and projection. This tendency is evident in Stokes's article of 1945, "Concerning Art and Metapsychology," in which he argues that Freud's pleasure principle should be expanded to include greater emphasis on the role the external world plays in our fantasies. As he stated, "It is perhaps astonishing that no general concept derived from the omnipresence of the external world as such, other than the reality principle, figures in psychoanalytic metapsychology" (p. 178). As he describes in *Venice: An Aspect of Art* (1945b), being in the world was nothing other than working out the subject–object dichotomy:

The new-born baby soon becomes aware that neither his mother nor the surrounding world is an extension of himself. Henceforth, to his dying day, there remains the huge division between himself and objects, people or things. Throughout life, we seek to rival the externality of things. The world as we perceive it, our animal habitat, is the language of every passing mood or contemplative state. Indeed, without this canvas on which to apply ourselves, by which we project and transmute as well as satisfy more direct biological needs, we cannot conceive the flow of the mind any more than the activity of the body. The body is obviously meaningless without a further external world: but so, too, is the mind. Mental as well as physical life is a laying out of strength within, in rivalry, as it were, with the laid-out instantaneous world of space [p. 137].

If one goes back to Freud, we see that he thought phantasy played a role in the making of art, but as an avoidance, as opposed to an enhancement, of reality. As he describes in his "Formulations on Two Principles of Mental Functioning,"

An artist is originally a man who turns away from reality because he cannot come to terms with the demand for the renunciation of instinctual satisfaction which it at first demands, and who allows his erotic and ambiguous wishes full play in the life of phantasy. He finds the way back to reality, however, from this world of phantasy by making use of special gifts to mould his phantasies into truths of a new kind [Freud, 1911, p. 224].

Stokes's view of art, as must be obvious by now, was radically different, in direct proportion to the reformulation he, via Klein, made of phantasy. Instead of seeing reality as that which is denied in art, he suggested, again in his "Concerning Art and Metapsychology," that, "As a mirror of man's overall physical situation, art . . . contains a further and even more general connection with reality," one which "allows sufficient weight to the perennial challenge of the wide, open world of the senses," in which "physical substitution [is] viewed as the means of the wider organization" (Stokes, 1945a, p. 179). His faith in substitution and the pattern of exchange that results in this enactment—his faith in art's form and not merely the artist's psyche, his faith in art as an ideal and not as an escape—is spelled out clearly in this long but evocative passage called "Notes for a book beginning August 1943: Argument" from his personal notebooks:

The mind, I believe, is constantly busy with the correlation of its patterns, and had I to name the content of the indubitable yeast for life which, although it varies, so seldom is altogether lost, I should say that, in terms of animal satisfaction, of accomplishment of idealism or whatever, this ever-growing store and ever-enlarging complication of patterns were the essence. For the greater part of the day for most lives—though not the night—the range is severely restricted. . . .

A transition now to consider the nature of art as the impulse to create patterns, is easy. Indeed, there is no need to point out the analogy. Art typifies the mental flow in which much is expressed within a simple datum of the senses [Stokes, 1943, pp. 40–41].

It is then precisely this structuralist model of the mind that points to Stokes's particular fascination with architecture: it mirrors the structure of the mind at the same time that it calls us to phantasy/substitution. In "Three Essays on the Painting of Our Time" (1961), he writes, "We will agree that the work of art is a construction. Inasmuch as man both physically and psychologically is a structure carefully amassed, a coalescence and a pattern, a balance imposed upon opposite drives, building is likely to be not only the most common but the most general symbol of our living and breathing" (p. 149). At times, this analogy takes on an anthropomorphic cast, but the deeper analysis investigates architecture's unique capacity to demonstrate—not through its shape or iconography, but rather through its material, textures and apertures—its own dialectic nature of inside-out transference:

We partake of an inexhaustible feeding mother (a fine building announces), though we have bitten, torn, dirtied and pinched her, though we thought we have lost her utterly, to have destroyed her utterly in fantasy and act. We are grateful to stone buildings for their stubborn material, hacked and hewed but put together carefully, restored in better shape than those pieces that the infant imagined he had chewed or scattered, for which he searched. Much crude rock stands rearranged; now in the form of apertures, of suffusion at the sides of the apertures, the bites, the tears, the pinches are miraculously identified with the recipient passages of the body, with the sense organs, with features; as well with the good mother which we would eat more mercifully for preservation and safety within, and for our own. . . . Colours, textures, smooth and rough planes, apertures, symbolize reciprocity, a thriving in a thorough partnership. The landscape's center is fashioned by plain houses in a cobbled street, by the dichotomy of wall-face and opening. Dichotomy is the unavoidable means of architectural effect. It has, of course, many embodiments, a sense of growth and a sense of thrust, for instance, heaviness and lightness, sheerness and recession or projection, rectangularity and rotundity, lit surface and shadowed surfaces, a thematic contrast between two principal textures, that is to say, between smooth and rough. I take this last to symbolize all, because it best marks the "bite" of architectural pleasure upon the memory: the dichotomy that permeates our final impression [Stokes, 1951, p. 241–242].

A whole cosmology of sense apparati and formal paradigms support and prefigure this position. His archetype in all of the arts was work whose spatial essence was presented flatly and immediately for the eye, whether it be the stone of a sculpture or a building façade, or the pigment and color of a painting. His hope for objects was that they would demonstrate and make us experience their otherness; only in its otherness would we both lose ourselves and, ironically, find ourselves. And vision was the sense par excellence for negotiating and providing this otherness. Only the eye allowed an immediate—a whole, unsplit, unsequential—grasp of the object, and only in this grasping of and onto the object could the subject find the mirror, the essence of his or her inner world, his or her psyche. He also appreciated vision as a physical phenomenon. The body, he noted, was literally present in the physical housing of the eye in the torso. All of the ocular muscles, mucous, and nerve-endings were experienced in the act of seeing and prevented sight from merely "floating" around ambivalently. But ironically—or again, dialectically—vision, as he liked to point out, is the one sense whose effects are not experienced as belonging to our bodies.

Likewise, the supposed flatness of vision was pivotal. Using but transforming the British empirical tradition of Berkley and Locke, in which vision's assumed two-dimensionality made it inferior to and dependent on touch, Stokes, like Ruskin, valorized the flatness as both an aspect of its immediacy and an essential condition for its ability to symbolize. Moreover, vision comes to us instantaneously. As such, it is not mediated by our internal intellect, but comes to us purely. "I would isolate and stress this far more pregnant quality of mass, its appeal to the quickness of the eye, its power to captivate in the one second or less. Exploring the sense of touch, I admit, introduces a succession, and therefore entails an element of time though it be turned into an impression by the quickness of the eye" (Stokes, 1932, pp. 134–135). At the same time, however, the full gamut of physical sensations was lodged in the eye. Despite Stokes's insistence that the visual was superior to the tactile, the body was nevertheless wholly present in vision; vision absorbed the other senses into itself. This is his fascination with textures. As he writes in *Smooth and Rough*, "In employing smooth and rough as generic terms of architectural dichotomy, I am better able to preserve both the oral and the tactile notions that underlie the visual" (1951, p. 243).

Certain formal preferences result from Stokes's notion of vision and objective identification and contribute to an aesthetics of surface. Paintings should never be about their composition or their perspectival depiction of deep space; rather, they should register their layering. That is, the important relationships aren't those that operate across the lateral surface of the painting, but those that imply a layered relationship from front (the eye of the viewer) to back (an implicit space in, on, or behind the canvas). Color should be "surface" color, not "film" color, where the former is understood to be "out there," located on the object and not, like film color, experienced as floating aspatially in our mind's eye. In sculpture, "carving" was seen as being superior to "modeling"; in the process of carving, the material fights back, in layers and depth, and challenges the ego, while modelling allows the ego to just willfully mush things around. To a certain extent, this was a very literal understanding of carving in stone, and not just any stone, but limestone, the material that Stokes felt, in its water-based make-up, embodied symbolization or "identity-in-difference." Thus his love of the sculptor Agostino di Duccio, whose bas-reliefs ensured that not the figure, but the stone through the medium of the figure, is the content of the work. But in another sense, carving was a more general admiration of the tough, durable "otherness" of an object, whether of words, landscapes, or buildings; an otherness that allowed perception to be registered not in the body or psyche, but again on the object itself.

As has been suggested, Stokes, with this set of aesthetic and psychoanalytic "rules," arrived at architecture as the most robust of arts because it promotes the most complex and compelling of phantasies. But there is a certain irony in this fact, given that flatness and immediacy are essential attributes for phantasy, and architecture is primarily spatial and experienced sequentially. Indeed, Stokes dismissed modernism's interest in both space and plasticity. Space, a concept that had only been identified as a formal category in architectural history at the end of the nineteenth century and was the calling card of modernism, was not just ignored by Stokes, but seen, like film color, to be that mushy, indeterminate thing in which the psyche could get lost and warped. Likewise, plasticity, the pliability of form and shape, best exemplified by the works of Le Corbusier such as the chapel at Ronchamp, was seen by Stokes as problematic. It, like modeling in sculpture, allowed the artist to avoid the concreteness of the material world and apply his or her will arbitrarily on it with no resistance, with no lessons learned from the physical world. (This is what made Stokes such an ambiguous figure in architectural history and criticism at the time: he was seen as deeply conservative with regard to architecture, even as his psychoanalytic framework made him scarily radical.) For Stokes, in architecture as well as sculpture, the textures are paramount and the juxtaposition of rough and smooth, especially around the apertures of a façade, are of major significance. Again, the registration of the exchange of inside and outside was of paramount importance because it was the analogue of our own psychic exchanges of introjection and projection; and as analogue, it objectified subjectivity at the same time that it allowed us to experience it visually and sensually. (Later he seemingly saw that this good/bad polarity was itself "unhealthy"—that is, split—and advocated that a psychoanalytically successful work of art would allow one to experience both sides of the equation; but he didn't give up on an aesthetic that praises the all-over clear figure–ground distinctions and the hierarchically composed.)

As Stokes (1951) wrote:

The building, which provokes by its beauty a positive response, resuscitates an early hunger or greed in the disposition of morsels that are smooth with morsels that are rough, or of wall spaces with the apertures; an impression, I have said, composed as well from other architectural sensations. To repeat: it is as if those apertures had been torn in that body by our revengeful teeth so that we experience as a beautiful form, and indeed as indispensable shelter also, the outcome of sadistic attacks, fierce yet smoothed, healed into a source of health which we would take inside us and preserve there unharmed for the source of our goodness: as if also . . . the smooth body of the wall-face, or the smooth vacancy within the apertures, were the shining breast, while the mouldings, the projections, the rustications, the tiles, were the head, the feeding nipple of that breast [p. 243].

Pre-Conclusion by Way of Example

Regardless of what one thinks about the aesthetic formula that Stokes's psychoanalytic framework gives him, the reader of his texts can't help but feel that his phantasies-cum-descriptions of architecture bear witness to someone who indeed finds not just pleasure but psychic sustenance from architecture. Just as Heinrich Wolffin's five principles of art/architecture style allow us to see much more in the buildings he analyzes than we might otherwise perceive, Stokes's own reveries—their own form of psychoanalytic transference—open up a world of unexpected associations for the reader. So here are examples from his *Venice: An Aspect of Art*, in which he is analyzing photographs of Venice—all that he has available as he writes from Carbis Bay, England, where he was a market gardener during the war. The fact that he is looking at photographs isn't incidental. They preview and aid the flattening of the architectural object that his analysis desires anyway; the flattening makes the buildings abstract and symbolic; they are already analogues. In this abstraction, the normal hierarchy of meaning that would make the building itself more important than, say, the laundry or birds that are caught incidentally in the frame, is eliminated. This book is made up of a series of photographs, identified by the name of the building, and Stokes's short descriptions of the photos' content. The simplicity of the travelogue approach belies the extravagance of phantasy. Here he describes "A Venetian House of the Seventeenth Century":

> Once again, the white squares of the thick stone surrounding the barred lower window, in a manner of clear and white arrest, epitomizes transaction within. The washing above hangs white and listless: but the liston below of the Isterian stone takes an added density as the sum of apparel. We see approximation and differences as in a family. The monolith Isterian jambs to the door give added density to the layer upon layer of thin transverse bricks and even to the worn horizontal planks of canal door. Yet brick and wood seem to partake of the stone from their intercourse. These static things appear teeming things arrested and ordered for the eye. In terms of distinctness, we have the sense of things fused [Stokes, 1945b, pp. 104–105].

Regarding Palladio's church, Il Redentore:

> At sunset the water reflects the sky. That which the water reflected all day it now clasps and incorporates. Fusion is complete: the sky itself now rocks beneath the grandeur of yet whiter stone. This same rock, one feels, sets the more distant churches swaying and swimming, sets their evening bells to roll. The brown prayers of the Redentore are loosed at evening in the unmoored sound: and the church slips in upon the sky-and-water, the white embannered Christ aloft upon the dome [Stokes, 1945b, pp. 92–93].

And finally, regarding the Manzoni-Angaran palace:

> It is low tide, as you see from the dark bottom stones of the palace and for the height of the water stair. The marble walls encrusted with disks and divided by the long narrow blackness of the windows, are reflected on the horizontal plane of the water. The tide flows over these reflected divisions slightly blurring them. Since to such Quattro Cento building we attribute a compulsive solidifying of what is successive, our imagination reverses the roles of object and reflection. The palace, then, shows us in marble, spatial form, full of the daylight, the brightness and darkness of the water. As we ride across such water its image stands indestructible upwards to the side, a lightness honeycombed with regular dark eddies, sometimes deep, sometimes no deeper that the oblong panel with a pilaster. The straight

threads of water are immobilized or made simultaneous by the light and dark lines of the fluted pilasters on the upper storeys. . . . Movement and depth of water are converted into stone. There is light and dark: all is precious, all weighty; nothing obtrudes. This architecture solidifies the continuity of water [Stokes, 1945b, p. 102].

Conclusion

What is of interest, in the context of this paper, is not only that these phantasies seem so indicative of the part-object world described by Melanie Klein, but that they also suggest a theory of surface that illuminates both phantasy's contribution to architectural appreciation and architecture's contribution to a theory of phantasy. The surface of perception, understood to be the almost physical surface of the eyeball, and the surface of the architectural object, equated with the surface of the photograph, get collapsed on a single conceptual plane, one that is thinned for its instantaneous visual consumption. But this thinness sustains enormous tension as it is challenged by the thickness of the imagined part-objects that are bodily, three-dimensional, and highly active. Here, architecture is illuminated by a condition that seems antithetical to it; it is appreciated not for the space it encloses and the subsequent sequential experience offered our bodies as we move thorugh space, but for the immediate images of space made available on the façade/image plane itself. It suggests that the space that is most (or at least equally) important is our psychical inner space which architecture of the façade and of surface texture both mimics and ignites. Likewise, phantasy is illuminated by the architectural structure it is given; that is, phantasy as a phenomenon is highly structured, not simply by the architectural content it gazes upon, but by the conceptual structure of flatness, layering, juxtaposition, identity-in-difference—all the things that make the image a specifically-formed symbol and not just transparent to the external world. While Stokes demonstrates this primarily when the content of the image is architectural, he wants to suggest that this conceptual structure is the condition for all images of the external world to connect with our inner world. It is this exploration of the architectural structure of phantasy, as well as the phantasical nature of architecture, that makes Stokes's writing so unique in psychoanalysis.

References

Freud, S. (1900), The interpretation of dreams. *Standard Edition*, 4 & 5. London: Hogarth Press, 1953.

——— (1911), Formulations on two principles of mental functioning. *Standard Edition*, 12:215–226. London: Hogarth Press, 1958.

——— (1925), Negation. *Standard Edition*, 19:235–239. London: Hogarth Press, 1961.

Olson, Nancy. (2003), Pictures into words: Visual models and data in psychoanalysis. Presented at Yale University School of Architecture, October, New Haven, Connecticut.

Stokes, A. (1932), The Quattro Cento. In: *The Critical Writings of Adrian Stokes*, 1:29–180. London: Thames & Hudson, 1978.

——— (1934), Stones of Rimini. In: *The Critical Writings of Adrian Stokes*, 1:181–302. London: Thames & Hudson, 1978.

——— (1937), Colour and form. In: *The Critical Writings of Adrian Stokes*, 2:7–84. London: Thames & Hudson, 1978.

——— (1943), Notes for a book beginning August 1943: Argument. *PN Review 15*, 7(1):40–41.

——— (1945a), Concerning art and metapsychology. *Internat. J. Psycho-Anal.*, 26:177–179.

——— (1945b), Venice: An aspect of art. In: *The Critical Writings of Adrian Stokes*, 2:85–138. London: Thames & Hudson, 1978.

——— (1947), Inside out. In: *The Critical Writings of Adrian Stokes*, 2:139–182. London: Thames & Hudson, 1978.

——— (1951), Smooth and rough. In: *The Critical Writings of Adrian Stokes*, 2:213–256. London: Thames & Hudson, 1978.

——— (1961), Three essays on the painting of our time. In: *The Critical Writings of Adrian Stokes*, 3:143–184. London: Thames & Hudson, 1978.

——— (1965), The invitation in art. In: *The Critical Writings of Adrian Stokes*, 3:261–300. London: Thames & Hudson, 1978.

Adrian Stokes and the "Aesthetic Position"
Envelopment and Otherness

STEPHEN KITE

In Adrian Stokes's (1902–1972) post World War II writings, the viewpoint of art and architecture that had previously foregrounded "carving" and the artistic achievements of the depressive Kleinian position, transmutes to a more complex analysis whereby greater credence is given to the "modelling" process and the role that fusion plays in the creation and appreciation of the art object, *together with* object-otherness. Stokes now defines an "aesthetic position" in which the "incantatory" aspects of art act in concert, and in simultaneity with, his long-held assertion of "otherness." This essay examines how Stokes arrives at this more inter-related spatiality within the context of contemporary attempts to define a Kleinian aesthetic and investigates how these psychoanalytical concepts are actually experienced and played out in the situatedness of architectonic reality (see also Kite, 2002 and 2003).

Positioning Aesthetics—Klein, Stokes, Segal, Milner

Adrian Stokes—aesthete, critic, painter and poet—is linked to John Ruskin and Walter Pater as one of the greatest writers in the English aesthetic tradition. The vision of art his writing conveys is humanistic and intensely corporeal and his influence was a notable factor in the formation of English Modernism in the 1930s—affecting artists of the stature of Ben Nicholson and Barbara Hepworth. Of especial import here is the seven-year analysis he began with Melanie Klein in 1930: her ideas, and the language of psychoanalysis, become increasingly evident in his post-World War II writings which, in their totality, represent a significant project to understand the nature of art and the creative dynamics of the psyche.

Contemplating a painting by Adrian Stokes, we are driven to conclude that it actually draws us into intermediary spaces far more equivocal than the "otherness" often espoused in his writings.

In his paper *Form in Art*, Stokes (1955) reiterates this lapidary standpoint: "The work of art, then, because it is expressively self-subsistent, should invoke in us some such idea as one of 'entity.' It is as if the various emotions had been rounded like a stone" (p. 406). Yet, in the same essay—together with his long-held assertion of the pebble-like apartness of the artwork—he begins to entertain the role that fusion plays in the making and appreciation of art, *together with* object-otherness. Here he is taking into account two things: his own aesthetic researches into artists of a more *modelling* disposition—predominantly Michelangelo—and shifts within the aesthetic discourse of Freudian psychoanalysis that gave increasing credence to the creative role of the paranoid-schizoid position. *Form in Art* appeared in an important collection of papers—*New Directions in Psychoanalysis* (1955), edited by Melanie Klein, Paula Heimann, and R. E. Money-Kyrle—that reflects debates about art within the object-relations school of psychoanalysis concerning the relative roles in creativity of the paranoid-schizoid and the depressive positions. In the same year, Stokes published *Michelangelo: A Study in the Nature of Art*. In the introduction to this work he provides new ways of thinking about the relations between *carving* and *modelling*; the latter is now associated to Freud's adopted phrase, the "oceanic feeling," which refers to the sense of oneness with the universe associated with the "feeding infant's contentment at the breast." In this new configuration, carving is not privileged over modelling but participates in a "doubling of roles." "Roles" can oscillate within the work, or from period to period: the Early Renaissance is distinguished by its Quattro Cento "love for the self-sufficient object," while the Baroque—of which Michelangelo is the herald—is characterized by homogenizing tensions and plasticity. As Richard Wollheim (1972) points out, what up to the writing of works like *Michelangelo* "had been comparatively neglected [namely, the modelling tendency], at times indeed despised, is systematically reconstructed, and then in its reconstructed form is brought into association with the earlier of the two positions" (p. 27).

This paper follows Stokes into the intermediary and multivalent spaces that he charts between the "carving" and "modelling" modes, and attempts to define the architectonic implications of this richer reading of spatiality.[1] In *Form in Art*,

---

[1] This is Stokes's so-called "Tavistock" period, when, under the imprint of a new publisher—Tavistock—in a densely argued series of works (*Michelangelo*, 1955; *Greek Culture and the Ego*, 1958; *Three Essays on the Painting of Our Time*, 1961; *Painting and the Inner World*, 1963; *The Invitation in Art*, 1965; and *Reflections on the Nude*, 1967), he wrestles with the question of form

Stokes attempts to articulate the contested spaces that lie between two significant papers in the same collection, *New Directions in Psychoanalysis*: Hanna Segal's "A Psychoanalytical Approach to Aesthetics" and Marion Milner's "The Role of Illusion in Symbol Formation." As Glover (2000) points out, Segal "was the first to fully elaborate a Kleinian aesthetic" and "it was largely through the work of Segal and Stokes that Kleinian aesthetics became fully established as a coherent approach to the visual arts." Segal's (1955) aesthetics are firmly Kleinian in the significance they accord to the depressive position: "The task of the artist", she declares, "lies in the creation of a world of his own." Taking Proust as a supreme example of an artist who sacrificed a life to the reconstruction of the past, she avers that "all creation is really a re-creation of a once loved and once whole, but now lost and ruined object, a ruined internal world and self" (p. 390). Klein, herself, has little to say on aesthetics. However, in an early paper from 1929, "Infantile Anxiety-Situations Reflected in a Work of Art and in the Creative Impulse" (see Klein, 1929), she takes two case studies in which "for the first time Klein connects creativity with deep early anxieties, and . . . regards the urge to create [as] arising from the impulse to restore and repair the injured object after a destructive attack" (Glover, 2000, p. 17). Milner's 1955 paper, on the other hand, departs from Klein's reparative stance, in asserting a positive creative role to regression to the earlier positions of the infantile unconscious. She takes Berenson's definition of "the aesthetic moment" from his *Aesthetics and History* (1950)—that "fleeting instant . . . when the spectator is at one with the work of art"—to support her assertion of the creative role of "oneness" in making and understanding art. Milner argues that creativity demands "an ability to tolerate a temporary loss of sense of self, a temporary giving up of the discriminating ego which stands apart and tries to see things objectively and rationally" (Milner, 1955, p. 97).

Stokes's difficulty in negotiating between these standpoints—between his loyalty to Klein and his predisposition to the notion of reparation—is evident in *Form in Art*, and his growing recognition that *fusion* was an indispensable ingredient of art. These were not peripheral matters in post-war English psychoanalysis. Glover (2000) reminds us that Klein regarded regression to states of fusion as a "manic defence," yet nonetheless allowed Milner's paper to be included in this collection that celebrated her seventieth birthday. But Winnicott's important paper

---

in art, in relation to the outcomes of psychoanalytical research. Some studies that engage with this territory are: Stonebridge (1998), *The Destructive Element: British Psychoanalysis and Modernism*; Pinkney (1984), *Women in the Poetry of T. S. Eliot: A Psychoanalytic Approach*; and Glover (2000), *Psychoanalytic Aesthetics: The British School*. Newton's (2001) *Painting, Psychoanalysis, and Spirituality*, a study of the object-relations school, stresses the role of the unconscious in creativity with particular reference to the theories of Anton Ehrenzweig.

on *Transitional Objects and Transitional Phenomena* (1951) was rejected, and Winnicott was forced to leave the editorial meeting remarking that "Mrs. Klein no longer considers me a Kleinian" (Glover, ch. 6, p. 13).

At a certain moment in *Form in Art*, Stokes's argument appears to reach an impasse. He confesses to a "muddle," to "have reached entire genetic confusion" (Stokes, 1955, p. 414): there is full object-otherness, certainly; there is the role of fusion and "oceanic" feeling; but the Kleinian insistence that the full "grip of psychic reality" must also disavow the "manic denial" of regression to the undifferentiated states of infanthood. He identifies the crux of the problem as follows:

> How can it be that the homogeneity associated with idealisation (the inexhaustible breast), is harnessed by the work of art to an acute sense of otherness and actuality? (Thus, space is a homogeneous "state" into which we are drawn and freely plunged by the representations of visual art; concurrently it figures there as the mode of order and distinctiveness for "pre-existent" objects.) It is my conviction not only that these are contrary elements fused in art but that there is a just proportion, founded upon a once simple link between them, which make their harmony poignant and health-giving [Stokes, 1955, pp. 414–415].

I hope to show here that these concepts—sometimes difficult to grasp in psychoanalytical terminology, or in the aesthetic interpretation of the graphic arts or sculpture—are matters of common experience in architectural space and form. Out of this impasse—into the standoff between the creative function that might be ascribed to the paranoid-schizoid or depressive positions—Stokes (1955) inserts a new position, "the aesthetic position." This aesthetic position, he maintains, "deserves a category of its own," a position that exists in reciprocity between the two fundamental Kleinian positions, encompassing "homogeneity or fusion combined, in differing proportions, with the sense of object-otherness" (p. 407). Ironically, we might also suspect a manic element in too fierce a masculine grip on the "psychic reality" of the depressive position. Pinkney (1984) certainly detects in Stokes an over-masculinized stress on objectivization that he traces back to modernism's roots—to Hulme, and to Eliot and Pound's rejection of what was regarded as the merging, effeminate and decadent tendencies lurking in late Romanticism and Symbolism (see also Stonebridge, 1998, p. 115). But now, in positing the "aesthetic position" and an increasing role to "oceanic feeling," Stokes came to place a greater emphasis on the so-called "feminine" aspects of creativity. Thus, in a paper originally published in 1956, "Psycho-Analytic Reflections on the Development of Ball Games, Particularly Cricket," he wrote: "Modern team games can serve as a substitute for [art], being in some ways a parallel re-creation, though composed largely of a crude genital sublimation that ignores the sustained feminine receptivity whose collaboration is needed for aesthetic experience" (Stokes, 1973, p. 40). Equally, in this context Storr (1976) deplores the stubborn resistance of Freudian psychoanalysis to allow a greater creative role to the unconscious—and its inability to discern the artist's positive creative engagement with these earlier states from the more negative eruptions of repressed and chaotic material. But Storr credits the part that Marion Milner, Anton Ehrenzweig, and D. W. Winnicott have played in opening up this territory to investigation. With the post–World War II series of books published by Tavistock, Stokes must be numbered among this important group of thinkers. Many commentators have spotted the parallels between Stokes's "aesthetic position" and Winnicott's notion of "potential space," "the hypothetical area that exists . . . between the baby and the object (mother or part of mother) during the phase of the repudiation of the object as not-me, that is, at the end of being merged in with the object" (cited in Pinkney, 1984, p. 14). Winnicott (1957) argues that it is in this space that the first objects are created out of the child's imagination, including the "transitional object"—such as the "special woollen square, or the mother's handkerchief." These found objects represent "the beginning of the infant's creation of the world." Moreover, "we have to admit that in the case of every infant the world has to be created anew. The world as it presents itself is of no meaning to the newly-developing human being unless it is created as well as discovered" (p. 133).

"In-here," "Out-there," and "In-between"

"Homogeneity," "otherness," and the "aesthetic position" can be subtle notions to grasp in the scrutiny of painting and sculpture: but in situated encounters with architecture and landscape, the spectrums of "envelopment" and "exposure" are readily recognized as familiar experiences. As a friend and enthusiastic reader of Stokes, Colin St. John Wilson (architect of The British Library, London) early realized the import of what Stokes was trying to articulate to the practice of architecture. In a significant essay, "The Natural Imagination: An Essay on the Experience of Architecture" (published in *The Architectural Review* of January 1989), he later sought to explicate these theories to a wide architectural audience (see also Menin and Kite, 2005). Wilson states that envelopment (equated to Klein's paranoid-schizoid position) finds its architectural analogue in "the architectural experience of interior space that is modelled in rhythmic forms of flowing and merging continuity" (1989, p. 66). Scharoun's Philharmonic Hall (1956–1963) for the Berlin Philharmonic epitomizes these womb-like spaces; the concert audience is gathered onto interlocking terraces within the great, enfolding, tent-like roof of the hall. In the contrary position of exposure (equated to Klein's depressive position), the detached awareness of object-otherness is demonstrated by the architectural experience "of open space and the external confrontation with a building's wholeness and self-sufficiency, the carved and massive frontality of its stance over-against you" (p. 66). Wilson illustrates this "position" with the frontality of Le Corbusier's Villa Stein at Garches of 1927. Wilson then points out the originality of Stokes's insight that it is "uniquely the role of the masterpiece to make possible the *simultaneous* experience of these two polar modes [described by Melanie Klein]; enjoyment at the same time of intense sensations of being inside and outside, of envelopment and detachment, of oneness and separateness" (p. 66). Stokes alone, he argues, "perceives the secret to lie in [the] *fusion* [of these two polar modes] and upon this rests the originality and significance of his vision" (p. 66).

Masterpieces, such as those modernist works cited by Wilson, or more everyday architectures, can be "womb substitutes in whose passages we move with freedom" or "hardly less obviously the exterior comes to symbolise the post-natal world, the mother's divorced original aspects or parts smoothed into the momentous whole" as Stokes writes in his *Smooth and Rough* (1951, p. 241). But, importantly, his later texts multiply instances of those architectural elements that intermarry the two experiences: "The great work of art," he writes, "is surrounded by silence. It remains palpably 'out there,' yet none the less enwraps us; we do not so much absorb as become ourselves absorbed" (1961, p. 158). As early as "Pisanello," his first mature essay written in 1928, Stokes lists the kinds of architectural elements that allow this simultaneity of experience:

> Externalisation is the mode of existence . . . freedom is when all can be taken in and all given out created, so living progresses neither within nor without . . . outdoors approximating to indoors while houses make answering assurance . . . exterior staircases, flat roofs from which one steps to the higher terrace, loggias suspended balconies with the neutral shade beneath pergola . . . doubly restful [Stokes, 1995, p. 163].

In his article Wilson takes the head of Schinkel's staircase in the Altes Museum, Berlin (1822–1830) as a masterly demonstration of the fusion of elation and calm evoked by these mediating spaces. The feeling is almost one of suspension in the grove of Ionic columns of the great portico of the museum as the museumgoer gazes through and beyond them to the open spaces of the Lustgarten.

Foraging and Nesting

Stokes arrived at these insights regarding the fusion of oneness and distinctness through deep reflection on the nature of art and spatial experience, and through the discourse of psychoanalysis. Interesting confirmation of his theories can be found in later research into the psychology of landscape and environmental behavior, especially the notion of *prospect and refuge* advanced by the English geographer Jay Appleton in his *The Experience of Landscape* of 1975.[2] Appleton arrived at his theory of prospect and refuge from a different direction than that of Stokes—from the angle of evolutionary behaviorism—yet his conclusions are strikingly similar. Although Appleton (1996) is clearly aware of the sexually charged interpretations of landscape that both precede and postdate Freud—notions that the relationship of humanity to the habitat is that of "the child to the 'Earth-Mother'"; that the morphology of gorges suggests vaginas; that "ivy-mantled towers" suggest the phallus; and so on—he insists that however valid such considerations may be, they should not deter us "from enquiring into the implications of the hypothetical assumption that a universal characteristic of primitive man, transmitted innately to his modern descendants, is the desire to see without being seen" (p. 76). Human beings, like most creatures, have two key requirements of the habitat: a *foraging-ground* to provide food and other requirements, and a *nesting-place*, related to the foraging ground, in which to shelter and raise the young. In these twin concepts, he contends, will be found "the basis of that interaction between a creature and its habitat on which the survival of the species ultimately depends" (Appleton, 1993, p. 74). There is only one short paper in which Appleton extends prospect-refuge theory into the territory of architectural spaces—his "Landscape and Architecture" paper of 1993. Here the conclusions he draws strikingly parallel those of Stokes: "Among environmental scientists," he writes, "there is an increasing recognition

---

[2] See Appleton (1996), *The Experience of Landscape* (rev. ed). For Appleton's own reflections on the theory and its later commentators and critics, see Appleton (1984), "Prospects and Refuges Re-Visited." Appleton only extended his theory into architectural space in one short paper: "Landscape and Architecture" (1993). One of the most coherent and successful attempts to apply prospect and refuge theory to architecture is Hildebrand's 1991 study of Frank Lloyd Wright's houses, *The Wright Space: Pattern and Meaning in Frank Lloyd Wright's Houses*, where Hildebrand makes, via Wilson (1989), an intriguing comparison to Stokes. The Kaplans have extended and developed Appleton's ideas from an evolutionary perspective. See Kaplan (1987), *Aesthetics, Affect, and Cognition: Environmental Preference from an Evolutionary Perspective*, and Kaplan and Kaplan (1989), *The Experience of Nature: A Psychological Perspective*. For overviews of the competing theories and literature, see Bourassa (1991), *The Aesthetics of Landscape* and Aoki (1999), "Review Article: Trends in the Study of the Psychological Evaluation of Landscape." I am grateful to Ian Thompson for conversations in the area of landscape theory.

FIGURE 1. Palace of Urbino; *torricini* enframing loggias and landscape. Photograph © by Stephen Kite.

that we are attached to both of these contrasting elements [foraging-ground and nesting-place] by deep bonds of association involving attraction, anxiety, repulsion and other feelings" (Appleton, 1993, p. 74). "To everyone," he continues, "the terms 'indoors' and 'outdoors' suggest a pair of complementary concepts whose importance can be easily understood in everyday environmental experience. . . . [The] many problems of architectural aesthetics hinge on the interaction between these two conditions" (p. 74). Like Stokes in "Pisanello," he lists those architectural elements that offer a "potential place of refuge from the 'great outdoors,'" namely "arcades, porticoes, verandas, balconies, overhanging eaves, exterior staircases, and recesses of all kinds." Elements that "render the separation of indoors and outdoors to some degree less absolute" (p. 74).

Others who have studied the cognition of space from the angle of environmental aesthetics, such as the Kaplans (1987, 1989), conclude that the ultimate spatial preference is for neither the agoraphobic extremes of exposure out in the foraging-ground of the savannah landscape, nor for immersion in the primary refuge of the dark forest depths. Rather, "these opposing vectors will tend to place the individual right at the forest edge"; a place that offers both safety and the possibilities of exploration and encounter. Moreover, ecologists tell us that it is these edge biomes that are the richest in terms of life-forms and biodiversity.

Urbino: Hanging Garden, *Studiolo*, and Loggia

In conclusion to the argument of this paper around the outworkings of this intermediary "aesthetic position," it seems appropriate to return to Stokes's confessed aesthetic starting point—the Palace of Urbino in the Marche region of Italy—and to address the positions of envelopment and exposure as evidenced in its architecture.

In the mid-fifteenth century, Federico da Montefeltro began construction of a palace on land acquired between an earlier family palace at the top of the southern hill of Urbino and a *castellare* 150 meters to the north, on the edge of the Valbona precipice. (See Benevolo, 1978 and Rotondi, 1969.) The spatial ambition and complexity of the palace increased dramatically as work progressed; the long early Renaissance wing facing the town was superseded by the new organism, organized around Luciano Laurana's *cortile* which encompassed a complete reversal of the city and palace's orientation. Instead of looking eastwards towards Rimini, the palace was planned to confront the traveller approaching Urbino from Rome, Tuscany, and Umbria over the pass of Bocca Trabaria. The heart of the new complex, Federigo's apartments and loggias, framed by its slender towers, the *torricini*, is pivoted out over the precipice of the gorge to directly confront this viewpoint (figure 1).

This reordering reflects the new Renaissance sense of homology between the city as entity and the countryside. In the nearly contemporary work ordered by Pius II at Pienza, between 1458 and 1464, Smith (1992) notes this new simultaneity— how the "experience of being in the urban fabric is defined and clarified by the viewer's simultaneous perception of its opposite the countryside" (p. 125). The Palace of Urbino itself mediates between the dense, enveloping streets of the earlier medieval condition, and these new prospect realizations; for Benevolo (1978), it now reads as "a long diaphragm between town and countryside, between the limited spaces of streets and squares, and the boundless space of the landscape" (p. 167). The "aesthetic position"—"the simultaneous perception of opposites"—that the palace organizes at the city–countryside level, is, as I shall describe, reflected

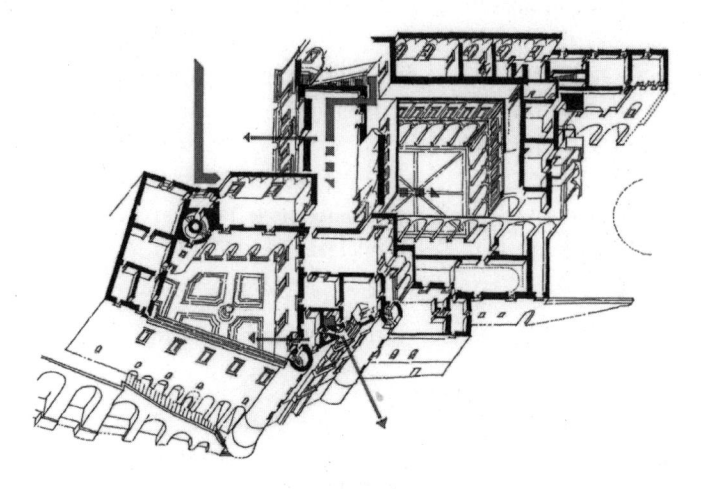

FIGURE 2. Axonometric of Ducal Palace showing route via courtyard and staircase to the Throne Room on the *piano nobile*, and the complex of the Ducal *studiolo* and chapel. After P. Rotondi, 1969, fig. 54.

in the experience of moving through the palace complex; a sequence of subtle displacements, mediated enclosures, and prospect opportunities that concludes, for Duke Federigo himself, in his personal suite of studiolo, chapel, and loggia (figure 2).

This suite is a simulacrum of the city–region organization instituted by the palace as a whole that allows, in a few strides, progression from the complete womb-like envelopment of the *studiolo* to the exhilarating release of the loggia.

The entry sequence to the palace is initiated on the southeastern city side by the Piazza Duca Federico; this is an urban space defined by the palace façade shaped on an L-plan that links the first phase of the long Palazzetto della Iole wing— aligned with the principal route spining the southern hill of the city—to the earlier *castellare*. But within the enfolding "L," the palace façade remains aristocratically aloof, a sufficient symbol of the postnatal world, of "parts smoothed into [a] momentous whole" (Stokes, 1951, p. 241). Di Giorgio devised a strong base-story of flat, rusticated stonework, to pull together the inchoate elements of the façade (left incomplete), superimposed in response to the differing rhythms of the *piano nobile*, by aedicular stone surrounds planted on the rough brickwork of the body of the building—a body pocked with scaffolding holes and scarred with traces of the building's history. This mauled, yet ultimately noble façade, shows the Italians'

FIGURE 3. Main portal leading to courtyard. From Rotondi, 1969, plate 80.

ability to live at ease with the *non finito* aspects of even their most monumental buildings. The reassurance such a survivor offers to depressive anxieties recalls Stokes's gratitude in *Smooth and Rough* to the "inexhaustible feeding mother a fine building announces." "We are grateful," he writes, "to stone buildings, for their stubborn material, hacked and hewed but put together carefully, restored in better shape than those pieces that the infant imagined he had chewed or scattered, for which he searched" (Stokes, 1951, p. 241). Hanna Segal, who, as discussed above, was among the first to develop a Kleinian aesthetic, was insistent that art must accommodate both beauty and ugliness. In his *Painting, Psychoanalysis, and Spirituality*, Stephen Newton (2001) notes Segal's contention that art must exhibit "a balance between the tragic ugliness of aggression, loss, mourning, and death, and their resolution and the ultimate redemption in beauty" (p. 10). In painting, he argues, art can do this by making evident all aspects of the creative dynamic. In the *facture* of the artwork's surface—in its scratches, scrubbings, erasures, and impasto—we read the material evidence whereby this balance has been achieved. The experience of process, "ugliness" and "resolution," in a façade like that at Urbino, can be similarly nourishing.

Among the many difficulties the palace façade had to address was the fact that the entrance axis of Laurana's *cortile d'onore* forced the principal entrance of the palace towards the internal angle of the "L." Anticipated by the semi-enclosure of the piazza, this portal—almost at the crotch of the palace's wings—begins the entry sequence into the palace proper (see figure 3).

Through the length of a shadowed, segmentally vaulted entrance atrium we gain the first sight of Laurana's luminous *cortile*. Beyond, the vista is projected into the garden spaces of the Cortile del Pasquino. Here are Appleton's (1984) primordial prospect-refuge conditions: a sheltering, subdued, edge-of-forest light, from which—through the "arched perspective" of a screen of columns (evoking the forest edge)—we glimpse a bright, more open prospect beyond. In *Three Essays on the Painting of Our Time* (1961), Stokes likens the language of architecture— its "oracle of spatial relationships" and its slow construction—to the "carefully amassed" physical and psychological structure of the person in resonant images of the body-language of architecture and of passage. As this discussion embodies so many of the themes under scrutiny here, it deserves citation at length:

> We will agree that the work of art is a construction. Inasmuch as man both physically and psychologically is a structure carefully amassed, a coalescence and a pattern, a balance imposed upon opposite drives, building is likely to be not only the most common but the most general symbol of our living and breathing: the house, besides, is the home and symbol of the Mother: it is our upright bodies built cell by cell: a ledge is the foot, the knee and the brow. While we project our own being on to all things, the works of man, particularly houses or any of the shelters he inhabits, reflect ourselves more directly than will organic material that has not been cultivated thus. . . . The ordered stone and brick encloses and defines: whether we will it or not, the eye explores these surfaces as if compelled to consult an oracle, the oracle of spatial relationships and of the texture that they serve. Hurt, hindered, and inspired by wall and ledge, the graphic artist has bestowed upon flat surfaces an expressiveness of space, volume and texture equivalent to the impact, at the very least, of phantasies, events, moods. Architecture has provided the original terms of this "language" that can rarely be put into words, though words may sometimes be found for the simple employment of the "language" by

FIGURE 4 (top). Main courtyard of the palace. Photograph © by Stephen Kite.
FIGURE 5 (bottom). Detail of pierced wall to the hanging garden. Photograph © by Laboratorio Fotografico Soprintendenza per I Beni Ambientali e Architettonici Delle Marche.

building when taken in conjunction with the natural scene. For instance, in the fascination of gazing along a dark passage into the outside light that invades an entrance, in a subject not uncommon for seventeenth-century Dutch painters, we may become aware that we contemplate under an image of dark, calm enclosure and of seeping light, the traumatic struggles that accompany our entry and our exit in birth and death [Stokes, 1961, pp. 149–50].

Thus the atrium passage leads to the court designed by Luciano Laurana, under the ethos of Piero della Francesca; this *cortile* is considered by Stokes the epitome of this "oracle of spatial relationships" (see figure 4).

Moving to the left, the Piero della Francesca-like perspective of the *cortile* arcade draws us towards the foot of the Grand Staircase. If we accept Stokes's analysis of this arcade, as we move towards the stair we will experience something rarely achieved in architecture: a "non-temporal synthesis where arches roll in succession," due to the perfect equation Laurana calibrated between the corporeal presence of the columns and arches, and the almost tangible quality of the spaces and intervals between them. To enter the body of the palace—the suite of apartments on the *piano nobile*—requires the negotiation of another barrel vaulted passage: the palely lit Grand Staircase, which tunnels up to the first floor. The Grand Staircase engenders feelings of compression, so that on arrival at the upper loggias overlooking the courtyard, and the almost immediate turn into the major reception space of the Throne Room (lit by three great windows allowing prospect over the Piazza Duca Federico, where the entry sequence began), we feel to the maximum the release and scale of the palace's principal reception room. The sense of release is intensified by the luminous ceilings, which seem to billow above the space like spring clouds. Rotondi (1969) speaks of Urbino's "elegant and slender vaults which seem to hold and contain in their cavity the weightless volume of air" (p. 63). Thereafter, progression becomes a more privileged spatial diminuendo as movement continues into the increasingly intimate reception rooms of the Duke (to the west) and the Duchess (to the north), arranged around the shared refuge of the secret garden, which is hidden to the outside world and the semipublic parts of the palace.

This hanging garden (*giardino pensile*) is a highly poetic example of the subtleties with which envelopment-prospect conditions are configured throughout the palace complex. The garden parterres and fountain occupy the trapezium-shaped space formed between the angled wing of the old *castellare* and the ducal block with the *torricini* frontispiece.

Within the shelter of these wings, the garden could simply have been designed to command an unbroken panorama over the landscape to the west, similar to the

FIGURE 6. *Virgin and Child*, Lorenzo di Credi, *c.* 1458–1537. Oil and egg tempera on wood, 71.1 × 49.5 cms. Photograph © by National Gallery, London.

elevated panoramas found in many hill towns, such as the Piazza della Signoria in Gubbio, where the Dukes of Montefeltro also built a Palazzo Ducale modelled on that of Urbino. Instead, Francesco di Giorgio defined a far more nuanced relationship of "hereness" and "thereness"; he reinforced the sanctum-like enclosure of the garden with a wall that, at the same time, allows framed views of the hillside beyond, through five beautiful Quattrocento apertures (see figure 5).

These openings rhyme with those of the palace wings, confirming the character of the parterre as an outdoor room. As Fiore (1993) points out, similar openings onto the landscape figure in the paintings of the period; in those of Francesco di Giorgio himself, in Vecchietta, Mantegna, and so on. In *The Experience of Landscape*, Appleton (1996) discusses how paintings of this period hold prospect and refuge in balance, avoiding either prospect and refuge dominance, through the "device of a marginal vista flanking a central refuge." Among the examples he chooses to illustrate this is Lorenzo di Credi's Virgin and Child in London's National Gallery (see figure 6).

The sense of refuge induced by the Virgin cradling and breast-feeding the infant Jesus, is balanced by the arched openings on either side of the mother's head that

FIGURE 7. *Studiolo.* Detail of east side. From Rotondi, 1969, plate 207.

disclose miniature landscapes of hills, trees, and water. In this connection, Appleton, uses the stagecraft term "coulisse" to describe the refuge device of framing wings that intensify the sense of recession of a prospect, while, on a behavioral level, allowing opportunities of concealment. This condition is evident in the person who peeps through a window, down into the street, masked by the shelter and security of the flanking walls. (Stokes, also a balletomane, was well aware of such devices.) Returning this account of the *giardino pensile* to the object-relations theory of psychoanalysis, we have noted Stokes's increasing recognition of the role that part-object relationships play in the creation and appreciation of art. In the final chapter ("Landscape, Art, and Ritual") of *The Invitation in Art* (1965), he asks: "Why does aesthetic contemplation demand closeness as well as detachment of the viewer?" (p. 290). The answer he gives is that in contemplating a work of art, we read aspects of our inner states "in the sense of varied attachment to objects both internal and external." In the language of Kleinian "object relations," the psyche is involved in a constant process of projection and introjection of "objects"—these may be real figures and objects, or feelings and emotions that can be psychically internalized, or projected outwards, particularly in the case of feelings that are denied, or linked to frustration or anxiety. From this it "follows that there is also an introjection which the work of art in fact solicits and facilitates by enveloping us with the delineation of overriding processes at work. And so we are immersed, a part of ourselves is immersed, in communion, though it be far short of a hypnosis, since our separateness, and many kinds of judgement, are evoked at the same time" (p. 290). Note Stokes's continued insistence that the immersion should be "far short of a hypnosis." Extreme part-object identification is still to be associated with "narcissistic or schizoid illnesses" that "tend to confuse, to split open, both subject and object." Nonetheless, in these later essays, Stokes is now prepared to concede that "paranoid-schizoid mechanisms, even of the most disruptive kind, can find embodiment in art as long as the overall ceremony of integration, and indeed that of reparation, have been instituted at the same time" (p. 291).

Turning again to the architectonic symbolism of the landscape Madonnas of Bellini and other Renaissance painters, he is struck by Donald Meltzer's observation that in the backgrounds described above, we discover "the child's exploration of the mother's inside; between mother and child . . . a later external relationship is reconstructed by the foreground figures." He continues, "In many works of visual art . . . we clamour to enter in the pursuit of a part-object relationship, while at the same time we are standing back in full acceptance of self-sufficient figures or—to take the case particularly of some landscape—in an acceptance of the work considered for its entirety" (p. 294). Part at least, of the moving power of this garden, and of other similar spaces throughout the palace, is the ability to enjoy, in the situatedness of the physical world, what the Lorenzo di Credi *Virgin and Child* offers: a complete sense of protective enclosure, with a concurrent apprehension of the ideal landscapes, that the openings of the screen wall fetch for us from the outer world.

Returning from the *giardino pensile* to our spatial progression within the palace, the first reception room of the Duke's suite, after the great Throne Room, is the Sala degli Angeli, considered by Stokes "the finest of Quattro Cento rooms" (Stokes, 1932, p. 164). Here, in Domenico Rosselli's carving, Stokes finds an "unusual love of stone" evident in the *putti* that dance in stillness along the frieze of the fireplace.

The sense of time suspended becomes yet more intense as movement continues through the audience room, to enter, via a small vestibular space, the absolute enclosure of the Duke's *studiolo*, a chamber less than four meters square. The sense of absolute seclusion from the outside world is reinforced by the dark golden tones of intarsia work that completely enclose the chamber to a height of some two meters (see figure 7). When closed, the doors to the vestibules on either side disappear into the intarsia composition that catches an instant in the Duke's life, as Rotondi (1969) describes:

The artist . . . depicted [the intarsia] as if the Duke, having opened them and taken out his favourite books after laying down his cuirass and arms, casually left the various tomes here and there. Musical instruments were placed in readiness and musical scores with martial songs opened, as if he had been called away, leaving his presence felt [pp. 81–82].

Nearness might border on claustrophobia in this panelled cave, without the fictive release prospects of the landscape panoramas realized in the wood, or without the relationship the *studiolo's* intense enclosure holds to the complex it forms with the adjoining chapel and prospect loggia. These exquisite spaces were skillfully projected by Laurana in the triangular zone created between the general westerly orientation of the Ducal wing and the inflection of the *torricini* wing to confront the pass from Rome, described above.

There is a Piero della Francescan ethos that underpins the spatial achievements at Urbino. Stokes understands Piero della Francesca's architectural settings, his halls and loggias, as unaffected enlargements of ordinary Italian streets and urban spaces. The progression from the Urbino landscape, through the bright loggia into the dimly lit study, is to be understood as a spatial reciprocity. As in Piero's backgrounds, we witness "open doors and windows revealing a greater and more simple darkness. Outside, the sun, inside a generous darkness beyond the edges of neutral-toned apertures" (Stokes, 1949, p. 197). In the few steps from the absolute enclosure of the *studiolo*, through the nodal vestibule, to the prospect-dominant loggia, the play of simultaneity explored in this essay between the opposed "positions" of closeness and detachment, attains an especial intensity (see figure 8).

It is undoubtedly this loggia—and the linking of the *studiolo* "sanctum" to the "thunderous day" of the Marche landscape—that Stokes has in mind when he writes in *Smooth and Rough*:

A loggia of fine proportion may enchant us, particularly when built aloft, when light strikes up from the floor to reveal over every inch the recesses of coffered ceiling or of vault. The quality of sanctum, of privacy, joins the thunderous day. A loggia eases the bitterness of birth: it secures the interior to the exterior: affirms that in adopting a wider existence, we activate the pristine peace [1951, p. 240].

The in-betweenness of the "aesthetic position" that Stokes thus defines with such psychological insight is one of the legacies of modernity. Accordingly, for example, the twentieth-century Dutch architect, Aldo van Eyck (1918–1999), in

FIGURE 8. Loggias of the Ducal Palace, Urbino. Photograph © by Stephen Kite.

designing his Hubertus House (1973–1978) refuge for mothers and their children in Amsterdam, also sought a making of "in-between places" to mitigate the "psychic strain" of its occupants. Inspired by the space–subject mutuality discovered by the Postimpressionists and Cubism, Van Eyck declared that humanity's "home-realm is the in-between realm—the realm architecture sets out to articulate" (Hertzberger et al., 1982, p. 44). In Stokes, as we have seen, there is an equally attuned sense of the reciprocity between substance *and* space; in opposition to the spatial essentialism that—in another modernist tendency—tends to collapse both space and mass in the craving for transparency. Stokes argues, rather, that "mass reveals an entirety, reveals space, just as music dramatises succession" (1932, p.

135), as in the disclosure of space-form he discerned in the Urbino *cortile* or in Piero della Francesca's art. Aldo Van Eyck, in his modernist practice, and Stokes, in his later twentieth-century writings, consequently arrived at a common belief that the mediation of these twin-phenomena of envelopment and otherness is vital to human well-being in an urban scenario of progressively tyrannous polarities.

References

Aoki, Y. (1999), Review article: Trends in the study of the psychological evaluation of landscape. *Landscape Research*, 24:85–94.

Appleton, J. (1984), Prospects and refuges re-visited. *Landscape Journal*, 3:91–103.

——— (1993), Landscape and architecture. In: *Companion to Contemporary Architectural Thought*, ed. B. Farmer & H. Louw. London: Routledge, pp. 74–77.

——— (1996), *The Experience of Landscape*. Revised edition. Chichester: Wiley. (Original work published 1975.)

Benevolo, L. (1978), *The Architecture of the Renaissance*. Vol. 1, trans. J. Landry. London: Routledge & Kegan Paul. (Original work published 1968 as *Storia dell' architettura del Rinascimento*.)

——— (1980), *The History of the City*, trans. G. Culverwell. London: Scolar Press. (Original work published 1975 as *Storia della Città*.)

Bourassa, S. C. (1991), *The Aesthetics of Landscape*. London: Belhaven Press.

Fiore, F. P. (1993), L' architettura civile di Francesco di Giorgio. In: *Francesco di Giorgio Architetto*, ed. F. P. Fiore & M. Tafuri. Milan: Electa, pp. 74–125.

Glover, N. (2000), *Psychoanalytic Aesthetics: The British School*. http://www.human-nature.com/free-associations/glover/index.html (paginated by chapter).

Hertzberger, H., Van Roijen-Wortmann, A. & Strauven, F. (1982), *Aldo Van Eyck: Hubertus House*. Amsterdam: Stichting Wonen.

Hildebrand, G. (1991), *The Wright Space: Pattern and Meaning in Frank Lloyd Wright's Houses*. Seattle: University of Washington Press.

Kaplan, R. & Kaplan, S. (1989), *The Experience of Nature: A Psychological Perspective*. Cambridge: Cambridge University Press.

Kaplan, S. (1987), Aesthetics, affect, and cognition: Environmental preference from an evolutionary perspective. *Environment and Behaviour,* 19(1):3–32.

Kite, S. (2002), Introduction to *Stones of Rimini*. In republication of A. Stokes, *The Quattro Cento and Stones of Rimini*. Pittsburgh: Pennsylvania State University Press, pp. 1–18. (Works originally published 1932, 1934.)

——— (2003), Adrian Stokes (1902–1972): British critic. In: *Key Writers on Art: The Twentieth Century*, ed. C. Murray. London: Routledge, pp. 256–262.

Klein, M. (1929), Infantile anxiety-situations reflected in a work of art and in the creative impulse. *Internat. J. Psycho-Anal.*, 10:436–434.

Menin, S. & Kite, S. (2005), *An Architecture of Invitation: Colin St. John Wilson*. London: Ashgate.

Milner, M. (1955), The role of illusion in symbol formation. In: *New Directions in Psycho-Analysis: The Significance of Infant Conflict in the Pattern of Adult Behaviour*, ed. M. Klein, P. Heimann & R. E. Money-Kyrle. London: Tavistock, pp. 82–108.

Newton, S. J. (2001), *Painting, Psychoanalysis, and Spirituality*. Cambridge: Cambridge University Press.

Pinkney, T. (1984), *Women in the Poetry of T. S. Eliot: A Psychological Approach*. London: Macmillan Press.

Rotondi, P. (1969), *The Ducal Palace of Urbino: Its Architecture and Decoration*. London: Alec Tiranti.

Segal, H. (1955). A psycho-analytical approach to aesthetics. In: *New Directions in Psycho-Analysis: The Significance of Infant Conflict in the Pattern of Adult Behaviour*, ed. M. Klein, P. Heimann & R. E. Money-Kyrle. London: Tavistock, pp. 384–405.

Smith, C. (1992), *Architecture in the Culture of Early Humanism: Ethics, Aesthetics, and Eloquence 1400–1470*. New York: Oxford University Press.

Stokes, A. (1932), The Quattro Cento. In: *The Critical Writings of Adrian Stokes*, 1:29–180. London: Thames & Hudson, 1978.

Stokes, A. (1949), Art and science. In: *The Critical Writings of Adrian Stokes*, 2:183–212. London: Thames & Hudson, 1978.

——— (1951), Smooth and rough. In: *The Critical Writings of Adrian Stokes*, 2:213–256. London: Thames & Hudson, 1978.

——— (1955), Form in art. In: *New Directions in Psycho-Analysis: The Significance of Infant Conflict in the Pattern of Adult Behaviour*, ed. M. Klein, P. Heimann & R. E. Money-Kyrle. London: Tavistock, pp. 406–420. (A shortened version of this paper is collected in Stokes [1973], *A Game That Must be Lost*.)

——— (1956), Psycho-analytic reflections on the development of ball games, particularly cricket. *Internat. J. Psycho-Anal.*, 37(2–3):185–192. (Also collected in A. Stokes [1973], *A Game that Must be Lost*.)

——— (1961), Three essays on the painting of our time. In: *The Critical Writings of Adrian Stokes*, 3:143–184. London: Thames & Hudson, 1978.

——— (1965), The invitation in art. In: *The Critical Writings of Adrian Stokes*, 3:261–300. London: Thames & Hudson, 1978.

——— (1973), *A Game that Must be Lost: Collected Papers by Adrian Stokes*, ed. E. Rhode. Cheadle Hulme: Carcanet Press.

——— (1995), Pisanello: First of four essays on the Tempio Malatestiano at Rimini, ed. R.

Read. In: *Comparative Criticism: Walter Pater and the Culture of the Fin de Siècle*, ed. E. S. Shaffer. Cambridge: Cambridge University Press, pp. 161–207.

Stonebridge, L. (1998), *The Destructive Element: British Psychoanalysis and Modernism*. Basingstoke: Macmillan.

Storr, A. (1976), *The Dynamics of Creation*. London: Penguin.

Wilson, C. St. J. (1989), The natural imagination: An essay on the experience of architecture. *The Architectural Review,* 185:64–70.

Winnicott, D. W. (1957), *The Child and the Family: First Relationships*, ed. J. Hardenberg. London: Tavistock.

Wollheim, R. (1972), *The Image in Form: Selected Writings of Adrian Stokes*. Harmondsworth: Penguin.

III
FRANK LLOYD WRIGHT

Frank Lloyd Wright
A Psychobiographical Exploration

JAMES WILLIAM ANDERSON

Once while testifying in court, Frank Lloyd Wright referred to himself as the world's greatest architect. Asked later how he could make such an excessive claim, he replied, "Well, I was under oath, wasn't I?" (Secrest, 1998, p. 376).

If declarations in court call for honesty, there is another situation that is even more likely to elicit truthfulness: when a person is alone, or thinks he is alone. One day a young apprentice named Jonathan Lipman happened to be working underneath the piano in Wright's studio at Taliesen, trying to repair the legs. Wright fussed around the room for a few minutes without noticing Lipman. The famous architect finally strolled out of the room, singing to himself, "I am the greatest" (Secrest, 1998, p. 251).

These two anecdotes capture Wright's primary conception of himself. He viewed himself as special, unparalleled, outstanding; I call this his exalted self. In looking at how this self-image developed, along with another competing view of himself, I will examine his early life.

Wright's Early Life

Wright tells us in his autobiography (1977, pp. 31–33) that, even before he was born, his mother wanted him to become an architect and hung engravings of English cathedrals in the nursery. Later, he notes, she provided Froebel building blocks with which he could play. While the specifics have been questioned (Gill, 1988, p. 44), Wright's recounting of these legends reflects his belief that his mother was invested in his achieving greatness and that his success as an architect had fulfilled her wish.

Anna Lloyd Jones's family was poor as she grew up. She had an interest in education and achievement and became a teacher, but her family could not pay for her to have formal training as they could, later on, for two of her younger sisters (Secrest, 1998, p. 47).

In her late twenties, Anna married William Carey Wright, a widower with three small children. Few people had as extreme a combination of impressive ability and meager accomplishment. A college graduate, William studied medicine but gave it up, learned to be a lawyer and was admitted to the bar, then began his main career as a minister. He was also a skilled musician who could play Bach and Beethoven beautifully and composed his own music. Both before and after his marriage to Anna, William held a succession of jobs. He always seemed to start out with a flourish, only to lose or quit his position sooner or later. Anna was increasingly frustrated as the family struggled to get by (Gill, 1988, pp. 30–39).

It seems to me that Anna was attracted by William's promise—she thought he would make a name for himself—but soon became disillusioned. She gave up on her husband and instead concentrated her hopes on her first child, Frank, who was born in 1867.

Frank Lloyd Wright is unambiguous in his autobiography about his mother's expectations for him. In his words, she saw him as a "means to realize her vision." She had "extraordinary devotion" to her son (Wright, 1977, p. 31). As he became older, one "direction" was "encouraged in skillful ways by the mother. Her son was to become an architect. He was to get beautiful buildings built" (Wright, 1977, p. 55).

In childhood Frank Lloyd Wright also had some unusual gifts: high intelligence, extraordinary spatial ability, a sense for color, and a talent for drawing. The combination of his sense of his capacities, along with his mother's view of his specialness, coalesced into what I am calling his exalted self, his view of himself as great.

But his father did not see him that way at all. Wright's impression was that his father "never made much" of him. "Perhaps the father," Wright (1977, p. 69) speculated, "never loved or wanted the son at any time." Wright had a vivid memory (Wright, 1977, p. 32) of his father playing the organ in church while he, only seven years old, pumped air into the bellows. His arms and back ached, and he was afraid of what would happen if he failed to supply the needed air. He notes that he "felt forgotten." He was unable to hold out, and his father became angry.

His father's way of viewing him was very different from his mother's. His father saw him as a nonentity, as someone who was not special. In the organ anecdote, he is his father's menial servant and, furthermore, a servant who is inadequate to the task. Many of the children in school also looked down on Frank; they saw him as a mama's boy with long golden curls. Frank was always threatened by what I call the denigrated self, by a self-image that reflected his understanding of his father's way of seeing him. One should also keep in mind that his exalted self was never secure. His mother doted on him and supported him, but the expectation was that he would achieve great things, and if he did not, he feared, she would be disappointed and would give up on him as she had given up on her husband.

Throughout his long life, Wright sought to live out of his exalted self and to sidestep the mortification that would come from experiencing his denigrated self.

In this light, we can understand his quest to become a renowned architect. He never cared to be just workmanlike, competent, and respected; he had to be extolled, admired, and adored. He, furthermore, formed the pattern of making others anxious that he would be a disastrous failure. I see a psychological meaning to this pattern. He was constantly threatened by his sense of himself as being a failure and the object of derision. Mere successes did not completely keep this inner sense at bay. He had to provoke others to consider him to be fatally inadequate—sometimes even a fraud and a fool—and then by proving them wrong he would demonstrate to himself that he was not the denigrated person he feared himself to be.

Theoretical Interlude

My analysis of Wright's personality revolves around the concept of the self, or, to be more precise, around my positing of his exalted and denigrated selves. According to *The Oxford English Dictionary*, one meaning of "self" is "an assemblage of characteristics and dispositions which may be conceived as constituting one of the various conflicting personalities within a human being," with the earliest such usage dating from 1595 (*Compact Edition of the Oxford English Dictionary*, 1971, p. 2715). In psychology, William James is the theorist who first provided a detailed analysis of the self. In his chapter on "The Consciousness of Self" in *The Principles of Psychology*, James (1890, I, 291–401) described various selves such as the empirical self, the social self, and the spiritual self. Sigmund Freud did not make consistent use of a concept of the self. His term "ego" does not refer to someone's organized personality but rather to a collection of functions and capacities that an individual uses in mediating among the demands of the id, superego, and external reality. The British object-relations theorists introduced the "self" to psychoanalysis. Although not providing a systematic analysis of the self, D. W. Winnicott (1960) put forth his influential concepts of the true self and the false self. Harry Guntrip (1969) was the first psychoanalyst to place the self at the center of his thinking. Heinz Kohut founded a school of thought within psychoanalysis called the psychology of the self. Kohut (1977) not only spoke of a "nuclear self" that is "the basis for our sense of being an independent center of initiative and perception" (p. 177) but also conceptualized certain specific selves that some individuals will have, such as the "grandiose self."

Kohut's concept of the "grandiose self" may seem to have much in common with what I am calling Wright's "exalted self," but there are two reasons why I deliberately chose not to use Kohut's term. First, Kohut posited an explicit etiology for the "grandiose self" that I consider to be possible but not certain. He believed that the "grandiose self" is grounded in a period early in life in which the child has a phase-appropriate experience of feeling outstanding and special as a result of the enthusiastic response of the "mirroring selfobject." Second, Kohut saw the "grandiose self" in adulthood as pathological, while I am attempting to describe Wright's personality but not to judge him as being sick. Rather, in my opinion, he had a personality, as do many people, that helps account for his accomplishments and that also got him into difficulties at times. It would be simplistic, not to mention dismissive, to categorize him as pathological.

Building on Kohut's psychology of the self, Arnold Goldberg (1999) was concerned with what is called the "vertical split." He argued that a person may seem to be "of two minds," such that an individual has two different personalities. For example, Goldberg (1999, pp. 68–71) discussed a patient, Roger. When acting on the basis of his "reality sector," the patient could work and derive satisfaction from his achievements: "[t]his was the Roger of propriety, dignity, and morality." There was also a "bad boy" Roger who would drink heavily and become involved with prostitutes.

I have made use of the concept of different selves, as described by Goldberg and others, but have not adopted any specific self that one of the theorists has postulated, such as Kohut's "grandiose self." In looking at the use of theory in psychobiography, I have argued (Anderson, 2003) that one misses the individuality of the subject if one tries to apply psychological concepts directly to that person's life, as in looking for someone's "grandiose self" or for "castration anxiety." What I have tried to do in this essay is to use the general category of selves and to discover the organized selves that developed in Wright from his experience of childhood, and, on the basis of which, he approached his work as an architect. I have posited that he had two selves that were not exactly the same as the selves that anyone else might have, and I have given them the names the "exalted self" and the "denigrated self" to capture the nature of these selves as they operated in Wright's life.

Wright's Early Career

After a brief period studying at the University of Wisconsin, Wright worked for some architectural firms in Chicago, most notably the successful partnership of Dankmar Adler and Louis Sullivan.

FIGURE 1. Romeo and Juliet Windmill (1896), Spring Green, Wisconsin.

In 1889, just before he became 22, he married Catherine Tobin, who was 18 years old, and they went on to have six children.

Not long after Sullivan fired him for moonlighting, Wright received a commission from a lawyer named Nathan G. Moore to design a house in the English half-timber style. As Wright later saw it, he agreed to copy this traditional, so-called Tudor style because he was worried about supporting his family. In looking back, he regretted having given in. Wright found it unfulfilling to design a building that was not out of himself, that was not special; he notes that he never made the same error again (Wright, 1977, pp. 152–153).

When the possibility of designing a windmill came up, he sought to do something different than was expected. Two of his mother's sisters, Nell and Jane, the same sisters who had received training as teachers, ran the Hillside Home School on the site of the family homestead in Wisconsin. They put in a new water system and wanted a windmill. Instead of the usual steel tower, Wright proposed an unconventional wooden tower that looks like two interlocking towers, one diamond-shaped, the other octagonal (see figure 1). He later named it the Romeo and Juliet Windmill, because of the two intertwining parts. As Wright relates the

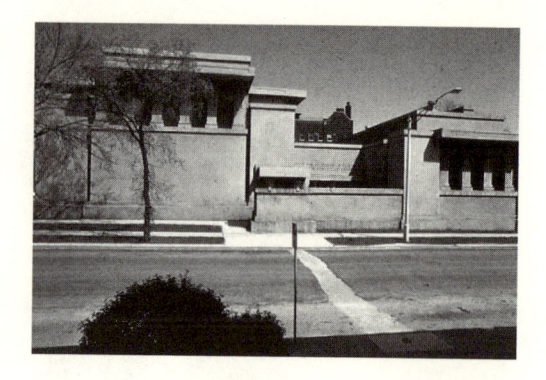

FIGURE 2 (top left, top right). Unity Temple (1904), Oak Park, Illinois.

FIGURE 3 (bottom left). Imperial Hotel (1915), Tokyo, Japan.

FIGURE 4 (bottom right). Fallingwater (1935), Ohiopyle (Bear Run), Pennsylvania.

Photographs © 2005 by Thomas A. Heinz.

FIGURE 5 (top left). Interior of S. C. Johnson Administration Building (1936), Racine, Wisconsin.

FIGURE 6 (bottom left). Westhope, Richard Lloyd Jones Residence (1929), Tulsa, Oklahoma.

FIGURE 7 (top right). Price Company Tower (1952), Bartlesville, Oklahoma.

Photographs © 2005 by Thomas A. Heinz.

story, his uncles thought his plan was foolish, and they consulted a builder who told them it was certain to fall over once heavy winds came. The aunts overruled their brothers and allowed Wright to proceed.

There were two choices: either there would be an extraordinary tower, radically different from the usual windmill, or the construction would come crashing to the ground and Wright would be shown to be ignorant. Wright recalls how, for years, the uncles would look at the windmill after there were high winds and expect to see it had fallen. Decades went by, and the uncles and aunts slowly died off or moved away. Finally, the youngest of the uncles, Enos, was the only one left. "Aged and alone now," Wright (1977) observed, "[he] never failed true to the habit of that long vigil, to come to the door after a storm and shading his eyes with his hand peer over at the tower to see the damage it had suffered at last" (p. 161). Now more than a century has passed, and the tower still stands.

Let us consider, too, the emotional impact of the tower. A plain, steel tower would be strictly utilitarian; one almost wants to pretend, as with a telephone pole, that it is not there. Wright says that his aunts were pleased with his design because they "thought it becoming to the dignity of the beloved school" (Wright, 1977, p. 157). The aunts had a school that they thought was outstanding, and they wanted a tower that would express their vision of the school. Wright's inner purpose, of creating a construction that would reflect his personal specialness, dovetailed with the aunts' purpose of having a tower that would express the school's specialness.

Much the same pattern took place when Wright designed his first major structure, the Unity Temple in Oak Park (see figure 2). Wright had no interest in building a conventional church topped by a steeple. He came up with the novel idea of a monumental building made of concrete blocks and covered with a concrete roof. In Wright's telling, there was difficulty winning over the building committee, but finally he did so. With this building, made of reinforced concrete, there was no fear that it would fall down. But the dissenters had their complaints. Not only did they feel that it did not look the way they thought a church should look, but they claimed that the auditorium would be too dark and the acoustics would be poor. One member of the committee, a Mr. Skillin, remained outspoken in his complaints, even after being outvoted.

When the building was completed, it was a resounding success. Mr. Skillin, Wright recounts, came up to him after the dedication and took back all of his criticisms and told Wright how pleased he was with the building (Wright, 1977, p. 184).

While Wright's career was flourishing, his marriage was not. His comment on the Romeo and Juliet Windmill helps explain his failed marriage. "Each," Wright (1977) says about the two intertwining parts of the tower, "is indispensable to the other . . . neither could stand without the other. Romeo . . . will do all the work and Juliet cuddle alongside to support and exalt him" (p. 159). That is exactly what he desired from his partner; he wanted someone who would support and exalt him.

I think he did not receive the attention and devotion he sought from his wife, and that is why he left her, after 20 years of marriage, and ran off with Mamah Cheney, who was married to one of his clients. Wright built the first version of Taliesin, his house and studio in Wisconsin, as a home for Mamah and himself. For the location, he chose the family homestead in Wisconsin near his aunts' school.

In 1915, while Wright was in Chicago attending to a building project, Mamah was at Taliesin. A disaffected servant went on a rampage. He murdered Mamah and six other people at Taliesin, including two of her children, and he set a fire that burned down most of Taliesin. Wright, as would be expected, was overwhelmed by the tragedy. Wright (1977) notes in his autobiography, "A horrible loneliness now began to clutch at me" (p. 212).

Another woman entered his life two years later. Miriam Noel, no doubt looking for a man to idealize, wrote Wright a letter in which she referred to his tragic loss and offered her sympathy. She received an invitation to visit him in his office in Chicago. They soon began a torrid affair. Only two weeks after her first letter, she wrote him, addressing him as "Lord of my Waking Dreams!" She told him he was her first true love and, in one biographer's paraphrase, "together they would soar starward where . . . they would find emblazoned the eternally conjoined names of Frank [and Miriam]" (Secrest, 1998, p. 241). She had found just the way to appeal to him. She looked at him almost as if he were a god; she idolized him. Wright, I would argue, found her irresistible because she reinforced his exalted self; she made him feel wonderful and special, rather than alone and empty.

Wright's Career as an Acclaimed but Controversial Architect

Throughout his career Wright reveled in courting triumph while risking disaster but never more dramatically than in one of his grandest projects, the Imperial Hotel in Tokyo, Japan (see figure 3). As Wright (1977, pp. 236–246) tells the story, his main concern in designing the hotel was the danger of an earthquake. He invented a new type of construction, which he described as being similar to "the balance of a tray on a waiter's fingers" (Hitchcock, 1975, p. 68). Just at the time when the directors had to provide more money, they were told that Wright was "mad" and that in an earthquake "the whole thing would tumble apart" (Wright, 1977, p. 241). But, according to Wright, the chairman of the board, Baron Okura, believed in Wright and told the others that he would provide the necessary money; the other directors, "red and angry to a man" (p. 243), left the room.

In 1923, two years after Wright returned to the United States, Tokyo was hit by the most devastating earthquake in the country's recorded history. Wright was filled with anxiety for ten days as he waited to hear the fate of his hotel. He finally received a telegram from Baron Okura, saying "HOTEL STANDS UNDAMAGED AS MONUMENT TO YOUR GENIUS" (Wright, 1977, p. 246). Skeptics have pointed out that Wright may have overstated his accomplishment. The Imperial Hotel was not as unique as Wright alleges; many other buildings survived the earthquake. And it is not even certain that the telegram is authentic (Gill, 1988, p. 264). It is undeniable, though, that Wright once again constructed a situation in which he could be a heroic success or an ignoble failure, and he understood the outcome as illustrating his exalted self.

Meanwhile, Wright's relationship with Miriam Noel was deteriorating. Noel no longer made him feel special and fabulous, as she had at the beginning of their relationship. Instead, she was acidly critical of him, as can be seen clearly in a remarkable letter in which he explains to her that she makes him feel like someone who deceives himself and slips, slides, and cheats (Gill, 1988, pp. 254–256). Wright became so mortified, I would argue, because Noel's disillusionment with him touched on the sense of himself that lurked beneath the surface and that he constantly tried to escape, his denigrated self.

Wright found another woman, Olgivanna Lazovich, who worshipped him, flattered him, and adored him. He obtained a divorce from Miriam, who had become his second wife, and married Olgivanna. They were together for the last 34 years of his life.

In 1931 Wright, with the active involvement of Olgivanna, had the idea of establishing a fellowship at Taliesin. Young apprentices would pay tuition in order to live at Taliesin. They would be expected to help around the institution: working on the buildings, keeping the boiler going, planting the garden. The chief benefit to them was that they got to watch the master at work. They could learn about architecture through observation; some of them, as their skills increased, could participate more and more in the designing process.

Critics argue that Wright exploited these young people; they say he did not merely get cheap labor—rather, he got the laborers to pay him for the privilege of laboring for him. But it is hard to question the testimony of the vast majority of the apprentices who found their time at Taliesin to be the most bracing, the most inspiring, the most memorable experience of their lives (Secrest, 1998, pp. 407–412). Wright was able to build up a group feeling in which the participants saw themselves as a part of something grand, special, and epochal; and indeed, they did participate in creating many acclaimed buildings.

Wright (1977) let slip in his autobiography what the payoff was for him. Talking about the apprentices, he admits he was "fond of the flattery of young people" (p.

259). I would expand on his statement by pointing out that he created a situation that supported his exalted self. He had not only his wife who worshipped him, but a whole crowd of enthusiastic younger people who were enchanted with him, who had reorganized their lives just to be around him, and who were proud to be associated with the world's greatest architect. One of the reasons for Wright's enormous productivity during the latter decades of his life was that his exalted self was strengthened and supported by the Taliesin fellows.

Four of Wright's Buildings

Now that I have described what I see as a central dynamic of Wright's personality, the tension between his exalted and denigrated selves, I would like to look at four of his buildings, beginning with Fallingwater, which is often described as the most outstanding example of residential architecture in the United States.

Wright's client was Edgar J. Kaufman, a wealthy department-store owner from Pittsburgh. One biographer argues that Kaufman, despite his success in business, felt inferior about his social status. He was the son of an immigrant peddler (Secrest, 1998, pp. 421–422).

Kaufman asked Wright to build a country home for him. Wright visited the location twice and quickly developed his conception of a dramatic house cantilevered over a waterfall. But time went on, and Wright courted failure again by not putting anything on paper. One morning while on business in Milwaukee, Kaufman called Wright and said he was coming over to see the plans for the house. Wright went to his studio and began drawing. His apprentices watched awe-struck and handed him sharp pencils as the great architect's rapid drawing dulled one pencil after another. By the time Kaufman arrived, Wright told him he had been expecting him and showed him the plans, which thrilled Kaufman (Secrest, 1998, p. 419) (see figure 4).

There was the usual trouble with Wright trying something daring and new. "The house seems to soar in all directions," notes Bruce Brooks Pfeiffer (1997, p. 115), "defying the laws of gravity." Kaufman was worried and consulted engineers who thought the house would collapse, but Wright succeeded in getting the house built his way.

Now the question I ask is, what is the emotional impact of this building? In my view, it expressed Wright's exalted self. And it did the same thing for Kaufman. The house helped the businessman feel not socially inferior, but the inhabitant of a great work of art: a country gentleman living in a home so magnificent that thousands of people would visit it to admire it.

Wright accomplished all this with the building's beauty and drama. The romance of nature transfers to the building: not only with the waterfall but also with the cliff, the trees, and the outcropping of rocks that is built into the interior of the living room. In short, with a building such as Fallingwater, Wright created within himself a feeling of being special, unparalleled, outstanding. The client, as the owner of the home, felt much the same way. Wright (1977) noted once, "I suspect the ego in [me] invited or repelled you [that is, the client] as you happened to be made yourself" (p. 153). He recognized that his ego—that is, his sense of specialness and importance—attracted a client if there existed a similarity between the client and him, and it pushed away a client if the client's ego did not correspond to Wright's. His buildings were most successful when he and the client had the same inner need to feel exalted.

We have looked at the most celebrated Wright home; next we will consider one of his most celebrated commercial buildings, the headquarters of Johnson Wax. For this building he created a grand, indoor atrium. Slender columns of reinforced concrete spread out at the ceiling into what looks like lily pads (see figure 5).

Once again Wright came into conflict with those who believed that his conception was faulty; state officials refused to allow him to build such thin columns. In a daring public-relations coup, Wright arranged to test a sample column with government bureaucrats, a horde of reporters, and newsreel cameras as witnesses. Workmen piled sacks of sand on top of the column. When the column supported 12 tons, twice the weight that it was required to support, the officials conceded that Wright could use his columns in the building. But Wright expansively exclaimed, "Keep piling!" until the column was holding up 60 tons (Gill, 1988, pp. 364–365).

On the floor of the vast central room of the S. C. Johnson Administration Building, the workers had desks, custom designed by Wright. Balconies, housing middle management, encircled the space. Not only were the employees given a spacious work area, but they also were provided with squash courts and a theater. As William J. R. Curtis (1983) has noted, the leaders of the company "wished their organization to maintain the character of a sort of extended family under a beneficent patriarchy." Wright grasped what they wanted and in his design "attempted to form an inward-looking community which would foster togetherness while mirroring the hierarchy of the firm" (p. 201). Another way of putting it, I think, is that the building captured the same spirit as that of the Taliesin Fellowship.

The firm's leaders, in particular Herbert F. Johnson, the president, were clearly in charge, but they were in a position to provide a special working life for their employees. The contentment of the employees, much like the satisfaction of Wright's apprentices, redounded to the credit of the person at the pinnacle. Once again, there was consonance between Wright's personality and that of his clients.

While my approach may help explain the emotions generated by Wright's highly successful buildings, can it help us make sense of his failures?

One Wright building that does not seem to work is the house he designed for a cousin, Richard Lloyd Jones, publisher of the *Tulsa Tribune*. Much of the correspondence between architect and client has survived. Lloyd Jones was highly suspicious of Wright. He knew Wright had talent but saw him as arrogant and unreliable. Lloyd Jones's attitude was something like that of his father, who had been the ringleader of the uncles who opposed the Romeo and Juliet Windmill.

Wright set off Lloyd Jones by calling him a "Puritan . . . of the worst stripe" and added that he was a hypocrite (Secrest, 1998, p. 365). Outraged, Lloyd Jones attacked Wright for his "'I-own-the-world' ways, his outlandish appearance, his selfish determination to have his own way at all costs, his contempt for society, [and] his lack of sympathy for others" (Secrest, 1998, p. 365). Later, Lloyd Jones pointed out the architect's "self-centeredness, his arrogance, his intolerance of others and his vaingloriousness" (p. 367). Lloyd Jones further noted that their family had been divided into two factions. There were those, like Wright, "who put on airs, wove fictional romances around themselves, and thought themselves too good for the rest of the world" and those, like Lloyd Jones's father, who had contempt for such fakery (p. 367). Wright made a rare admission; in the face of his cousin's attacks, he noted that "behind his own apparent 'bravado' was a hidden sadness" (p. 368).

Here are some of the descriptions of the resulting house (see figure 6). It is "stripped-down, forbidding, and almost belligerently lacking in charm. From certain aspects it . . . looks like an armed camp, 'the window slits acting as gun emplacements'" (Secrest, 1998, p. 371). "Disastrously ugly" (Twombly, 1973, p. 197). "It could readily be mistaken for an immense penitentiary" (Gill, 1988, p. 334). Lloyd Jones himself called it a "pickle factory" (Secrest, 1998, p. 372).

With this building, Wright probably first used a line he was to repeat other times. The house leaked. One rainy day Lloyd Jones went to his desk and called Wright in a rage. "Dammit Frank," he said, "it's leaking on my desk." Wright's reply: "Richard, why don't you move your desk?" (Secrest, 1998, p. 372).

Here is what I think went wrong. Lloyd Jones not only did not share in Wright's desire to be exalted and special but despised this quality in Wright. Lloyd Jones's attacks exposed Wright's denigrated self; Wright was threatened with feeling worthless, fake, a charlatan. Wright, as a result, designed a building that reflected his need to buttress himself against this painful way of seeing himself. The building makes a person feel safe and protected from a hostile outer world. The interior is not as unsuccessful as the exterior. While inside, a person does not have the openness to the natural surroundings that is typical of a Wright country house. But the interior works in another way. It gives one a sense of being in a spacious, comfortable, secure environment.

The final building I will discuss, the Price Company Tower, reflects what happened when there was an ideal fit between Wright and his client.

Harold (Hal) Price owned a company in Bartlesville, Oklahoma, that built pipelines. Price wanted a simple two- or three-story building for his modest business and asked Wright to design it. Wright agreed to work on a building but talked Price into accepting a 19-story skyscraper. Wright resurrected old plans for a New York skyscraper that was never built, and he based the Price Tower on that project (Gill, 1988, pp. 453–466).

The resulting building, graceful and beautiful, looks down on and dwarfs everything for miles around (see figure 7). It gives the sense that it houses a great company. In constructing the tower, Wright once again used a daring design that might be seen as risking disaster. The building has a shaft at its center with each floor cantilevered to the shaft much as branches of a tree extend from its trunk. The outer walls of the building are like screens hanging from the floors and are not load-bearing. Price, with a personality much like Wright's, found the building to be thrilling. During construction, he would stand on the periphery of one of the floors that was cantilevered more than 100 feet above the ground. Because the rigid walls were not yet fully in place, he could jump up and down and the floor would bounce much like a diving board. The construction workers down below were afraid (Gill, 1988, p. 457). Price joined Wright in soaring above the pedestrian world.

Price's office is impressive. It is on the top floor and has a commanding view. Wright designed the furniture and created a mural for it (Constantino, 1998, p. 131). One can imagine that, sitting in the office, Price felt as extraordinary and powerful as Wright liked to feel.

The chairs Wright designed were uncomfortable and could easily tip over. The architect heard that the Governor of Oklahoma had visited Hal Price in his office and had fallen over when he sat down. Wright wrote Price, "I learn by grapevine ... that as your architect I got the governor down on the floor. Well, Hal, he can't be much of a governor if the poor devil can't even negotiate a Price Tower official chair?" (Gill, 1988. p. 460). Wright's response once again illustrates my central theme. Wright avoided feeling inferior and foolish for designing an inadequate chair. He turned the incident around and declared that it showed his superiority—and by extension his client's superiority—to the most powerful official in the State of Oklahoma.

Conclusion

The keynote of many of Wright's buildings is that they express and reinforce his exalted self. The design of the buildings is grand, thrilling, beautiful, and unconventional. They elicit in the viewer an emotional reaction: here is something special and fabulous. The clients, if they have personalities similar to Wright's, feel enhanced by owning such remarkable buildings. Some of Wright's buildings produce an additional rush by flirting with and triumphing over the possibility of an embarrassing failure. Throughout his life Wright feared and played with the threat of experiencing himself as a fraud and an object of derision; he was never completely free of his denigrated self, which was a countervailing force underneath his exalted self. He pulled many of his clients into his internal drama. As we saw most clearly with Kaufman, in the case of Fallingwater, these clients sometimes feared that the building would collapse but ended up sharing in Wright's victory. There was an ongoing tension during Wright's career that fueled his achievements and played a part in shaping his creations.

References

Anderson, J. W. (2003), A psychological pespective on the relationship of William and Henry James. In: *Up Close and Personal: The Teaching and Learning of Narrative Research*, ed. R. Josselson, A. Lieblich & D. P. McAdams. Washington, DC: American Psychological Association, 2003.

The Compact Edition of the Oxford English Dictionary (1971). Oxford: Oxford University Press.

Constantino, M. (1998), *The Life and Works of Frank Lloyd Wright*. Philadelphia: Courage Books.

Curtis, W. J. R. (1983), *Modern Architecture Since 1900*. Englewood Cliffs, NJ: Prentice-Hall.

Gill, B. (1988), *Many Masks: A Life of Frank Lloyd Wright*. New York: Ballantine.

Goldberg, A. (1999), *Being of Two Minds*. Hillsdale, NJ: The Analytic Press.

Guntrip, H. (1969), *Schizoid Phenomena, Object-Relations, and the Self*. New York: International Universities Press.

Hitchcock, H.-R. (1975), *In the Nature of Materials: The Buildings of Frank Lloyd Wright, 1887–1941*. New York: Da Capo Press.

James, W. (1890), *The Principles of Psychology* (2 vols.). New York: Henry Holt.

Kohut, H. (1977), *The Restoration of the Self*. New York: International Universities Press.

Pfeiffer, B. B. (1997), *Frank Lloyd Wright: Master Builder*. New York: Universe Publishing.

Secrest, M. (1998), *Frank Lloyd Wright: A Biography*. Chicago: University of Chicago Press.

Twombly, R. C. (1973), *Frank Lloyd Wright: An Interpretive Biography*. New York: Harper & Row.

Winnicott, D. W. (1960), Ego distortion in terms of true and false self. In D. W. Winnicott, *The Maturational Processes and the Facilitating Environment*. New York: International Universities Press, 1965, pp. 140–152.

Wright, F. L. (1977). *An Autobiography*. New York: Horizon Press.

Frank Lloyd Wright
Power, Powerlessness, and Charisma

JEROME A. WINER

Frank Lloyd Wright was an architectural genius. In this essay, I will tackle two areas of his amazing career. First, how Wright established charismatic relationships with many he knew personally or professionally. To do that, I will explore how interacting with Wright transformed many people who had an unconscious sense of being passive or unappreciated into individuals who felt they were active figures of merit and importance. Sometimes this transformation occurred because they lived in a house that he had designed for them, or because they had commissioned one of his buildings. With his Taliesin apprentices, it was because they worked in his fields, ate in his presence, listened to the music he loved, and stood at his elbow as he worked. To yet others, it might have been the way he made them feel personally important. Brendan Gill, *New Yorker* writer and later one of Wright's biographers, gives us an example of this: Despite the half-century difference in their ages Wright insisted on the young writer calling him Frank. "When he came to New York he would ring me up from the Plaza Hotel and say 'Hello Brendan, this is Frank.' And I felt as if George Washington were telephoning me from Mt. Vernon and saying, 'Hello Brendan, this is George'" (Gill, 1998, p. 17).

    The second major area I will discuss is how Wright's use of space resonates with core aspects of the personalities of many of us who view or enter his buildings. Wright abhorred what he called "boxes." By doing away with traditional compartmentalization, he gives many a sense of freedom and soothing that often approaches awe. Wright removed boundaries in a way that served to blend his houses with their surroundings and the nature that lay beyond them—and beyond the world as we know it. In larger buildings he removed boundaries between workers, turned office buildings into cathedrals and temples, turned an art gallery from the housing for art into the art itself. To those who feel confined by internal, over-strict unconscious demarcations, Wright's life and work has a special appeal.

Wright as a Charismatic Figure

Let me begin exploring the first topic, Frank Lloyd Wright's charisma, by tracing the concept of charisma (Winer, Jobe, and Ferrono, 1985; Winer, 1989). Modern scholarship concerning charisma began with the German sociologist, Max Weber, who was born in 1864, just three years before Wright. Weber described charisma as "a certain quality of an individual personality by virtue of which he is set apart from ordinary men and treated as endowed with supernatural, superhuman, or at least specifically exceptional qualities" (quoted in Eisenstadt, 1968, p. xviii). To Weber, "charisma may involve a subjective or internal reorientation born out of suffering, conflicts or enthusiasm." The University of Chicago sociologist Edward Shils (1965) took the position that the charismatic bond between leader and follower is not necessarily abnormal. Shils included scientific discovery, artistic creativity, and all forms of genius as instances of things charismatic. Although most psychologically oriented writers have construed charismatic leadership in exclusively pathological terms with respect to both leader and follower, Erik Erikson (1958, 1969) gave it a more balanced view, showing that a leader's personal conflicts and resolution can provide a new ordering force that is constructive.

The Greek word *charisma* conveyed that the gods had bestowed special gifts on an individual. Instead of gifts of the gods, or the later Christian view that the power came from closeness to God, in previous work I posited that the charismatic figure's self-initiated reversal of enforced passivity and impotence into magnificent activity and power was an important aspect of his charismatic attraction. He is a magnetic personality who conveys to followers that by attaching themselves to him, his work, or mission, they can experience a similar reversal of passivity into activity, of weakness into strength. Of course, the charismatic leader also must possess great artistic, political, or spiritual qualities. His or her personality must convey greatness. Again and again, Wright turned extreme hardship, tragedy, rejection, and dismissal into triumph, thrilling accomplishment, adulation, and veneration. A quick example would be Frank Lloyd Wright's reversing his own six springs and summers of despised, exhausting labor on his mother's relatives' farms during his youth, into being the master of scores of Taliesin apprentices who worked his land exhaustively, trying their best to anticipate and to imitate his every action. "If he went to hoe, one should be hoeing; if he was going to work on the dam one rushed there" (Secrest, 1992, p. 407). Many of these apprentices were "dropouts" motivated to join the fellowship because they felt themselves to be lost and passive in a personal, subjective world that could not privilege them as individuals of merit and power. Merely to be in Frank Lloyd Wright's presence changed all of that, and offered a great sense of personal worth. Wright's charismatic attraction went far beyond his apprentices, however. It began with some of his early clients and has extended, in many ways, to the present day.

In order to better understand Wright's charismatic appeal, let's review Wright's family background. His father, William Carey Wright, was a handsome, rather small man, a university graduate, musician, preacher, lawyer, teacher, scholar, liked by everyone but incapable of making a solid living. After his first wife Permelia died, leaving him with three small children, he married one of the family boarders, the schoolteacher Anna Lloyd Jones, nearly a spinster at 24. He was 41. He needed considerable admiration, what psychoanalysts often call mirroring, from his new wife. Instead, he found her lavishing most of her attention on their first-born child, Frank. To Anna, this boy would actualize all of her unrealized hopes by becoming an architect, a builder of great buildings and great fame. If one believes Wright's autobiography (Pfeiffer, 1992), which is full of tall tales, she placed a picture of the great English cathedrals on his wall and bought wooden Froebel blocks of geometric forms to familiarize him with basic architectural shapes as a small child. His drive for greatness was inculcated by Anna from an early age, but she was a mother whose love and adoration was something he could not rely on since he had witnessed her fierce criticism and derogation of his father and stepsiblings. This reached such depths that William Carey Wright once asked the Lloyd Joneses if there was a history of mental illness in the family. Anna's clear favoritism of Frank over her husband contributed in a major way to William's obtaining a divorce and leaving his family behind. Frank never saw his father again. Wright both sought the approval of, and liberation from, his mother all of his life. When he married at 21 and designed his new home in Oak Park, she was ensconced next door before the house was even completed. When he deserted his wife and six children, it was in part to leave her behind as well. When he built Taliesin, his magnificent home and estate in Spring Green, Wisconsin, it was allegedly for his mother, although really for his mistress, Mamah Cheney. Anna had helped him obtain Lloyd Jones family land back in Wisconsin, to which Anna also returned. She was never too far away. When Wright fell ill in Japan, she was soon there to nurse him.

Wright's six springs and summers on the Lloyd-Jones family farm in Wisconsin fills a large percentage of *An Autobiography*'s description of his childhood and adolescence. The recurring phrase "adding tired to tired, and adding it again" (Pfeiffer, 1992, p.115), together with the animal smells and disgusting daily food that sickened him, characterized a period that only the surrounding beauty of nature and Sunday picnics, with an array of wonderful food, could soften. His father resented his wife's preference of the son for whom lightning and thunder at his birth served as presentiments of his greatness—at least according to her.

The mother sharply rebuked any failings of the boy. The father, on the other hand, is represented as forcing a seven-year-old Frank to pump the church organ as he played Bach until Frank nearly fainted.

In one of the few anecdotes from his adolescence in the autobiography, Wright describes how he rescued the crippled 14-year-old Robie Lamp, whose shriveled legs dangled dead as he moved along on crutches. Schoolboys teased Robie unmercifully, once burying him in leaves until Frank drove them off. Why did he include this story? Fantasy or not, the story portrays exactly the paradigmatic relationship that lay at the heart of Wright's drive to be charismatic. I believe Wright felt that to his father, and at times his mother, he was a Robie Lamp. Now he is the rescuer. Once he was his father's suffering son; later he is artistic father and nurturer to those who want him to build houses or buildings for them, those clients whose sense of mediocrity or ordinariness will be overcome by owning a Wright House or building. In fact, later in life he hoped to rescue all of American architecture and civilization as well. Wright called his plan "Broadacres," a decentralization where the city would be "everywhere but nowhere" (Tafel, 1993). After striking some chords on the piano, Wright once said to the assemblage at Taliesin,"If I had followed music and not architecture I could have surpassed Beethoven" (Tafel, 1993, p. 144); this expression, as much a lament as a boast, was a far cry from pumping the organ for his father to the point of exhaustion.

Identification with the "hero" who has reversed enforced passivity into exemplary activity is not enough to explain Wright's or any other charismatic figure's interpersonal power, however. Also important is the charismatic figure's empathic capacity to understand a person's wishes and needs in a way that gives that person both the feeling of being totally understood as well as the sense that these needs and wishes will be fulfilled. Over a period of several years, Chicago architect Wilbert Hasbrouck (personal communication, 2004) interviewed over 40 people for whom Wright built houses. Hasbrouck reports that Wright made the client feel he was building exactly the house that the client had wanted, that it was essentially the client's own design, that it was uniquely that individual's, and perfect. *Each one also felt that his or her house was Wright's favorite.*

Psychoanalysts focus exclusively on the patient; the analyst is interested in hearing every thought, every fantasy, every desire that the patient expresses. As a result, patients often experience a regression. Old wishes that they rarely think of, let alone talk about, come out. Frozen conflicts embedded in character defrost. It becomes possible to discover instinctual drive derivatives and defenses and to interpret them so that the patient can find new solutions for them. Wright seemed to be able to rapidly induce similar regressions even in an initial interview, in which clients felt that they had Wright's total attention and that they were uniquely important to him. He made them feel that he was going to make their fantasies a reality, rather than interpret them, of course.

Here is an excerpt from the letter W. E. Martin of Oak Park wrote to his brother, Darwin of Buffalo. "I have been—seen—talked to, admired one of nature's *noblemen*—Mr. Frank Lloyd Wright . . . a straightforward businessman—with high ideals. I met his mother, a *beautiful type* of woman . . . You will *fall* in *love* with him—in 10 min. conversation. He will build you the *finest*, most *sensible* house in Buffalo. You will be the envy of every rich man in Buffalo, it will be published in all of the Buffalo papers. It will be talked about all over the East. You will never grow tired of his work" (Gill, 1998, pp. 141–142). Darwin Martin was to bail out Wright repeatedly from desperate financial straits over the next decades. Darwin convinced his boss, John Larkin, in a similar letter to give Wright the commission for the new Larkin Company office building. Darwin Martin reported to Larkin that he and his wife had visited four Wright houses and talked to the owners. "You never witnessed such enthusiasm. No one will admit a fault in their house. They will admit faults in other of Wright's houses but not in theirs. That, Mr. Wright says, is because he studies his client and builds the house to fit him" (Gill, 1998, p. 143). Another proud Oak Park house owner wrote to a German architect that Wright was one of the most remarkable men he had ever met and that he was proud to call him his friend.

Wes Peters, who spent his lifetime working for Wright and Wright causes after Wright's death, described their initial meeting. "I had thought he was tall and he wasn't, but he dominated the room. I can't explain what happened but something did. I felt my whole life would be changed" (Secrest, 1992, p. 403). Regression to old wishes includes the magical wish for reversal of passivity into activity, from being controlled by one's environment or parents into living in an environment that is a representation of personal wishes that have come true. No wonder Wright identifies himself with Aladdin in his autobiography.

Many of us wish we could be children again providing we have the power to make our own choices. We would love to play at the beach, at sports where *we* can decide when *we* arrive, when *we* can leave, where to go, and how to participate. Wright was described by many as a child who never grew up. He did not pay his bills, and bought luxuries when the necessities went unpaid for. He loved to party, to picnic, and tell tall stories in which he exaggerated his accomplishments. He reports in his autobiography that as a boy of ten or so he told several peers that they could come to his house for a party. Because this party existed only in his wishful imagination, his mother had to quickly improvise refreshments when the guests arrived. Again this is one of the few anecdotes he reports from his early life and its theme is much like the Robie Lamp story. I will reverse your state—and enrich your experience. The fact that his mother immediately picked up on what was going on and supplied what was necessary to make the fantasy a reality demonstrates her role in Wright's lifelong pattern of great sensitivity to fulfilling the wishes of others and often charming outside sources to provide the wherewithal.

In even the most compliant child, there lies beneath the constraints of ego and superego development the wish to have it my way, not the way parents or teachers want it. Wright, like the Welsh mythological magical figure Taliesin, with his seer's wand and cape, was the unbridled child. Wright's lifelong fondness for a cape and cane conveyed a touch of that magician. To this day we are enchanted by tales of Wright's childlike overthrowing of adult boundaries. The August 20, 2003, *Wall Street Journal* recalled his May 1957 trip to Iraq. Invited by King Faisal II to build an Opera House, Wright impudently introduced himself to the monarch as "His Majesty the American Citizen." We are charmed as this child of nearly 90 turns the expected passivity of commoner before royalty into a complete reversal. Wright asked for an island in the Tigris. Faisal replied, "The island, Mr. Wright, is yours." But to be childlike, alone, is not charismatic. To actualize childlike fantasies with artistic powers far beyond those of the ordinary artist is charismatic.

Partly in a childlike way and partly out of a sense of narcissism, Wright considered himself above normal constraints both in his personal life and in his work. A hallmark of a charismatic leader according to Max Weber is disregard and transcendence of the traditional and bureaucratic societal rules, the everyday routine ("*Alltäglichkeit*"). Wright held a press conference on Christmas Day 1911 at Taliesin, his new home in Spring Green, Wisconsin, two years after leaving his first wife and six children for the married Mamah Cheney, and stated: "The ordinary man cannot live without rules to guide his conduct. . . . It is infinitely more difficult to live without rules, but that is what the really honest, sincere, thinking man is compelled to do" (Gill, 1998, p. 222). Although his comment was used as fuel for ever more scurrilous newspaper columns, Wright was altogether sincere. He believed that he was the greatest architect of all time and therefore his charismatic mission, in Weber's sense, was to bring about a new order using his special gifts available to no one else. I cannot tell you whence Wright obtained the skills that led to putting onto paper the design for Fallingwater (considered by many to be the finest residence ever constructed in America) in only three hours, nor his waking at 4:00 AM and designing three altogether different houses by the beginning of the regular work day. But nearness to such genius made those closest to him feel a touch of genius in themselves, too. This was especially true of Fallingwater's wealthy owner, E. J. Kaufman, who was sensitive about being the son of an itinerant peddler.

Max Weber claimed that "charisma knows only inner determination and inner restraint" (Gerth and Mills, 1958, p. 246). The capacity we have to identify vicariously with those who actively overthrow restraint brings us pleasure. In our tradition-bound passivity to societal rules, we delight in anecdotes such as the one told by biographer Meryle Secrest. She reports Wright talking the manager of Abercrombie and Fitch into giving him an expensive coat because it would be an advantage to the store to have HIM as a walking advertisement—and then demanding a second coat for his friend, architectural historian Henry-Russell Hitchcock, who was with him (Secrest, 1992, p. 441). Yet Hitchcock's own version of the story was that Wright insisted on seeing higher and higher officers of the company in order to have his personal check accepted, which was not allowed by store policy (Henry-Russell Hitchcock in Tafel, 2001, p. 223). How did the story grow? Is it an example of the biographer's own distortion or someone else's? No matter, for the small child's unresolved need to feel secure within the strength of another's strong presence, that is buried inside most of us, is quite likely at work (Kohut, 1971). When one has the capacity to deliver in the almost magical way the way that Wright could, charismatic attribution is borne out. Wright designed the Johnson Wax Building on thin pillars that no one but Wright believed could carry the weight they were to bear (figure 1). When authorities challenged the plan, Wright arranged a demonstration where ten times the necessary weight was added to a model pillar before it crumbled. When an earthquake destroyed most of Tokyo, Wright's Imperial Hotel remained standing; and he was not above spreading the word that it was the *only* building still in place. He also failed to credit the engineer who made the building's endurance possible. Hitchcock believed "Mr. Wright's entire life was staged. It was intended for an audience. It was above all, a projection of personality" (Tafel, 2001, p. 222).

Let us look at these facts psychoanalytically. A small child looks to parents for the sustaining "gleam in the mother's eye" that Kohut (1971) called "mirroring." The death-in-life produced by infants raised in impersonal institutions is an extreme example of the absence of this psychological nutrient. Although the young Frank experienced much of it from his mother, he certainly did not, according to his own account, receive it from his father. It also seems plausible that Frank's perception of Anna's true delight left him with a sense that she was "using him" to elevate her own self-esteem. Frank was consequently left with a lifelong need for admiration and praise. Kohut postulated an additional need in the developing child, the need for someone to idealize. Those adults in whom this childhood need was largely unfulfilled are constantly seeking a Wright-like figure to admire, even in adulthood. Wright spent a lifetime offering himself as an object for admiration. If you do a Google computer search on the name Frank Lloyd Wright, 377,000 entries come up as of this writing. This great collection of citations exists because of the quality of Wright's work, not because of his charisma alone.

FIGURE 1 (top). Johnson Wax Company.
FIGURE 2 (center). Taliesin.
FIGURE 3 (bottom). Guggenheim Museum.

Photographs © 2005 by Thomas A. Heinz.

Wright's Work and the Core Aspects of Personality

Let me turn now to my second major topic, a psychoanalytic perspective on the compelling power of Wright's buildings. I will explore how Wright's work resonates with core aspects of human personality so as to yield a sense of pleasure, comfort, and serenity. On first seeing Fallingwater, the architectural critic Paul Goldberger said he could not find words for the experience, that all he could think of was wanting to sing (Burns, 1998). I would like to suggest that Goldberger's experience is not unlike that of many of us. Because Wright worked for more than seven decades, finding common themes in his work is most challenging. Yet Wright's oft-repeated hatred of "boxes" gives us a clue. The objects of his derision ranged from the rooms of Victorian houses to the work of the International School, whom he called the "glass box boys." From the Prairie-style houses of a century ago, to the Guggenheim Museum essentially free of any of the rooms where art had been traditionally hung, to the boxless ziggurat planned by Wright for Baghdad at age 90, Wright continued to free his buildings from compartmentalization.

Wright believed that boundaries within a building, or between the inner space of a house and natural world, were as odious as were the constraints of bureaucratic society that hemmed in a creative, charismatic genius. (Of course, the boundary set by the anticipated cost of a project was another limitation that he frequently ignored.) Wright was acutely aware of the power that architecture can have on one's psyche and he was able to create a sense of liberation by the use of materials that blended with the natural world. This not only allowed the house to become part of its surrounding, but also enabled the person within the house to become one with nature, the essence of life that lay beyond the world before us. Wright's concept of nature, influenced by Emerson and Louis Sullivan, was not what is usually understood by that word. It was the unobservable experience of observable nature as processed through the human soul. For Wright, therefore, light was as natural as possible, windows were placed next to each other to provide a panoramic view; living space was above the street and its distractions; rooms coalesced; and colors were the green, gold, and gentle brown of the countryside. The hearth with its Inglenook served as the center of a Prairie house, enabling the family to live in unity, with even the boundaries between one another minimized. The architect, himself, is one with the natural world and especially capable of manifesting it for others through the houses and buildings *he* creates in a seamless fashion together with their furnishings which *he* designs. The architect/creator gives life and vitality to inert objects—bricks, stones, wood, glass—and in order to do so must have supreme confidence in himself (Samuelson, personal communication, July 2003).

Huxtable (2004) describes the early Prairie house as "a low horizontal structure

. . . with a relationship to the land that the rigidly vertical dwelling had never acknowledged . . . The conventional formal parlor was replaced by a living room, dining room, and study that flowed together in a hearth-centered single space" (p. 74). The individual flowed into the surround.

I suggest that Wright's buildings which free one from the constraints of boxes, from borders between self and environment, appeal to the depths of psychic organization. That is because they put one in touch with that period in one's life when he or she was free of the boxes of "should" and "never," "right" and "wrong," and "me and not me"—in other words, the serene preverbal state of human childhood before the anxiety caused by transgression exists. To my knowledge, Wright was in no way influenced by Freud; but Freud's concept of "the oceanic feeling," borrowed from his friend Romain Rolland (who in turn had discovered it in Rama Krishna), is quite pertinent: "it is a feeling of an indissoluble bond, of being one with the external world as a whole" (Freud, 1930, p. 65). Along with earliest childhood, typified by the infant at the breast, Freud tells us that there is only one state that approaches this loss of self-boundaries. "At the height of being in love the boundary between ego [self] and object [other] threatens to melt away" (p. 66). No wonder many who enter a Wright space such as Unity Temple, Taliesin, the Johnson Wax Building, or the Guggenheim Museum, feel a bit as if they are falling in love (see figures 2 and 3).

The workers in both the Larkin Building and the Johnson Wax Building were offered a compartmentless open space to perform their activities—not a usual room, divided space, or the even more odious modern cubicle. At the same time as they were constrained by being at work, they were free and in many ways within a cathedral—a subtle provision of an experience mildly reminiscent of an oceanic experience. Wright aimed to liberate them from the box that was their own work self with all its concerns.

The psychoanalyst Arnold Modell (2003) has defined metaphor as "the transfer of meaning between dissimilar domains" (p. 41). Wright's spaces can be seen as the metaphorical transferring of one's own wish for freedom from personal boundedness to the very space of the building or house—light, limitless, in touch with the infinite that lies beyond nature—and beyond the societal constraints we face as adults. This is what I believe Wright tried to convey when he so frequently used the term organic. Huxtable (2004) believed Wright meant by organic architecture "to unite man and his built world with nature, the human spirit, and the universe" (p. 28). Wright was quoted in his *New York Times* obituary (April 10, 1959) as denouncing the box houses of this country: "A box is more of a coffin for the human spirit than an inspiration." Wright liked to hide the entry to a house or building much like the tradition of having to seek to find the magic entrée to a different world.

I do not claim that the freedom that at its utmost approaches the oceanic feeling is appealing to everyone. To many, such lack of boundaries suggests a kind of chaos that yields only anxiety. Good fences often do make good neighbors.

In summary, I have examined the life and work of Frank Lloyd Wright from two vantage points. I have discussed his charismatic appeal to many as being rooted in the capacity to transform their own sense of passivity and powerlessness through the power of his personality. I have also discussed how Wright's abhorrence of compartmentalization and "boxes," and his merger of man-made structures with a greater natural world, produces a unique serenity in many observers because of its capacity to evoke the oceanic feeling. Hans Loewald (1978) has written of the aesthetic experience in the contemplation of art or "the proportions of a building" (p. 67) where rational processes continue to operate yet are overshadowed by the timelessness of the unconscious or primary process. Given Wright's capacity to reach our unconscious sense of timelessness, of the absence of borders and boundaries, it is no wonder Frank Lloyd Wright seems so much alive today.

References

Burns, K. (1998), *Frank Lloyd Wright: A Film by Ken Burns and Lynn Novick*. Los Angeles: Time-Warner.

Cohen, A. (2003, August 20), Frank Lloyd Wright 'builds' Baghdad. *The Wall Street Journal*.

Eisenstadt, S. N. (1968), Charisma and institution building: Max Weber and modern sociology. In: Weber, M., *On Charisma and Institution Building*, ed. S. N. Eisenstadt, pp. ix–ivi. Chicago: University of Chicago Press.

Erikson, E. (1958), *Young Man Luther*. New York: W. W. Norton.

—— (1969), *Gandhi's Truth: On the Origins of Militant Nonviolence*. New York: W. W. Norton.

Freud, S. (1930), Civilization and its discontents, *Standard Edition*, 21. London: Hogarth Press, 1961.

Gerth, H. H. & Mills, C. W., eds. (1958), *From Max Weber: Essays in Sociology*. New York: Oxford University Press.

Gill, B. (1998), *Many Masks: A Life of Frank Lloyd Wright*. New York: DaCapo Press.

Huxtable, H. (2004), *Frank Lloyd Wright*. New York: Viking.

Kohut, H. (1971), *The Analysis of the Self*. New York: International Universities Press,

Loewald, H. W. (1928), *Psychoanalysis and the History of the Individual*. New Haven, CT: Yale University Press.

Modell, A. (2003), *Imagination and the Meaningful Brain*. Cambridge, MA: MIT Press.

Pfeiffer, B. B., ed. (1992), *Frank Lloyd Wright: Collected Writings*, vol. 2. New York: Rizzoli.

Secrest, M. (1992), *Frank Lloyd Wright: A Biography*. Chicago: University of Chicago Press.

Shils, E. (1965), Charisma, order, and status. *American Sociological Review*, 30:199–213.

Tafel, E. (2001), *Frank Lloyd Wright: Recollection by those who Knew Him*. Toronto: Dover.

Winer, J. (1989), Charismatic followership as illustrated in George Eliot's *Romola*. *The Annual of Psychoanalysis*, 17:129–143. Hillsdale, NJ: The Analytic Press.

Winer, J., Jobe, T. & Ferrono, C. (1985), Toward a psychoanalytic theory of the charismatic relationship. *The Annual of Psychoanalysis*, 12/13:155–175. New York: International Universities Press.

Raumplan
Adolf Loos, Frank Lloyd Wright, Residential Space, and Modernity

ROBERT TWOMBLY

Frank Lloyd Wright and Adolf Loos were near contemporaries. Born in 1867, Wright designed his first houses when he was about 25: those half-dozen or so "boot-leg" commissions, he called them, of 1891 and 1892 in and around Chicago that, taken in violation of contract with his employers Dankmar Adler and Louis Sullivan, led to his dismissal from their firm. Born in 1870, Loos first built in 1897 when he was 27 and until 1903 he was known for shop and apartment renovations in Vienna. But beginning with his 1904 Villa Karma on Lake Geneva in Switzerland, Loos, like Wright, garnered acclaim for free-standing dwellings, although he, too, designed many other kinds of well-known, sometimes controversial, buildings. Neither one was, nor was content to be, exclusively a residential architect, but their reputations nevertheless stemmed in large measure from their pioneering work in villa design.

Raumplan—which is to say room plan or the arrangement of interior space—has come to be associated with Loos even though he never used the word and only late in life discussed it as a concept. The term was actually coined by associates assembling the 1931 book, *Adolf Loos: Architectural Works*, the editor of which, Heinrich Kulka, explained *raumplan* as "the arrangement of related spaces into a harmonic invisible whole and into a spatially-efficient composition" (Van Duzer and Kleinman, 1994, p. 38). Wright could surely have written that about his own work.

Here is what Loos himself wrote about room arrangement, in 1933, the year he died:

> I do not design plans, façades, sections, I design space. Actually there is neither a ground floor, an upper floor or a basement, there are merely interconnected

spaces, vestibules, terraces. Every room needs a special height—the dining room a different one from the pantry—therefore the floors are on varying levels. After this one must connect the spaces with one another so that the transition is unnoticeable and natural, but also the most practical [Van Duzer et. al., 1994, p. 38].

Possibly because Loos was rethinking architectural categories, he exaggerated a bit. Some of his villas *do* have ground floors, upper floors, and basements, and rooms do *not* always vary in height. But increasingly from the mid-1910s forward, his heights and levels—even within rooms—do indeed vary, all the way down into what is no longer a basement but a lower level. The reason for this—and here Loos did not exaggerate—is that, in his view, each space was unique because of its singular function, including psychological function, requiring its own architectural mood. Differences in ceiling height and floor level within and among rooms are two of several mechanisms for creating mood and enhancing singularity, but it was also Loos's view that spatial differences must of necessity be connected by "unnoticeable and natural" transitions into an harmonious, practical whole. This was a difficult feat to accomplish assuredly, and was Wright's goal as much as it was Loos's.

Here it is necessary to note that it is just as inaccurate to assign Loos's work to the misnamed "International Style" as it is to place Wright's work in that category. One of the few positive things to be said about Henry-Russell Hitchcock and Philip Johnson's 1932 book of that title is that both architects were omitted from it. Loos never adopted the so-called "open plan," Le Corbusier's "free plan," an important ingredient of which is the large principal salon, that multifunctional space containing dining and living areas, perhaps a reading or a conversation zone, the whole flowing through plate glass into a roof garden or a terrace. Nor did Wright use the "open plan" during his pre-World War I "Prairie" period, though he did with his "Usonian" and post-Usonian houses from the mid-1930s until his death in 1959. Loos designed discrete rooms, as Wright did early on, and it goes without saying that both gave priority to the beauty and efficiency of every space. But both accorded even higher priority to what Kulka called "harmonic invisible wholes," the creation of which was for each of them as much a social as an architectural undertaking. Loos and Wright believed that residential architecture was fundamentally a means of providing optimum facilities in which twentieth-century families might adjust to "modernity," specifically urban modernity. That their architectural provisions were so different was in large measure the outcome of quite different understandings of what modernity meant and of quite dissimilar readings of how space affected emotions. Loos and Wright, though virtual contemporaries, lived in different worlds; but geographical distance was only one measure, hardly the most important, of their several degrees of separation.

There is a good discussion of *raumplan* in a valuable 1994 monograph by Leslie van Duzer and Kent Kleinman entitled *Villa Müller*, about Loos's 1928 design in Prague. *Raumplan*, the authors contend, is formulated with two persons in mind: the stationary person and the ambulatory person, which could mean—they don't say—resident and visitor at the same moment, resident or visitor at different moments. Put another way, space must accommodate the sitter and walker at the same time or the sitter who later walks. So there is either simultaneous movement and stasis or sequential movement and stasis; that is, change and no change at once or separately.

On the one hand, Loos's room moods differ because domestic functions vary—entertaining, sleeping, eating, bathing, relaxing, and so on—and because people inhabit similar spaces differently, bedrooms, for instance. This requires not only appropriate furniture, utensils, and equipment but also appropriate emotional ambiance achieved by varying colors, materials and their grains, ceiling heights, floor levels, lighting, and fabrics, by sometimes substituting mirror for glass, laying carpets on the floor or not, draping windows or not, and so on. Each room is autonomous, conceived for the stationary person or persons.

On the other hand, there is the meanderer—the moving inhabitant and occasionally the visitor. Loos's rooms and furniture placement are usually symmetrical and orthogonal, to which lines of sight and movement do not always correspond. Circulation is ordinarily at the edge of a room, entry to the side near a corner, and unlike the stationary person focusing on the room itself, the ambulatory person, even when momentarily standing at its edge, sees through a succession of spaces frequently along diagonal lines, often through different levels.

To move or not to move is the question, when and where to move as well. Do I continue along the periphery into the next room—along the path, that is—or do I turn into this one? By entering, the person learns something about a fragment of the whole. Does this mean that discovering the whole is for the visitor? Unlikely. Visitors are unwelcome in the boudoir. Is discovering the whole for the resident? But isn't this a contradiction in terms? The resident already knows. That leaves not knowing the whole for the visitor and knowing it for the resident. Which is so obvious, so simple-minded, that one wonders if Loos was joking, pulling cognoscenti legs, by gratuitously transforming the self-evident into the ambiguous.

But Loos was deadly serious. The notion of *raumplan* is based on two dichotomies: distinctive, self-contained spaces versus an "harmonic invisible whole," and the stationary versus the ambulatory person. The two dichotomies that may be combined and reformulated to mean: simultaneous fragmentation and unity, difference and sameness, knowing and not knowing, change and stasis, reality and perception of it—ambiguities of modern life in which Loos participated enthusiastically. So if we assume that he understood a villa's circulatory system to be a street, the rooms it connected little buildings, and the ensemble to be a city, we might conclude that for him the villa was a representation of the urban life he saw around him, a metaphor for what observers were calling the modern condition.

Such considerations were Loos's meat and drink, for he had a great deal on his intellectual plate. In addition to being an architect, he was also a prolific journalist, a keen observer, and an insightful analyst writing, for example, about fashion, theater, shoes, automobiles, underwear, plumbing, art, printing, music, the crafts, sexuality, whatever interested him. He loved cabarets and music halls and was a denizen of café society. He adored Josephine Baker, for whom he designed a house in Paris. He was peripatetic: born in Moravia, schooled in Bohemia, Austria, and Germany at Dresden Technical Institute from 1890 to 1893, he traveled around the United States for three years after graduation, visiting New York, Philadelphia, St. Louis, and Chicago, where he was struck by Adler and Sullivan's buildings, supporting himself as a waiter, dishwasher, music critic, and corresponding journalist. He settled in Vienna to practice architecture in 1896, removed himself to Paris from 1923 to 1928, then returned to Vienna. He was a notorious womanizer: four wives and many affairs, which may or may not explain his 1933 death at age 63 from a venereal disease contracted in 1911. The extent to which he was or was not remembered fondly by Vienna's female population is unrecorded.

Loos's life pattern was that of the *raumplan* writ large: stationary, ambulatory, stay here, go there, live there, return here. He traveled constantly, including to places in which he designed: Prague, Berlin, Côte d'Azur, Alexandria, Mexico City, and Tientsin. As a cosmopolite he was restive, even within his own Vienna, prowling the city at all hours, displaying that intellectual and physical restlessness said to characterize the modern condition.

Loos knew the work of Charles Baudelaire, another journalist, among other things, whose flâneur was in some ways Loos's spiritual godfather. The flâneur is the meanderer, the stroller, the Parisian prowler, van Duzer and Kleinman's "ambulatory person." He roams the city recording what he sees, things of which he is not part. He empathizes but does not participate, at once the resident and the visitor. What he sees in Paris during the 1850s and 1860s is ambiguity, unpredictability, irony, the lack of an agreed-upon code of ethics, fleeting happiness, the unrequited search for love and community, loneliness, and above all, an anxiety exacerbated by the passing of an old social order coupled with the emergence of a physically new city. The Revolutionary Era was but a half-century removed, after all, the uprisings of 1848 barely over, and Baudelaire's Paris was at the time Georges-Eugène Haussmann's vast construction site. A century before David Riesman discovered the "lonely crowd," Baudelaire's flâneur was part of it.

Fast forward a half-century to Loos's Vienna of the 1920s and the Europe of which it was part. If anything, the pace of change had accelerated, and anxiety with it. Increasingly rapid and more modestly priced transportation, communications, and information dispersal were weakening old boundaries—of geography and of the mind. Revolutions in the arts were altering sensibilities; one need mention only James Joyce, Pablo Picasso, Igor Stravinsky, jazz, cinema, and photography. Industrial and financial capital had created huge proletarian and immensely powerful entrepreneurial classes which were at war, creating ideological and political dilemmas for burgeoning middle classes. Socialism was everywhere in the air, established on the ground in Russia, several Weimar regions and municipalities, and in Loos's own Vienna. Fascism was on the rise, Benito Mussolini already in power. A new era had come into being—call it the machine age, industrial capitalism, a new world order, or modernity. All was in flux, uncertainty ruled, values had been transformed, and the future was now. Much of this touched the United States as well, nowhere more so than in Chicago.

Frank Lloyd Wright was approaching professional maturity during the 1890s when he worked in Chicago for Adler and Sullivan before opening an office in his suburban Oak Park residence, just across the municipal border. If any city epitomized the new American economy at the time, it was the one Wright left, as its exploding commercial, industrial, transportation, and agricultural products transformation sectors stimulated phenomenal population growth. As a result Chicago was the United States hotbed of class warfare, pitting its numerous Socialist residents and exceptionally militant union movement—particularly in the building trades—against a notoriously uncompromising local plutocracy (Twombly, 1997).

So it was hardly accidental that Chicago's Haymarket Massacre of 1886 and Pullman Strike of 1894 remain to this day among the most blatant emblems of state-sponsored violence and entrepreneurial intransigence in the face of working class demands. Nor was it surprising that Chicago was the site of William Jennings Bryan's inflammatory "Cross of Gold" presidential nomination address delivered in 1896 to an angry, populist-oriented Democratic convention. Industrialization also brought with it a vast expansion of the ill-defined "middle classes"—professionals, suppliers, small to mid-size business owners, administrators, managers, and the like—of which Wright, Loos, and their clients were part.

But Frank Lloyd Wright was no Adolf Loos. As far as we know, he never contracted a venereal disease; nor did he prowl the demimonde or frequent cabarets or music halls, although in 1914 he designed one, the Midway Gardens in Chicago. Like Loos, however, he loved the cinema, expensive cars, and music, and wrote extensively, freely expounding on whatever struck his fancy, although unlike Loos his thoughts on nonarchitectural matters were often silly and uninformed. And he was a womanizer: he also married four times if we count Mamah Cheney, the love of his life, for whom he left his wife of 20 years in 1909, and with whom he lived on and off and on again until her death in 1914. Loos and Wright also shared a new architectural vision; more accurate to say, they each had a new vision for architecture, especially the villa.

Their visions were as disparate as their life experiences. Before he was 11 years old, Wright had moved from Wisconsin to Iowa, Massachusetts, Rhode Island, and back to Wisconsin, but prior to arriving in Chicago at age 20 in 1887, he never lived in what would qualify even as a mid-sized city. He spent his teen year summers on one or another maternal uncle's farm near Spring Green, Wisconsin, as part of a large, clannish, tight-knit extended family very different than his nuclear family in which an aloof, self-absorbed father distanced himself from his wife and children by retreating into his preaching and into the "popular" music he composed and performed. Always closer to his mother, Wright became even more dependent after she initiated and won divorce proceedings, a brave and scandalous undertaking for a woman in 1885. Wright moved to Chicago two years later, and after another two moved to Oak Park, installing his mother in a house next door, keeping her as close to him as possible until her death in 1923.

Wright attended college for a single year, and had no academic training in architecture or engineering. He did not travel abroad until 1905, when he was 38. Even after a decade of fame and fortune as an architect, he quit Oak Park in 1909, ultimately resettling in rural Wisconsin near his relatives; Wright brought his elderly mother with him, but none of his six children ranging in age from six to 19 (Twombly, 1979).

He returned to Wisconsin because, like his father, he had discovered that being a bourgeois parent was not his cup of tea. Instead, tucked away in his remote country retreat, he made of his assistants, other employees, his own and Cheney's children when they visited, and people who came and went, an extended family—not unlike those in which he had spent his teen year summers—with himself as the undisputed head. "Patriarchal" might be one description of his residential arrangement, but "feudal" would be better; he may have become a country gentleman, but more closely resembled a lord of the manor, especially as time passed and his student apprentices were obliged to pay tuition for the privilege of maintaining the physical plant and growing their own food. The vociferous advocate of American family life preferred not to have one, in the orthodox sense of the word, choosing instead to locate his unorthodox "family" as far from modern life, urban life, as was reasonably possible—Chicago was 160 miles away, Milwaukee 100—while still depending on urban clients. When he moved to Chicago in 1887, he carried all the trappings of a country bumpkin (Wright, 1943, pp. 53–55). But by the time he settled definitively in Spring Green in 1911, he had adopted the persona of a rural aristocrat, carefully cultivated ever after.

In their lifestyles and worldviews, urbane Loos and provincial Wright could not have been more unlike, except in one respect. During roughly the same time period, the first two decades of the twentieth century, they both reinvented the villa. Their work looked very different, but they had the same agenda: to come to grips with the social and psychological implications of living in a rapidly changing world.

A villa is a rural residence that "cannot be understood apart from the city," according to its eminent interpreter, James S. Ackerman. Although it satisfies "the perceived needs of the city dweller," including enjoyment and relaxation, at bottom those needs are "not material but psychological and ideological." Villas are historically of two types: the self-sustaining agricultural estate owned by an urban resident, and the non-agricultural retreat, the subject of this essay. The retreat, Ackerman continues, partakes of "the ideology that extols the country and scorns the city [and] is thus in part a paradoxical response to the dependence of the villa style of country life on the economic resources of the city."

When Wright announced his Prairie House in 1901, he said it was intended for "the city man going to the country." By the time he wrote that, however, the villa had long since evolved into a third type: the primary or sole residence of someone working in the city—the commuter, that is. As such, its psychological and ideological importance as a retreat resonated just as strongly—or perhaps just differently—for its inhabitants as it did for those whose villas served as "second" or "vacation" homes, because it continued to "provide a counterbalance to urban values and accommodations," as Ackerman observed of its more traditional counterparts, which is precisely what Wright and Loos knew their clients wanted (Ackerman, 1990, pp. 9–15).

For both architects, "the city man going to the country" meant predominantly male clients whose livelihoods depended upon the urban economy but who wished for whatever psychological, social, or ideological reasons to settle outside the urban center, either in leafy residential districts like Vienna's Hietzing or in more distant, even less-developed areas like Chicago's Oak Park. These clients had new money: they were professionals, small- to middle-scale manufacturers, businessmen, suppliers, in one way or another products of industrializing economies. Elsewhere I have written (Twombly, 1995) that in Western Europe and the United States, from roughly the 1890s to the 1920s, a new pool of architectural clients emerged, recently moneyed, not superrich but quite comfortable, who knew that acquiring impressive buildings would add luster to their social credentials—nothing new here, of course—but chose not to emulate plutocrats who historically preferred revival architectures, that is, the "neos"—Neoclassical, Neogothic, Neorenaissance, Neowhatever. Rather, these upper middle level, freshly minted arrivistes were drawn to architectures signaling their savviness and practicality, their progressive outlook; they chose architectures not wastefully flamboyant, showing independence of mind and judgment, and demonstrating that their owners understood the modern world in which they lived. I do no suggest that all second echelon, recently moneyed clients were of the same mind; plenty—most, in fact—emulated their betters when selecting a style in which to build. What distinguished them from purchasers of traditional architecture might best be investigated by social psychologists, not me. Nevertheless, this minority of clients was there, and Loos's and Wright's were among those who paid for what we now call "modern architecture."

Loos's villas revealed something startling going on that Le Corbusier, Mies van der Rohe, Walter Gropius, and the rest of the so-called International Style soon enough got hold of. And when they did, they followed his lead to a certain extent, more closely with exteriors than interiors. As a group, Loos's exteriors are spare, spartan, white or otherwise monochromatic cubes or assemblages of cubes, giving little indication of their richly textured, elaborately detailed, luxurious interiors. Especially at street side, windows are few, punched out of broad, severe surfaces that, like entries, have no moldings or frames. There is no ornament, unless the composition into which solids and voids coalesce qualifies as an abstract decorative field. Roofs are likely flat, street façades symmetrical. (One notable exception is the zebra-striped, asymmetrical 1928 project in Paris for Josephine Baker, who was, in keeping with her house proposal, a rather flamboyant, decidedly ostentatious cabaret performer.)

Loos said his façades were meant *not* to call attention to themselves, to be anonymous, to therefore suggest privacy and detachment, I would contend. But as might have been expected, just the opposite occurred. As with Wright's, they stood out from their neighbors like a certain sort of thumb, so radically different were they. Most people thought them rather strange. One Viennese matron crossed the street rather than pass too close to one on her daily walk. (Parenthetically: the Municipal Council of Vienna stopped construction on Loos's 1909–1911 Goldman and Salatsch commercial building because it lacked ornament, requiring him to install bronze window boxes on upper story sills where they remain. Ironically, the building is today called "*Looshuis*.")

Most people thought Wright's villas rather strange as well, although certainly not the hardheaded businessmen who commissioned them. Chicago's art docent, Harriet Monroe of *Poetry* magazine (but writing in this case for the *Chicago Examiner*) in 1907 called his work "unusual, at times even bizarre." Wright's houses looked nothing like Loos's blocklike, flat-roofed, monochromatic stacks of cubes without ornament which were a universe away from Wright's open-ended, layered, duo- or polychromed, hip-roofed rectangles or cross-axials with lots of decoration, principally in the form of art glass, large urns, and dark strips of wood trim. But for all their visual differences, they had much in common.

Take entry as an example. Both architects employed two strategies—sometimes combined—to signal a kind of disengagement with the world at large. One was to locate the principal entry at the side or in back. At Wright's 1908–1909 Robie House in Chicago, it is one or the other depending upon where one thinks the front is. Loos required arrivers at his 1912 Scheu House in Vienna to walk its length, pass through a gate, climb stairs, and then turn right to the door. Alternatively, if the main entry faced the street, it was covered and recessed, both at Wright's 1904–1907 Tomek House in Riverside, Illinois (by a shelf roof cantilevered from outsized piers acting as visual barriers) and at Loos's 1926 Moller House in Vienna (by a projecting second-story room). Both entrances appear to be set at the back of caves.

What happens next, with Wright and Loos, after getting through the door? One is likely to find oneself in a narrowish and/or lowish vestibule leading to a taller, broader reception area, sometimes up a step or two. The view from the vestibule suggests but does not fully reveal the burst of vertical and horizontal space that awaits, like a secret, when revealed after entry, and then leads to a hall, living and dining rooms, the kitchen, perhaps an office in Wright's case, or a sitting room in Loos's—but in both cases to the family's public realm.

So the entry sequences are somewhat ceremonial—initiations to the holy of holies—and somewhat similar: not so much inviting as allowing access to spaces that hint at, but do not divulge, what comes next. And as with Loos, Wright locates the public realm on the second floor, first floor European style—second level, more accurately, because Wright's is less than a full story above ground—thereby elevating residents above pedestrian and vehicular traffic. Wright provided substantially more windows than Loos, even at street side, but by tucking them deeply under far-extending eaves and partially filling them with patterned art glass, he created the sense of closed-inness that Loos achieved by simply reducing fenestration. In either case, sightlines of passersby were forced upward onto ceilings several feet inside the walls, leaving a protected zone nearer the windows where one might sit and observe the world without being seen, as if, perhaps, from a flâneurial roost.

What Loos rarely provided were the street-facing terraces that Wright again elevated and often hid behind plantings, setting the whole business in a garden. The American country boy thought that distancing one's self from urban life meant returning to bucolic ruralness—insofar as he could provide its simulacrum—whereas the Czecho-Austrian city kid saw no such need, although gardens he did provide. The difference was that a Wright villa stretched across the land, embracing it, while Loos's stood atop it resolutely, implying different attitudes toward nature, dominance as opposed to partnership, perhaps. In any event, Loos offered *faux* bunkers, not *faux* countryside; so while proposing different solutions, both architects nevertheless erected analogous physical and psychic walls around visually protected spaces for clients anxious about living in the city, especially Wright's clients.

Other similarities between their villas take us back indoors. By and large, Wright's rooms are also entered at corners with circulation along the edges, not for practical reasons alone, but also to enable people to look from one room through another room into yet another. At some of his houses, it is possible to stand on a terrace and, on a diagonal, see clearly through the house out the other end. These long sightlines took Loos's approach one step further, because one does not need to amble from room to room in a Wright residence to have a strong sense of the entire public realm. His rooms are also organized symmetrically, but orthogonally are even more insistent than Loos's. Furniture is placed accordingly: in the living room balanced left and right of, or facing, the ever-present hearth—the age-old comfort food for the psyche—set smack in the middle of a wall; while in the dining room furniture is squarely in the center, exactly positioned beneath a ceiling recess which is either painted a different color than its surrounds or is vividly articulated with wood trim or lighting. In both rooms and their connections, dropped ceilings along the periphery are like canopies over the circulation route.

These dining rooms, the most formal in Wright's houses, were unlike Loos's, which were neither more-nor-less formal than the other public spaces. Set directly below the central portion of the ceiling—so that if it were moved an inch it would compromise the room's exacting orthogonal geometry—Wright's dining table is surrounded by high-back chairs, like Charles Rennie Mackintosh's, occasionally extending above head height. At the time, elegant dining required candles or candelabra; but with Wright an overhead light box, built-in lamps at table corners, or carefully positioned wall sconces made an illuminating centerpiece unnecessary, in the same manner that table-corner plant holders sometimes replaced flower arrangements. What we have, then, is a room within a room, devoid of visual obstruction across the table, with chair backs acting as a secondary wall. This is to facilitate conversation, to focus people on each other, and to strengthen the family, because even then it was thought that the unrelenting demands of modern urban life were pulling it apart. So the evening meal became a ceremony, almost a sacrament, the one moment each weekday the family was assuredly together (see Twombly, 1975).

Wright's public rooms were reasonably autonomous, but not to the extent of Loos's, some of which had curtains but more likely doors, occasionally hidden pocket doors that could be closed or not, isolating the space or not. Wright did not provide this option, relying instead on the transitional zone between rooms to indicate spatial separation by lowering its ceiling (as part of the traffic route canopy); or inserting a lintel with an opening above; or with low dividing walls at times supporting spaced vertical slats. These devices allowed longer vistas than those of Loos's and permitted greater spatial and visual continuity between and among rooms than Loos provided. Within rooms, both Loos and Wright were amenable to subdividing spaces. Loos did it by changing floor levels, inserting columns and half-walls, to create partially screened, semiprivate areas that were part yet independent of the larger space. Wright did it with alcoves, inglenooks, and shallow wall interruptions fully open to view, therefore hardly private. I do not mean to imply that Loos's public rooms or portions thereof were meant to be sealed from each other. They could be, or the spaces could flow—albeit less freely than Wright's—but no matter how broadly they opened to each other, one constant remained: some or most of the materials and furnishings differed from room to room. With Wright, materials and furnishings and the way they were deployed were essentially the same throughout.

Here is a Loosian example not to be found in a Wright villa. Loos's 1930 Khuner House in Kreusberg, Austria, has a galleried, two-story sitting room that flows through what is perhaps a 20-foot closable opening into an adjacent dining room: free space itself, when wanted, vertically and laterally. And from the sitting room one sees it all: that the rear wall of one room is stone, of the other wood panel, with plaster walls in the gallery. Most telling is the floor's parquet pattern, identical in the sitting and dining rooms but different in the transitional area between, on the path, that is—the street—running through the house. The effect of this change in pattern is to indicate, however subtly, that the path is its own entity. Wright's peripheral, dropped-ceiling canopy is also a roadmap of sorts that, like Loos's path, is part of the room as well as the route, but noticeably more subordinate to the former than Loos's was.

Loos emphasized spatial distinctions with disparate household personalities in mind in order to ensure that mood, emotional content, and general ambiance varied appropriately from place to place. Wright had no interest in this, never spoke of or alluded to it, as far as one can tell, probably because he was less attracted by individual difference than by the "problem" of the modern family, and its alleged decomposition in face of urban demands. So in his houses the type and graining of wood, dimensions and pointing of brick, color combinations, fixtures like radiator covers and wall sconces, and floor, ceiling, wall, and art glass decorative patterns— in short, all the built-in or custom-made accessories and furnishings—hardly varied; they were virtually the same in every room. He offered, in other words, *one* mood, *one* emotional experience, a *single* ambiance: Loosian variety *versus* Wrightian holism, Loosian choice *versus* Wrightian lack of it, Loosian relativity *versus* Wrightian absolutism.

This brings us to the essential difference between Loos's and Wright's *raumplan*s. H. P. Berlage, the great Dutch architect, often said that, like the city, good design was "diversity in unity." Loos and Wright would probably have agreed, with Loos stressing the diversity and Wright stressing the unity. I think this means that Loos's diversified spatial arrangements were intended to highlight individual differences within households, and of each household from every other, whereas Wright's holistic *raumplan* downplayed individual differences within and among households but announced that, as a group, his differed from all others because his clients were exceptional people, as he almost literally wrote (Wright, 1908). No one would confuse a Wright or a Loos villa with one by another architect, so distinctive was each man's work. But just as Loos's *raumplan*s were more internally heterogeneous than Wright's, so did they vary more from one house to the next.

Similarly, if urban diversity attracted Loos, it had no appeal for Wright. If for Loos and his clients the city in some ways repelled, it was just as surely fascinating. For Wright and his clients, it was a necessary evil. So Loos gave his clients minicities, or representations thereof, while Wright gave them modernday farmhouses set in bucolic retreats. It will not do to point out that his Robie House and a handful of others are in the city proper, because once he had worked out his program for "the city man going to the country," he did not alter it for his urban commissions, not even for the few close to downtown.

If we allow a Loos villa to stand as a metaphor for civil society, its *raumplan* suggests that just as independent entities—household members—come together on family occasions but then return to their personal preoccupations, so the independent entities of a city—its residents—periodically cohere for collective events because public and private realms invariably intersect. Wright's *raumplan* suggests that independent entities—for him families, not their members—ought to be of sufficient solidity to go it alone, ignoring the collectivity, civil society at large, with which they need not inevitably intersect. His language is revealing: every family, he wrote, is "a little private club" requiring, as he put it, "shelter in the open," which is how he described his residential designs (Wright, 1938). A little private club sheltered in the open—"open" meant "away" from other houses as surely as it meant generous fenestration—suggests a private island without a bridge to the civic mainland, a place to hide, where one might establish control over, or psychic disengagement from, an unruly world. This might take place up there on his partly walled off, second-level terrace, for example, from which Frederick Robie happily reported that he could "look out and down the street to my neighbors without having them invade my privacy" (Robie, 1958, pp. 136–127). What *is* this really? Voyeurism? Flâneurism? Snobbery? Fear? And did Robie actually believe that someone seeing him on his terrace was thereby invading his privacy? One wonders how much exterior space he wanted to control. Shielded from the outside with which they were contestatory, if Robie's is any indication, Wright's villas opened up inside to strengthen family bonds, the solidity of which, or lack of it, troubled him, except when it came to his own family.

Loos's houses opened up inside, too, albeit less than Wright's, because he gave his clients options, and they also shielded residents from the external world. But they all had nearby neighbors and were close to the street, right there at the sidewalk even on large lots. Loos did not intend to remove his clients from the city but to give them safe retreats on its edges. By contrast, the occasional Wright villa within city limits was sited as far back from the street or elevated as high above it as he could manage, although he much preferred to tuck his clients away in verdant suburbs, as safely removed from the madding crowd as possible. But when he repeatedly told his later clients to select building sites ten times farther away from the city than they had thought to go, he had apparently concluded that, in truth, his early clients had not been safe enough.

There are conflicting views of modernity here. Loos's is that the world had changed irrevocably, there is no going back, so let us accommodate to it. Wright's is that the world had changed irrevocably, and while there may be no going back, perhaps we can hide somewhere. "Back in farm days," he wrote in 1954, "there was one big living room, a stove in it, and Ma was there cooking—looking after the children and talking to Pa—dogs and cats and tobacco smoke too—all gemütlich if all was orderly, but it seldom was; and the children were playing around. It created a certain atmosphere of a domestic nature which had charm and which is not, I think, a good thing to lose" (Wright, 1954, pp. 165–166). One can only imagine Loos's response to that.

As metaphors, Loos's villas accepted the city and the modernity that Wright's villas rejected. Loos's innovative architectural forms adjusted to twentieth-century changes in social formations; Wright's equally innovative forms implied that nineteenth-century formations ought still to be in place. Loos was a cultural progressive, immersed in modern life; Wright was a cultural reactionary, clinging to the past.

Alfred Loos's and Frank Lloyd Wright's quite different sets of psychological and emotional responses to modernity, as revealed to them in city life, profoundly influenced the form and substance of their residential work. Loos embraced modernity's physical and intellectual restlessness, enthusiastically participating in a broad swath of urban activities, including those of the demimonde. For him, the new was natural and normal. Wright believed modernity to be socially and psychologically destructive, precisely because of its restlessness—lack of rootedness, he might have said—rejecting the city as a place to live for himself and for his clients. For him, modernity was unnatural and abnormal.

Loos's *raumplan*, an outcome of his own observation and experience, encapsulated the innumerable options modernity offered. Wright's *raumplan*, equally based on experience and observation, offered a tightly organized retreat into an idealized memory. Although diametrically opposed, their *raumplan*s attracted strongly supportive clients, demonstrating that the personal, the psychological, and the emotional—the autobiographical, it might be said—is as fundamental a part of architectural consumption as it is of its production.

References

Ackerman, J. S. (1990), *The Villa: Form and Ideology of Country Houses*. Princeton, NJ: Princeton University Press.

Hitchcock, H.-R. & Johnson, P. (1932), *The International Style*. New York: W. W. Norton.

Robie, F. C., Jr. (1958), Mr. Robie knew what he wanted. *Architectural Forum*, 109, pp. 126–127, 206, 210.

Twombly, R. (1975), Saving the family: Middle-class attraction to Frank Lloyd Wright's Prairie Houses, 1901–1909. *American Quarterly*, 24:57–72.

—— (1979), *Frank Lloyd Wright: His Life and His Architecture*. New York: Wiley.

—— (1995), New forms, old functions: Social aspects of Prairie School design. *Museum Studies*, 21:85–90.

—— (1997), 'Cuds and Snipes': Labor at Chicago's Auditorium Building. *Journal of American Studies*, 31:79–101.

Van Duzer, L. & Kleinman, K. (1994), *Villa Müller: A Work of Adolf Loos*. Princeton, NJ: Princeton Architectural Press.
Wright, F. L. (1908), In the cause of architecture. *Architectural Record*, 23:155–222.
——— (1938). A little private club. *Life*, 5.
——— (1943), *An Autobiography*. New York: Duell, Sloan, and Pearce.
——— (1954), *The Natural House*. New York: Horizon Press.

IV
HISTORICAL AND CULTURAL APPROACHES

The Bauhaus *as a Creative Playspace*
Weimar, Dessau, Berlin, 1919–1933

PETER LOEWENBERG

> A house is said to be true that expresses the likeness of the form in the architect's mind.
> —Thomas Aquinas

> If children would continue to develop as they at first intimate, we would have many geniuses.
> —J. W. Goethe

The Problem: The Psychodynamics of a Creative Institution

The *Bauhaus* was a preeminent creative cultural institution of the modern world that decisively shaped much of twentieth-century architecture, furniture and interior design, graphics and typography, expressionist painting, and worldwide art education. Peter Gay (1976) terms the *Bauhaus* "possibly the most influential school of design since men began to teach design." The fertile space structured for the masters and the students in the *Bauhaus*, the leadership styles and struggles over policies and control, and the institutional functioning and group process between the masters (and between the masters and the students), are dimensions which may be enriched by psychodynamic understanding of this wonderful, creative group.

The *Bauhaus* aesthetics were a reaction to the concealing ornamentation of *art nouveau* and the elaborate decoration of *Jugendstil*. As *Bauhaus* founder Walter Gropius (1883–1969) wrote in 1910: "Instead of good proportions and practical simplicity, pomposity and a false romanticism have become the trend of our time" (Wingler, 1969, p. 20). *Bauhaus* principles of design symbolize modernism:

no historical allusions (such as Greek temples or Roman cornices); rejection of ornamentation; simplicity, directness and lack of concealment; function dictates form; standardization; and integrating design with the rationality and production needs of the modern machine age. All of these imperatives are invoked in the famous epigram of the *Bauhaus*'s last director, Mies van der Rohe (1886–1969): "less is more."

The *Bauhaus* was a community of teachers and students dedicated to practicing in their lives and work the unity of all the creative arts. Under Gropius the *Bauhaus* aimed at binding the arts together in a *Gesamtkunstwerk*, an all-inclusive "total work of art" as realized in the Medieval and High Baroque periods by Europe's great cathedrals, where architecture, design, engineering, craftsmanship, and fine arts coexisted as part of an integral whole. In the *Bauhaus* community, students and teachers lived, created, and partied together. They shared a common consciousness of a social responsibility. The group psychodynamic problem is how and why the *Bauhaus* and its leadership worked under the contentious, often adverse, political and economic conditions of the Weimar Republic, how it attracted eminent, world-class talent, and how it welded these together in a successful creative unit.

The Leader and His Mission

Walter Gropius was a collaborator in Peter Behren's Berlin architectural studio from June 1908 to March 1910, working on contracts for the office buildings, power stations, and turbine halls of the AEG (*Allgemeine Elektrizitätsgesellschaft*), one of Wilhelmine Germany's largest and most modern industrial corporations. In 1911, the 28-year-old Gropius, having just resigned from Behrens under a cloud, audaciously presented himself to factory owner Carl Benscheidt, who already had an architect and completed plans. The young architect's assertiveness and self-esteem was rewarded—Gropius was hired. He and his collaborator Adolf Meyer (1881–1929) made architectural history when they built the first curtain wall dissolving the two-thousand-year-old principle of massive bearing walls literally into glass at the Fagus shoe-last factory at Alfeld an der Leine. The Fagus-Werk far surpassed anything that Behrens had done and truly presaged the *Bauhaus* in its steel and reinforced concrete structure; its glass façade and transparent corners hung from a skeletal frame (see figure 1).

The first seat of the *Bauhaus* was the Grand-Ducal Saxon Academy of Art in Weimar, a small town that is Germany's eighteenth-century cultural shrine, where Goethe had been Minister and brought Schiller to the University at Jena. Gropius waged the initial political-ideological struggle for existence [*Existenzkampf*] of the *Bauhaus* against entrenched Weimar old guard right-wing political and conservative

FIGURE 1. Fagus-Werk (1911), Alfeld, Germany. Photo © 2005 by Peter Loewenberg.

artistic opposition in 1919 to 1921. As Gropius wrote, "90 percent of the incredible efforts invested by all participants in this enterprise had to be turned to defend against hostility on the local and national levels, and only 10 percent remained for the actual creative work" (Gropius, 1985, p. 14).

Although Gropius was a "modernist" among the masters, he often talked in the idioms of the medieval guilds. A student recalled,"In the Aula Gropius greeted us newcomers. He spoke of collaboration, of the feeling of belonging in the sense of the medieval craft guilds" (von Erffa, 1962, p. 31). He underscored the medieval guild identification by affecting the title "Master" (*Meister*), although to the world at large he went by "*Herr Direktor.*" Governance was participatory—the *Bauhaus* Council was made up of Masters of Form as well as Masters of Crafts and journeymen and elected student representatives who voted on the school's constitution and on selections and expulsions. The Council of Masters debated the pros and cons of major issues, such as the title issue, whether the faculty should be called "Master" or "Professor" (Wingler, 1969, pp. 54–56), or on the pedagogic and ideological conflicts concerning art and design education.

Gropius's emotional style was paternal, with both gracious generosity and institutional discipline evident. Times were hard in Germany in the early 1920s and many of the students were very poor. Gropius organized free midday meals and gifts of clothing. Said one student, "It was wonderful if you earned a Mark for a night's work as an extra at the theatre" (Droste, 1993, p. 38). Gropius insisted the students take work discipline seriously. When groups of students left the *Bauhaus* to go wandering in Italy, Gropius put up an announcement that those who absented themselves in midsemester should regard themselves as having been dismissed from the school (von Erffa, 1962, p. 413).

Political, Economic, and Social Setting

The history of the *Bauhaus* is inseparable from the political, economic, and social life and crises of the Weimar Republic, 1919–1933. Germany had lost a war and an empire. In 1923, the hyperinflation destroyed the middle class. The political support for the *Bauhaus* came from the center-left political coalitions of the early Weimar Republic. The fortunes of the *Bauhaus* responded to the reality of Weimar politics throughout its brief existence—its dates and migrations reflect the turbulent political years of the Weimar Republic.

From its inception, the budgets, policies, and style of the *Bauhaus* were controversial. Its creation was temporally, politically, and in spirit syncretic with the hopes and promise of the new democratic, socialist, and modern republic after the war. The *Bauhaus* was attacked on moral and social as well as aesthetic grounds. One Weimar newspaper wrote:

> There is no need to list the occasions on which *Bauhaus* people of both sexes have rolled around naked somewhere in the open air. . . . There is no need to associate oneself with the complaints arising from cases in which such unusually unrestrained fraternization between young people of both sexes has ultimately led, in the case of the females, to motherhood. But I must condemn all this as a result of an entirely irresponsible attitude and especially as a consequence of the damaging educational methods of the *Bauhaus* if, as has actually happened, such pregnancies are publically celebrated with all sorts of noise, and if, for example, a cradle is constructed in the *Bauhaus* Workshops for the resulting infant and then carried in triumph to the flat of the girl concerned [Whitford, 1992, p. 122].

The very existence of the *Bauhaus* depended on party politics in a polity where the Right was both anti-modern and anti-republican. It was virtually inevitable that every aesthetic and design issue was politicized in Germany in the 1920s. Modernity, standardization, mass production, functionalism, were of the Left. So also were the political convictions of most of the masters and students. In the end, the *Bauhaus* was inseparably tied to the fate of the short-lived Republic. Being wedded to the political fortunes of the Weimar Republic meant that the *Bauhaus* would also fall with the Republic. It was both the creature of, and the victim of, Weimar politics.

Creative Playspace

The social group process and creative play states,[1] particularly the frequent *Bauhaus* festivals (*Feste*), are especially significant because the psychoanalytic object relational understanding of creativity stresses the playful component of the creative process. Said Gropius, "the spirit was simply excellent, and some of the informal activities, like our celebrations—the *Feste*—when someone would set a theme, like 'black and white,' or 'square,' were splendid occasions" (Gay, 1976, p. 126). The *Feste* constituted a structured creative transitional space, a playspace, which complemented the play of design in the drafting studios and workshops. In the original 1919 *Bauhaus* Manifesto, Gropius wrote: "Theater, lectures, poetry, music, costume balls. Creation of festive ceremonies in these gatherings" (figure 2).

Gropius created four main festivals in the course of the year: the lantern party on his birthday, May 18, in which students made original lanterns; summer solstice; a kite festival in the fall, in which the students went out to the fields to fly their unique self-constructed kites; and the Christmas party. A White Festival and a Metallic Festival were added later. Some of the postcard invitations to these parties were executed as lithographs in the graphic print workshop with pupils and masters equally involved in their production. Paul Klee did the postcard for the Lantern Festival in 1921; Oskar Schlemmer created the one for 1922. Lothar Schreyer (1966), a graphic artist who directed the stage workshop, recalls:

> We had wonderful parties both large and small at the *Bauhaus*. Whenever a particularly fine piece of work was completed it was celebrated by the Workshop concerned. When [the student] Ida Kerkovius finished her first large rug we had a party in my small flat under the roof of the old house. . . . We surrounded it with burning candles and squatted around it on the floor chatting happily. . . . We also spent happy hours whenever Paul Klee, whom everyone loved, announced a musical evening in the hall and played Mozart for us on his violin. . . . The big celebrations—the Lantern Festival and the Kite Festival—are unforgettable. The

---

[1] Albert J. Solnit defines a "play state" as "play [that] not only involves physical activity and pretending, it also has a symbolizing capacity and usually has the characteristics of a synthesizing exercise or practicing to adapt or to resolve conflicts in an exploratory, make-believe manner. . . . Functionally, the play is exploring, trying out, and pretending another approach than that which would be realistically consequential. . . . Play allows thinking and acting (or behaving) to flow into each other with a looser connection, developmentally and experientially, than non-play thinking and acting usually permit" (Solnit, 1987, pp. 211, 214, and 218).

Workshops toiled for weeks simply preparing for these festivals. No effort was spared in turning the most fantastic shapes into functional lanterns. When the really warm summer nights arrived and the glow worms glowed in the bushes in the old Goethe Park we walked in a long crocodile through the park, up around the hill and through the town, a host of lanterns in the darkness, sometimes singing, sometimes keeping silent, but completely filled with the beauty of our lights in the beautiful night. One sunny autumn day on a small hill above Weimar we let the kites fly up, true works of art, fragile and large, birds, fishes, abstract shapes, trembling on their long strings, almost disappearing in the blue of the sky [pp. 120–121].

Gunta Stoelzl describes one of the Christmas parties:

Christmas was indescribably beautiful, something quite new, a "Festival of Love" in every detail. A beautiful tree, lights and apples, a long white table, big candles, beautifully laid, a big fir wreath, everything green. Under the tree everything white, on it countless presents. Gropius read the Christmas story, Emmy Heim sang. We were all given presents by Gropius, so kind and lovely and special to every *Bauhäusler*. Then a big meal. All in a spirit of celebration and a sense of the symbolism. Gropius served everyone their food in person. Like the washing of the feet [Droste, 1993, p. 38].

Another student recalled, "Soon the public lectures and musical evenings began; Erdmann played for us. It was the age of Expressionism. Theodor Däubler thundered his poems at us. Mrs. Lasker-Schüler held us spellbound with her staccato verses. A scholar read us Gilgamesh. The room was lit by a single candle which died away during the slow recitation of the death lament" (von Erffa, 1962, p. 413).

Johan Huizinga, who first advanced the ludic concept of culture, maintained that "civilization is, in its earliest phases, played. It does not come from play like a babe detaching itself from the womb: it arises in and as play, and never leaves it" (Huizinga, 1944, p. 173). He also noted the integral relationship between play and festivals:

Banquets, junketings and all kinds of wanton revels are going on all the time the feast lasts . . . the relationship between feast and play is very close. Both proclaim a standstill to ordinary life. In both mirth and joy dominate, though not necessarily—for the feast too can be serious; both are limited as to time and place; both combine strict rules with genuine freedom. In short, feast and play have their main characteristics in common [Huizinga, 1944, pp. 21–22].

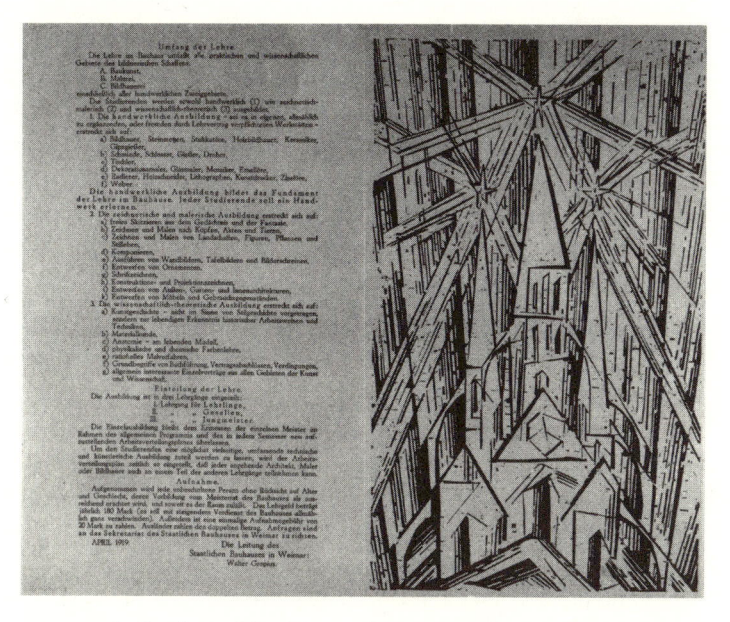

FIGURE 2. *Bauhaus* Manifesto with cathedral woodcut by Lionel Feininger. © Artist's Rights Society (ARS), New York / VG Bild-Kunst, Bonn. Courtesy of the Estate of Lionel Feininger and the Los Angeles County Museum of Art.

One plays within boundaries that define the players from "outsiders" who do not share the mystique and knowledge of play. Erik Erikson (1963) observed that

> the playing adult steps sideward into another reality. . . . I propose the theory that the child's play is the infantile form of the human ability to deal with experience by creating model situations and to master reality by experiment and planning. It is in certain phases of his work that the adult projects past experience into dimensions which seem manageable. In the laboratory, on the stage, and on the drawing board, he relives the past and thus relieves leftover affects; in reconstructing the model situation, he redeems his failures and strengthens his hopes. He anticipates the future from the point of view of a corrected and shared past [p. 222].

In the *Bauhaus* the masters and students could allow the most intimate of their preconscious and unconscious processes to be realized in an intermediate area of experience which D. W. Winnicott (1971) defined as the sphere of the transitional space: "This intermediate area of experience, unchallenged in respect of its belonging to inner or external [shared] reality, constitutes the greater part of the infant's experience, and throughout life is retained in the intense experiencing that belongs to the arts and to religion and to imaginative living, and to creative scientific work" (p. 14). The original space of symbolization, the initial creative space, is the transitional play space between mother and child. This is a space that we carry the rest of our lives and which becomes the model for all later spontaneous creative activity. Transitional space is the beginning of the capacity for symbol formation and representational thought. It is a me-extension, occupying an in-between space between inner and external reality. This is the place of play and of the first phase of cultural, artistic, architectural and planning creativity (see Winnicott, 1971).

Internal Ideological and Personal Conflict, 1921–1923

The fundamental ideological and educational policy struggle of the early years between Johannes Itten (1888–1967) and Gropius concerned the practical-modern versus the aesthetic-individual orientation of the school. Itten, a great art educator who hated commercialism and industrialism, advocated a spiritual cultivation of subjective artistic sensibility; Gropius fostered rationality, standardization, mass production, and contracts with industry. Gropius said that "the *Bauhaus* in its present form will stand or fall depending on whether it accepts or rejects the necessity of commissions" (Droste, 1993, p. 46). He wrote about the role architects could play in shaping a corporate public image. He believed in engaging with the needs of industry, in seeking outside commissions for work, in incorporating the technologies of commerce and mass production. He made it a policy to consistently meet with manufacturers and industrialists and to seek new contracts for the *Bauhaus* and its students.

Itten met Gropius in the spring of 1919 at a weekend invitation to the Semmering by Gropius's wife, Alma Mahler, and he was recruited to the *Bauhaus* upon her recommendation. He sought to cultivate artistic perceptivity and to create a new spiritual person. He organized the basic course (*Vorkurs*), which was the six-month trial course for new students and the only obligatory course in the school. Itten was an adherent of Mazdaznan, an ascetic Indian cult, and wore their smock which came to be known as the *Bauhaustracht*. He practiced a bio-vegetarian diet and fostered its introduction in the *Bauhaus* canteen. He applied his ideas of the awakening and harmonious development of the creative individual in the *Bauhaus*.

Johannes Itten's motto was "play becomes party—party becomes work—work becomes play." His ideas on creativity in education were to let the child fantasize and project these fantasies in art and artifacts without confronting him or her with the criteria of "correctness" or the measure of concordance with reality.

He was acutely aware that criticism is potentially humiliating and corrodes self confidence:

> A carelessly posed question: "What is that?" will be quickly answered, but in most cases the question breaks the flow of intuition. The child "wakes up" and the creative state is spoiled. . . . Therefore the works of the child, which he or she made with great interest—and only such have value—should not be criticized. The educator must allow mistakes to be corrected by subsequent cleverly chosen themes developed by the child himself, that is to say through his or her own efforts. Corrections and criticism are humiliating, constricting, for everyone, like frost in the summer—devastating [Rotzler, 1972, p. 263].

Itten's ideas are in concord with Winnicott's emphasis on bringing the "inner me" to outward expression in creativity, as when Itten said:

> Every morning for a week the students sat before a pot with a fern for a half an hour of studies drawing it. At the end of the week the students had to draw the fern from memory. The fern was drawn freehand for twenty minutes. This exercise demonstrates that the ideas of form [*Formvorstellungen*] must be clearly developed so that the inner sensation may objectively respond outwardly [Rotzler, 1972, p. 274].

Itten believed in the creative role of the unconscious in working out solutions after the cognitive work has been done:

> It could be that one wrestles for months and years with a theme and suddenly, overnight the brain finds the final connections in the unconscious—unexpectedly! . . . We see here one of the most important educational problems: the student must learn to see all sides of a problem and to precisely program it through logical thinking. And he must be able to wait until the unconscious can find the right solution [Rotzler, 1972, p. 282].

The wife of Oskar Schlemmer, the Master of the *Bauhaus* mural, wood, and sculpting workshops, and later of the dance and the experimental theater workshop, recounts Schlemmer's pain at the internecine fighting:

> A conflict of spirits, open or hidden as perhaps in no other place, a constant disquiet, which daily forced each individual to take a basic position toward deep fundamental questions. . . . One felt as on volcanic terrain, and one had to be

extremely careful not to be torn back and forth by all that stormed in on us. . . . There were the sharpest clashes—but they were always carried by a sense of responsibility toward the whole [Neumann, 1985, pp. 224–227].

Schlemmer described the situation as "a crisis" which "divides the *Bauhaus* into two camps, which also includes the masters" (Schlemmer, 1958, p. 120). He wrote at the time of his tension between the two positions:

This dualism seems to me to be very primary in today's Germany. On the one side, an invasion of Eastern culture, Indian cults, also the return to nature of the *Wandervogel* movement and more, housing estates, vegetarianism, Tolstoyism, reaction to the war—on the other side Americanism, progress, the miracles of technology and discovery, the metropolis. Gropius and Itten are the almost typical representatives and I must say, I again find myself happily-unhappily in the middle. I affirm both or wish for the interpenetration of the one by the other. Or, are progress and [expansion] and self-realization [deepening] really two different directions that are not simultaneously possible and practically exclude each other? [p. 121].

Schlemmer noted that Gropius was an outstanding diplomat, businessman, and pragmatist. He maintained his large private architectural practice in the *Bauhaus* and he passed contracts on to students to help them get started in their practices. Said Schlemmer (1958):

Not the best conditions for *Bauhaus* work. Itten is right if he attacks this and wishes the students to be secure in the tranquillity of labor. . . . Gropius wants the able and competent person who is seasoned by friction with reality and practice. Itten wants talent which is formed in calmness, Gropius wants character formed in the stream of life [and the talent that is required] [p. 121].

The conflict was resolved when Gropius commissioned the *Bauhaus* joinery workshop to build the seating for the Jena Municipal Theater (*Stadttheater*) for which he and Adolf Meyer had the commission to do the renovations. Itten, who refused commissions on principle, gave notice and left the *Bauhaus* in April 1923, going to Herrliberg near Zürich, the center of the Mazdaznan sect, where he taught and led workshops. His explanation 40 years later was, "A picture analysis lesson in 1923 gave Gropius occasion to say that he could no longer justify my instruction to the government. I decided spontaneously to leave the *Bauhaus* without any further discussion" (Wick, 1988, p. 9). The conclusion was that Gropius prevailed. Itten left to be replaced by Laszlo Moholy-Nagy, and the needs of industry were integrated in *Bauhaus* design.

Defeat and Expulsion from Weimar, 1924–1925

Following the victory of the political Right in the Thuringian state elections of February 10, 1924, the *Bauhaus* masters' contracts were terminated and the budget was slashed 50 percent. This was a crisis of threatened annihilation—the *Bauhaus* had to find a new home or die.

Now Gropius acted as a skilled political and media figure who mobilized public support and pressure on the government—and who planned fall-back positions for institutional survival. His first response was that privatization as an educational corporation (GmbH) was the solution. A group of investors, including the German General Trades Union Congress (*Allgemeine Deutsche Gewerkschaftsbund*), underwrote 121,000 marks of contributions, loans, and credits. Letters of protest to the Thuringian government were sent by, among others, Lovis Corinth, Hugo von Hofmannsthal, Max Reinhardt, and Hans Thoma (Bayer, Gropius, and Gropius, 1995, p. 95). A group of internationally prominent "Friends of the *Bauhaus*" was founded including Peter Behrens, Marc Chagall, Albert Einstein, Gerhart Hauptmann, Oskar Kokoschka, Arnold Schoenberg, Franz Werfel, and many others.

Dessau, seat of the House of Anhalt with its Renaissance castle, was an industrial center, home of the Junker aircraft factory, as well as chemical, machine, railway, sugar, and chocolate manufacture. The energetic Lord-Mayor, Dr. Fritz Hesse, a member of the Democratic Party, worked to bring the *Bauhaus* to Dessau and continued to be a strong supporter. Hesse led the Democratic/Social Democratic coalition in the municipal government, which voted to invite the *Bauhaus* to Dessau, prevailing over the parties of the Right by 26 to 15 in a vote on March 24, 1925 (Wingler, 1969, p. 103). He negotiated with Feininger, Klee, and Muche during February and March 1925 while Gropius was on holiday in Italy. When he heard, Gropius cabled: "Dessau impossible." Kurt Schwitters wrote to the van Doesburgs: "Dessau is the only German province [sic!] that has Socialist rule. It is therefore a Party matter that the *Bauhaus* has been taken up there" (Whitford, 1984, p. 154). Feininger grandly idealized the financial security of the new home: "They want us and need us, they plead with us. . . . We have an open checkbook there (*ein voller Kredit dort*) and none of Weimar's musty tradition" (Hochman, 1997, p. 184). The Masters, seeking a peaceful setting, negotiated the wrenching move to the industrial city of Dessau in Saxon-Anhalt where the *Bauhaus* remained until 1932.

Virtually all of the early masters went to Dessau in the relocation, including Feininger, Gropius, Kandinsky, Klee, Moholy-Nagy, Muche, and Schlemmer. Only Gerhard Marcks, who was opposed to the school's new industrial orientation, accepted an outside call to the Kunstgewerbeschule in Halle/Saale. The ceramic

FIGURE 3: *Bauhaus*, Dessau, 1925–1933. Glass and steel curtain wall. Designed by Walter Gropius as an integrated design school with workshops, faculty offices, student residence and living space, cafeteria, theater, and canteen. Photo © 2005 by Peter Loewenberg.

workshop, which Marcks led, was not moved to Dessau. Almost all the students relocated from Weimar to Dessau where their work immediately continued in temporary quarters. Six former students were made teachers and became members of the Master's Council (*Meisterrat*): Josef Albers, Herbert Bayer, Marcel Breuer, Hinnerk Scheper, Joost Schmidt, and Gunta Sharon-Stölzl. In Dessau the *Bauhaus* would develop in relative peace for the next half-decade.

The city agreed to finance a new building for the school to be designed by Gropius. He wished to build a showpiece and working exemplar of his concept that "to build is to shape the patterns of life" (Droste, 1993, p. 121). He designed a three-winged building: a workshop wing with a stunning glass façade held the studios, classrooms, and exhibition space; an arts and crafts wing including an auditorium, theater, foyer, and canteen which could be opened up to create a "festival level"; and a six-story student wing with 28 live-in studios, baths, laundry, a gymnasium, and a cafeteria. A three-floor bridge over a street with an administrative section, including faculty offices and Gropius's private atelier, connected the wings. Thus, the various functions were differentiated to parts of the building and then brought back into harmony as an interrelated, secure whole: a bounded "container" for work, living, eating, parties, recreation, sports, and theater functions integrated

FIGURE 4 (top). Preller Wing: student residences with a balcony to every room.
FIGURE 5 (bottom). Houses for the *Bauhaus* Masters (Kandinsky, Klee, Moholy-Nagy, Schlemmer, Scheper, Muche, and Gropius), Dessau, 1925. Photos © 2005 by Peter Loewenberg.

under one roof, in what came to be one of the most influential buildings of the twentieth century (figures 3 and 4).

Writing of the *Bauhaus* campus in 1927, Rudolf Arnheim noted that

> it is a triumph of purity, clarity, and generosity. Looking in through the large windows, you can see people hard at work or relaxing in private. Every object displays its construction, no screw is concealed, no decorative chasing hides the raw material being worked. It is very tempting to see this architectural honesty as moral, too [Droste, 1993, p. 122].

When Gropius designed the new *Bauhaus* in Dessau, he had the background of cathedrals and palaces, the great public buildings of European culture, in mind. Against this tradition he wished to postulate a conscious contrast:

> The typical building of the Renaissance, the Baroque, has a symmetrical façade which is approached by a path to the central axis. The picture offered to the approaching viewer is flat and two dimensional. A building erected in the contemporary spirit departs from the representative appearance of the symmetrical façade. One must go all around this building to see its physical contours and to grasp its function and structure [Bayer et al., 1955, p. 100].

The city of Dessau also authorized the construction of seven residences, including a detached home for Gropius and three semidetached houses for the *Bauhaus* masters (figure 5). Klee and Kandinsky shared one house, Muche and Schlemmer a second, and Feininger and Moholy-Nagy the third. Kandinsky said, "Only a fireproof wall divides the house, but we can visit each other in spite of that without going outside, by a short walk through the cellar" (Geelhaar, 1973, p. 19). These model residences had open and flexible living/dining areas, indirect ceiling lighting, and built-in book shelves, ironing boards, irons, and even a built-in sewing cupboard. Since the walls were not bearing walls, they could contain convenient built-in cupboards for dishes and utensils between the dining and dishwashing areas as well as pass-through openings from the eating areas to the kitchen. The kitchen had a dish rack for drying directly above the sink so that clean dishes could dry on the spot rather than have to be wiped and carried elsewhere to be put away.

The final phases of *Bauhaus* history were a turn to the Left followed by a turn to the Right. Hannes Meyer led the turn to the Left in 1928 to 1930, initiating a functional-collectivist-socialist phase of cooperative utilitarian ideals. The *Bauhaus* became a school of architecture committed to social solutions rather than personal experiments. Moholy-Nagy, Breuer, and Beyer resigned; Ludwig Hilbersheimer was appointed to teach mass housing and city planning. Oskar Schlemmer resigned in 1929. Meyer was terminated for being a Marxist and politicizing the *Bauhaus*. Meyer then led a left-radical "Red Brigade" to Moscow where he was Director of the WASI Architectural College, leaving in 1936. Between 1939 and 1949 he worked as an architect and town planner in Mexico. Mies van der Rohe led a turn to the Right in 1930 to 1933. While Gropius was dedicated to teamwork at the *Bauhaus,* Mies was autocratic. When Gropius praised the virtues of collaboration in the creation of a building, Mies asked, "But Gropius, if you decide to have a baby, do you call in the neighbors?" (Schulze, 1985, p. 338). Mies depreciated Gropius as an architect as when he said that "the best thing Gropius has done was to invent the name *Bauhaus*" (Schulze, 1985, p. 177).

When Leftist students held noisy mass meetings in the cafeteria, Mies called in the police and threw them out. The students were officially expelled. Readmission depended on painstaking personal interviews with him, intended to flush the radicals out. Approximately 180 of the 200 students returned to the *Bauhaus* (Schulze, 1985, p. 175). When the Dessau *Bauhaus* was closed on October 1, 1932, Mies reopened the school in an abandoned telephone factory in Berlin-Steglitz on October 25. He attempted to accommodate to National Socialism by being "nonpolitical." His effort at ingratiation failed, ending in closure of the *Bauhaus* by the Gestapo on April 11, 1933, with the dispersal of its teachers, students, and heritage. Mies signed a public proclamation endorsing Adolf Hitler, published in *Völkischer Beobachter*, August 18, 1934: "We believe in this *Führer* who has fulfilled our passionate wish for harmony. We trust his work which fosters sacrifice . . . we set our hope on this man." Most of the masters went into exile in the five years after the *Bauhaus* closure: Gropius to Harvard; Mies to Chicago; Lyonel Feininger to New York; Lazlo Moholy-Nagy to Chicago; Josef and Anni Albers to Black Mountain College; Paul Klee to Bern; Wassily Kandinsky to Paris; Marcel Breuer to London and New York.

Cultural History and the Psychoanalysis of Group Creativity

The essential precondition of creativity is the protection of an intermediate area of experience between the inner life and the external shared reality. The *Bauhaus* provided such a secure place for its masters and students, where the realization of their fantasies was nurtured and inspired by interdisciplinary exchanges, and where taking "inside-me" ideas and making them "not-me" was encouraged. The institution of the *Bauhaus* protected creative fantasy from immediate repression through inner inhibition and suppression by outer criticism. The intense group process of creative interaction in the *Bauhaus* was one of personal and functional interpenetration. Boundaries between individuals, between masters and students, were partially dissolved in significant ways, in an ongoing group process of regressive fusion and creativity (Bion, 1959, pp. 152–153). The institutional limits set by Gropius and Mies, such as insistence on attendance and performance, were an important antidote to institutional dissolution and disintegration. The personal boundary in many important aspects came to be the group of innovators itself, which stood in creative competition to the cultural message, style, methods, and content of the tradition-oriented outside world, but was enthusiastically received by *avant garde* modernists.

This regressive group phenomenon was exciting and exhilarating. It provided intense emotional closeness coupled with aesthetic and cultural cross-fertilization and stimulation. The *Bauhäusler*, both masters and students, were still attached to their *Bauhaus* experience and mourned it decades after it was over (see Neumann, 1985). In the *Bauhaus*, transferences were enacted and competitive rivalries and jealousies were accentuated—as in the struggles for dominance and control between Gropius and Itten, and in the envious depreciation of Gropius by Mies.

The term *Spielraum*, playspace, has meanings related to flexible and receptive attitudes toward ideas and concepts, things and people, fantasies and objects. It refers to the idea of "play" in instruments and mechanics, as in "the play of the wheel." In both literal and figurative terms it represents an ability to come close, handle, touch, feel, and "play with" new, different, strange, unusual, unexpected, unsanctioned, and forbidden concepts and objects (Dorn, 1974, p. 108). Our ability to create depends upon our capacity to "play," which Hutter (1982) defines as "to experiment with and interact with an object outside of the self and to use this interaction to expand the boundaries of the ego and of the cultural space which each of us creates and inhabits" (p. 314).

The *Bauhaus* was a holding environment in Winnicott's sense of being a secure space in which the artists and craftsmen could be playful and safely try out ideas. All works are created with some fantasied recipient in mind. For architects, designers, and artists it is the community of their peers and colleagues and the commercial world of patrons and clients who confer external validation. The point where a new idea is launched, when the manuscript is given over to its first reader, when the artist shows his painting or sculpture for the first time, is absolutely critical because until that moment the creation was still a part of the self. Now, it has become a transitional object in a transitional space. The idea, text, or creation stands between the observer and the creator's self. It is a self-extension that is transitioned from the inner world of nothing-but-me into a world of people and objects outside of omnipotent control. The use of this space happens only when there is a feeling of confidence in the relationship that the fragile new parts of the self will be sheltered. As Winnicott (1971) put it: "We experience life in the area of transitional phenomena, in the exciting interweave of subjectivity and objective observation, and in an area that is intermediate between the inner reality of the individual and the shared reality of the world that is external to individuals" (p. 64).

The *Bauhaus* was a cultural playspace that was safe: a good holding environment for the first finding, leaking, spilling, and reflection of pedagogical methods and radical design ideas that the *Bauhaus* as playspace permitted. In the group "playspace" of the *Bauhaus*, we see the interplay between separateness and union, between regressive fusion among masters and students. This was, to paraphrase Ernst Kris (1952), a regression in the service of creativity. The creativity occurred in the institutional space where the individuals could comfortably allow themselves the freedom to regress to sharing their nascent work, projects, sketches, and their regressive fantasies, play, and behavior. This space served both individual growth and group creativity in their mutual enterprise of furthering the *Bauhaus* "idea" of clarity, regularity, and simplicity in design; functionalism in building; and community in creativity.

References

Bayer, H., Gropius, W. & Gropius, I. (1955), *Bauhaus: 1919–1928*. Stuttgart: Verlag Gerd Hatje.

Bion, W. R. (1959), *Experiences in Groups and Other Papers*. New York: Basic Books.

Dorn, R. M. (1974), The geography of play, child analysis, and the psychoanalysis of the adult. *Internat. J. Psychoanal. Psychother.*, 3(1):90–115.

Droste, M. (1993), *Bauhaus 1919–1933*. Cologne: Benedickt Taschen Verlag.

Erikson, E. (1963), *Childhood and Society*. 2nd ed. New York: Norton.

Gay, P. (1976), *Art and Act: On Causes in History—Manet, Gropius, Mondrian*. New York: Harper & Row.

Geelhaar, C. (1973), *Paul Klee and the Bauhaus*. New York: Graphic Society.

Gropius, W. (1985), Die Bauhaus-Idee-Kampf um neue Erziehungsgrundlagen. In: Eckhard Neumann, ed., *Bauhaus und Bauhäusler Erinnerungen und Bekenntnisse*. Cologne: DuMont Buchverlag, pp. 12–18.

Hochman, E. (1997), *Bauhaus: Crucible for Modernism*. New York: Fromm International.

Huizinga, J. (1944), *Homo Ludens: A Study of the Play-Element in Culture*. Boston: Beacon Press, 1950.

Hutter, A. (1982), Poetry in psychoanalysis: Hopkins, Rossetti, Winnicott. *Internat. Rev. of*

Psycho-Anal., 9:303–316.

Kris, E. (1952), *Psychoanalytic Explorations in Art*. New York: International Universities Press.

Neumann, E., ed. (1985), *Bauhaus und Bauhäusler: Erinnerungen und Bekenntnisse*. Cologne: DuMont.

Rotzler, W., ed. (1972), *Johannes Itten: Werke und Schriften*. Zürich: Orell Füssli Verlag.

Schlemmer, T., ed. (1958), *Oskar Schlemmer, Briefe und Tagebuecher*. Munich: Albert Langen–Georg Mueller.

Schreyer, L. (1966), Memories of *Der Sturm* and the Bauhaus. In: F. Whitford, *The Bauhaus: Masters and Students by Themselves*. London: Conran Octopus, 1992.

Schulze, F. (1985), *Mies van der Rohe: A Critical Biography*. Chicago: University of Chicago Press.

Solnit, A. J. (1987), A psychoanalytic view of play. *Psychoanal. Study Child*, 42:205–219.

von Erffa, H. (1962), Das frühe Bauhaus: Jahre der Entwicklung 1919–1923. In: *Wallraf-Richartz-Jahrbuch: Westdeutsches Jahrbuch fuer Kunstgeschichte*, 24:413–414. Cologne: Verlag M. Dumont Schauberg.

Wick, R., ed. (1988), *Johannes Itten: Bildanalysen*. Ravensburg: Otto Maier.

Wingler, H. M. (1969), *The Bauhaus: Weimar, Dessau, Berlin, Chicago*. Cambridge, MA: MIT Press, 1969.

Whitford, F. (1984), *Bauhaus*. Thames & Hudson, 1984.

Whitford, F., ed. (1992), *The Bauhaus: Masters and Students by Themselves*. London: Conran Octopus.

Winnicott, D. W. (1971), *Playing and Reality*. London: Tavistock, 1974.

The Designer in Architectural Practice

ROBERT GUTMAN

Ever since my book on practice was published 16 years ago, I have spent some of my time away from the university consulting to architectural firms. Although most architectural firms make considerable use of consultants these days, mostly to advise them on technical problems of building, my own work focuses on management issues: for example, improved ways of organizing the office, how to formulate strategic plans for getting more work, what might be done to better the quality of their product, and whether or not to add certain specialties, such as interior design. I am fortunate that I am able to concentrate on the issues I like best, which is to help small design firms, often called "boutiques," to increase the number of jobs they get, or to help firms which are successful commercially to improve the quality of their design.

In dealing with the problems designers face as practitioners, I find that I understand them best and can be most helpful to them by making use of the ideas borrowed from the psychoanalytic tradition that address the subject of the creative individual. The creative process is a subject that psychoanalysts have attended to beginning with Freud, who made a variety of studies of artists, including Leonardo and Michelangelo, and who treated several patients who were artists.

The question I would like to focus on in this paper is this: what difficulties do the psychodynamics of creativity as they are exhibited in the personality of designers

---

A version of this paper was read to Architecture Students and Faculty at Washington University, St. Louis on November 15, 2004. I want to thank Dr. Larry Hirschhorn of the Center for Applied Research for his invaluable counsel in thinking through the ideas developed in this paper. This paper, or any part of it, may not be duplicated or reproduced without the permission of the author.

foster in an enterprise, such as an architectural firm, that deploys a building design as a commercial asset?

For most jobs, this is what a firm sells, and the quality of their design, judged from many points of view, distinguishes the better firms from the poorer ones. How do the characteristics of the creative process influence how design architects in a firm deal with colleagues and, in turn, how do colleagues with other roles and specialties deal with them? How do designers cope with criticisms of their work coming from inside the firm? And in what way does the designer's relation to her colleagues influence their methods for dealing with clients?

The organization of the paper is as follows. First, I will make some general comments about the salient role of the designer in architectural practice. Then I will turn to the subject of the psychological processes involved in creativity. Third, I will discuss the way in which the psychodynamics of creativity affect life within firms. Fourth, I will examine what firms often do, or can do, to resolve the tensions that emerge between designers and other types of professionals. Finally, I will conclude with a few general remarks about the role of creative individuals in modern organizational life.

Architectural firms in the United States today vary in size from one or two persons to 1,800, which is the number of persons employed by HOK (Helmuth, Obata, and Kassabaum), now the largest architectural firm in the world.[1] HOK was started in St. Louis and still has its world headquarters there.

Although the importance of the design architect (as distinguished from the architect who deals with construction or makes sure the building will function well) obviously has a well-established lineage in the profession, it has acquired a new prominence in the past 30 years. This prominence results partly from the tremendous growth of popular and client interest in visual culture and art generally, but it is also enhanced by new, sturdier, flexible building materials and advances in building technology that make it possible to construct seemingly bizarre or puzzling, but very intriguing, building forms. These developments, especially the new public interest and attention to design, reinforce the narcissism and pride of design architects in what they do.

As is the case with other prima donnas, the attitude within the profession toward the design architect is characterized by a good deal of ambivalence. He or she is the cock of the walk, the heroic figure, the individual on whose identity the public seizes; and for these reasons, the design architect often infuriates his or her more pragmatic colleagues, who correctly argue that without their services

---

[1] Of course, included among the 1,800 are many employees who are not trained as architects, and they are distributed among HOK's many offices around the world.

buildings would not get built and would not hold up. As with other artists, the design architect often has mixed feelings about himself, too. He recognizes the fragility of his achievement, how the resolution of the design problem may have been won through some intense battle with his inner self, and the ease with which the public's admiration fades quickly.

This happens especially in this era where the audience for artistic production appears to be continually searching for something new and different. The trend is perhaps more apparent in painting and graphics than it is in architecture, because not all buildings are conceived with public attention and popularity as a primary focus of concern. But this concern is particularly true whenever the success of a building is measured in terms of its attraction to a mass audience, or to potential donors. Colleges and universities are prime targets in this respect, as are museums.

The Psychodynamics of Creativity

Within the psychoanalytic tradition, no group of analysts has paid as much attention to the creative process as has Melanie Klein and her colleagues in the British School of psychoanalysis.[2] This school is often regarded as the prime innovator in psychoanalytic thought in the 1920s and much of the 1930s. It was also the tradition that generated, through the agency of the Tavistock Institute in London, the most active application of psychoanalytic ideas to the study of social institutions.[3] This makes the Kleinian tradition especially useful to me because my principal interest is to understand more about practice. In this context, I want to examine the behavior of designers in the setting of an architectural firm.

Klein's thrust, and that of her followers, has been to emphasize how artistic work helps the artist to repair her inner world. Most artists, Klein believed, are people who are riven by internal psychological conflicts. In some cases these conflicts are founded on infant and childhood experiences; in other cases, the Kleinians argued, they arise from the intrinsic complexity of artistic work. But whatever the source, Klein believed that the artistic object—the painting, the sculpture, the play, the novel, the poem, the building design—can resolve the conflict by enabling the

---

[2] Klein's best-known paper on the relation between artistic production and the development of the self is "Infantile Anxiety Situations Reflected in a Work of Art and in the Creative Impulse." The paper is included in Melanie Klein (1975), *Love, Guilt and Reparation and Other Works, 1921–1945*. Klein's ideas on art are elaborated in several essays by her followers in the volume *New Directions in Psychoanalysis*.

[3] A good history of the Tavistock Clinic and its use of psychoanalytic ideas to improve organizational life has been published recently by Amy Fraher (2004), *A History of Group Study and Psychoanalytic Organizations*.

artist to introject the wholeness of the work as an antidote to the fragmentation of her inner or unconscious world. Klein believed that it is this process which gives to the work of art or design its healing aspect. I want to repeat the phrase I just used: "to introject the wholeness of the work as an antidote to the fragmentation of her inner world." In other words, the finished design, the resolution of the design problem, provides a psychological benefit to the artist or architect. This is the special advantage of being an artist, a good artist, the Kleinians believed—something that is not available to people without this talent, who must find other ways to handle the struggles that go on within their psyches.

However, it is also important to point out that the process of creation often, perhaps usually, entails substantial destruction and significant risk and anxiety. The process of revision, which is contained within the creative process, and which has been experienced by many of us here, is itself a destructive process. It means that the artist tears down what he has lovingly created. The wish contained in the first draft is mercilessly critiqued. This process of creating, destroying, redrawing, and expunging goes on in all work, the literary as well as the visual arts. Manuscript versions of a poet's or novelist's work illustrate this process in abundance, as do the architect's notes and drawings. There are very few artistic or creative people who do not revise their own work.

For architects, as for most artists and creative people, this process of internal critique is preceded by the experience of being critiqued by a mentor or teacher. The artist gains the psychological resources to tear down his or her own work by internalizing the critical and sometimes humiliating voice of the teacher. Novice architects inherit, so to speak, an artistic superego or conscience as a precondition for their own effective artistry. Many artists are familiar with the experience of hating their early drafts, of finding them contemptible.

In architecture schools, where design problems necessarily dominate the curriculum, students are frequently exposed to a particularly harsh review process of their work. This happens in studio classes where the student meets with the instructor one-on-one, and also, even more scathingly, in public reviews, in which several critics focus collectively on the production of a single student. I have seen a similar process at work in some architecture firms. A junior colleague or partner will present his or her design idea to the senior design partner. The senior designer then will take a piece of tracing paper and impose his design over the colleague's proposal—thus erasing it. The junior colleague is humiliated by this encounter but defers to it—because the person who is superimposing it is the great designer and also is senior to her. You can see on the face of the person whose design has been effaced (the word itself is significant)—this mixture of admiration and hostility. Of course, design architects, if they are worth their salt, constantly engage in the same process with their own work.

The process of becoming a design architect can thus be injurious and generally creates a special artistic persona, a character structure, giving a distinctive shape to the designer's personality. We all know that designers carry with them a certain conceit, and the narcissism that accompanies it. The architectural culture is replete with stories in which the heroic architect cares only about the aesthetic and formal properties of his buildings. The designers' conceit can be associated with an idea of their irresponsibility, on the assumption that since they are artists distinguished for their creative ability, they are freed of the obligation to consider other issues of building. A similar conceit applies in all the arts; the idea resembles the concept of "poetic license."

The idea of irresponsibility probably is linked to the psychological disturbance architects have undergone in learning how to design, the harsh criticism that is a traditional feature of studio education in architecture, along with the attacks architects deploy against themselves in revising their own work. Because they are battle-scarred they deserve special treatment, so they often think. Their victimization confers privileges.[4]

This conceit is matched by what we might call a "thin-skinned/thick-skinned" persona. For design architects to survive their own education, they must become to some degree thick-skinned. Part of their thick skin consists of the rationalizations they develop to make their work appear logical, necessary, and correct. For many design architects, it is important to provide an oral or written account of the logic of their work—why, in fact, all its parts truly hang together. This is especially true for designers who also are faculty members. But, of course, such accounts are rationalizations only. After all, an aesthetic solution is not something that is logically constructed—it is an imaginative leap—and this makes it fragile and vulnerable to attack. Thus the thick skin, which makes architects so often appear to colleagues or clients as people impervious to rational debate, is a defense against the thin skin.

Another aspect of their thick skin, I think, is that designers learn through the studio experience to adopt an offensive stance as a way of quelling criticism before it comes. This creates a certain touchiness. I knew a gifted designer, for whom

---

[4] There have been frequent efforts to moderate the brutality of criticism in architecture schools by educators and others who believe that the traumatic experiences of many students in jury situations can have only debilitating effects on their future performance as architects, and thus will diminish their capacity for responsible behavior to clients when they undertake practice. Although one can sympathize with these campaigns, from our point of view we would have to say that these criticisms fail to understand the psychodynamic processes which contribute to the sustained development of the creative design architect. On the shortcomings of the studio system, see the excellent white paper on "The Redesign of Studio Culture," available on the website of the American Institute of Architecture Students.

I did some consulting work, who was very insecure and behaved childishly. To protect himself, he imagined that he was much more aggressive than he actually was capable of being. He reported often how he "told people off." "I wiped so and so off the floor," he would say. But the next day you would run into this "so and so." "I heard that X let you have it." The other person typically would say to me, "No, what do you mean? We had a nice conversation." The designer had the fantasy that he had wiped the guy off the floor. We might say that his acute insecurity prevented him from actually being aggressive and instead he created a fantasy of his aggressiveness to protect his self-esteem. This way of behaving did not, as you might imagine, help him to clarify his relationship with clients.

I want to suggest that the design architects' thin skin is not only linked to the provisional nature of their aesthetic solution, to the fact that, as an imaginative product, it can never be "proven." It is also linked to the fact that the design solution is so much tied up with the artistic vision as a solution to the inner conflict. The artist succeeds in transforming an inner conflict by using it as raw material to create something whole and fine and beautiful. But if the product should fail to be beautiful, what is exposed, once again, is the inner conflict in all its chaos. One is reminded here of the stories of writers, painters, or poets who commit suicide shortly after finishing an important work of art. We may be puzzled at this level of despair. But if we see the work of art as a temporary solution to an inner conflict, the art which may be defined as insufficient only brings to the surface the inner conflict once again. The demon returns despite all the heroic efforts undertaken to suppress it.

We could say that the prospect, indeed the danger of failing, is itself a source of significant anxiety and sustained vigilance for the designer, just because of the close relationship between the success of designs in winning an audience and the role of the design itself in the designer's personal psyche. Designers who lose their following seem to experience an unusually precipitous decline in their self-regard and their ability to maintain their confidence in competing with fellow architects. Architects who were once at the top of the heap but then lose their stature understandably find it hard to cope with their reduced position. Their new designs seem to have lost their force and vigor. They often try desperately to regain their hold by adopting a new style, a signature that is different from what they were best known for previously. But the strategy rarely succeeds, perhaps because it is too inauthentic, and its connection to the process—which Klein and her colleagues labeled "reparation"—is too artificial. The probability of decline creates, I suggest, powerful anxieties: not simply because it augurs death, but because it can and often reveals a hidden deficiency of character.

The Designer in Context

I want to turn now to some of the problems design architects encounter in the setting of the firm. What are the psychodynamics of creativity among a group of people rather than just within one person?

Let me given an example of one dynamic. I was called up by the managing partner of a 20-person firm, which is headed by an extremely gifted and successful young designer whose interior designs have garnered tremendous attention and praise within the architectural and fashion industries. We will call the managing partner Will and the designer George. Will had very mixed feelings toward George. He wanted George to give him an ownership share in the firm, but George was reluctant to do so. I met with the managing partner first by himself—he revealed to me all of his many disagreements with George and the hostility he felt toward him. Then George entered, dressed—if you can believe it—in a black cape, looking like a painter or poet of the Parisian demimonde of the late nineteenth century. Will's tone changed completely. He became extremely deferential, as if he were kissing George's feet. The whole matter of the managing partner's desire for ownership in the firm, which I was ostensibly called in to help facilitate, completely disappeared from the agenda. Will didn't have the nerve to bring up the matter. Sensing Will's cowardice, George played his role as the artist/enfant terrible for all its worth. I thought to myself, "Will will be out on his ear soon." George could only have contempt for him. I learned later that the managing partner spent his life in a secondary position to a succession of famous designers in different firms. He told me that "he wished he had their gift." Will is unable to liberate himself to engage in another kind of creative process—his desire to be a designer himself runs so deep that he is only able to function in architecture by associating himself as closely as he can with design architects.

The profession is chock-full of people like Will. Even though they occupy a support role, often a peripheral position in such firms, they still are able to think of themselves as closer to the core of the field than other managerial types who work in firms that are not distinguished for design quality. Of course, from the point of view of the design firm, such architects are a welcome resource. Who is to say that these people are not better off positioned as they are, despite the personal humiliation and pain they often suffer? At least when they are asked where they work, they can point proudly to the renown of their firm within architectural circles.

The artist as prima donna is an acknowledged figure in our culture, and, of course, in the psychoanalytic tradition as well, where it is often linked to the idea of the narcissistic artist. Architecture borrows from this tradition just as do the other arts. Young architects will often endure considerable financial sacrifice to apprentice themselves to these canonical leaders, hoping that somehow the gifts of the master will be passed on to them. The psychological meaning of this process is interesting to contemplate. Do the young, for example, hope that they will acquire from the master a design resolution of their own inner conflicts, which they can internalize? It may be something like this, because it is not uncommon for gifted younger architects to spend part of their careers working for a succession of great or good designers, hoping somehow to borrow from the knowledge and insight of all of them. The best of the younger generation don't last very long at any single firm. If they are very good themselves, they can pick up what is valuable in the personality and language of the prima donna rather quickly. Also, if they are searching to develop their own original design vocabulary, it is useful to become familiar with the range of attitudes dominating the generation just before their own. Perhaps the most critical factor in their own development is the discovery that the great design architects of any period insist on running their own show; and they don't like criticism. Or to put it in psychodynamic terms, a design language that will resolve one architect's inner conflicts works for that particular individual, and rarely for anyone else.

Firms respond in their own destructive ways to the designer. The creative achievements of designers violate the self-esteem of the other principals and associates. It is as if the violence and pain stirred up in the creative process is then introjected by the bystander, who, as much as he admires the work of beauty, feels diminished by it. I believe this is one reason we give critics such authority—their violent, passionate attack on the artists protects our own self-esteem. Other architects, whose time has passed, or who lack the gift of the masters, often cherish the words of the harsh critic and cite their commentaries over and over again in an effort to bolster their self-esteem. And in a manner that makes no sense except psychodynamically, they often praise the work of architects who are ignored by the critics.

Consider the following case. A senior partner in a 150-person, well-established practice—we will call him Robert—is upset that his firm has not won any meaningful design awards. The firm is very successful; it has a good reputation for its capacity to address pragmatic building problems in several industries. One global company gives all its work to just three firms; this firm is one of the three, on a rotating basis. As the firm became more successful, Robert began to wonder if it was not time to achieve a certain renown in terms of design—where it really counted. In addition, a new factor entered from the point of view of clients. The GSA (General Services Administration), which has responsibility for all federal government construction, was introducing a new criterion in awarding contracts. They asked bidders to respond to the question: "Have you won any design awards?"

That had never appeared before, and suddenly from a practical point of view in getting work, Robert and his partners worried that they would be excluded from the competition because they had not won any design awards of importance.

The firm asked me to help them consider this issue. Before I started with them, Robert, with the lackluster concurrence of his partners, had gotten approval to hire two designers. They "scoured" the country, or so they told me, for two guys who were regarded as good designers; but amazingly, given the reason why the firm was hiring them, the two had not won awards before. When I viewed the work done under the direction of the new designers, and examined the material that they submitted to design award juries, I concluded that the firm had not gone after really first-rate talent.

What were the dynamics operating here? I believe that although Robert recognized the advantages to the firm of improving its reputation in design circles, he and his partners did not really want to have anyone on staff who was too good, who the partners would feel was looking down on them, and whose talents and achievements they obviously could not begin to match. I provided the partners with a five-point program, which I thought addressed their problem but also recognized their apprehension over hiring top design talent. None of the recommendations I had made could achieve miracles overnight, especially because, as I later learned, even my moderate proposals had led to a certain backlash in the higher reaches of the organization. It did not surprise me, therefore, when I visited the firm one year later, to find that they still had not been able to win a major design award.

On this occasion, a senior partner asked to see me alone for an hour. He had been very skeptical of Robert's attempt to hire good designers. Then berating me for my advice, he spent the hour showing me *his* design work, crowing that surely it was much better than the work of the "la-di-das," his term for characterizing the two new designers. Just as the individual designer launches preemptive attacks on potential critics, and must act this way because of the special function the design plays in resolving his inner conflicts, so we can say that this firm launched a preemptive attack on the designers they hired.

This process of first integrating and then ejecting the designer is a very familiar one in the history of architecture firms. A very successful New York firm was concerned about the media's attention to new designers. So they hired a talented young designer, I will call him Jay, whose work attracted the attention of Herbert Muschamp, then architecture critic of *The New York Times*. Jay was the most prominent designer in this firm for a period of three years. Then suddenly his name disappeared from the ranks. It was clear that his presence irritated the other partners. They felt that the publicity he was getting them was obscuring their identity. Some partners thought that he was commanding too much time and attention in terms of the firm's resources; and the more publicity he got, the more he demanded that he be given the best projects. So they kicked him out. In my experience, this same response to major design talent occurs often in large, comprehensive practices.

We might wonder why Jay, or someone like him, could not have been both brilliant and modest; then surely the firm would not have ejected him. But as my description of the psychodynamics of creativity suggest, this is like wishing for the tooth fairy. The latter's existence is logically possible, but hardly plausible. I have been arguing, following Klein, that the artist designer grows into his talent only by being injured and remaining fragile, which typically he compensates for by being narcissistic or aggressive, or often both.

It is interesting in this regard to consider another anecdote. In one firm with which I also did some consulting work to management, the partners chose to cope with the personalities of their designers by organizing a systematic review process. At the quarterly meetings of the partnership, two days would be spent reviewing the total output of the firm from different perspectives: aesthetic, construction time, match to user needs, client satisfaction, and cost. The chairman of the firm and several partners told me that they thought the process had achieved its goals: the firm was profitable, and it had a reputation among clients and designers throughout the world for doing superior work. None of them told me, however—because most of them did not know—what I found out later to be the case: that the leading designers in the firm experienced these meetings as tremendously disturbing. In fact, before each set of meetings, the design architects as a group met for an entire day among themselves at their home offices, going over all the questions that they feared might be raised about their work. They made sure to exclude all engineering staff, construction administrators, and managerial personnel from these sessions.

Provisional Solutions

I would like now to turn to the fourth question I posed at the outset.

How are firms able to support and integrate the brilliant designer for as long as they do? I am asking the question with respect to so-called comprehensive firms, which work on a broad range of building types, and include partners representing the many specialties that are required for the production of a building. Obviously the problem is quite different when design architects are heads of their own firms. Then the problem is how architects with other skills learn to tolerate the personality of the head of the firm, or how proficient the designer is in generating a viable working situation for architects who are not designers. There is also another model of practice that cannot be ignored, namely the design firm that is set up by a group of talented designers. These firms are often started by young architects who formerly worked in a practice led by a single master, and then left it together, hoping to capitalize on their experience and talents as a collectivity. Some of the issues that emerge in the relations between design architects and other types can also develop in these settings. It is well known that no opera production can sustain too many prima donnas on stage during a single performance. And when design stars have to perform together every day, it is not surprising that these firms break apart after a while.

For the medium- or large-sized comprehensive firm, the solution is twofold. First, you need partners who feel that they themselves are sufficiently accomplished in some other sphere of architectural practice (for example, technology, construction management, or marketing). At that point they can afford, or at least can tolerate, the encounter with the designer. Still, the tension is always present, and privately these non-design types will complain about what they have had to endure from the designers; they make fun of their foibles, tell jokes about their shortcomings, and, indeed, make them out to be more unworldly than in fact successful designers actually are.

A second thing firms do is to isolate the designer. It is as if the psychosocial condition of the artist, in which he stands alone in the struggle to resolve his own inner conflicts, is reproduced in the structure of the firm. But firms are often wary of interfering too much with the conditions under which a successful designer functions, even though they are constantly fearful that what he does and how he operates could wreck morale and cohesion.

I am familiar with one very successful firm owned by a master architectural entrepreneur. I will call him Daniel. Only in the last few years has he become psychologically capable of hiring a distinguished designer in his firm and giving him sufficient influence—so that he can reach partnership. When Daniel first hired the designer, he announced to the world that he was going to make him director of design and that this person would have general responsibility for overseeing and critiquing all the projects that went through the firm. But the other architects could not tolerate this. The designer went around telling people how lousy their work was. Daniel recognized that this person was valuable. So Daniel set him up in a separate department, and he let the designer run that department, but allowed him no authority in the rest of the firm. This department also specializes in the part of the market where clients give extra weight to superior design quality, for example, museum, university, and prep school buildings. In other words, Daniel developed a structure to isolate a talented but understandably opinionated architect from the rest of the organization. On appropriate occasions, the other architects in the firm could take pleasure and credit in the designer's achievement while in other situations they could simply shunt him aside.

Like most students of organizations who operate in a psychoanalytic tradition, I value integration—that which is whole and complete. The integrated organization usually provides the best setting in which to work, it is most successful in the market place, and it has a very good chance to survive. This bias, however, does not serve us well when we try to understand the role of the creative person in the organization. The case of the architect-designer may be an unusual one, since it represents the only situation where an artistic activity is actually licensed as a profession. But I do think it highlights some general principles:

1. The process of becoming creative is an injurious one. It involves experiences of submission and humiliation.

2. The process of creating requires destruction. The successful artist revises his work "in cold blood" by introjecting the voices of his teachers and mentors whom he once experienced as cruel.

3. People are driven to create in order to resolve inner conflicts, to overcome the chaotic qualities of their inner world, by introjecting the created work they have produced, and by identifying with the creation whose raw materials may in fact have been the partial, scattered objects of their inner world.

4. The creative accomplishment is always fragile. This is because it rests on an imaginative leap rather than a scientific formula, and because the conflict that stimulates it can be relived innumerable times. This fragility, in turn, sustains a climate of chaos and abuse as the artist relates defensively to critics and also to admirers.

5. In architecture firms there can arise the need or wish to integrate the creative designers into the firm, to make her creative process and products part of the firm's culture and achievements. This sets up its own climate of destructiveness as people wrestle with the feelings of having been diminished by another's talent. This experience recalls for some their own failed attempts to become a creative designer.

6. The best way to contain the stresses created by this socialized creative process is to isolate the designer, but in way that will harness his talents for the benefit of the enterprise as a whole. The diminution that occurs over time in the quality of work in even the best design firms is an indication of how difficult it is to harness this process effectively.

7. By understanding how the creative process operates in a large-firm setting, I believe we also acquire a better understanding of why good designers—men and

The Myth of the Masterbuilder
A Psychoanalytic Perspective

RUXANDRA ION
JAMES WILLIAM ANDERSON

At first glance, architecture may seem to be far removed from psychoanalysis. Architecture refers to the design of buildings. Psychoanalysis can be thought of as the study of inner meaning. Buildings are literally materials that have been shaped by their designers so that they fulfill particular functions: first, to remain standing; then, to provide a residence, a place of business, or a house of worship. But on further thought it becomes obvious that architecture is suffused with meaning. Even the rudest of structures has meaning to its occupants; for example, a simple hovel may feel to its users as if it is a sturdy refuge from the elements. A house of worship has meaning far beyond its primary function of serving as a place for reverence to the divine; such a building touches on and interacts with an abundance of complicated emotions in those who practice their faith within it.

The question is not whether buildings have meaning for those who use them but rather how to get at such meaning.

We propose to exploit an unusual opportunity for gaining entrée to the inner experience of those who make use of a particular religious structure. Mythical stories have a hold on people—and last for many years—because they express, play with, and resolve the conflicts and stresses that are crucial in a given culture. Such stories, then, when explored psychoanalytically, yield up inner meanings connected to the subject matter of the story. In Romania, mythical stories have played an especially central role. "Dominated by foreign power and subjected to corrupt leadership," notes Ted Anton (1996), "Romanians survived primarily through the shared experience of telling stories" (p. 30). One of these stories, perhaps the most widely celebrated, takes, as its subject matter, architecture; it describes the legend of the building of the Monastery of Arges in the town of Curtea de Arges[1] (see figure 1).

In this paper we will investigate the mythical story about the building of this church. Our goal is to analyze the story and to use this understanding of the underlying psychological and cultural function of the story to gain insight into the effect that the building has on those who make use of it.

The Myth of the Masterbuilder[2]

As the story begins, the Black Prince, the upper-class ruler, is walking along the Arges River with the masterbuilder, Manole, and nine skilled workmen. They are searching for a site where they can build a church. They come upon a shepherd who is playing a "*doina*" on his flute; a "*doina*" is a gentle, sad song. The Prince asks him whether he has seen any locations where there was an unsuccessful attempt to construct a building. The shepherd says that there is such a place, a place where "my dogs bark and bay." The Prince chooses that location for the church and charges Manole to build the tallest church ever.

The workers build during the day, only to have their structure collapse during the night. The same thing happens day after day. The Black Prince threatens them with death if they cannot complete the church. One night Manole has a dream in which "a whisper from above" tells him that the building will continue to fall down unless they sacrifice a human being by enclosing her in one of the walls. And that person cannot be just anyone. It has to be the first woman, the beloved wife or sister of one of the builders, who comes to them the next day with their midday meal. They are enjoined not to warn their loved ones to stay away.

The next morning Manole climbs on the scaffolding and sees his wife, Ana, on the road bringing them their food and drink. He prays to God to send torrential rain that will prevent her from reaching him. Soon there is a horrible storm, but Ana somehow keeps coming closer and closer. Then he prays for a powerful wind that will stop her. God listens to his prayer. There is a gale, but she forges ahead and

---

[1] When using its formal name, we will call it the "Monastery of Arges"; at other times, we will refer to it as "the church." It was originally built as a church and has remained a church. A building for a monastery was added in the seventeenth century, and the "Monastery of Arges" became the name of the complex. The name also became attached to the church but is inaccurate, as the building has been in continuous use as a church.

[2] The myth was first recorded in 1793 (Talos, 1973). Vasile Alecsandri published what is considered the standard version in 1852 (Ricketts, 1988, p. 1143). Specialists in Romanian folklore (Pop and Ruxandoiu, 1976; Itu, 1994) do not speculate when the myth originated. The earliest possible date would be the time when the church was built, the early sixteenth century. After the first version

reaches the builders.

Manole, who loves his wife deeply, puts her within the construction site and says they will pretend to wall her in. As the building covers her more and more, she cries out about how scared she is and how much it hurts, but Manole continues building. She mentions that the wall is breaking her womb and the baby within it. Although enraged, Manole keeps constructing the wall around her. The language of the story is sensuous as it describes how "the wall covers Ana, up to her small ankles, up to her thin calves, up to her fragile ribs, up to her soft lips, up to her pretty eyes."

Some time later, the Black Prince comes to pray at the completed church, which is the most splendid and stately house of worship in the world. He asks Manole and the workers, who are on the roof, whether they are capable of constructing another building that is even more beautiful. They boast that they are. The Black Prince proceeds to attempt to murder them by taking away the scaffolding and trapping them on the roof. Manole and the workers have a desperate plan for survival. They make wings out of shingles so that they might try to fly off the roof. In attempting to escape, the workers fall to their deaths. When Manole is about to jump, he hears a voice from within the wall, "Manole, Manole, Master Manole, this wall is hurting me so. This wall is breaking my baby. My life is wasting away." As he is listening to his wife's voice, he jumps, crashes onto the ground, and dies there. The story ends, "And from that very spot, a quiet spring emerged. It was a spring with salty water like teardrops" (see figure 2).

The Message of the Myth

What is the central message of this folk story that became possibly the most celebrated myth in a country that especially valued its folklore?

One of us (Ruxandra Ion) spent her childhood in Romania in Curtea de Arges and was familiar with the myth from a young age. She recalls the following anecdote.

Growing up under communism, I attended a class on political ideology that was designed to indoctrinate us. The theme of the class was that communism, as

---

of the myth was composed, it would have evolved as it was transmitted orally until it was finally written down. Our quotations from the myth are taken from the standard version (in Toma, 1988, pp. 159–167), as translated by Ruxandra Ion. A number of scholars point out that similar stories about other structures exist throughout Europe, with notable examples existing in Greek, Serbo-Croatian, Hungarian, Albanian, Bulgarian, and Macedo-Romanian cultures; there is also evidence of such stories in India (see especially the detailed examination in Dundes, 1996). Mircea Eliade (1992; 1994) had a great interest in the Myth of the Masterbuilder and wrote an entire book exploring it. He notes that it is "a myth central to the spirituality of the Romanian people" (Ricketts, 1988, p. 1142).

FIGURE 1. The Monastery of Arges as it appears in modern times. Photograph by Ruxandra Ion.

developed by the Romanian dictator, Nicolae Ceausescu, was the perfect system. At the age of 12, I remember asking the teacher, "If communism is so perfect, why is television broadcast for only two hours per day, why do we not have reliable heat in the winter, and why do we often suffer from hunger?" The teacher could not deny these facts. He said that we all had to make "sacrifices" in constructing the ideal society. He noted that we had an honorable mission in assisting the Communist Party in its heroic endeavor. He pointed out that such "selfless sacrifice" had been known throughout Romanian history. Nothing could illustrate this better than the legendary story of the building of the Monastery of Arges in our town. Manole, for the sake of a higher purpose, had sacrificed his wife and walled her into the foundation of the building. We should all feel proud, he concluded, to be part of

FIGURE 2. Monument built in the nineteenth century to memorialize Manole's spring. Photograph by Ruxandra Ion.

the collective effort of making sacrifices so that the ideal society could be built for the future.

A textbook (Toma, 1988) from the communist era in Romania takes a similar approach to the myth. It instructs the students to write an essay including the point that "the sacrifice makes Manole stronger; he sacrifices what he holds dearest in the world: his beloved wife and his own life ultimately" (p. 167). The textbook requires the students to conclude their essays by expanding on this passage: "The legend has the following meaning: It symbolizes in dynamic metaphors the sacrifice on behalf of creation. It is one of the most valuable Romanian folk creations" (Toma, 1988, p. 167).

A teacher of communist ideology and the writer of the textbook during the communist era saw the central message of the story as extolling sacrifice for the sake of a higher purpose. It is striking that the view from the bitterest enemies of the communists was much the same. Constantin Davidescu (n.d.), a political scientist, studied the Iron Guard, a fascist movement in Romania during the 1930s and 1940s. He noted the viewpoint of the Iron Guard: "The sacrifice, as a heroic act necessary to the reconstruction of the Romanian nation, has its representation in the popular legend of [Master] Manole."

We bring up the evidence from these three sources because it is so consistent; in each case the myth is seen as extolling self-sacrifice for the sake of a higher cause. The communists and the fascists could appeal to this understanding of the myth because it rang true to the way the Romanian people had responded to the story for many years. It should be added, though, that both the communists and the fascists distorted the meaning of the myth for their own purposes. They saw the myth as encouraging self-sacrifice for a higher cause, but they substituted their own preference of a higher cause for the cause that the myth describes. The Iron Guard saw the higher cause as the ruthless, dictatorial, intolerant form of government that they wanted, while the communists saw the cause as the failing economic system that the party was perpetrating on the country. Both ignored the higher cause around which the myth is organized, namely, the building of a church for the greater glory of God.

The Myth of the Masterbuilder developed through the oral tradition (the period of its creation began sometime after the completion of the church in the early sixteenth century and ended when the myth was written down in the middle of the nineteenth century). There is one large generalization that holds true for this entire span of time: life was miserable for the vast majority of the Romanian people (Georgescu, 1991; Pop, 1999). Most Romanians lived in three principalities (Wallachia, in which the Monastery of Arges is located; Moldavia; and Transylvania). Nearly all the Romanians were peasants; many were serfs. The three principalities were independent only for the briefest time; usually they were under the control of the surrounding powers (the Ottoman empire, Hungary, Austria, and Russia). The large countries exploited the principalities. As an example, from the second half of the sixteenth century until 1821, Wallachia, except for some short periods, was under Ottoman control. During much of this time the Ottomans extracted large payments from Wallachia, and these payments ensured that most of the Romanians in the principality, who were peasants, would be kept impoverished. Wars were frequently a part of Romanian life. At times the principalities revolted; at other times the surrounding powers invaded the principalities. Often the larger countries fought each other on Romanian soil, and the people living there suffered. Many Romanian men were drafted into the armies of the larger countries and fought and died in their wars. Romanians suffered from poverty, illness, and the threat of violent death.

The concept of collective or group trauma, developed by psychoanalytic historians (e.g., Volkan, 1997; Welsh-Jouve, 2003; Binion, 2003) applies to the experience of the Romanian people in this era. Unless defended against, a trauma leaves a great many people feeling helpless, ashamed, enraged, and humiliated (Volkan, 2003, p. 223).

Another effect of the Romanians' tragic experience over so many years was a view of the omnipresence of dark forces, along with the belief that with faith in the divine one might hope for protection, and could seek it, but could not count on it. Even today it is common for Romanian peasants to look at many happenings and say either "*e lucrarea disvolului*" (it's the Devil's doing) or "*e lucrarea Domnului*" (it's God's doing). There was a general sense that a person had little power; one's life was in the hands of larger forces.

The Myth of the Masterbuilder, we would argue, provided a collective defense that helped the Romanian people cope with their group trauma. The story does not deny the lived reality of the people that the world is dangerous and hurtful. It does not extend to listeners the hope of gaining control over their lives. But it says, in essence, if you persist through the pain of living, see the pain as a sacrifice, and remain faithful to a higher calling, you will find meaning in life, and you will be able to connect to the positive forces, the divine presence, which will offer you protection or rewards after death. Moreover, through such sacrifice a person is enabled to feel self-esteem, to have a satisfying sense of who one is that helps offset physical discomfort and pain; as a result, the physical discomfort and pain feed a positive sense of who one is.

How the Psychological Experience of the Characters Carries the Message of the Myth

Our next task is to analyze the psychological experience of the characters. One may ask, why would we treat the characters as if they are real people? They are merely fictional creations. The reason is that the listeners to the story identify with the characters, and the listeners' psychological reaction to the story is based on these identifications. In looking at the characters' experience, we concentrate on their emotions, because emotions point to what is most important for an individual. A story has its greatest impact when the listeners experience the emotions of the characters in the story.

The main character in the story is Manole, the masterbuilder. The listener is quickly put into the mood of the story when Manole and the others come across the shepherd who is playing melancholy music. It is possible that the story itself was sung and was in the form of a "doina," the kind of sad tune that the shepherd is playing (Itu, 1994). After Manole learns that a beloved wife or sister will have to be immolated within the walls in order for the structure to be built, he is so dedicated to the higher purpose of completing the church that he is committed to following through on the murder; and he remains committed even when he sees that his beloved wife will be the victim. There is no doubt that he loves his wife and that the sacrifice is an enormous one for him. When she keeps coming toward the work site despite the rainstorm, Manole's "heart [is] aching" and he cries; and when she arrives, he is "enraged." The sensuous description of her loveliness underlines to the listener how severe his loss is, and the revelation that she is pregnant makes his suffering excruciating. As he is about to leap off the building with his wings made of shingles, he hears her voice, and the pain is so unbearable that he loses consciousness. A stream is created at the spot where he crashes to his death. His sadness is so great that it continues to be expressed for centuries as the salty water, like tear drops, continues to flow.

Manole's experience is poignant. He makes the ultimate sacrifice; he undergoes extraordinary suffering in order to remain true to his higher calling of building a house of worship, a tribute, in stone, to God. The extent of his suffering defines the power of his creation. Manole provides the model of an ego ideal for the listener, who vicariously experiences what Manole has experienced. The listener comes away from the story with the lesson that suffering has its rewards. It enables one to feel esteem for oneself; it justifies the misery of one's life.

There is also a secondary message that is expressed through Manole's experience. Manole is the masterbuilder; he is described as "the best of all." We may think of him as a great architect; in the mythical story, he has designed a church "that is more splendid and more stately than any other [church] in the whole world." In other words, he is an artist with surpassing talent. In Romania, during the period in which the story was composed, there was an emphasis on being modest, on not standing out, on not having pride. Eliade (1992) notes that there was a pervasive avoidance of perfection, so that one did not appear too skilled, too much like God. For example, a builder would often leave some small part undone, or a peasant creating a piece of needlework would leave one line unfinished.

The situation of an artist created a dilemma. For a building to be outstanding, as was appropriate for a tribute to the divine, the creator had to be outstanding; but to be outstanding meant to stand out, and that was discouraged. In the story, the builders suffer a punishment because of their pride in their accomplishment. After they boast that they are capable of constructing a more gorgeous church, the Black Prince sentences them to death. The ostensible reason, of course, is that he does not want another church built that would surpass the one he has commissioned. But the message to the listener is that it is wrong and dangerous to be too prideful. While Manole is among those who is killed, it is not clear whether he is one of those who participated in the boasting. The story, we think, was constructed in this way so that the emphasis would not be taken away from the main theme, of Manole's suffering for a higher purpose. But the secondary message still comes through, that pride is to be avoided.

While female listeners could hear about Manole's experience and take in the message of the story, one could not expect them to identify with Manole as easily as men would. Perhaps one reason for the mythical story's great impact among Romanians is that it also provides a woman, Ana, with whom female listeners can identify, and it is striking that the message Ana's psychological experience expresses is complementary to the message that stems from Manole's experience.

Ana is selfless, nurturing, and giving. She provides an ego ideal for women. She is intent on taking care of her husband and the other men by bringing them food and drink. After the torrential rain, she falls down again and again but still keeps forging ahead. Even the gale-force winds cannot stop her. She shows enormous strength in fulfilling her duties.

An anonymous woman from a farming background in Curtea de Arges recalled the following anecdote in a personal interview:

> I remember how the women in our agrarian community needed great strength and will power to help the family get by. My mother often brought lunch to the men in the field, to the men of the family and the hired workers. She would take me along during the period when I was two to five years old, and sometimes we walked with the food as far as ten kilometers. I used to complain that the walking was tiresome and the bags were too heavy. She told me how important and honorable it was for us as women to feed the men on time. When the women contributed in this way, it helped them to be well thought of in the community and to feel positively about themselves.

Ana makes the ultimate sacrifice. She suffers as the wall encloses her. She expresses how it feels, "The wall hurts me so." She cries out that the baby within her womb is being crushed. Manole sacrifices his beloved wife for the church, but Ana herself is sacrificed. She is the key ingredient that enables the building to stand.

A female listener to the story takes away a similar message to that of a male listener who identifies with Manole. The typical female listener shares in Ana's pain, and she feels that Ana's suffering was justified ultimately in that it played an essential role in the construction of this church that honors God. Without Ana's loyalty, and without her tragic death, the building would never have been completed. Women, as well as men, were enabled to feel that their sacrifices, for a higher calling, justify their lives. A woman, adopting Ana as an ego ideal, could strive to be as nurturing and as giving as Ana is in the story. One must also add that Ana's obedience is valorized. When Manole asks her to stand in the wall so they might play at walling her in, she accedes to his request.

Here we feel we must comment on the role of women as it is depicted in the story. The Myth of the Masterbuilder both assumes and reinforces the patriarchal structure of society. Ana's chief role is to take care of the men and to bear and nurture children. In the story she functions as the object that Manole most values, and it is shown that he values her for her loyalty, her obedience, her beauty, her sexuality, and her childbearing. She is the possession that makes his loss so enormous. She has no part in any decisions. He is the one who must choose whether or not to murder her for the sake of the building. She is not consulted; in fact, he deceives her in order to encourage her to comply. As Ileana Alexandra Orlich (2002) has noted, Ana has "limited participation at the social, political and cultural levels" and the story "communicates to the reader . . . the sources of authority in Romanian society and their hierarchical order" (p. 14). (On Ana's role, see also Antoniu, 1996.)

We think, though, that women may have had a role in composing the parts of the story that tell of Ana, because ultimately she is given personhood and a voice. As we noted, she is allowed, within the patriarchal structure of society, to feel that she has a valued role and acts heroically, especially in her battling the elements to bring the food and drink to the men. And as she is walled in, she is permitted to express her pain. She is more than an object that Manole sacrifices; she is a person whose cry of agony is heard. Even well after her death, her voice comes to Manole: "This wall is hurting me so. This wall is breaking my baby. My life is wasting away!"

There is one more character named individually in the story: the Black Prince. While Ana is treated as a real person with whom listeners can identity, the Black Prince is not. The depiction of him reveals the attitude of the people who created this folk legend towards their rulers. He is portrayed as being evil, selfish, ruthless, and grandiose. He does not care for his workers or for the populace or even for God; he builds the church as a reflection of his own greatness, not to honor the Lord. In the beginning, he does not hesitate to threaten the builders with murder if they are unable to construct a church, at his chosen spot, that will remain standing. The workers build a magnificent church; Manole goes so far as to sacrifice his beloved wife so that the church can be completed. How does the Black Prince reward them? He is afraid that they will build a more beautiful church elsewhere.

If he cared about serving the Lord, he would be grateful to see other churches that contributed to the greater glory of God; but no, his interest is that his church would surpass all others. He kills Manole and the other skilled workers.

The people of the peasant class, as suggested by the Myth of the Masterbuilder, had contempt for the aristocratic rulers and saw these rulers as being dominated by selfish motives and as having no concern for their well-being. It is notable that there is not a hint of revolt in the story. It seems that the people believed that the political order, organized around the autocratic rule of the royal family, was immutable; it was the way things were. They considered themselves powerless to influence the structure of society.

An enduring folktale like the Myth of the Masterbuilder can have a complexity that enables it to work at different levels. We wonder about a countervailing interpretation of the story that many people in Romania who have reverence for the myth would find to be shocking.

If Manole were a real person, one would have to consider the following interpretation of his experience. His dream that he should murder someone as a sacrifice to the success of his building does not come from some mystical source; it comes from within him. He has a wish to commit this murder, and he surely knows from the first that it is his wife who is to be sacrificed. By unconsciously depicting the message in his dream as forced on him from above, he provides the perfect rationalization for killing his wife; he did not want to do it, but had to do it, in order to accomplish a higher purpose. The story offers few possible hints as to why he would want his wife dead. The text states that, while dead, she assures the success of the building; the implication is that, alive, she stands in the way of its creation. Or one might consider the story's mention that she is pregnant. Does Manole feel jealous of this future rival for her affection, or does he, as an artist, feel envious of a woman who can create something, a life, that surpasses the creation of any man?

Manole, of course, is not a real person. But listeners to a story identify with the main character's experience. Might something else have been operating for many male listeners? Might the story have unconsciously transmitted to them an additional message: that it is acceptable to have murderous wishes toward your wife? Through neglect or domination, you might well sacrifice her to your work or your other higher goals. She does not matter as much as your own personal interests.

While we are far from insisting on the validity of this interpretation, we note that it does seem to solve one puzzle that we found in the literature on the myth; commentators seem to have a surprising lack of concern about Ana's homicide. For example, in the textbook from the communist era, the instructions to the students in writing an essay on the myth guide them to talk about Manole's loss but see it as fully justified as a "sacrifice for the higher cause"; Ana's tragic experience of getting killed while having no say in her fate is ignored (Toma, 1988).

How the Myth Mediates the Worshiper's Experience of the Monastery of Arges

We now turn to the topic of the emotional experience of those who viewed and made use of the Monastery of Arges (see figure 3). How does the mythical story of its construction, known intimately by many people who worshiped in this church, help reveal to us their emotional experience?

Our starting point is the belief, central to Romanian culture, and further reinforced by Christianity, that the universe is divided between the sacred and the mundane, between the spiritual realm and the physical world. The spiritual realm has a profound impact on everyday life. The demonic forces are of great power and make life perilous. The only hope people have is to align themselves with the positive forces, that is, the protection of the divine. A church allows people to come into the presence of Providence.

In the Myth of the Masterbuilder, the Black Prince wants to build his church at the spot where something eerie has been happening. At this location, attempts to construct a building have failed, and dogs, who can sense otherworldly vibrations, "bark and bay" when they come nearby. A portal into the supernatural realm resides there. No simple building can withstand the forces that are at large. It is an apt location for a church, because a church encloses on earth a portion of the spiritual realm. But a church must be worthy of fulfilling this awesome role; it must be powerful and special in order to serve as God's dwelling.

When Manole and his workers try to build the walls, they collapse. In a dream, Manole learns what would transform the building into one that would stand. He must sacrifice a human being by walling her into the building, and this person cannot be anyone but must be the beloved wife or sister of one of the workers; no doubt, it is decided from the beginning that the person is to be Manole's wife.

There is a long tradition of human sacrifice; one need only think of the story of Abraham's attempt to sacrifice his son Isaac in the Old Testament and the Christian motif of the sacrifice of Jesus. Eliade notes that there are many myths, as well as documented instances, of a person being walled into a structure to assure its completion. The various stories, Eliade (1972) argues, have in common a single ideology: "[a] construction . . . must be animated, that is, must receive both life and a soul. The 'transference' of the soul is possible only by means of a sacrifice; in other words, by a violent death" (pp. 182–183). We see two separate ideas expressed

FIGURE 3. The Monastery of Arges by J. Schönbrunner as it appeared in the nineteenth century.

in Ana's immolation in the Myth of the Masterbuilder. First, the church, by being animated, by receiving her soul, becomes powerful enough to serve its sacred function. The sacrifice, moreover, demonstrates that Manole is willing to give of himself. Through his sacrifice, he makes himself worthy of creating a building that is suitable to its profound purposes.

One question sometimes asked is why the "whisper from above" that appeared in Manole's dream would require him to undertake such a dreadful act. This question ties into the nature of the positive forces, as understood in Romanian culture. A divine voice is doing Manole the favor of telling him what the world is like. If he wants to build the church, he can do so only by carrying out the sacrifice. It is beyond God's power to make things different. When Manole prays to God to prevent Ana from reaching him, God listens and tries to help. But His power is limited. He can create forceful storms, but He cannot change the unfolding events.

Worshipers at the Monastery of Arges are readied to approach it by means of their intimate acquaintance with the legendary story of its construction. With the myth in mind, they view the building as awesome. It has to it a great power, a power strong enough to enable the building to serve as an enclosure, on earth, of a piece of God's realm. The building is animated; it has a soul. Ana's vital presence has been transmitted to it. The church is numinous; the special circumstances of its construction assure that it has the Holy Spirit within it. Its being built in a location that has access to the spiritual forces further guarantees that the building is in vital contact with the divine realm. Worshipers are also primed to appreciate its beauty and majesty, because they understand that the church was so magnificent that the Black Prince murdered the builders to prevent another comparable structure from being erected.

The single most important lesson of the story involves sacrifice. As we have argued, the story enjoins people to be selfless and to withstand sacrifice in their lives in order to contribute to a higher purpose. Just as Manole sacrificed in order to build a church that could fulfill its demanding and sacred role, the worshipers must sacrifice in order to be worthy of praying in the church. The worshipers, moreover, by sacrificing in the service of the divine, identify themselves not only with the holy figures and martyrs of Christian history but also with Jesus himself. Confronted by the Monastery of Arges, a church associated with the Myth of the Masterbuilder, they are reminded of their sacred task of devoting themselves to the service of the Lord.

A passage (Pop and Ruxandoiu, 1976, p. 334) in a variant of the myth makes these themes explicit. It begins with Ana's lament:

"Manole, Manole,
My beloved,
My sweet lover,
The wall is hurting me.
It breaks me."
Manole heard her, sighed and said:
"Be quiet, my dear, beautiful lover.
God wants to bring you to him.
And God wants us to complete this church,
To be a place where people celebrate His might."

The passage states directly what is implicit in the standard version of the myth: Ana is being sacrificed so that the church will be powerful enough to be a building in which worshipers may celebrate God's might.

The architecture of the building works together with the legendary story of the church's construction to produce the emotional effect that the building has on those who worship there.

In 1512, Prince Neagoe Basarab of Wallachia began building the church, which was dedicated to the Virgin Mary. His son-in-law, Prince Radu of Afumati, completed it in 1526. In 1517, although not yet finished, the church was consecrated on the day of the Assumption of the Virgin with great pomp; even the Patriarch of Constantinople was in attendance. The close connection between the church and the Virgin Mary underlines the theme of sacrifice that the church inspires in the minds of those who worship there.[3]

Over the centuries the church suffered damage from minor earthquakes and fires, but it has maintained its integrity. Three major renovations were undertaken, two in the seventeenth century and one in the ninteenth century.

Let us consider how a typical worshiper who knew and believed in the Myth of the Masterbuilder might have viewed the church.

The worshiper is struck first by the church's height; for centuries it was far taller than any other building in sight. The verticality of the building is emphasized by its four domed towers, three surmounting the entry vestibule and the largest, central dome rising to a height of 86 feet over the center of the sanctuary. At its pinnacle, each dome is surmounted by a triple-barred cross elevated on a golden, pear-shaped orb, and additional triple-barred crosses decorate the building. With so many large crosses, which represent the Trinity, the building is clearly identified as a Christian sanctum. Looking up at the soaring domes, the worshiper pictures the building as reaching toward the heavens. The nearby spring, said to have formed at the spot where Manole plunged to his death, draws the worshiper's attention to the church's height. (In the late 1800s, a small building was constructed in a French style to memorialize Manole's spring; see figure 2.) Trapped on such a high roof, Manole and his workers, according to the myth, tried to fly off with wings made of shingles, but the worshiper can see that they could not survive a leap from such a height.

---

[3] The description of the church and the account of its history are based on the following sources: Reissenberger, 1867; Samuelson, 1883; Sinigalia, 2005; and two websites: Curta de Arges Monastery, n.d., and The Monastery of Curtea de Arges, n.d. The authors wish to thank Ann Marie Yasin, Ph.D., of Northwestern University for her expert advice regarding church architecture.

The church's bulk and solidity impress the worshiper. The sanctuary of the church is trefoil in plan, with a large central apse and smaller apses projecting to either side. The rectangular entry vestibule (*narthex*) spans the width of the church and creates the impression on the exterior of an elongated building. The church was designed to withstand the seismic torsion forces caused by earthquakes in the area, and therefore it departed from the standard Greek Orthodox cross-in-square model, which has a square sanctuary with a central dome and apse on axis with the entrance, flanked by two smaller side apses. While the purpose was to withstand tremors (the existence of earthquakes in the area no doubt played a role in the genesis of the story in which it is a challenge to build walls that will remain standing), the meaning to the worshiper is that the church has the strength to contain within it powerful spiritual forces. For the worshiper, the sense of the building's strength is reinforced by the image of Ana being entombed within the walls.

The church was built of limestone masonry and adorned with marble and mosaic; Neagoe Basarab is said to have brought some of the materials from Constantinople. An architectural molding carved to resemble a rope encircles the exterior of the church and divides the exterior walls into two registers. The lower portion of the wall features tall, narrow windows encased by heavy stone frames. The upper register is adorned with sculpted blind arcades, the centers of which feature square and circular relief panels carved with intricate Arabian, Persian, and Georgian motifs. A worshiper was surely meant to understand the church with its rich decoration and harmonious design as honoring the Divine.

Such a building, moreover, is a suitable home for the positive forces of Christianity, and the dark forces of Romanian folklore clearly have no place there. The earliest surviving description of the church, from 1517, notes that it "resemble[s] God's paradise" (Monastery of Curtea de Arges, n.d.). The church, in other words, was seen from the beginning as being consonant with God's realm.

The worshiper receives similar impressions of sanctity, beauty, and strength from the interior of the church. There are rich decorations, including twelve columns with floral ornaments, votive frescoes, and liberal use of marble and gilded bronze. In 1526 Dobromir of Targoviste painted two mural frescoes. The royal court of Neagoe Basarab and his wife, Princess Despina, is the subject of one of them. The other fresco portrays their daughter Roxanda with her husband, Radu of Afumati. The fresco depicts Princess Roxanda as the official founder, holding the model of the church, even though her father was the founder. The emphasis on this angelic-looking woman may remind the worshiper of the church's connection to two women, the Virgin Mary and Ana, both of whom are associated with the ideal of sacrifice. The theme of death further comes to mind as one sees the necropolis, where Neagoe Basarab and other royal figures are entombed.

Additional frescoes from later times depict Jesus, the Virgin Mary, and Apostles, along with scenes from the Old and New Testament. The impression is of being in a safe, secure, and holy sanctum, with reminders of death and religious sacrifice all around. The worshiper may well think, "It is this for which Manole sacrificed his wife's life, as well as his own." The building seems all the more somber and sacred as the worshiper recalls the Myth of the Masterbuilder.

Conclusion

Using an interpretive method that draws on psychoanalysis, we have attempted to accomplish two purposes. We analyzed an influential Romanian story, the Myth of the Masterbuilder. Our starting point was the assumption that, for a story to retain its power and popularity over centuries, it must serve a function within the culture. Unless people are moved by and benefit from the story, they will not pass it on from generation to generation. We concluded that the chief function of the story was to offer a defense against the group trauma from which the Romanian people suffered. The story told people: If you tolerate your suffering and you sacrifice for a higher purpose, you will be rewarded. You will have the satisfaction of making a contribution, and you will have reason to have justifiable pride in yourselves. This message helped lessen the chronic despair that can stem from a group trauma.

We chose to analyze this myth for a particular reason: it revolves around an architectural theme. It describes the legend of how the Monastery of Arges was built. We saw this as an opportunity to explore the meaning of this structure; in other words, to discover the emotions that the building elicits in its users. We found that the story prompts worshipers to feel awe at the building, to see it as powerful, numinous, and magnificent. The story encourages them to be inspired to sacrifice themselves in their service to the divine. We argued that the architectural features of the building work together with the influence of the story to produce a joint effect on those who worship there. This essay, then, can be described as a case study of the emotional impact of a building.

References

Anton, T. (1996), *Eros, Magic, and the Murder of Professor Culianu*. Evanston, IL: Northwestern University Press.

Antoniu, M. (1996), The walled-up bride: Architecture of eternal return. In: *Architecture and Feminism*, ed. D. Coleman, E. Danze & C. Henderson. Princeton, NJ: Princeton Architecture Press, pp. 109–129.

Binion, R. (2003), Traumatic reliving in history. *Annual of Psychoanalysis*, 31:237–250.

Curtea de Arges Monastery (n.d.), Retrieved 2004 August 9, from http://www.rotravel.com/romania/monasteries/arges.php

Davidescu, C. (n.d.), Totalitarian discourse as rejection of modernity: The Iron Guard, a case study. Retrieved 2004 July 22, from http://www.crvp.org/book/Series04/IVA-22/chapter_viii.html

Dundes, A., ed. (1996), *The Walled-up Wife: A Casebook*. Madison: University of Wisconsin Press.

Eliade, M. (1972), *Zalmoxis: The Vanishing God*. Chicago: University of Chicago Press.

——— (1992), *Mesterul Manole: Studii de Etnologie si Mitologie*. Iasi, Romania: Editura Junimea.

——— (1994), *Commentaires sur la Légende de Maître Manole*. Paris: L'Herne.

Georgescu, V. (1991), *The Romanians: A History*. Columbus: Ohio State University Press.

Itu, I. (1994), *Poemele Sacre: Miorita si Mesterul Manole*. Brasov, Romania: Editura Orientul Latin.

The Monastery of Curtea de Arges (n.d.). Retrieved 2004 August 9, from http://www.ici.ro/romania/en/cultura/a_curteadearges.html

Orlich, I. A. (2002), *Silent Bodies: (Re)discovering the Women of Romanian Fiction*. Boulder, CO: East European Monographs.

Pop, I. A. (1999), *Romanians and Romania: A Brief History*. Boulder, CO: East European Monographs.

Pop, M. & Ruxandoiu, P. (1976), *Folclor Literar Românesc*. Bucharest: Editura Didactica si Pedagogica.

Reissenberger, L. (1867), *L'Eglise du Monastère Episcopal de Kurtea D'Argis en Valachie*. Vienna: Charles Gerold Fils.

Ricketts, M. L. (1988), *Mircea Eliade: The Romanian Roots, 1907–1945*. Boulder, CO: East European Monographs.

Samuelson, J. (1883), *Roumania: Past and Present*. London: Longmans, Green, and Co. [Electronic version]. Retrieved 2004 August 10, from http://depts.washington.edu/cartah/text_archive/sam/meta_pag.shtml

Sinigalia, T.-I. (2005), Curtea de Arges. Grove Art Online. New York: Oxford University Press [Electronic version]. Retrieved 2005 April 18, from http://www.groveart.com/

Talos, I. (1973), *Mesterul Manole: Contributie la Studiul Unei Teme de Folclor European*. Bucharest, Romania: Editura Minerva.

Toma, M. (1988), *Limba Romana-Lecturi Literare*. Bucharest, Romania: Editura Didactica si Pedagogica.

Volkan, V. D. (1997), *Blood Lines: From Ethnic Pride to Ethnic Terrorism*. New York: Farrar, Straus, and Giroux.

——— (2003), Traumatized societies. In: *Violence or Dialogue?: Psychoanalytic Insights on Terror and Terrorism*, ed. S. Varvin & V. D. Volkan. London: International Psychoanalytical Association, pp. 217–236.

Welsh-Jouve, G. (2003), Silence in the aftermath. In: *Violence or Dialogue?: Psychoanalytic Insights on Terror and Terrorism*, ed. S. Varvin & V. D. Volkan. London: International Psychoanalytical Association, pp. 179–194.

Tracking the Emotion in the Stone
An Essay on Psychoanalysis and Architecture

PETER HOMANS
DIANE JONTE-PACE

> Our design is not only functional; it is an emotional skyscraper.
>
> —Wolf D. Prix, Coop Himmelb(l)au[1]

In this paper we address the relationship between psychoanalysis and architecture by focusing on two contemporary architectural structures, the Vietnam Veterans Memorial in Washington, D.C. and the Jewish Museum, in Berlin, Germany. We ask whether there are "emotions in the stone," that is, whether buildings, structures, and interior physical spaces affect us emotionally. And we ask whether psychoanalysis can help us answer this question. In particular, we draw upon two of Freud's essays, "Mourning and Melancholia" and "The Uncanny," to illuminate this inquiry.

In one sense this paper attempts a classic "interpretation" or "application" of psychoanalytic theory: it uses psychoanalytic concepts to uncover psychological meanings along the lines of the applications of clinical psychoanalysis to art. Yet there are significant differences: the first psychoanalysts applied clinical concepts to culture the way one might apply a coat of paint to a wall in one's house. Our observations and interpretations are grounded in psychological interpretations that have been made by architects and historians—and not, for the most part, by psychoanalysts. The house, in a sense, is already painted in psychological hues—

The authors would like to thank Bertram Cohler, James Anderson, and William Parsons for their assistance with this essay.

[1] Managing partner of Coop Himmelb(l)au, architect Wolf D. Prix, is describing here the design for the new headquarters of the European Central Bank in Frankfurt, Germany (Landler, 2005, p. B34).

the housepainters have psychological paints and tools at hand. This situation necessitates a new stance in the project of psychoanalytic "interpretation."

What is the new stance required of psychoanalytic interpreters? In a nutshell, it involves one of the most important achievements of the social sciences, the notion of culture. The idea of "culture," as a set of symbols representing meanings and tying the present to the past, emerged at the end of the nineteenth century, first in anthropology and sociology, and later, in psychology. In this view, culture is a "whole way of life," and the template or blueprint for that "way" is a set of symbols. This network or web of symbols contains meanings, generates communities, and maintains links to tradition. From this perspective, symbols are the "structure," so to speak, of culture. The explanatory capacities of this concept of culture pushed to one side the older terminology, "civilization," both in the social sciences and in the humanities.

Although Freud commented on the debate over "culture" and "civilization" in his 1927 publication *The Future of an Illusion* (1927, p. 6), this concept of culture was not available to him in his earlier work. Nor was it available to the turn-of-the-century architects. Turn of the century psychoanalysts, architects, and other thinkers simply did not realize that the culture surrounding them had an influence upon them: the Coop Himmelb(l)au statement in the epigraph above could not have been made a century ago.

The development of this new understanding of culture coincided with an optimistic and bold thinking associated with the modernism of the early twentieth century. Both the psychoanalysts and the architects of this period expressed a sense of discovery, an excitement about the future and about the new possibilities of using creative new ideas and materials. Around mid-century, however, we see the beginnings of a "sea change," a "notable or unexpected transformation" (Thompson, 1996), as this modernist optimism began to fade or dissolve. By the end of the century, this sea change had led to new styles of thinking expressing fragmentation, self-reflection, and loss—ideas associated with postmodernism.

Both psychoanalysis and architecture in the late twentieth century show the marks of this sea change: in reaction to the tragedies and terrors of two world wars, the Holocaust, and Vietnam, a sense of loss appeared in the literature of psychoanalysis and in public memorials and architectural structures. Freud's work on loss and mourning, for example was adapted for cultural analysis only after the 1950s: "Mourning and Melancholia," although written in 1917, was applied to culture in the work of such scholars as Gorer (1965), Fussell (1975), Mitscherlich (1975), Santner (1990), Halbwachs (1992), and Homans (2000) only after mid-century.

The two architectural structures studied here, we believe, are "about" loss: not the loss of a father or a mother or a child, but the loss of "the past," the loss of another, earlier culture. The Vietnam Veterans Memorial works with loss within (and beyond) a "modern" context, whereas the Jewish Museum works with loss within the context of "postmodernity."

Contemporary psychoanalytic interpretation must take into account the "sea change" marking the end of modernist optimism. It must also take a self-reflexive stance, for psychoanalysis has become part of the culture it once interpreted. The interpretive project no longer involves the discovery of hidden Oedipus complexes, hidden homoerotic desires, or hidden psychosexual/developmental issues. Rather, the psychoanalytic interpreter must now be attentive to the ubiquity of psychological ideas within the culture. In addition, psychoanalysis itself has been interpreted by that culture: a new "class" or "type" of interpreter has emerged, the "cultural studies" scholar, who stands alongside the analysts and the architects. Residing in universities, in humanities and social science departments, these scholars write about psychoanalysis, architecture, and other disciplines as forms of culture. Thus any discussion of psychoanalysis and architecture will have to consult not only the analysts and the architects, but also the scholars of cultural studies (Hall, 1980; Williams, 1983; de Berg, 2002).

This paper thus not only asks, "What is the psychoanalytic meaning of architecture?" It also asks, "What is the meaning of psychoanalytic interpretation in a context in which psychoanalysis is interpreting a culture that is already psychological?" Central to these questions are the phenomena of culture and loss. Culture and loss will function as the red threads holding together this argument.

Theories of Culture

We will proceed below not by immediately developing an interpretation of our two architectural structures, but rather with a short discussion of the concept of culture. We'll briefly examine its inception as a new idea in the social sciences early in the twentieth century, its significance in shaping the twentieth century as "the psychological century," and its relevance to the discussion of loss, modernity, and postmodernity. We will then turn more specifically to a psychoanalytic interpretation of the monument and the museum.

During the early twentieth century, as the social sciences grew, their practitioners became more interested in and concerned about the representations of meaning in the form of symbols shared by communities to form a common culture (Kroeber and Kluckhohn, 2001). These scholars argued that groups and societies not only carry meaning systems, they can also lose systems of meaning over time. The symbol systems that tie the present to the past, in other words, are fragile: symbols and ties can be broken.

This view of culture, meaning, and loss was expressed first in the work of the sociologist Max Weber (1958), who articulated the sense of "disenchantment" associated with the loss of meanings and the loss of the past. Historian Carl Schorske took an important further step describing history in terms of "culture-making" and "culture breaking." In fin de siècle Vienna, Schorske (1980) studied the leading Viennese artists, musicians, architects, and writers—including Freud—who together created the culture that was modernism. These "culture makers" saw themselves as breaking all ties to the past. They were indifferent to the way that history can serve "as a continuing nourishing tradition," as a source of meaning, identity, and community. To put the same point in a different way, Schorske's work described the way that modernist culture involved a refusal to remember, a forgetting of history and the past, a breaking of memories of and attachments to the past.

Anthropologist Clifford Geertz, in *The Interpretation of Cultures* (1977), elaborates upon some aspects of Weber's formulation, noting that we are caught in webs of meaning that we ourselves have spun. Geertz explains that "the concept of culture I espouse is essentially a semiotic (i.e., symbolic and linguistic) one . . . Believing, with Max Weber, that man is an animal suspended in webs of significance he himself has spun, I take culture to be those webs, and the analysis of it to be therefore . . . an interpretive one in search of meaning" (p. 5).

The work of Geertz suggests that paintings, buildings, music, literature, etc., are ways of symbolizing what life means and who we are. In his view, we weave webs of significance in a process that involves the projection of meanings through these cultural creations. This is "culture-making." The work of Weber and Schorske helps us understand that when these artists, writers, musicians, and architects created modern culture, they were not only culture-makers; they were also culture-breakers. To "spin a web," to project something new, is to replace the old.

Psychoanalysis and Architecture in the Twentieth Century

We can now turn to a discussion of the connections between psychoanalysis and architecture. Three historical moments provide the frame or context for this discussion: First is the culture of modernism which began to develop at the end of the nineteenth century and the beginning of the twentieth. Second is the shift we have called a "sea change," by which the culture of modernism progressively weakened and then disintegrated. Third is the contemporary late modern or postmodern culture that began to take shape in the postwar period and continues to evolve today.

Psychoanalysis and architecture traversed these three moments, each in its own way. Each progressively revised its own understanding of culture and of the way its cultural surround influenced it. These three moments provide the framework for our exploration of how and why our two architectural structures are psychoanalytically psychological, even though their builders have no formal interest in, or knowledge of, psychoanalysis as it is understood in its institutes and by its practitioners.

Psychoanalysis emerged from and embodied the spirit of modernism in the context of late nineteenth-century Europe. The loss of the past initiated by the forces of industrialization, urbanization, and modernization, as Homans (1989) has shown, created a turn inward among many thinkers: a more introspective view of the self emerged. Psychoanalytic introspection is one of the products of modernization. Freud saw his method as part of a modernist trajectory: he saw psychoanalysis as a new science that could be used to understand not only the individual but also all the major forms of culture. In his modernist enthusiasm to interpret all of culture, he relegated the self-representations of art, religion and society itself, to the past; he embraced a sense of breaking from the past and attempted to leave behind the traditions and symbols of the past.

The sea change in psychoanalysis—the weakening of the modernist vision and the shift to postmodernity—was gradual and progressive. It was not clearly recognizable in psychoanalysis until near the century's end. Works like Philip Rieff's *Freud: The Mind of the Moralist* (1979), Peter Gay's *The Naked Heart* (1995), and Ely Zaretsky's *Secrets of the Soul* (2004), chart the slow realization that psychoanalysis was not so much a great new theory of mental illness, but, rather, a new form of culture. Ironically, at the same time that the psychoanalytic claim to be a science was discredited, its incorporation by the culture as a worldview had already begun: the sea change imperceptibly gave way to the postmodern.

By century's end psychoanalysis had produced a society in the West in which psychological perspectives informed and shaped modern and postmodern culture—they are now embedded in literature, film, art, popular culture, and so forth. Historians and cultural theorists are now calling the twentieth century the "psychological century" or the "psychoanalytic century" (Zaretsky, 2004): we can trace a gradual migration of psychological thinking into the self-understandings of our own contemporaries. In the West, psychological thinking "becomes" culture (as in for example, "Mourning Becomes Electra" by Eugene O'Neill). Micale and Porter (1994) express this clearly: "Plainly the psychological revolution that has taken place around us represents much more than the expansion of a single medical sub-specialty. Rather . . . it constitutes one of the major cultural transformations of the twentieth century" (p. 14).

The earlier, modernist, self-understanding of psychoanalysis thus gave way to a more complex view: psychoanalysis could no longer understand itself as free from the past and from culture because it had become part of the culture; it had become part of what would eventually be the past. This, in our view, is part of what enables psychoanalysis now to understand culture, loss, and the past in a way that it could not do in its modernist phase. It represents a kind of psychoanalytic postmodernism.

In the case of architecture, a similar shift can be seen. Modern architecture in the first quarter of the twentieth century was not psychological or introspective, but it did emerge from, and embrace, a process of breaking away from the past not unlike the trajectory we have traced in psychoanalysis. Industrialization, urbanization, and modernization, along with the development of new materials and the discovery of new engineering techniques, led to utopian visions of physical and social structures that would be free from tradition. The skyscraper was created and new designs and structures emerged for private homes. Both sorts of buildings expressed a spirit of optimism and confidence over the promise of progress and prosperity (Scully, 1988; Jackson, 1994). These designers took it for granted that architecture need no longer simply produce new imitations of the past: it had no longer any need for a past.

After the middle of the century, however, the modernist movement in architecture began to weaken. Robert Venturi's assault on the dominant modes of architectural modernism in *Learning from Las Vegas* initiated this shift, challenging modernism by calling for a greater receptivity to "commonplace" tastes, values, and structures, and for an abandonment of the obsession with the new. In an effort to "make the case for a new but old direction in architecture," Venturi quoted Wallace Stevens: "Incessant new beginnings lead to sterility" (1977, p. 87).

Both a theorist and an architect himself, Venturi is significant for his effort to bring psychological or emotional questions into the heart of architectural discourse as well as for his attempt to reclaim a focus on the past. He argued, for example, that "architecture depends in its perception and creation on past experience and emotional association" (p. 87). And in his critique of modernism he expresses a perspective that is broadly psychological, although he does not specifically mention Freud: the "formal languages and associated systems" of modern architecture, he states, "become tyrannies when we are unconscious of them" (p. 162). Venturi can thus be seen as one of the initiators of a sea change in architecture: he attacked modernism, he sparked an architectural shift that led to postmodernism, and he spoke psychologically about architecture, referring to emotions and the unconscious.

Venturi's critique of modern architecture has been echoed by others as well. Most significant among these, perhaps, is Anthony Vidler, professor of the history and philosophy of architecture. With the concept of "the architectural uncanny," Vidler (1992) documented and challenged the philosophical stance of modernist architecture: he exposed a denial of the need for history and a past. Vidler's argument, and the broader question of how architecture became psychological, will be discussed further below, but at this point it is important to note that Vidler and Venturi are not alone in their critique of modernism. As the twentieth century has drawn to a close, writers in a number of disciplines have expressed concern over the modernist rejection or denial of the past. Loss, and the denial of that loss, have gradually become a central concern for an increasing number of scholars in a variety of disciplines. In these studies loss is often linked to mourning and memory (see, for example, Cheng, 2000; Homans, 2000; Young, 2000; Eng and Kazanjian, 2003), themes that are deeply significant for the two structures we will examine.

Interpretive Tools

A number of Freud's writings provide interpretive tools valuable for the understanding of the phenomenon of cultural loss, memory, and the question of "emotions in the stone." The essay "Mourning and Melancholia" is particularly important for our purposes. Here, Freud argues that there are two ways we can encounter loss. Mourning is the successful encounter with loss—the experience involves loss, grief, and recovery. Melancholia, on the other hand, involves an inability to mourn or an entrapment in the process of grief. Freud described the causes and contexts for mourning: mourning occurs not only in "reaction to the loss of a loved person"; it can also be caused by "the loss of some abstraction . . . such as one's country, liberty, an ideal, and so on" (1917, p. 243). Freud knew that the loss of the past, or the loss of ideals, could cause us to grieve and mourn or to be trapped in melancholia. He was attentive to the cultural dimensions of mourning and loss. He articulated an insight that would be more widely understood and applied only later.

Memory is an important piece of Freud's understanding of how mourning happens, both for the individual and for the culture. Memory, he suggested, is the crux of the psychological process, supported by cultural rituals and structures, of working through loss and grief by remembering the lost object before one can let it go. The process is painful, it is "carried out bit by bit" over a long period of time, and it requires the engagement of memory: the "memories and expectations by which the libido is bound to the object" are recalled, "hypercathected," and gradually "detached." When the work of memory and mourning is completed "the ego becomes free and uninhibited again" (1917, p. 245). He reiterates the role of memory in "Remembering, Repeating, and Working Through" (1914, pp. 145–156), where he emphasizes the role of memory or "remembering" in healing. In melancholia, in contrast, memories cannot be engaged: the "object loss is withdrawn from consciousness" and the process of remembering the loved and lost object "bit by bit" cannot occur. Freud also describes the role of memory in relation to repression and the return of the repressed in "Remembering, Repeating, and Working Through": the patient does not remember anything of what he has forgotten and repressed, but acts it out, reproducing it not as a memory but as an action. Freud notes, "he cannot escape from the compulsion to repeat, and in the end we understand that this is his way of remembering" (1914, p. 150). This point is echoed in Freud's essay "The Uncanny," where he links the uncanny with the compulsion to repeat (1919, p. 238). Freud's understandings of mourning, memory, and cultural loss will be important to our inquiry into "emotions in stone."

Freud's essay on "The Uncanny" (*Das Unheimlich*) will provide another important piece of our analysis. In "The Uncanny" Freud explored the psychodynamics of "that which arouses dread and horror" (1919, p. 219). Freud was interested in the duality inherent in the meaning of the term *unheimlich* in the German: it "develops in the direction of ambivalence, until it finally coincides with its opposite" (p. 226). The *heimlich* (literally, the homelike) involves all that is associated with house, home, and hearth, and can flip into the *unheimlich* (literally, the unhomelike), the uncanny or unfamiliar. He explains further that it is associated with the unconscious, the hidden, or the unseen: "on the one hand it means what is familiar and agreeable, and on the other, what is concealed and kept out of sight" (pp. 224–225). He emphasizes that the sense of the uncanny emerges under certain conditions: it involves something that we feel "ought to have remained hidden but has come to light"; it involves "something which is familiar and old-established in the mind and which has become alienated from it" (p. 241).

The sense of the uncanny might be said to be a replacement for a memory. Rather than remembering that which is "familiar and old-established," we experience the sensation of the uncanny: it is a signifier of an old memory that we are unable to reclaim, a signifier without a signified, a symbol without content, a "void." Freud's understanding of the uncanny, with its sense of dread, its sense of alienation from all that is homelike, and its association with inaccessible memories will be useful in our discussion below.

Let us now turn to the main work of the essay, a set of psychological and cultural reflections on the Vietnam Veterans Memorial (a form of memorial architecture) and the Jewish Museum Berlin (a form of museum architecture). In one sense, of course, all monuments and museums are expressions of cultural memory and attempts to build bridges between past and present. But our inquiry will offer a fresh perspective on culture and loss, memory and mourning, and the interrelationship of emotions and stones in the twentieth-century context.

The Vietnam Veterans Memorial: Mourning and Melancholia in a Modern Monument

Although America's war with Vietnam officially ended in 1975 with North Vietnam's capture of Saigon, the Vietnam Veterans Memorial was not dedicated until 1982. Another decade or more passed before the nation as a whole reached a consensus with regard to the memorial's fundamental meaning. Once the nation reached that closure, or understood the way the memorial really "worked," its meaning finally could be fixed.

In retrospect, we can see that the 20 years or so between the mid-1970s and the mid-1990s were years of collective grief work, during which the nation mourned the enormity of the war—first by simply recognizing it, and then gradually letting go of it. Some of this grief was worked out through a process of debating, creating, authorizing, and interpreting the monument. This process involved journalists, veterans, politicians, artists, critics, and others. We can now ask what, exactly—that is, psychologically—did the nation do throughout this period, and what exactly is the meaning of the memorial? In what sense can we speak of "the emotion in the stone"?

The place to start is the memorial's polished surface and the meanings it has generated. At times the polished surface is seen as a window, at other times as a mirror (see figures 1 and 2). If one sees the monument as a window, one is imaginatively drawn into the past and the war itself, into memories or imaginings, a bit like the memories of the elderly veteran that serve as the prologue of Stephen Spielberg's film, *Saving Private Ryan*. On the other hand, if one sees it as a mirror, one's attention is deflected away from the wall and the past, and outwards onto the Mall and its surroundings: one is drawn by the pull of the present.

Maya Lin, the architect and designer of the memorial, was aware that the monument can function in these two ways: it is, she said, "a memory and a personal experience" (Smith, 2000). Yet, it must be noted, she made these remarks only after the memorial was completed, a month after it had been dedicated. Lin had initially understood the monument as a window onto the past. Only later did she see it as a mirror of the self and the surrounding environment. Maya Lin's understanding of the memorial reflects the same evolution as the evolution of meaning that can be observed among critics and interpreters in the broader culture.

This evolution of meaning has been traced by Levi Smith, a preeminent historian of the memorial, who analyzes the cultural discourse in popular and scholarly media around the symbolism of the polished surface. The earliest interpretations, he shows, consistently emphasized the surface as a window onto the past. These readings later gave way to interpretations stressing the mirroring or reflective quality of the surface. And, still later, interpretations emerged that stressed multiplicity or fragmentation in the reflections. It is Smith's view that these evolving interpretations of the polished surface of the memorial reveal the gradual "progress of cultural mourning of the Vietnam War" (2000, p. 107): only through the process of memorial design, dedication, and interpretation was America able to let go of the past and reembrace the present.

Smith has also suggested that the two major interpretations of the polished surface, as window or mirror, embody not only two distinct phases of collective mourning, but also two different kinds of mourners—two cohesive and continuing groups of veterans. One group cannot let go of the past. They continue to seek each others' company as solace: they continue to see the memorial as a window. They sometimes gather at the memorial at night when the wall's reflexivity is radically reduced: "by visiting the memorial at night" he explains, "they find comfort in the presence of their comrades." These comrades are both the living and the dead: "the dead seem closer at night" (2000, p. 111). The second group of veterans, on the other hand, can let go and do so: they look through the "window" back to the past, and then through the "mirror" out to the present.[2]

This leads us back to Freud. Although neither Levi Smith, the historian, nor Maya Lin, the architect, were trained in psychology, the monument and its interpretations are deeply psychological. The two types of mourners and two kinds of mourning outlined by Smith are precise embodiments of the two ways of approaching loss that Freud described in "Mourning and Melancholia." Those who were able to unite window and mirror, to remember the losses they experienced and to eventually let go of the past, correspond to Freud's mourners. Those who could not let go, who could see the memorial only in one way, as either mirror or window but not both, correspond to Freud's "melancholics." The melancholics share a psychological

---

[2] We might also speak of a third group, the intellectuals. With their customary detachments from most collectivities and commitments, intellectuals of many different stripes were nonetheless able to join together in the repeated attempts to make sense of a war which did not make sense through a memorial that allowed them to look both into the past and into the present. They encountered the memorial, in other words, as both a window and a mirror; yet they also saw the reflectivity as fragmenting and complex. Encountering it as a window, they looked into the past, they saw the names of the dead, they engaged with the memories and losses associated with the war. Encountering it as a mirror, they saw the Mall, they saw themselves, and they saw the present. And, as intellectuals, they reflected on this process and its dynamics, emphasizing the ambiguity of the symbolism, and the "phenomenological complexity of the experience of reading the engraved names in their glittering field of reflection" (Smith, 2000, p. 115). For these theorists, the effort of reading the wall involves a complex process of struggling for meaning, of holding onto multiple, fragmented accounts that contain truth but "resist easy interpretation" (p. 115).

FIGURES 1 and 2. Vietnam Veterans Memorial.

framework with the subjects of the Mitscherlichs's volume, *The Inability to Mourn*: they are either caught in the past, unable to move forward, or they are caught in the present, unable to look back, resisting both memory and the past. For those who can do both, those who can see the interplay between mirror and window, the interrelation of present and past, the monument provides, in a sense, a visual representation of the psychological process of mourning through remembrance and "working through" that Freud described: bit by bit one remembers the loss, bit by bit one detaches from the past and returns to the present.

Freud's remark at the end of his short essay "On Transience," is, perhaps, appropriate here. Speaking of the losses associated with the first world war, he stated, "however painful it may be [mourning] comes to a spontaneous end . . . It is to be hoped that the same will be true of the losses caused by this war. When once the mourning is over, it will be found that our high opinion of the riches of civilization has lost nothing from our discovery of their fragility. We shall build up again all that war has destroyed, and perhaps on firmer ground and more lastingly than before" (1916, p. 307). Maya Lin's monument expresses some of the same sentiment: it conveys a deep sense of the tragedy of the war, the fragility of culture, and the grief associated with the loss of both lives and cultural ideals. Yet, at the same time, it allows the viewer to look forward with a cautious or hesitant optimism.

It is important to ask how Maya Lin, who knew nothing about psychology, could design such a psychological structure, and how Levi Smith, who similarly knew little about Freud, could describe this cultural mourning process and these two types of mourners in a way that was so astute in psychoanalytic insight. We believe that two factors are crucial in explaining the psychological nature of this monument and its symbolism. First, due to the broad cultural shift—the sea change—that we've described, the entire culture experienced a sense of loss that had a psychologizing effect. This psychological effect emerged visibly in its monuments even without the conscious intentions of the designers. The second factor is the shift to postmodernism, particularly the migration of psychoanalytic ideas from the institutes (where they were located in the height of the modernist period) into the broader culture and the academy. Freud's ideas, in other words, were taken for granted so thoroughly that they could be absorbed into Maya Lin's design of the memorial and into the interpretations of the monument in the popular press and the works of critics and scholars, even without any explicit psychological intention.

We suggested earlier that one of the marks of modernism is a dramatic break from the past and a denial of the loss of the past. How can we describe the Vietnam Veterans Memorial as a "modern" monument if, as a monument, its role is precisely to name the losses associated with the war, or to symbolize and support national mourning? Let us look at this question more closely. First, we should acknowledge that the monument is "modern" in its appearance: it differs dramatically from traditional civic monuments to fallen heroes and soldiers of wars. It lacks anthropomorphism—it contains no human figures. As Levi Smith points out, it eschews "the traditional iconography of heroism, service, or sacrifice" (2000, p. 106). Its structure and materials are modern: its reflective black granite is sleek and shiny like modern urban buildings. It is also modern in its optimism, in its ability to direct the viewer's gaze to the present or future. Although this is a limited optimism, it does express a hopeful sense that cultural healing is possible. We believe it is successful as a modernist structure, however, precisely because it breaks through the limitations of modernism: the ambiguity of its surface— as window and mirror—echoes the ambiguity of its time-reference—past and present. Its hesitant optimism links it with, and at the same time, distances it from, modernism: the optimism is modernist; the hesitation transcends the modernist impulse.

The Jewish Museum Berlin: The Uncanny in Postmodern Architecture

The concept of an "architectural uncanny" is one of the most interesting and promising examples of a psychology of architecture, but at the same time it is also one of the most difficult to describe and illustrate. That is in part because the concept of the uncanny owes its origins to nineteenth-century literature, philosophy and psychology. Only from there did it migrate to Freud and psychoanalysis, and, still later, from Freud into architecture. But the concept of the uncanny did not simply get swept into architecture; rather, it entered architectural thinking via a small cluster of neo-avant-garde architects greatly influenced by the postmodern philosophy of Jacques Derrida and the surrealist art movement of Salvador Dali. Its complexity has rendered it as yet inaccessible to the wider public.

Yet we want to make a case for an architectural uncanny—that is, for an architecture which organizes space in such a way that one is likely to find oneself in the presence of uncanny thoughts, feelings, and images upon entering the space. We refer to the architecture of the Jewish Museum Berlin, designed by the architect Daniel Libeskind. Here we draw from the historical and interpretive work of cultural historian James E. Young (2000) as well as the theoretical perspective of Anthony Vidler (1992), although the argument is our own.

In this section we shall proceed in four steps: we will review our earlier discussion of Freud's concept of the uncanny; we will explain and illustrate what, in the hands of Anthony Vidler, the architectural uncanny looks like and why he has found it so important for the understanding of "modernity" and "postmodernity"; we will explain Libeskind's central architectural concept, "the void," illustrating how voids generate the "architectural uncanny" in the minds and bodies of visitors; and we will conclude by explaining how voids and the uncanny shape not only Libeskind's interiors, but every other principal aspect of his entire museum.

As we noted above, Freud describes the uncanny as the unsettling sensation of the spooky or terrifying, focusing on the tension or ambivalence between the familiar and the unfamiliar, the alien and the safe, the *unheimlich* and the *heimlich*: "the uncanny is that class of the frightening which leads back to what is known of old and long familiar" (1919, p. 220). It involves all that nurtures, protects, and supports. It is linked to "house" or "home" or "hearth." The *unheimlich* or uncanny, emerges when everything that once was and always has been *heimlich* is suddenly or unexpectedly transformed and experienced as its opposite. One of the oldest and strongest meanings of "uncanny" is that which is the opposite of feeling "at home." This connotation carries us right into the midst of Anthony Vidler's "architectural uncanny" and Daniel Libeskind's Jewish Museum Berlin.

Vidler, who developed the term "the architectural uncanny" (and who uses the term "unhomely" to describe it), argues that, toward the end of the nineteenth century, a number of intellectual disciplines became increasingly aware of the existence and presence of the uncanny in modern life. In the case of architecture in particular, he argues, the uncanny is more and more found in the interstices between "psyche and dwelling," between "body and space," between "the unconscious and its habitat."

Vidler believes that as architects have increasingly studied domesticity, and as more and more people have had to accept the ways in which architects have organized the spaces which make up their homes and houses, "a deep structure of the uncanny" has evolved. He argues that the uncanny has virtually become a metaphor for a "fundamentally unlivable modern condition."

One of the best known—and profoundly tragic—examples of Vidler's understanding of this "modern condition," its uncanny qualities, and its unlivability, we suggest, is the Pruit-Igoe public-housing project built in the city of St. Louis during the 1950s. At the time of its construction, it was highly touted as a great achievement, not only socially but also technologically and architecturally. However, by the end of the 1960s, the buildings had been so badly vandalized and crime-ridden that the entire project was submitted to demolition.

What went wrong? Looking back on the project some years later, a sadder but wiser architectural consensus observed that "the best of modernist thought, owing to its aloof indifference to the small-scale personal requirements of privacy, context, and sense of place, could do nothing to make Pruit-Igoe housing a workable home for the economically disadvantaged persons whose living conditions it was meant to improve" (Arnason, 1998, p. 691).

Indeed, the housing project consisted of box-like buildings filled with box-like rooms. It provided little in the way of human dignity, personal warmth, familiarity and domesticity. What should have been "homey" was experienced as decidedly "unhomey" (or "unhomely," in Vidler's terminology), alien, and strange—that is to say, as uncanny. Modern architecture, with its distance from the past and from tradition, had been exposed as a strategy that cannot help people feel at home. Modernism, in this case, had failed to attend to the emotions in the stones.

It is but a short step from Vidler's work on the uncanny to Libeskind's architectural design. His word for the uncanny is the "void." Voids are the building blocks of his design. The entire structure of the Jewish Museum is made up of voids. But, it is also the case that, for Libeskind, voids are not only psychologically uncanny, they are also deeply historical: the entire architectural design bears the stamp of history, that is, the memory of the Holocaust (Libeskind, 1999; Young, 2000).

To understand the link between architecture, the void, and the uncanny, it is necessary to begin by describing the museum's historical context. In this case two museums—not only the Jewish Museum Berlin but also the Berlin Museum—are located right next to each other and are, at the same time, completely apart from each other.

What is today known as the Berlin Museum, first known as the Markische Museum, was built in 1876 as the official institution whose goal it was to tell the history of the city of Berlin. Many years later the Berlin Wall went up. The Markische Museum was in the east, and the west no longer had a museum to represent the city's history. In 1962, the Berlin Senate approved and funded a new Berlin Museum in the western sector. In 1969, this museum was moved to its permanent site on Lindenstrasse.

What is today known as The Jewish Museum Berlin originated in 1917. At that time it consisted of three exhibition rooms in the synagogue complex at Oranienberger Strasse, and was designated "The Art Collection of the Jewish Community in Berlin." This small collection subsequently grew to become a permanent home for the presentation to the city of Jewish art and cultural history. It officially opened as The Jewish Museum in 1933. At that point the Nazis became more and more belligerent, first turning the museum into an exhibition of "decadent" art, and then, in 1938, destroying it entirely on Kristallnacht.

During the 1970s and early 1980s, concern about the future of a Jewish museum, and discussion of how its relationship to the Berlin Museum might be represented, became more and more urgent. In 1988, the Berlin Senate approved financing for building an entirely new Jewish Museum, and its planners instructed the architect-to-be as follows:

> The history of the Jews of Berlin is so closely tied up with the history of the city that it is virtually impossible to separate the two; i.e., an autonomous Jewish Museum is necessary but almost inconceivable without the history of Berlin, in the same way as, conversely, a Berlin Museum of urban history would lose all meaning if it did not take its Jewish citizens into consideration [Young, 2000, p. 162].

James Young has summarized these discussions by noting that "the aim of the museum would be to show that Jewish history is part of and separate from German history, a balancing act demanding almost impossible discretion, diplomacy, and tact" (p. 162).

This was the mandate Libeskind accepted. In effect, it requested that he translate the planners' words into his architecture. To him this meant that the entire building would reflect and symbolize this charge—not only the interiors (such as the shape of the walls, the corridors, the rooms, and so forth), but also the site (where the museum was located and how it was positioned), and the façade (what its sides and roof look like). Indeed, even Libeskind's concept of the purpose of a museum is revised in the service of carrying out the planners' charge.

Obvious and important as all these features of the building are, they are all shaped by an even more primary structure, "the void." Voids are the key to Libeskind's entire design. They not only generate the uncanny, they also link it to history, for they shape not only the interiors but also the symbolic structure of the museum as a whole. What is a void and how do voids evoke the uncanny?

A "void," of course, is both an adjective and a noun meaning "empty" or "emptiness," as in the phrase, "an empty space." As we walk through this museum, we come across voids—spaces which we expect to be filled with something familiar but which in fact turn out to be empty (see figure 3). The experience is distressing, even frightening, often uncanny as the visitor encounters, for example, "the Holocaust void" and "the interior view of bridges and voids."

The experience of having one's expectations frustrated—of finding nothing when one expects something—resembles what some have called "culture shock" or "defamiliarization." The flow of experience, as one moves through the museum, encountering one void after another, is sometimes referred to as an "open narrative." An open narrative by definition does not provide the familiar sense of continuity of experience as one walks from one space to another. Open narratives are "void-like," strange, often uncanny.

These voids also have historical resonance. They are "empty," but they are

FIGURE 3. First Void Underground, Jewish Museum, Berlin. Photo © Bitter Bredt, Berlin.

also "full": they "contain," "in absentia," all that is missing, that is, all the Jews of Berlin, all the memories of those who were murdered and whose homes were destroyed, so that nothing remains, except nothingness itself. Young describes the historical meanings of the museum's voids:

> [Libeskind] has simply built into it any number of voided spaces, so that visitors are never where they think they are ... they [these voids] are not meant to instruct, but to throw previously received instruction into question. Their aim is not to reassure or console, but to haunt visitors with the unpleasant—uncanny—sensation of calling into consciousness that which has been previously—even happily—repressed. The voids are reminders of the abyss into which this culture once sank and from which it never really emerges. . . . voids embody the absence of Berlin's Jews [p. 180].

Although Young, the premier interpreter of the Jewish Museum, rarely cites Freud explicitly (2000, p. 154), and has often said that he has no use for Freud, his description of the "uncanny sensation of calling into consciousness that which has been repressed" is not far from Freud's thought. Let us recall Freud's suggestion that we feel the frightening or spooky sense of the uncanny when something we once knew—an old memory, perhaps—is evoked but not recalled, and when the homelike and familiar suddenly seems alien and unfamiliar. The structure of Young's analysis is implicitly psychoanalytic at the same time that it is historical and cultural. We can build upon Young's interpretation: we noted above that the feeling of the uncanny becomes a kind of signifier without a meaning—a feeling without content—we might call this a "void." Libeskind's voids, as Young suggests, are signifiers of the lost Jews, and of our cultural repression of the memory of the atrocities that led to their deaths. The uncanny experience of the museum, and the voids out of which it is constructed, confront us with our own and our culture's impossible memories (Levine, 2004).

The Jewish Museum Berlin has little to do with mourning, loss, and recovery in the sense of the Vietnam Veterans Memorial: there is no possibility of successful "working through," of putting the past behind us and looking forward toward the future. There is neither recovery nor mourning. Here, for some visitors, it is a question of crime and punishment, of the denial of guilt and the realization of guilt. The museum engages visitors with something almost like the Christian concept of original sin: it evokes a sense of a terrible mark or stain which all share and all struggle to deny. While traditional museums may provide anesthetic illusions allowing viewers to deny the truths of history (as Young's postmodern critique of monuments suggests), the Jewish Museum Berlin asks viewers, in contrast, to stand in the presence of the uncanny truth of responsibility and culpability for the tragedy of the Holocaust. Mourning is not possible: the museum asks us not to mourn, but

FIGURE 4. Jewish Museum in Berlin.

to let the wound remain open. The experience echoes Freud's description of the melancholic "open wound": "the complex of melancholia behaves like an open wound, drawing to itself cathectic energies . . . from all directions" (1917, p. 253). Memories, in this context, cannot be recalled and reintegrated nor put aside "bit by bit." The visitor must simply experience the void and face the uncanny.

It is important to note that the sense of the uncanny is communicated through several aspects of the museum's structure and architecture. In addition to the voids found in the interiors of the museum, the building's site, setting, façade, and exteriors also convey the uncanny. Libeskind deliberately built the Jewish Museum Berlin directly adjacent to the Berlin Museum, yet, at the same time, he fragmented the connection between the two structures. They are only a few feet apart, but they are far apart: an underground tunnel is the only connection between the two. If one wants to learn about the history of the Jews of Berlin, one cannot do so by visiting the museum of the city of Berlin, for the Jews of Berlin were "voided" out of the city of Berlin; rather, one must enter the Jewish Museum through the tunnel. This distanced proximity, this proximity of distance, vividly conveys a message regarding the murder of the Jews by their German neighbors. It also communicates a powerfully ambiguous message about memory and forgetting. Even the façade of the Jewish Museum is uncanny (see figure 4). It is made entirely of zinc plating and appears reminiscent of a prison. A jagged, menacing line of windows, and an overall zig-zag shape of the entire building contrast jarringly with the baroque elegance of the Berlin Museum next door.

Indeed, Libeskind has designed a museum that inverts all we have learned to expect when we go to museums. A museum, we assume, will be an assembly of spaces of varying sizes, shapes, and meanings; these spaces will be filled with objects from its collections which we, the museumgoers, want to see. We also assume that nothing is hidden. Most of all, we think of museums as positive and self-enhancing: we assume they are filled with the best of what there is to know and remember from the past. We do not expect museums to challenge these assumptions. The Jewish Museum is unsettling and uncanny. It asks us to become aware of the way our culture has disguised or denied the existence of the past. Unlike the Vietnam Veterans Memorial, it does not allow us to grieve, mourn, and move on. It holds us in a kind of stasis. We are asked to stand in the presence of unresolvable suffering and tragedy.[3]

Finally, we must return to the question we posed earlier in relation to the Vietnam Veterans Memorial. We asked how Maya Lin, without any psychological training, created a monument that mirrored so precisely Freud's psychoanalytic reading of the response to loss, and how Levi Smith constructed such a Freudian reading of the monument. Here we must expand our question to incorporate the Jewish Museum Berlin: how did Daniel Libeskind and his interpreter James Young develop such psychological structures and theories? As we noted above, the answer brings us back to the cultural changes we have discussed. It may be useful here to differentiate three factors. First, as the cultural optimism associated with modernism waned, a widespread sense of loss led to introspection and psychologization within Western, industrially advanced cultures. Second, the terrible events of the twentieth century compounded this sense of loss. In this context, psychoanalytic ideas, once located primarily in the psychoanalytic institutes, were broadly adopted throughout both popular and academic culture, often without specific attribution to Freud. A third factor emerged: cultural studies arose as a discipline within the academy; in this development, a cadre of intellectuals within the humanities and social sciences began to read Freud, just as the nineteenth-century intellectuals had all read Marx.

A whole culture, in other words, experienced the loss of an optimistic sense of progress and hope; a whole culture experienced the unspeakable tragedies of the twentieth century; a whole culture grieved, and began to think more and more psychologically. Psychological ideas were incorporated into popular culture, media, advertising, and other arenas; a culture of the "therapeutic" (Rieff, 1966) infused both education and the church. And psychological ideas permeated the academy: just as Freud was being abandoned by psychology departments his

---

[3] It should be noted that Libeskind himself does not precisely share this view of the museum. He is more positive: every architectural structure, he says, embodies an optimism of some sort.

work became required reading among scholars influenced by cultural studies. As architecture itself became postmodern, it did not seek out psychology; rather, embedded as it was in its "cultural surround," architecture created psychological buildings, museums, and monuments. Architects and theorists of architecture knew, consciously or unconsciously, explicitly or implicitly, that there were "emotions in the stone."

How can we weave together these cultural and interpretive reflections? First, an historical-cultural reflection is possible: Both psychoanalysis and architecture began the twentieth century with a stance that denied the significance of the traditions of the past, a stance that looked forward with great optimism and enthusiasm regarding new methods, materials, and possibilities for change. Memory was irrelevant—only the future mattered. By the end of the twentieth century, however, both psychoanalysis and architecture had changed. In a sense, both had become more introspective or psychological: both were seeking ways to understand the past, to work with memory (and the impossibility of certain memories), to deal with loss, and to address the ways we fail to deal with it.

Second, an interpretive reflection can be made: Psychoanalysis began the century thinking that the interpretive act was a strategy that worked in one direction: culture was the object of interpretation; psychoanalysis was the method or the tool. By the end of the century, however, this one-directional strategy was clearly impossible: architecture, like many other cultural phenomena, had adopted psychological ideas (the uncanny, the void, the emotional structure); the tools no longer belonged exclusively to the analysts. Interpretation became a more complex process.

Third, a psychological reflection is possible: Acknowledging the historical-cultural realities and the hermeneutical complexities of the situation, we can nevertheless attempt an answer to the question we posed at the beginning of this essay: Are there emotions in stones? There are indeed "emotions in stones." And there are memories in stones. The Vietnam Veterans Memorial and the Jewish Museum Berlin provide vivid examples of these emotions and memories. Within these two architectural structures, the psychological and the architectural, "the emotions and the stones" interact with each other. In the Vietnam Veterans Memorial the locus of this interaction is the "window" or "mirror": the viewer sees the past, then grieves or lets go of what has been. The monument is a visual or structural portrayal of Freud's "Mourning and Melancholia." In the Jewish Museum Berlin, the locus of the interaction is the architectural space of the void. The void is experienced as uncanny, unsettling. It demands of us that we return to old knowledge, old memories that we cannot integrate. It asks us to hold on to the awareness of the unthinkable, to reside in or with the unlivable, uncanny, knowledge of the Holocaust. The museum can be seen as a visual or structural portrayal of Freud's essay, "The Uncanny." It does not allow us to complete the process of mourning: there is no "mirroring" moment when we can feel healed, when we can return to the present, when we can feel, to use Freud's words from another essay, "at home in the uncanny" (1927, p. 17).

And finally, a reflection on the process of culture-making: Through their own innovative work of design, Daniel Libeskind and Maya Lin created these powerful and evocative structures in which "emotions" can be felt within "stones": clearly Libeskind and Lin are culture-makers. Our psychological analysis has given us an understanding—or perhaps we should say, a glimpse of an understanding—of the way we feel when we come into the presence of these stones. Although psychological interpretations may never fully grasp how "stones work" or how they produce emotions, such interpretations can, nevertheless, bring us a step closer to the creativity of the architects. Like the work of the architects, the work of the psychoanalytic interpreter contributes something to the creative process of culture making.

References

Arnason, H. H. (1968), *History of Modern Art: Painting, Sculpture, Architecture.* New York: Prentice-Hall.

Cheng, A. A. (2000), *The Melancholy of Race: Psychoanalysis, Assimilation, and Hidden Grief.* New York: Oxford University Press.

De Berg, H. (2002), *Freud's Theory and its Use in Literary and Cultural Studies.* Rochester, NY: Camden House.

Eng, D. & Kazanjian, D., eds. (2003), *Loss: The Politics of Mourning.* Berkeley: University of California Press.

Freud, S. (1914), Remembering, repeating, and working through. *Standard Edition*, 12:145–156. London: Hogarth Press, 1958.

―――― (1916), On transience. *Standard Edition*, 14:303–307. London: Hogarth Press, 1957.

―――― (1917), Mourning and melancholia. *Standard Edition*, 14:239–257. London: Hogarth Press, 1957.

―――― (1919), The uncanny. *Standard Edition*, 17:217–256. London: Hogarth Press, 1955.

―――― (1927), The future of an illusion. *Standard Edition*, 21:1–56. London: Hogarth Press, 1961.

Fussell, P. (1995), *The Great War and Modern Memory.* New York: Oxford University Press.

Gay, P. (1995), *The Naked Heart.* New York: Oxford University Press.

Geertz, C. (1977), *The Interpretation of Cultures.* New York: Basic Books.

Gorer, G. (1965), *Death, Grief, and Mourning*. Garden City, NY: Doubleday.

Halbwachs, M. (1992), *On Collective Memory*, ed. and trans. L. Coser. Chicago: University of Chicago Press.

Hall, S. (1980), *Culture, Media, Language: Working Papers in Cultural Studies 1972–1979*. London: Hutchinson.

Homans, P. (1989), *The Ability to Mourn: Disillusionment and the Social Origins of Psychoanalysis*. Chicago: University of Chicago Press.

——— (2000), Introduction. In: *Symbolic Loss: The Ambiguity of Mourning and Memory at Century's End*, ed. P. Homans. Charlottesville: University of Virginia Press.

Jackson, L. (1994), *Contemporary: Architecture and Interiors of the 1950s*. Boston: Phaidon.

Kroeber, C. & Kluckhohn, C. (2001), *Culture: A Critical Review of Concepts and Definitions*. Westport, CT: Greenwood Press.

Landler, M. (2005), Europe's ambitious bank picks a bold design. *The New York Times*, Jan. 14, p. B34.

Levine, P. (2004), Seeing the past in present tense: Working thoughts on monuments. *Camerawork: A Journal of Photographic Arts*, 31(2):9–13.

Libeskind, D. & Schneider, B. (1999), *Daniel Libeskind Jewish Museum Berlin: Between the Lines*. New York: Prestel Publishing.

Micale, M. & Porter, R., eds. (1994), *Discovering the History of Psychiatry*. New York: Oxford University Press.

Mitscherlich, A. & Mitscherlich, M. (1975), *The Inability to Mourn: Principles of Collective Behavior*. New York: Grove.

Rieff, P. (1966), *The Triumph of the Therapeutic*. New York: Harper & Row.

——— (1979), *Freud: The Mind of the Moralist*. Chicago: University of Chicago Press.

Santner, E. (1990), *Stranded Objects: Mourning, Memory, and Film in Postwar Germany*. Ithaca, NY: Cornell University Press.

Schorske, C. (1980), *Fin de Siècle Vienna: Politics and Culture*. New York: Vintage.

Scully, V. (1988), *American Architecture and Urbanism*. New York: Holt.

Smith, L. (2000), Window or mirror: The Vietnam Veterans Memorial and the ambiguity of remembrance. In: *Symbolic Loss: The Ambiguity of Mourning and Memory at Century's End*, ed. P. Homans. Charlottesville: University of Virginia Press.

Thompson, D., ed. (1996), *Oxford Modern English Dictionary*. New York: Oxford University Press.

Venturi, R. (1977), *Learning From Las Vegas: The Forgotten Symbolism of Architectural Form*. Cambridge, MA: MIT Press.

Vidler, A. (1992), *The Architectural Uncanny: Essays in the Modern Unhomely*. Cambridge, MA: MIT Press.

Weber, M. (1958), *From Max Weber: Essays in Sociology*. New York: Oxford University Press.

Williams, R. (1983), *Culture and Society 1780–1915*. New York: Columbia University Press.

Young, J. (2000), *At Memory's Edge: After Images of the Holocaust in Contemporary Art and Architecture*. New Haven, CT: Yale University Press.

Zaretsky, E. (2004), *Secrets of the Soul: A Social and Cultural History of Psychoanalysis*. New York: Knopf.

Architecture at the Sonia Shankman Orthogenic School of the University of Chicago

JACQUELYN SANDERS

"Whatever a human activity may be, its success is facilitated by a particular setting; the more so when complex and subtle issues are at stake. The structure of family life, and the nature of the human relations within it, will be quite different in a one-room hovel and in a palace, though either may be less than ideal when the goal is to promote good mental health" (Bettelheim, 1974, p. 7).

Thus Bruno Bettelheim begins his last of four books about the Sonia Shankman Orthogenic School, the University of Chicago's residential institution for the study and treatment of children and adolescents with severe emotional disturbances. Bettelheim, who started at the school in 1944, was director for more than two decades. I was at the helm from 1973 to 1993. Though he had not been formally trained in psychoanalysis, he developed an approach, psychoanalytically oriented milieu therapy, that brought to him and the school worldwide acclaim. Those years were the heyday of residential treatment for children, years when a number of eminent professionals were applying the lessons of psychoanalytic theory to the treatment of children so disturbed as to require residential care; children whose disturbances before that time had been considered untreatable. Bruno was the most publicly known spokesperson for this effort.

He devoted a good third of this last book on the school, *A Home for the Heart*, to the physical surround of the mental patient, using the example of the Orthogenic School to explicate and elaborate his meaning. He explains the importance of the physical environment in treatment thus:

"For the patient, once we can convince him to try climbing our ladder out of his dark hole, it is a long pull, rung by rung, toward self-discovery and rediscovery of the world; most of all toward finding and facing what meaningful, good, and enduring human relations are possible and available to him.

"If we wish to build the unique ladder which will permit this particular patient to use it, we must be able to understand those hidden messages which alone enable us to help persons who suffer from severe emotional disorders. To do so we must pay attention to the minute details of human behavior. Our intentions too are conveyed by the smallest details of our behavior and of the physical environment with which we surround the patients. The underlying concepts which we use both to read correctly their hidden messages, and to convey our intentions to them, are derived from psychoanalytic thinking as it is applied to all aspects of living" (Bettelheim, 1974, p. 9).

While Bettelheim is not entirely systematic in his application of psychoanalytic theory, he does both explicitly and implicitly use an approach that meets the criteria of Winer and Anderson in which they refer to psychoanalytic application "in its broad sense to refer to psychological approaches that take the unconscious into account, consider the effect of childhood on adult thinking and behavior and account for the interplay of forces in the mind" (Anderson and Winer, 2003, p. 1).

Consideration of the kind of message that the architecture of an environment can send to the unconscious of its inhabitants was an intrinsic part of all deliberations on the architecture and accouterments of the Orthogenic School. The name, *A Home for the Heart*, is schmaltzy—but not too off the mark of what we always tried to convey. This is reflected in the first sight of the Orthogenic School. Throughout the 48 years during which Bettelheim and I were consecutive directors, any visitor, child, parent or staff member, would find that haven at the side of the grassy stretch called the Midway, at the edge of the University of Chicago's campus. Its red brick was a welcome, warm contrast to the Gothic gray of the University (figure 1). One would walk up the short flight of stairs from the street to the welcoming, bright yellow door of a house, not an "institution."

While the message of its façade was surely one that we wanted to convey to parent and child from their very first sight—that the place where their child would be living is warm and welcoming—it was a building that Bettelheim had not chosen, so he could not claim initial responsibility for its selection. But his decision over the years, when he undertook two major and costly reconstructions, was to keep the old place: to improve and add to it, but never tear it down. He saw this as a powerful metaphor for those whose need it was to reconstruct their psyches while at the same time maintaining the valuable aspects of their selves.

The yellow door was always opened by a person. Though I sometimes contemplated, even investigated, the installation of a buzzer system, I never could bring myself to agree to anything but a personal first greeting for a child and parents. This was, after all, the beginning of treatment.

JACQUELYN SANDERS

FIGURE 1. Front of the Sonia Shankman Orthogenic School.

Once through the yellow door, one continues to see and feel the welcoming warmth and openness. Before you is a gracious staircase; to the right, behind French doors, is an office; and to the left, behind matching French doors, a living room where the visitor can wait, and never for long. The impact of this area was so apparent, even to city and state fire inspectors, that I managed to convince these officials of its therapeutic value so that they did not insist on enclosing the staircase. If the stair hall had been enclosed, no longer would the first statement to the child ("patient") have been one of transparency—of comfort in the living room, on the one hand, and of careful organization in the office on the other. When a prospective associate saw me in this entrance discussing with a carpenter the replacement of a newel post on the staircase, his reaction was: "if they can spend such careful time attending to the detail of a stair, how attentive must they be to children and staff—this is where I want to be."

Walking through the school, one has to feel that this is a place of brightness and hope for children. Some of this message is set in place deliberately, some not. There is a ceramic mural in one of the stair halls depicting Americana, going from the bottom of the sea to the top of the heavens (figure 2). Bettelheim, in his collaboration with Harold Haydn, the artist, wanted an uplifting theme, showing children able to explore every part of the world and to reach its heights. The other stair hall is of colored brick, comprised of all variety of bright and wild animals. In every artistic endeavor that was incorporated in the school's structure, Bettelheim was a significant collaborator, intent on convincing our charges that the world was a place worth entering and that they could succeed in it.

Bettelheim very deliberately tried to build into the very walls the message that the school was for them. The colors in the dormitories shouted this out. They were always bright; there were always at least two different colors in each room, and sometimes four. This was the result of a standard practice that the dormitory group chooses the colors of the wall—and the decision had to be unanimous. A frequent solution to the issue of unanimity was that there would be almost as many colors as inhabitants. If a child could have his or her choice on one wall, he or she could tolerate a color that was not a favorite on another wall. That the inhabitants liked what they saw and felt that it was theirs was much more important than the aesthetic correctness of the color scheme.

All around the school there was artwork, mostly chosen by Bettelheim (though the walls beside a youngster's bed were decorated completely to that child's taste), often conveying symbolic messages (as art is wont to do). The message of the very large play sculpture of a woman lying down is pretty obvious and was very deliberately planned. The staff met with a class from the Illinois Institute of Technology who had taken on the project of designing and building a structure for our play yard. The class came with several proposals from which we were to select one. None were completely satisfactory. Then Bettelheim proposed the "Lady." When he had this idea, we counselors understood exactly what he had in mind, and proceeded to demonstrate how we would lie on the floor while playing with our younger autistic children. This, then, was the model from which the class made a sand figure. They cast it into a mold in their studio and installed the play figure in our back yard under the careful observation of the entire school.

On every summer vacation or speaking trip abroad, Bettelheim collected artwork for the school. Though this work could frequently be interpreted in terms of its symbolic significance, I very much doubt that Bettelheim actually consciously deliberated such things when he made the purchase. The furnishing of the living room reflected this. One year he came back from Cape Cod with a wooden seahorse from an antique merry-go-round; another time he came back from Europe with an antique wood cradle; the head of buildings and grounds at the university found a king and a queen's chair in storage that he thought we would like; a parent gave us an old doll house; and I found in the Merchandise Mart an old-fashioned book ladder for access to the high shelves of the bookcases that lined one wall with psychoanalytic literature. It's easy to make an interpretation of the value of such symbolism for the welcome room of a children's institution, but my impression was that Bettelheim acquired these things simply because he liked them and thought that our kids would. Though it might not fit psychoanalytic theory comfortably, his method always did entail a careful and empathic reflection on how our youngsters

FIGURE 2. Stair halls.

would experience each addition. The conviction that the unconscious impact of every detail was of great importance pervaded every decision, whether or not the interpretation was accurate.

In true psychoanalytic spirit, facilitation of attention to oral and anal issues was built into the structure in 1952, when Bettelheim made an addition. This new dormitory building extended back from the minister's house, which was the original site of the school. Though the dining room and full kitchen were on the basement floor of the three-story structure, there was a kitchenette on each of the two dormitory floors, within a few feet of the doors of each of the three large dormitory rooms where the youngsters lived. Food was to be always easily available. A counselor could cook a special snack without ever being out of earshot of his or her charges, and any kids who needed constant supervision could easily accompany the counselor to the cooking center. Since a stove can be a hazard, when not in use and attended, the kitchenette was safely behind a locked door.

The dining room was a plain rectangular room, fit for easy visibility and for family style serving. It was sized to accommodate a table for each group and a table for the staff—with room between the two rows of tables for the serving staff to bring the food. After first trying rectangular tables, Bettelheim changed to round ones. A round table enables a counselor to serve each of the children directly and makes it easier for a conversation at a table for seven or eight to include everyone. Family style serving, without concern for preparation or cleaning up, enables the

FIGURE 3. Bathroom.

staff member to concentrate entirely on the feeding experience, the basis of the development of all relationships. And a meal without the necessity of moving about is most likely to engender a calm and comfortable atmosphere.

That there is no separate dining room for the staff reflects an attitude of respect toward the "patients" and interest in the rhythm of their lives. The presence of the staff who are not working with the children at the meal, contributes to an atmosphere of calm. Volatile youngsters are much less likely to act up if there are extra adults around, particularly those in positions of authority, like the school's director.

When Bettelheim did the next reconstructive addition, in 1965, he made sure that food was even more readily available. He had the very large cookie and candy closet built into the wall of the passageway by which the adolescents went from the playroom or dining room to their rooms. Unfortunately, it sometimes became an opportunity to satisfy the instinctual need to deprive others as well as that of satisfying oneself. The cabinet was filled every week, and now and then a youngster would take the whole week's supply of his or her favorite candy. Another drawback was that the easy availability of sweets could be perceived as an impersonal seduction. When a child could take several candy bars from a shelf, the comfort of a small candy from the pocket of a counselor became less comforting.

In the design of the 1952 addition, the importance of attention to the bodily functions is apparent from the location of the bathrooms. They were placed at one end of each of the dormitory rooms. It was possible, then, for a counselor to be available for a child in the bath or on the toilet without leaving the area where the other members of the group were engaged. That we wished the experience in this room to be a pleasurable one was dramatically manifest in Bettelheim's 1965 construction. In this "adolescent unit" there were double rooms, each with its own bathroom (figure 3). Each bathroom had beautiful colored mosaic tile on the floor and imported Italian tile on its walls. There was a different tile for each of the bathrooms. I witnessed again another of the many examples of Bettelheim's careful and intense investment in the details of comfort for our "patients" when this 1965 construction was in progress. It was his custom to go over to the addition every day to observe the progress of the work. One day he came back extremely agitated, insisting that his secretary immediately get the architect on the phone. The holes for the toilets had been put in. His distress came from the fact that the distance from the toilet to the toilet paper holder would make the retrieval of the paper uncomfortable for someone on the toilet.

When I returned to the school in 1972, some architectural features were giving messages that I didn't like. While I was gone, the adolescent unit, an additional building, was completed and we had yet more space available for our use—space that had formerly been used by the university. A significant part of this was the nave of a Universalist church. This had been refurbished in all its glory, with the addition of flags of Sienna hanging halfway up to the soaring ceiling. One could not help feel some touch of gloriousness when this was the place where one lived. I loved it and the rich medieval texture of the arched windows and gold wallpaper of the unit's living room. But Bettelheim had opted to integrate all the disparate buildings—the unit was built between the minister's house and the church—and everything was connected on at least two levels by corridors. While such integration had much to commend it, it was very confusing. There was a certain route along which I would, for a couple of months, invariably take the wrong direction. I had always thought it a great advantage that, when a new child came to visit, I could show him or her around and the child could fairly easily become completely oriented. No longer could he or she grasp the geography of this new home in such a short time.

I was further distressed by the allocation of space; the percentage of both indoor and outdoor space allocated to active pursuits had been significantly reduced. This was again an unconscious message, but one I did not like. It seemed to reflect Robert Hutchins's credo "whenever I feel the urge to exercise, I lie down until it passes," rather than "*mens sana in corpore sano.*"

I. W. Coburn was the architect with whom Bettelheim worked on the 1965 addition to the school. I had met him during the period of that collaboration and, on my return to Chicago, called on him for further collaboration on the architectural construction and reconstruction projects that I undertook. He told me how much he enjoyed working with Bettelheim because of his psychological perspective on all that they did. He expected no less of me. An aspect that impressed him, and colored his work with Bettelheim, was Bettleheim's very different view of space. Space was not an aesthetic. It was essential for our population that space be clearly defined. There should be no doubt when one walked into a living room that it was a place for quiet relaxation—and a playroom was a place to play (figure 4). I believe that this relates to the consideration for the fragile structure of our kids. Since they did not have the internal strength and structure to create a definition of their surroundings, it was important that the external structure be clear. This would be very obvious when an inexperienced person would spend time with a group. It was almost as though every large space was an invitation to be filled with their internal chaos, while a smaller, clearly defined space could contain that chaos.

Our first big project together was to change the balance of activity space in our outdoor area. Behind the school was a very large piece of undeveloped property that the university had purchased and had designated for our use. I wanted our children to not only get the message that we encouraged the active use of their bodies, but to have the actual space to do it in. Since it was a good-sized area, I wanted a variety of activities to be available: climbing on equipment, digging in a sandbox, gardening, picnicking, and ball playing. I wanted the spaces to be well defined, not only for the nature of their activity, but so a group of children could easily be restricted to a particular area. But I did not want this definition to be a restrictive barrier. Coburn understood the necessity for these ego supports to offer structure but not to be overly rigid. So he designed the area with hedges delineating the various activity areas.

In designing an institution such as ours, the building in of structure for safety, to support the fragile ego structure of youngsters who cannot themselves contain destructive impulses, is a persistent issue. The large rooms are without L-shapes or alcoves so that there is no part that the adult in charge cannot see. Thus continuous supervision is easily possible in a way that is ego supportive rather than overtly restrictive. On the windows are safety screens that do not look much different from regular screens, but are impossible to break through. And the closeness and integration of all parts makes help easily available, usually within seconds—at most, minutes.

Our other major project was undertaken to mark the significance of education in our children's lives. There had been no improvement to the classroom building in years. We completely gutted one wing and constructed three classrooms in it. Each classroom had its own washroom, thus eliminating the problem of supervision

FIGURE 4. Playroom.

of washrooms at a distance, and conveyed the message discussed above—bodily functions should not be dissociated from the rest of life.

An issue that needs constantly to be addressed in an institution whose purpose it is to promote psychological health is the infringement on selfhood that uniformity imposes. In our classrooms, I asked Coburn to address this by making each unique. To a large extent a teacher does this by the way he or she furnishes the classroom—posters, children's work, etc. I wanted it to be built into the structure. Every classroom had a different floor: two of different woods, and one of tile. Each had different walls: one wood, one textured, and one vinyl-like. And the windows in each were treated differently—two with window seats of different woods and one without.

In deciding on the size and shape of the rooms, we considered what space would be desirable and necessary for the various educational activities that we wanted to take place. We thought about the need for both privacy and group interaction so that the students could have individual space and group space; and we thought about optimal distances—how far a teacher could be from his or her students and still be "connected." Bettelheim discussed this issue at some length in *Home for the Heart*. We wanted a child entering any of these rooms to immediately know that this was a place where he or she would be warmly welcomed, where each student would have a place of his or her own, and where each would learn.

FIGURE 5. Inner courtyard.

In summary, Bruno Bettelheim, in his last book about the Sonia Shankman Orthogenic School of the University of Chicago, explicated his application of psychoanalytic ego psychology to the architecture of a residential treatment facility for severely emotionally disturbed children and adolescents. In this paper I have described and explained some of the processes of this application as I observed them during his tenure and as I practiced them during my tenure.

I have described how, with the help of a talented and sympathetic architect, we were able to create a physical environment that could contribute to the healing and healthful growth of our residents. With the construction and reconstruction of various parts of the building we carefully considered the messages that were being sent and how to build in the messages that we wanted—from the warmth of the façade to the hopefulness of rebuilding. All of our considerations, though having multiple influences, were psychoanalytically informed. This dictated, for example, that our planning of spaces relate to oral and anal needs: kitchen and dining areas and bathrooms. A very important element in all of the design was the use of space. Our major concern was that the space be ego supportive. Thus, the clear definition of space was more important than any aesthetic.

When Bettelheim wrote *A Home for the Heart* in the early 1970s, his aim was to influence the dismal architecture of mental hospitals. Since then, society's drive has, of course, been to close them. However, my personal observation of institutions for children over the years leads me to believe that Bettelheim's efforts have had some of the desired influence. While those in charge may not think in terms of unconscious messages and ego support, the vast change in the ambiance of such institutions reflects more positive unconscious messages and more ego-syntonic physical environments.

References

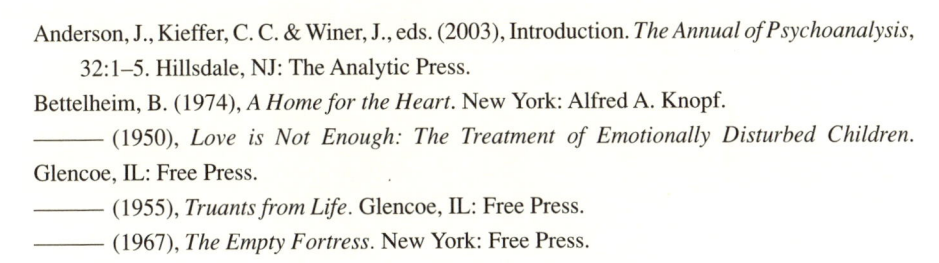

Anderson, J., Kieffer, C. C. & Winer, J., eds. (2003), Introduction. *The Annual of Psychoanalysis*, 32:1–5. Hillsdale, NJ: The Analytic Press.

Bettelheim, B. (1974), *A Home for the Heart*. New York: Alfred A. Knopf.

────── (1950), *Love is Not Enough: The Treatment of Emotionally Disturbed Children*. Glencoe, IL: Free Press.

────── (1955), *Truants from Life*. Glencoe, IL: Free Press.

────── (1967), *The Empty Fortress*. New York: Free Press.

Index

Figures in italics refer to bibliographical citations.

A
Abraham, K., 127
Ackerman, James S., 197, *204*
acoustic intimacy, 117–118
Acropolis (Athens)
    Freud's reaction to, 3, 40–41, 45–46
    "*informal*" and, 49–50
active room, 113–115
Adams, Henry, 58
Adams, L., 20, 22, *23*
Adler, Dankmar, 166, 191, 194, 195
Adorno, Theodor, 65
aesthetic position, 4, 139–160
Albers, Anni, 223
Albers, Josef, 220, 223
Alecsandri, Vasile, 242n
Alltäglichkeit, 184
alone, being, 3, 60
Altes Museum (Berlin), 144
Ambasz, Emilio, 93, 103–107
analytic listening, 51–54
analytic space, 3, 109–124
anamorphosis, 98
Anderson, James William, *177, 295*
    "emotion in the stone," 261n, 286
    introduction, 1–6
    Myth of the Masterbuilder, 241–259
    Rodman and, 57n
    on Wright, 163–177
Anton, Ted, 241, *257*
Antoniu, M., 250, *257*
Aoki, Y., 145n, *158*

Appleton, Jay, 145–146, 150, 153, 154, *158*
Aquinas, Thomas, 209
architecture
    awareness of, 39–56
    creativity and, 1
    dreams and, 3, 20, 25–37
    inspiring self-inquiry, 3
    landscape over, 104
    phantasy and, 4, 125–137
    references to human body, 17, 32, 33
    subjective responses to, 9–24
    "surrendering" to, 21
    time in, 104
    tracking emotion in, 261–284
    and true self, 57–66
    in twentieth century, 264–267
    violence of, 110
Arnason, H. H., 275, *282*
Arnheim, R., 21, 22, *23,* 222
art
    as antidote, 229–230
    criticism of, 230–231
    expression through, 67
    immersion in, 22
    layers of meaning in, 21
    objects of, 118–120
    pride in, 248–249
    Stokes on, 132–133
    as vanity, 31
artistic creation. *See* creativity
AT&T Building (New York), 96

attitude, 113
authenticity, 3
awareness
    of architecture and design, 39–56
    of consciousness, 34, 35, 79
    Quattro Cento buildings, 125
    of windows, 115

B
Bachelard, G., 113, 114, 116–117, *124*
Baker, Josephine, 194, 198
Balmond, Cecil, 46–50, 51, *55*
Baroque period, 140
Basarab, Neagoe (Prince), 255, 256, 257
Basilica of the Mission Dolores (San Francisco), 2, 9–24
Baudelaire, Charles, 194, 195
Bauhaus, 5, 6, 209–226
Bayer, H., 219, 220, 222, *225*
Behrens, Peter, 210, 219
being alone, 3, 60
being in relation with others, 3, 60
Benevolo, L., 147, *158*
Benjamin, Walter, 80, 85–89
Benscheidt, Carl, 210
Berenson, Bernhard, 141
Berkeley, George, 132
Berlage, H. P., 202
Berlin
    Bauhaus and, 209–226
    Benjamin's analysis of, 80, 85–89
    Neue Synagoge in, 3, 39n, 41–46, 49
    Philharmonic Hall, 143–144
Berlin Museum, 275
Bettelheim, Bruno, 5, 285–295
bifocal insight, 87
Binion, R., 247, *258*
Bion, W. R., 224, *225*
Blum, H. P., 39, 40, *55*
Bock, C. C., 67, *75*
Bollas, C., 89, *90*
Bouchard, F., 40, *55*
Bourassa, S. C., 145n, *158*

Breuer, Marcel, 220, 223
Brody, M., 20, 21, *23*
Bryan, William Jennings, 195
Burns, K., *189*
Bush, M., 20, *23*

C
carving, modeling and, 140
Casa de Retiro Espiritual (Córdoba), 105
Ceausescu, Nicolae, 244
Chagall, Marc, 219
chaos theory, 47, 50
charisma, 180–185
Chartres cathedral, 58–59
Cheney, Mamah, 171, 181, 184, 196
Cheng, A. A., 267, *282*
city space, 79, 89
CNN Center (Atlanta), 73
Coburn, I. W., 5, 291–293
Cohen, A., *189*
Cohler, Bertram, 261n
collective trauma, 247
color
    Sonia Shankman Orthogenic School, 288
    Stokes on, 125, 133
community, sense of, 43, 44, 249
complex systems, theory of, 50
composite memory, 34
composites, 84
condensation, dream-work and, 81, 82, 83, 84
consciousness
    awareness of, 34, 35, 79
    repression and, 278
    therapeutic action and, 39
Constantino, M., 176, *177*
construction, 97, 99
convergence, dream-work and, 81–82
Coop Himmelb(l)au, 261, 262
Cooper, Jerome, 68–69, 74, 75
Corinth, Lovis, 219
couches, analyst's office, 111–113

Index

coulisse, 154
countertransference, 20, 112
courtship, process of, 21
creativity
    architecture and, 1
    charisma and, 180
    feminine aspects of, 142
    psychodynamics of, 227–239
    regressive, 5
    unconscious in, 141n, 143
    violence of, 110
Credi, Lorenzo di, 153, 155
Crick, Francis, 26
crime and punishment, 278
criticism, artists and, 230–231
culture, 262–265, 280
Curtea de Arges Monastery, *258*
Curtis, William J. R., 174, *177*

D

da Vinci, Leonardo, 34, 94
Dali, Salivador, 273
Daniels, Stanley, 70–72, 75
Danze, Elizabeth A., 1–6, 109–124
Däubler, Theodor, 214
Daudet, Alphonse, 82
Davidescu, Constantin, 246, *258*
de Berg, H., 263, *282*
de Young Museum (California), 102
Deamer, Peggy, 4, 125–137
death
    Basilica of Mission Dolores and, 16, 18
    as disappearance, 30–31
death drive, 99–100
defamiliarization, 276
dehumanization, war and, 44
démontage, 95
Derrida, Jacques, 95, 273
design
    awareness of, 39–56
    psychodynamics of creativity, 227–239

    for safety, 68
    for sanctuary, 68–69
Despina (Princess), 256
destroy, urge to, 63–64
di Giorgio, Francesco, 148, 153
disintegration *vs.* integration, 65
disorder, 51, 64
disorientation, 51, 113
displacement, dream-work and, 81, 83
distinctness, 4, 145
divergence, dream-work and, 81, 83
Dobromir of Targoviste, 256
Dodson, Eva, 68
doors as "tears" in houses, 27, 29
Dorn, R. M., 224, *225*
dreams
    architecture and, 3, 20, 25–37
    awakening from, 35
    Freud on, 25, 26, 33, 80–85, 86
    of houses as parents, 60
    politics of, 89–90
    reality and, 86, 89
    space and, 3, 76, 79–91
    of storefront, 59–60, 61–62
Droste, M., 211, 214, 216, 220, 222, *225*
Duccio, Agostino di, 133
Dundes, A., 243n, *258*

E

Ecclesiastes, 34
ego
    Freud on, 35, 36, 95, 128, 165
    Klein on, 127, 128
    mental space of, 94
    splitting of, 127, 128
Egypt, 93, 94
Ehrenzweig, Anton, 141n, 143
Einstein, Albert, 35, 219
Eisenman, Peter, 95
Eisenstadt, S. N., 180, *189*
Elam, Merrill, 70
Eliade, Mircea, 243n, 248, 252, *258*
Eliot, T. S., 142

Emerson, Ralph Waldo, 187
emotion
    architecture eliciting, 20
    "emotion in the stone," 5, 6, 261–284, 286
    Myth of Masterbuilder and, 252–257
Eng, D., 267, *282*
English Modernism, 139
envelopment, 139–160
environmental aesthetics, 147
Erikson, Erik, 180, *189,* 215, *225*

F
Fagus-Werk, 210–211
Faisal II (King), 184
Fallingwater (Pennsylvania), 168, 173–174, 184, 187
fantasy (phantasy)
    architecture and, 4, 125–137
    of being aggressive, 232
    intrapsychic space, 44
    unconscious, 96, 97
feelings. *See* inner experience
Feininger, Lionel, 215, 219, 222, 223
Ferenczi, S., 127
Ferrono, C., 180, *190*
fetishism, 127
Fiore, F. P., 153, *158*
Flanders, S., 80, *90*
Flannery, J. G., 41, *55*
Flavell, J. H., 27, *37*
Fonagy, P., 39, *55*
foraging-ground, 145–147
Fraher, Amy, 229n, *239*
Frank, Karen A., 113, *124*
freedom, sense of, 4, 6
Freud, Alexander, 40
Freud, Sigmund, *37, 55, 90–91, 107, 124, 189, 282*
    architecture of phantasy, 125–130
    concept of uncanny and, 273, 274
    on culture and civilization, 262
    as culture maker, 264

    dream model, 25, 26, 33, 80–85, 86, 89
    on ego, 35, 36, 95, 128, 165
    on hovering attention, 54
    on instincts, 34, 128
    intellectuals and, 280
    introspective space, 111–112
    on loss and mourning, 261–262, 267–268, 272, 281
    on modernization, 265
    on object relations, 61
    objects in office, 118
    "oceanic feeling," 140, 142, 188
    on open wounds, 279
    picture of study, 111
    reaction to Acropolis, 3, 40–41, 46
    on second theory of anxiety, 39
    self-analysis and, 41
    use of space, 3, 93–107
    "Wolfman," 97–98, 101
    Wright and, 188
    Young on, 278
Fussell, P., 262, *282*

G
Galatzer-Levy, R. M., 40, 50, 51, *55*
Gamwell, L., 118, *124*
Gauguin, Paul, 65
Gay, Peter, 209, 213, *225,* 265, *282*
Gedo, J. E., 40, *55*
Gedo, M., 22, *23*
Geelhaar, C., 222, *225*
Geertz, Clifford, 264, *282*
Gehry, Frank, 65–66, 103
genetic epistemology, 27
Georgescu, V., 246, *258*
Georgia Tech, 68, 70, 74
Gerhardt, J., 20, 22, *23*
Gerth, H. H., 184, *189*
ghosts in dreams, 87–88
Gilbert, G., 20, 22, *23*
Gill, B., *177, 189*
    on Wright's career, 172, 174, 176

Index 301

on Wright's charisma, 179, 183, 184
on Wright's early life, 163, 164
Gilloch, G., 85, *91*
Globus, G., 20, 22, *23*
Glover, N., 141, 142, *158*
Goethe, J. W., 209, 210
Goldberg, Arnold, 166, *177*
Goldberger, Paul, 187
golden section, 34
Goldman and Salatsch building (Austria), 198
Gorer, G., 262, *283*
Graham Foundation, 1, 2
"grandiose self," 166
Greenberg, C., 21, 22, *23*
Gropius, I., 219, 222, *225*
Gropius, Walter, 5, 198, 209–226
group trauma, 247
GSA (General Services Administration), 234–235
Guggenheim Museum
    Bilbao, Spain, 103
    New York, 186, 187, 188
Guillaumin, J., 40, *55*
guilt, 278
Guntrip, Harry, 165, *177*
Gutman, Robert, 5

H
Halbwachs, M., 262, *283*
Hall, S., 263, *283*
Halpern, J. R., 40, *55*
harmony
    Ambasz and, 104
    with surroundings, 68
    Wright and Loos on, 192
Harris, Robert F., 2, 6, 9–24
Harrison, I. B., 41, *55*
Hasbrouck, Wilbert, 182
Hauptmann, Gerhart, 219
Haussmann, Eugène, 195
Haydn, Harold, 287
Heaney, S., *37*

Hegel, Georg, 103
Heidegger, Martin, 95
Heim, Emily, 214
Heimann, Paula, 140
heimlich, 268, 274
Heinz, Thomas, 168, 186
Hepworth, Barbara, 139
Hertzberger, H., 157, *158*
Herzog, Jacques, 102
Hesse, Fritz, 219
Hilbersheimer, Ludwig, 223
Hildebrand, G., 145n, *158*
Hirschhorn, Larry, 227n
Hitchcock, H.-R., 171, *177,* 185, 192, *204*
Hitler, Adolf, 223
Hochman, E., 219, *225*
Hoffman, I. Z., 39, *55*
Hofmannsthal, Hugo von, 219
HOK architectural firm, 228
Holl, S., 116, 119, *124*
Holocaust
    Jewish Museum (Berlin), 275, 276, 278, 282
    Neue Synagoge and, 41–44, 50–51
    sense of loss and, 262
Homans, Peter, 5, 6, 261–284
Homer, 34
homogeneity, 143
homosexuality, 129
Hopper, Edward, 119
houses
    of architects, 3, 67–75
    as extensions of human body, 32
    interior space. *See Raumplan*
    with "tear" in, 27, 29
Hubertus House (Amsterdam), 157
Huizinga, J., 214, *225*
Hulme, T. E., 142
human body
    architecture and references to, 17, 32, 33
    golden section, 34
Hutchins, Robert, 291

Hutter, A., 224, *225*
Huxtable, H., 187, 188, *189*

I
id, 94, 126–127
identification (defense), 127
Il Rendentore church, 135
Imperial Hotel (Japan), 168, 171–172, 185
impulsion, 99
incommunicado nature (true self), 61
"*informal*" environment
    Balmond on, 46–50
    effective analysis and, 54
    psychoanalytic restatement, 50–51
inner experience
    encountering architecture, 9–24
    memorials and, 269
    psychoanalysis and, 1, 6
instincts, Freud on, 34, 128
integration *vs.* disintegration, 65
interior space of houses. *See Raumplan*
International Style, 192, 198
intrapsychic space, 44
introjection (defense), 127, 128, 134
introspective space, 109–124
Ion, Ruxandra, 5, 6, 241–259
Iraq, Wright in, 184, 187
irresponsibility, 231
Itten, Johannes, 216–218, 224
Itu, I., 248, *258*

J
Jackson, L., 266, *283*
James, William, 164, *177*
Jencks, Charles, 47, *55*
Jewish Museum (Berlin)
    "emotion in the stone" and, 261, 263, 268, 281
    process of mourning and, 5
    uncanny in postmodern architecture, 273–282
Jobe, T., 180, *190*

Johnson, Herbert F., 174
Johnson, Philip, 96, 192, *204*
Johnson Wax Building (Wisconsin), 169, 174, 185–186, 188
Jonte-Pace, Diane, 5, 6, 261–284
jouissance, 96, 97, 100
Joyce, James, 195
Judaism, 43, 276

K
Kahn, Louis, 74, 121
Kandinsky, Wassily, 219, 221, 222, 223
Kant, Immanuel, 95
Kaplan, R., 145n, 147, *158*
Kaplan, S., 145n, 147, *158*
Kaufman, Edgar J., 173, 184
Kazanjian, D., 267, *282*
Kerkovius, Ida, 213
Khuner House (Austria), 201
Kieckhefer, R., 22, *23*
Kieffer, C. C., 286, *295*
Kimbell Art Museum (Texas), 121
Kirshner, L., 21, *23*
Kite, Stephen, 4, 139–160
Klee, Paul, 213, 219, 221, 222, 223
Klein, Melanie, *159,* 239
    aesthetics of, 141
    architecture of phantasy, 125–130, 136
    on creative process, 229–230, 239
    New Directions in Psychoanalysis, 140, 141
    on object relations, 154
    paranoid-schizoid mechanisms, 126, 140, 142, 143, 145, 155
    on polar modes, 144
    on reparation, 232
    Stokes and, 4, 139
    Winnicott and, 141–142
Kleinman, K., 191–192, 193, 194, *205*
Kluckhohn, C., 263, *283*
Kohut, Heinz, 165–166, *177,* 185, *189*
Kokoschka, Oskar, 219

Index

Koolhas, Rem, 102
Kris, E., 20, 21, *23,* 225, *226*
Kristallnacht, 43, 275
Kroeber, C., 263, *283*
Kuhn, T. S., 39, *55*
Kuhns, R., 21, *23*
Kulka, Heinrich, 191, 192
Kuspit, D., 20, 22, *23,* 65, *66*

L

Lacan, J., *107*
    on anamorphosis, 98
    on the death drive, 100
    on the elementary form of desire, 105
    filmmaking and, 93
    on FreudSpace, 95, 99
    on *jouissance,* 96
Lamp, Robie, 182
Landler, M., 261n, *283*
landscape, architecture and, 104
Larkin, John, 183
latent content (dreams), 80–81, 89
Laurana, Luciano, 147, 150, 152, 156
Lazovich, Olgivanna, 172
Le Corbusier, 133, 144, 192, 198
Lebovitz, Phil S., 3, 67–75
Ledofsky, L., 95, 104, *107*
Lefebvre, Henri, 79, *91*
Lepori, R. Bianca, 113, *124*
Levine, P., 278, *283*
Libeskind, Daniel, 273–282, *283*
light
    analyst's office and, 115–117
    Basilica of Mission Dolores and, 17, 18
    designing in, 70, 72, 74
    dreams of, 59–60
    homogeneous, 115
    recording, 35
Lin, Maya, 269, 270, 272, 280, 282
Lipman, Jonathan, 163
Lipscomb, P., 21, 22, *23*
Little, Margaret, 64–65, *66*

Lloyd Jones, Anna, 163–164, 181
Lloyd Jones, Richard, 169, 175
Locke, John, 132
Loewald, Hans, *189*
Loewenberg, Peter, 4–5, 6, 209–226
Loos, Adolf, 4, 191–205
loss. *See* mourning process
Lucy Daniels Foundation, 2, 57n

M

MacCannell, Juliet Flower, 3, 93–107
Mackintosh, Charles Rennie, 200
Mahler, Alma, 216
Mahon, Eugene, 2, 25–37
Malner, J., 120, *124*
manifest content (dreams), 81, 89
Mantegna, Andrea, 153
Manzoni-Angaran palace, 135–136
Marcks, Gerhard, 219–220
Marcus, L., 80, *91*
Markische Museum (Berlin), 275
Martin, Darwin, 183
Martin, W. E., 183
Marx, Karl, 79, 86, *91,* 280
Masson, J. M., 40, *55*
Masson, T. C., 40, *55*
Masterbuilder, Myth of, 5, 6, 241–259
McLuhan, Marshall, 33
meaning
    architecture conveying, 20
    of dreams, 80
    layers of, 21
    loss of, 264
    memorials and, 269
    of self-designed homes, 67
Meissner, W. W., 67, *75*
melancholia, 267, 270
Meltzer, Donald, 155
memorials, 5, 41, 269–273
memories. *See also* inner experience
    bifocal insight, 87
    forgetting and, 279
    irrelevance of, 281

memorials and, 269, 279
mourning and, 267–268
repressed, 94
Menin, S., 143, *159*
mental space, 94, 95
Meuron, Pierre de, 102
Meyer, Adolf, 210, 218
Meyer, Hannes, 222, 223
Micale, M., 265, *283*
Michelangelo, 94, 140
Midway Gardens (Illinois), 196
Mies van der Rohe, Ludwig, 5, 198, 210, 223, 224
Mills, C. W., 184, *189*
Milner, Marion, 141, 143, *159*
Mitscherlich, A., 262, 272, *283*
Mitscherlich, M., 262, 272, *283*
modeling, carving and, 140
Modell, Arnold, 188, *189*
modernism
    aesthestic position and, 144
    Bauhaus principles and, 209–210
    challenges to, 266–267
    cultural optimism, 280
    development of, 264–265
    Freud and, 264
    Pruit-Igoe housing project, 274–275
    Raumplan and, 191–205
    roots of, 142, 272
    "sea change" and, 263
Moholy-Nagy, Laszlo, 218, 219, 221, 223
Moller House (Austria), 199
The Monastery of Curtea de Arges, 241–259
Money-Kyrle, R. E., 140
Monroe, Harriet, 199
Montefeltro, Federico da, 147, 148
Moore, Nathan G., 167
Moraitis, G., 110, *124*
Moses, R., 22, *23*
mourning process
    Freud on, 261, 262, 281
    memorials and, 5, 267–273, 278–279

Muche, Georg, 219, 221, 222
Municipal Court building (Austria), 198
Muschamp, Herbert, 235
Mussolini, Benito, 195
muteness, 114
Myth of the Masterbuilder, 5, 6, 241–259

N
nature, integration with, 68–69, 74, 75
nesting-space, 145–147
Neue Synagoge (Berlin), 3, 39n, 41–46, 49
Neumann, E., 218, 224, *226*
Newton, S. J., 141n, 149–150, *159*
Nicholson, Ben, 139
Nietszche, Friedrich, 17
Noel, Miriam, 171, 172
Nora, P., 85, *91*
Noy, P., 20, *23*

O
object-otherness, 139–160
objects
    part objects, 127, 129
    relationships among, 61
    in rooms, 118–120
"oceanic feeling," 140, 142, 188
Ogden, T., 20, *24*
O'Gorman, J. F., 26, *37*
Olson, Nancy, 128n, *137*
O'Neill, Eugene, 265
oneness, 4, 145
open narrative, 276–278
optimism, 280
Orlich, Ileana Alexandra, 250, *258*

P
Palace of Urbino, 146, 147–158
Palladio, Andrea, 135
Pallasmaa, J., *124*
    on acoustics, 117, 118
    on architectural scale, 114
    on homogeneous light, 115

on space, 121–123
paranoid-schizoid mechanisms
    creative role of, 140, 142
    envelopment and, 143
    Klein on, 126
    Stokes on, 155
parergon, 95
Parsons, William, 261n
part objects, 127, 129
Pascal, Blaise, 34, *37*
passage, themes of, 22
past
    connection to, 18
    loss of, 262–264
    memorials as windows to, 269–273
Pater, Walter, 139
peace, sense of, 16, 104
Persky, Seymour, 2
personal experience. *See* inner experience
Peters, Wes, 183
Pfeiffer, Bruce Books, 173, *177*, 181, *189*
phantasy. *See* fantasy
phobias, 93
Piaget, Jean, 27, 28, 35, 36
piano nobile, 148, 152
Picasso, Pablo, 195
Piero della Francesca, 152, 156, 158
Pile, Steve, 3, 79–91
Pinkney, T., 141n, 142, 143, *159*
Pius II (Pope), 147
Poe, Edgar Allan, 32
politics of dreams, 89–90
Pop, I. A., 246, *258*
Pop, M., 242n, 246, 254, *258*
Porter, R., 265, *283*
postmodernism
    culture and, 263–265, 272
    ideas associated with, 103, 262
    Jewish Museum (Berlin), 273–282
    Venturi and, 266
"potential space," 143
Pound, Ezra, 142
Prairie House, 192, 197

Price, Harold, 176
Price Company Tower (Oklahoma), 169, 175–176
prima donnas, 233–234
primal events, 94, 97
Prix, Wolf D., 261
projection (defense), 127, 134
Proust, Marcel, 28, 34, *37*, 94, 141
Pruit-Igoe public-housing project, 274–275
psyche, 79–80, 84, 274
psycho-aesthetics, 129–134
psychoanalysis
    inner experience and, 1, 6
    office space and, 109–124
    space and, 79–91
    in twentieth century, 264–267
pulsion, 99
pure pleasure principle, 127

Q
Quattro Cento period, 125, 140

R
Radu (Prince), 255, 256
Rasmussen, S., 116, 117, *124*
Raumplan, 4, 191–205
reality
    dreams and, 86, 89
    energy and, 99
    primal events and, 98
    splitting of the ego and, 127, 128
reality testing, 35
Reinhardt, Max, 219
Reissenberger, L., 255n, *258*
relational opportunity, 112
Renaissance period, 147
reparation, 232
representation, dream-work and, 83–84
repression, 94, 127, 278
residential space, 191–205
Ricketts, M. L., 242n, 243n, *258*
Rieff, Philip, 265, 280, *283*

Riesman, David, 195
Rizzuto, A., 22, *24*
Robie, F. C., Jr., 203, *204*
Robie House (Illinois), 199, 202
Rodman, F. Robert, 3, 57–66
Rolland, Romain, 40, 46, 188
Romanian church myth, 5, 6, 241–259
Romanticism, 142
Romeo and Juliet windmill, 167, 170
room arrangement, 191–192
Rose, G., 20, 23, *24*
Rosselli, Domenico, 155
Rotondi, P., 147–149, 152, 154–156, *159*
Rotzler, W., 217, *226*
Roxanda (Princess), 256
Ruskin, John, 126, 139
Ruxandoiu, P., 242n, 254, *258*

S
sacrifices, 243–252
safety, designing, 68, 289
Samuelson, J., 255n, *258*
sanctuary, designing in, 68–69
Sanders, Jacquelyn, 5, 6, 285–295
Santner, E., 262, *283*
Saving Private Ryan (film), 269
Scharoun, Hans, 143
Scheper, Hinnerk, 220, 221
Scheu House (Austria), 199
Schiller, Friedrich, 210
Schinkel, Karl Friedrich, 144
Schlemmer, Oskar, *226*
　　at Dessau, 219, 221, 222
　　pain at internecine fighting, 217–218
　　postcard invitation created by, 213
　　resignation of, 223
Schmidt, Joost, 220
Schneider, B., 275, *283*
Schoenberg, Arnold, 219
Schönbrunner, J., 253
Schorske, C., 264, *283*
Schreyer, Lothar, 213–214, *226*
Schuetz, Chana C., 39n

Schulze, F., 223, *226*
Schwitters, Kurt, 219
Scogin, Mark, 69–70, 71, 74, 75
Scully, V., 266, *283*
sculpture, 69, 143
"sea change," 262–266
secondary revision, dream-work and, 84, 85
Secrest, M., *177, 189*
　　on Kaufman, 173
　　on Miriam Noel, 171
　　on Peters, 183
　　on Wright and Lloyd Jones, 175
　　on Wright as advertisement, 185
　　on Wright as greatest architect, 163–164
　　on Wright's apprentices, 172, 180
Segal, Hanna, 141, 149, *159*
self
　　concept of, 165–166
　　fostering, 3
　　"grandiose self," 166
　　incommunicado nature, 61
　　marriage and, 60
self-inquiry
　　analytic environment and, 40
　　building elements inspiring, 3
　　Neue Synagoge and, 41–46
self-portraits, houses as, 67–75
separateness, 4
sexual references
　　buildings and, 22, 33
　　dream-work and, 83, 84
　　humanity to habitat, 145
　　in images, 16
　　"Wolfman," 98
Shakespeare, William, 26
shared perplexity, 52
Sharon-Stötzl, Gunta, 220
Shils, Edward, 180, *189*
shudder, 65
Sinai, 93, 94
Sinigalia, T.-I., 255n, *258*

Index 307

sleepwalking, space and, 88
Slochower, H., 40, *55*
Smith, C., 147, *159*
Smith, J., 47, 48, *55*
Smith, Levi, 269–270, 272–273, 280, *283*
Solnit, Albert J., 213n, *226*
Sonia Shankman Orthogenic School (Chicago), 5, 6, 285–295
Sonnenberg, Stephen M., 3, 39–56
soothing, sense of, 4, 16, 19
Sorkin, M., 103, *107*
Sottsass, Ettore, 104
space
    between analyst and analysand, 111–113
    analytic, 3, 109–124
    architecture and, 25–26
    avoiding taking up, 61–62
    Bettelheim on, 292
    city space, 79, 89
    dreams and, 3, 26, 79–91
    expansiveness to, 72
    Freud and, 3, 93–107
    house interiors. *See Raumplan*
    impact of, 6
    interrelationships with, 72
    intrapsychic, 44
    introspective, 109–124
    "lightness" of, 14
    loss of orientation to, 46, 51
    mental, 94, 95
    "potential space," 143
    psyche and, 79
    psychoanalysis and, 79–91
    residential space, 191–205
    and sleepwalking, 88
    sunken living room, 68
    time and, 44, 99
    transitional, 215–216
    uncanny and, 274
    Winnicott on, 143, 215–216, 224, 225
    Wright's use of, 4, 179, 201
spatial relationships
    between analyst and analysand, 111–113
    in analyst's office, 120–124
    construction and, 97
    design and, 72
    dreams and, 84
Sperling, S., 21, *24*
Spielberg, Stephen, 269
Spielraum, 224
Spitz, E., 20, 21, 22, *24*
splitting of the ego (defense), 127, 128
Stevens, Wallace, 266
Stoelzl, Gunta, 214
Stokes, Adrian
    aesthetic position, 139–160
    architecture of phantasy, 125–137
    Klein and, 4, 139
    on refuge, 146
Stonebridge, L., 141n, 142, *160*
Storr, A., 143, *160*
Strauven, F., 157
Stravinsky, Igor, 195
structuralist model of mind, 131
suffering, feeling of, 19, 248, 280
Sullivan, Louis, 166–167, 187, 191, 194–195
superego, 94, 127, 230
surface, theory of, 4
surprise, 52
survivability, 3, 62–65
Sweetnam, A., 20, 22, *23*
Symbolism, 142
symmetry, space and, 14

T
Tafel, E., 182, 185, *189*
Taliesin (Wisconsin), 171–172, 180–182, 184, 186, 188
Talos, I., 242n, *258*
Tanizaki, J., *124*
Tavistock Institute, 140n–141n, 143, 229
"tears" in houses, doors as, 27, 29
territory, 118–120

texture, 4, 133, 293
Thebes, 93
Thoma, Hans, 219
Thompson, D., 262, *283*
Thompson, Ian, 145n
time
    in architecture, 104
    and space, 44, 99
    "time lost," 94
Tobin, Catherine, 167
Toma, M., 243n, 245, 252, *258*
Tomek House (Illinois), 199
transference, 112
transparency, 287
trauma, 97, 247
true self, 57–66
Twombly, Robert, 4, 175, *177*, 191–205

U
uncanny, 268, 273–282
unconscious
    in creativity, 141n, 143
    fantasy and, 128
    uncanny and, 274
unheimlich, 268, 273–282
Unity Temple (Illinois), 168, 170, 188
Urbino, Palaco of, 146, 147–158

V
van Duzer, L., 191–192, 193, 194, *205*
Van Eyck, Aldo, 156, 157, 158
Van Roijen-Wortmann, A., 157
Vecchietta, 153
Venice, Stokes on, 135–136
Ventulett, Thomas, 73–74, 75
Venturi, Robert, 266, *283*
Vidler, Anthony, 266–267, 273–275, *283*
Vietnam Veterans Memorial (Washington, D.C.)
    "emotion in the stone" and, 261, 263, 268, 281
    mourning and melancholia in, 5, 269–273
Villa Karma (Switzerland), 191
Villa Müller (Hungary), 193
Villa Stein (Garches, France), 144
Vitruvius, Marcus, 28, 33, 34, *37*
Vodvarka, F., 120, *124*
voids, 275–279
Volkan, V. D., 247, *258*
von Erffa, H., 211, 212, 214, *226*

W
Wallerstein, R. S., 39, *56*
war
    dehumanization and, 44
    memorials and, 270
Watson, James, 26
Weber, Max, 180, 184, 264, *283*
Wells, R., 118, *124*
Welsh-Jouve, G., 247, *259*
Werfel, Franz, 219
Werman, D. S., 40, *56*
Westhope (Oklahoma), 169, 175
Whitford, F., 212, 219, *226*
wholeness, 3
Wick, R., 218, *226*
Williams, R., 263, *284*
Wilson, Colin St. John, 143, 144, 145n, *160*
windmill, Romeo and Juliet, 167, 170
windows
    analyst's office and, 115–117
    memorials as, 269–270
Winer, Jerome A, 1–6, 179–190, 286, *295*
Wines, Robert, 104, *107*
Wingler, H. M., 209, 211, 219, *226*
Winnicott, D. W., *66, 124, 160, 177*
    on babies' relationships, 59
    on borderlines, 64
    on Freud, 114
    Klein and, 141–142
    Rodman on, 3
    on self, 165

Index

    on space, 143, 215–216, 224, 225
    on true self, 58, 61
    on unconscious, 143
Wollheim, R., 20, 21, 22, *24*, 140, *160*
wonder, 52
World War II, 41, 43, 45, 275
Wright, Frank Lloyd
    conference on, 1, 4
    discomfort on being enclosed, 6
    power, powerlessness, and charisma, 179–190
    psychobiography, 163–177
    Raumplan and, 191–205
Wright, Permelia, 181

Wright, William Carey, 164, 181

Y
Yale University, 2
Yasin, Ann Marie, 255n
Young, J., 267, 273, 275–276, 278, 280, *284*

Z
Zaretsky, Ely, 265, *284*
zeitgeist, 33
Žižek, Slavoj, 96, 100–103, 106, *107*
Zumthor, Peter, 119, 120, *124*